# Computer Vision with OpenCV 3 and Qt5

Build visually appealing, multithreaded, cross-platform computer vision applications

**Amin Ahmadi Tazehkandi**

BIRMINGHAM - MUMBAI

# Computer Vision with OpenCV 3 and Qt5

Copyright © 2018 Packt Publishing

All rights reserved. No part of this book may be reproduced, stored in a retrieval system, or transmitted in any form or by any means, without the prior written permission of the publisher, except in the case of brief quotations embedded in critical articles or reviews.

Every effort has been made in the preparation of this book to ensure the accuracy of the information presented. However, the information contained in this book is sold without warranty, either express or implied. Neither the author, nor Packt Publishing or its dealers and distributors, will be held liable for any damages caused or alleged to have been caused directly or indirectly by this book.

Packt Publishing has endeavored to provide trademark information about all of the companies and products mentioned in this book by the appropriate use of capitals. However, Packt Publishing cannot guarantee the accuracy of this information.

**Commissioning Editor:** Aaron Lazar
**Acquisition Editor:** Parth Kothari
**Content Development Editor:** Lawrence Veigas
**Technical Editor:** Supriya Thabe
**Copy Editor:** Zainab Bootwala
**Project Coordinator:** Prajakta Naik
**Proofreader:** Safis Editing
**Indexers:** Rekha Nair
**Graphics:** Jason Monteiro
**Production Coordinator:** Nilesh Mohite

First published: January 2018

Production reference: 1291217

Published by Packt Publishing Ltd.
Livery Place
35 Livery Street
Birmingham
B3 2PB, UK.

ISBN 978-1-78847-239-5

www.packtpub.com

*This book is dedicated to the open source communities and you, the bright minded developers,
working hard to build a better world for all of us.*

`mapt.io`

Mapt is an online digital library that gives you full access to over 5,000 books and videos, as well as industry leading tools to help you plan your personal development and advance your career. For more information, please visit our website.

# Why subscribe?

- Spend less time learning and more time coding with practical eBooks and Videos from over 4,000 industry professionals

- Improve your learning with Skill Plans built especially for you

- Get a free eBook or video every month

- Mapt is fully searchable

- Copy and paste, print, and bookmark content

# PacktPub.com

Did you know that Packt offers eBook versions of every book published, with PDF and ePub files available? You can upgrade to the eBook version at `www.PacktPub.com` and as a print book customer, you are entitled to a discount on the eBook copy. Get in touch with us at `service@packtpub.com` for more details.

At `www.PacktPub.com`, you can also read a collection of free technical articles, sign up for a range of free newsletters, and receive exclusive discounts and offers on Packt books and eBooks.

# Foreword

Around 20 years ago, when I was graduating from university, development of large and complex applications that included a graphical user interface was a time-consuming and difficult task. The APIs and tools that existed at that time to create those applications were difficult to use and understand. Creating applications for multiple platforms required writing a large part of it several times.

It was at that time that I discovered Qt, a framework that fixed both of these problems. It came with an easy-to-use, intuitive API and worked across all major desktop operating systems. Suddenly, programming these applications went from being hard work to something I really enjoyed. I wasn't limited to one operating system anymore—I could have my application running on multiple operating systems with a simple recompile.
Since then, many things have improved for application developers. Frameworks have put a lot more effort into having easy-to-use APIs. The operating system landscape has changed, and having APIs that are available cross-platform is more important than ever.

OpenCV has, over the last few years, evolved into the leading API for computer vision. It contains a large set of functionalities and algorithms that can be used for things such as face recognition, tracking camera or eye movements, track markers for augmented reality, and much more.

Qt has also, over the same period, turned into one of the leading cross-platform frameworks for application development. Its comprehensive feature set contains most of the functionality you will need to develop a complex graphical application.

Making Qt the best technology to create cross-platform applications has been my mission for the last 17 years. One of the goals has always been to make it easy to combine Qt with other technologies. This book gives you a great example on how this can be done.

Both Qt and OpenCV feature cross-platform C++ APIs, making it straightforward to use them together. By combining them, you will have a powerful set of tools at hand, making it easy to create applications that combine computer vision with a graphical user interface. I hope that this book will help you on your way to becoming an expert in both Qt and OpenCV.

**Lars Knoll**
Qt Chief Maintainer and CTO at The Qt Company

# Contributors

## About the author

**Amin Ahmadi Tazehkandi** is an Iranian developer and a computer vision expert. He completed his computer software engineering studies in Iran and has worked for numerous software and industrial companies, including Paxan (Turkey) and Petroleum Software (UK). Amin is a passionate blogger and a longtime volunteer and supporter of the Computer Vision community. He currently resides in Vienna, Austria, where he continues to research, develop, and write about cross-platform computer vision software development.

*I would like to thank my wife, Senem, who is a symbol of passion, love, and strength for me. I would also like to thank my family, a big pack of brilliant engineers born to an Iranian inventor father and a loving mother, for all of their unconditional love and support.*

# About the reviewers

**Karl Phillip Buhr** has a BSc in computer science (2006), an MSc in applied computing (2010), and is a Data Science and Machine Learning enthusiast. He developed many cross-platform and computer vision systems for the private sector and enjoys answering questions on Stack Overflow. He spent years lecturing classes and doing research projects for a computing engineering course in Santa Catarina, Brazil. Nowadays, he runs a software company focused on developing solutions for challenging industry problems.

**Vinícius Godoy** is a professor at PUCPR and a proud owner of a game development website, Ponto V!. He has a master's degree in computer vision and image processing (PUCPR), a specialization degree in game development (Universidade Positivo), and has graduation in Technology in Informatics—Networking (UFPR). He has been in the software development field for more than 20 years and is the author of the book *OpenCV by Example* by Packt Publishing.

# Packt is searching for authors like you

If you're interested in becoming an author for Packt, please visit `authors.packtpub.com` and apply today. We have worked with thousands of developers and tech professionals, just like you, to help them share their insight with the global tech community. You can make a general application, apply for a specific hot topic that we are recruiting an author for, or submit your own idea.

# Table of Contents

# Preface

There has never been a better time to be a software developer than now. Just look around you and, most probably, you'll see at least a couple of different devices such as computers, smartphones, smart watches, or tablets running some applications on them that help you with various daily tasks or entertain you with music, movies, video games, and so on. Every year, hundreds of new devices are introduced into the market and new versions of operating systems are required to keep up with them in order to provide better interfaces for application developers to create software that makes better use of the underlying resources such as high-resolution displays, various sensors, and so on. As a consequence, software development frameworks have to adapt to and support the ever growing number of platforms. Considering this, Qt is probably one of the most successful cross-platform software development frameworks that offers power, speed, flexibility and ease of use, all at the same time, and it is a top choice when it comes to creating software that needs to look appealing and consistent across a wide range of platforms.

In recent years, and especially with the rise of more powerful processors at lower costs, the role of desktop computers and their handheld counterparts has shifted toward performing the more demanding and complex tasks such as computer vision. Whether it is for intelligent movie or photo editing, securing a sensitive building, counting objects in a production line, or detecting traffic signs, lanes, or pedestrians by an autonomous car, computer vision is being used more and more to solve such real-time problems that once were expected to be solved only by humans. This is where OpenCV Framework enters the scene. In the past few years, OpenCV has grown into a full-fledged cross-platform computer vision framework, with a focus on speed and performance. All around the world, developers and researchers are using OpenCV to realize their computer vision application ideas and algorithms.

This book aims to get you to grips with both Qt and OpenCV frameworks by taking you through their basic concepts and taking you up to the point where you can easily continue on your own to develop and deliver computer vision applications across a wide range of platforms. The only assumption made for being able to easily follow the topics covered in this book is that you are familiar and comfortable with C++ programming concepts such as classes, templates, inheritance, and so on. Even though the tutorials, screenshots, and examples covered throughout the book are based on the Windows operating system, the difference on macOS and Linux operating systems are also mentioned wherever necessary.

This book is the result of months of hard work, and it would have not been possible without the invaluable help of Lawrence Veigas, for his perfect editing; Karl Phillip Buhr, for his honest and insightful reviews and comments; Parth Kothari, without whom this book would have not been a reality; and Zainab Bootwala, Prajakta Naik, Aaron Lazar, Supriya Thabe, Tiksha Sarang, Rekha Nair, Jason Monteiro, Nilesh Mohite, and everyone at Packt Publishing who helped create and deliver this book as it is to you, our readers from all around the world.

# Who this book is for

This book is for readers interested in building computer vision applications. Intermediate knowledge of C++ programming is expected. Even though no knowledge of Qt5 and OpenCV 3 is assumed, if you're familiar with these frameworks, you'll benefit.

# What this book covers

Chapter 1, *Introduction to OpenCV and Qt*, goes through all the required initializations. Starting with from where and how to get Qt and OpenCV frameworks, this chapter will describe how to install, configure, and make sure that everything is correctly set in your development environment.

Chapter 2, *Creating Our First Qt and OpenCV Project*, takes you through the Qt Creator IDE, which we'll use to develop all of our applications. In this chapter, you'll learn how to create and run your application projects.

Chapter 3, *Creating a Comprehensive Qt+OpenCV Project*, goes through the most common capabilities required for a comprehensive application, including styles, internationalization, and support for various languages, plugins, and so on. Through this process, we'll create a comprehensive computer vision application ourselves.

Chapter 4, *Mat and QImage*, lays out the foundation and teaches you the basic concepts needed to write computer vision applications. In this chapter, you'll learn all about the OpenCV Mat class and the Qt QImage class, how to convert and pass them between the two frameworks, and a lot more.

Chapter 5, *The Graphics View Framework*, teaches you how to use the Qt Graphics View framework and its underlying classes in order to easily and efficiently display and manipulate graphics in an application.

Chapter 6, *Image Processing in OpenCV*, takes you through the image processing capabilities offered by OpenCV framework. You'll learn about transformations, filters, color spaces, template matching, and so on.

Chapter 7, *Features and Descriptors*, is all about detecting keypoints from images, extracting descriptors from keypoints, and matching them with each other. In this chapter, you'll learn about various keypoint and descriptor extraction algorithms and end up using them to detect and locate a known object inside an image.

Chapter 8, *Multithreading*, teaches you all about the multithreading capabilities offered by the Qt framework. You'll learn about mutexes, read-write locks, semaphores, and various thread synchronization tools. This chapter will also teach you about both the low-level (QThread) and high-level (QtConcurrent) multithreading technologies in Qt.

Chapter 9, *Video Analysis*, covers how to correctly process videos using Qt and OpenCV frameworks. You'll learn about object tracking using MeanShift and CAMShift algorithms and other video processing functionalities. This chapter also includes a comprehensive overview of all the essential and basic concepts for video processing, such as Histograms and back-projection images.

Chapter 10, *Debugging and Testing*, takes you through the debugging capabilities of the Qt Creator IDE and how it is configured and set up. In this chapter, you'll also learn about the unit testing capabilities offered by the Qt framework by writing example unit tests that can be run manually or automatically every time our project is built.

Chapter 11, *Linking and Deployment*, teaches you to build both OpenCV and Qt frameworks dynamically or statically. In this chapter, you'll also learn about deploying Qt and OpenCV applications on various platforms. At the end of this chapter, we'll create an installer using Qt Installer Framework.

Chapter 12, *Qt Quick Applications*, introduces you to Qt Quick Applications and the QML language. In this chapter, you'll learn about the QML language syntax and how to use it along with Qt Quick Designer to create beautiful Qt Quick Applications for desktop and mobile platform. You'll also learn about integrating QML and C++ in this chapter.

# To get the most out of this book

Although every required tool and software, the correct version, and how it is installed and configured is covered in the initial chapters of the book, the following is a list that can be used as a quick reference:

- A regular computer with a more recent version of Windows, macOS, or Linux (such as Ubuntu) operating system installed on it.
- Microsoft Visual Studio (on Windows)
- Xcode (on macOS)
- CMake
- Qt Framework
- OpenCV Framework

To get an idea of what a regular computer is these days, you can search online or ask a local shop; however, the one you already have is most probably enough to get you started.

# Download the example code files

You can download the example code files for this book from your account at www.packtpub.com. If you purchased this book elsewhere, you can visit www.packtpub.com/support and register to have the files emailed directly to you.

You can download the code files by following these steps:

1. Log in or register at www.packtpub.com.
2. Select the **SUPPORT** tab.
3. Click on **Code Downloads & Errata**.
4. Enter the name of the book in the **Search** box and follow the onscreen instructions.

Once the file is downloaded, please make sure that you unzip or extract the folder using the latest version of:

- WinRAR/7-Zip for Windows
- Zipeg/iZip/UnRarX for Mac
- 7-Zip/PeaZip for Linux

The code bundle for the book is also hosted on GitHub at `https://github.com/ PacktPublishing/Computer-Vision-with-OpenCV-3-and-Qt5`. We also have other code bundles from our rich catalog of books and videos available at `https://github.com/ PacktPublishing/`. Check them out!

# Download the color images

We also provide a PDF file that has color images of the screenshots/diagrams used in this book. You can download it here: `https://www.packtpub.com/sites/default/files/ downloads/ComputerVisionwithOpenCV3andQt5_ColorImages.pdf`.

# Conventions used

There are a number of text conventions used throughout this book.

`CodeInText`: Indicates code words in text, database table names, folder names, filenames, file extensions, pathnames, dummy URLs, user input, and Twitter handles. Here is an example: "The `QApplication` class is the main class responsible for controlling the application's control flow, settings, and so on."

A block of code is set as follows:

```
#include "mainwindow.h"
#include
int main(int argc, char *argv[])
{
    QApplication a(argc, argv);
    MainWindow w;
    w.show();
    return a.exec();
}
```

When we wish to draw your attention to a particular part of a code block, the relevant lines or items are set in bold:

```
#include "mainwindow.h"
#include
int main(int argc, char *argv[])
{
    QApplication a(argc, argv);
    MainWindow w;
    w.show();
    return a.exec();
}
```

Any command-line input or output is written as follows:

```
binarycreator -p packages -c config.xml myinstaller
```

**Bold**: Indicates a new term, an important word, or words that you see onscreen. For example, words in menus or dialog boxes appear in the text like this. Here is an example: "Clicking the **Next** button moves you to the next screen."

Warnings or important notes appear like this.

Tips and tricks appear like this.

# Get in touch

Feedback from our readers is always welcome.

**General feedback**: Email feedback@packtpub.com and mention the book title in the subject of your message. If you have questions about any aspect of this book, please email us at questions@packtpub.com.

**Errata**: Although we have taken every care to ensure the accuracy of our content, mistakes do happen. If you have found a mistake in this book, we would be grateful if you would report this to us. Please visit www.packtpub.com/submit-errata, selecting your book, clicking on the Errata Submission Form link, and entering the details.

**Piracy**: If you come across any illegal copies of our works in any form on the Internet, we would be grateful if you would provide us with the location address or website name. Please contact us at copyright@packtpub.com with a link to the material.

**If you are interested in becoming an author**: If there is a topic that you have expertise in and you are interested in either writing or contributing to a book, please visit authors.packtpub.com.

# Reviews

Please leave a review. Once you have read and used this book, why not leave a review on the site that you purchased it from? Potential readers can then see and use your unbiased opinion to make purchase decisions, we at Packt can understand what you think about our products, and our authors can see your feedback on their book. Thank you!

For more information about Packt, please visit packtpub.com.

# 1
# Introduction to OpenCV and Qt

In its most basic form and shape, Computer Vision is the term that is used to identify all methods and algorithms that are used to empower digital devices with a sense of vision. What does that mean? Well, it means exactly what it sounds like. Ideally, computers should be able to see the world through the lens of a standard camera (or any other type of camera for that matter), and by applying various Computer Vision algorithms, they should be able to detect faces, even recognize them, count objects in an image, detect motion in video feeds, and do many more, which, at first guess, would only be expected of a human being. So, to understand what Computer Vision really is, it's better to know that Computer Vision aims to develop methods to achieve the ideal that was mentioned, empowering digital devices with the power of seeing and understanding the surrounding environment. It is worth noting that most of the time Computer Vision and Image Processing are used interchangeably (although, a historical study of the subject may prove that it should be otherwise). But nevertheless, throughout this book we'll stick to the term Computer Vision since that is the more popular and widely used term nowadays in computer science communities and also because, as we'll see later in this chapter, Image Processing is a module of OpenCV library that we'll also be introduced to in the upcoming pages of this chapter, and it will also be covered in a complete chapter of its own.

Computer Vision is one of the today's most popular subjects in computer science and it's used in a variety of applications ranging from medical tools that detect cancerous tissues to video editing software that helps make all those shiny music videos and movies, and from military grade target detectors that help locate a specific location on the map to traffic sign detectors that help driverless cars find their way around. Well, it's obvious that we can't finish naming all possibilities for Computer Vision, but we can be sure it's an interesting subject that will be around for a long time. It's also worth mentioning that there is a fast-expanding market for jobs and careers in the field of Computer Vision and it's growing day by day.

Among the most popular tools used by Computer Vision developers and experts, come two of the most prominent frameworks of open source community, which are also in the title of the book you have in hand, OpenCV and Qt. Every day, literally thousands of developers around the world, ranging from established corporations to innovative startup companies, work with these two frameworks to build applications for various sets of industries, such as the ones we mentioned, and that is exactly what you will learn in this book.

In this chapter, we will cover the following topics:

- Introducing Qt, an open source, and cross-platform application development framework
- Introducing OpenCV, an open source, and cross-platform computer vision framework
- How to install Qt on Windows, macOS, and Linux operating systems
- How to build OpenCV from sources on Windows, macOS, and Linux operating systems
- Configuring your development environment to build applications using a combination of both Qt and OpenCV frameworks
- Build your very first application using Qt and OpenCV

# What is required?

This is the most obvious question after what was said in the introduction of this chapter, but the answer for it is also the first step in our journey to learn Computer Vision. This book is intended for developers who are familiar with C++ programming language and want to develop powerful and good-looking computer vision applications that perform well on different operating systems without much effort. This book aims to take you on an exciting journey through different topics of Computer Vision with a focus on hands-on exercises and developing whatever you learn, one step at a time.

Anyone with enough C++ experience knows that it's not an easy task to write visually rich applications using raw C++ code and depending on OS-specific APIs. So, almost every C++ developer (or at least serious developers with an active career in C++), use one or another framework to ease the process. Among the most widely known frameworks for C++ comes Qt. It is, in fact, one of the top choices, if not *the* top choice for that matter. On the other hand, if your aim is to develop an application dealing with images or visualized datasets, the OpenCV Framework is perhaps the first (and perhaps the most popular) address to visit. So, that's why this book focuses on the combination of Qt and OpenCV. Developing Computer Vision applications for different desktop and mobile platforms that perform with the highest possible performance would not be possible without using a combination of powerful frameworks such as Qt and OpenCV.

To summarize what was said, make sure you have at least an intermediate level of knowledge in C++ programming language. If terms such as class, abstract class, inheritance, templates, or pointers sound unfamiliar to you, then consider reading a book on C++ first. For all the rest of the topics, especially all of the hands-on topics that are covered, this book promises you crystal clear explanations (or reference to specific documentation pages) for all of the examples and tutorials included. Of course, to get a very detailed and deep understanding of how modules and classes are implemented in Qt and OpenCV, you need to be familiar with many more resources, studies, sometimes even hard-core mathematical calculations or low-level understanding of how a computer or operating system performs in the real world, which is totally out of the scope of this book. However, for all the algorithms and methods covered in this book, you will get a brief description of what they are, how and when and where they are used, and enough guidelines to let you continue digging deeper if you feel like it.

# Introduction to Qt

You have heard about it or maybe even used it without knowing it. It's the foundation of many world famous commercial and open source applications, such as VLC Player, Calibre, and so many more. The Qt Framework is used by a majority of the so-called Fortune 500 companies, and we can't even begin to define how widely used and popular it is among the many application development teams and companies in the world. So, we'll start with an introduction and take it from there.

Let's first go through a brief introduction to the Qt Framework to get us on our feet. Nothing can make you feel more comfortable with a framework than having a clear picture of the whole thing in your mind. So, here we go, currently built and managed by The Qt Company, Qt Framework is an open source application development framework that is widely used to create visually rich and cross-platform applications that can be run on different operating systems or devices with very little or no effort at all. To break it down further, open source is the most obvious part of it. It means you can access all of the source code for Qt. By visually rich, we mean enough resources and capabilities are present in Qt Framework to write very beautiful applications. As for the last part, cross-platform, this basically means that, if you develop an application using Qt Framework modules and classes for Microsoft Windows operating system, for instance, then it can be compiled and built for macOS or Linux exactly as it is, without changing a single line of code (almost), provided that you don't use any non-Qt or platform-specific libraries in your application.

At the time of writing this book, Qt framework (or simply Qt from here on) is at version 5.9.X and it contains many modules for almost any purpose in developing applications. Qt divides those modules into these four main categories:

- Qt Essentials
- Qt Add-Ons
- Value-Add Modules
- Technology Preview Modules

Let's see what they are and what they include since we'll be dealing with them a lot throughout this book.

# Qt Essentials

These are the modules promised by Qt to be available on all supported platforms. They are basically the foundation of Qt and they contain the majority of the classes that are used by almost all Qt applications. Qt Essential modules include all of the general-purpose modules and classes. Pay real attention to the words *general-purpose*, since it's exactly what these modules are used for. The following is a brief list for a quick study of the existing modules and for later reference purposes:

| Module | Description |
|--------|-------------|
| Qt Core | These are core non-graphical classes used by other modules. |
| Qt GUI | These are base classes for graphical user interface (GUI) components. These include OpenGL. |

| Qt Multimedia | These are classes for audio, video, radio, and camera functionality. |
|---|---|
| Qt Multimedia Widgets | These are widget-based classes to implement multimedia functionality. |
| Qt Network | These are classes to make network programming easier and more portable. |
| Qt QML | These are classes for QML and JavaScript languages. |
| Qt Quick | This is a declarative framework to build highly dynamic applications with custom user interfaces. |
| Qt Quick Controls | These are reusable Qt Quick based UI controls to create classic desktop-style user interfaces. |
| Qt Quick Dialogs | These are types to create and interact with system dialogs from a Qt Quick application. |
| Qt Quick Layouts | These layouts are items that are used to arrange Qt Quick 2 based items in the user interface. |
| Qt SQL | These are classes for database integration using SQL. |
| Qt Test | These are classes for unit testing Qt applications and libraries. |
| Qt Widgets | These are classes to extend Qt GUI with C++ widgets. |

For more information, refer to `http://doc.qt.io/qt-5/qtmodules.html`.

Note that it's not possible and perhaps not a good idea to cover all modules and all classes in this book, and, for the most part we will stick to whatever module and class we require; however, by the end of the book you'll feel comfortable enough exploring all the numerous and powerful modules and classes within Qt by yourself. You'll learn how to include a module and class in your projects in the upcoming chapters, so for now, let's not bother with too much detail and just focus on having a picture of what Qt really is and what it contains in our minds.

# Qt Add-Ons

These modules may or may not be available on all platforms. This means they are used for developing specific capabilities as opposed to the general-purpose nature of Qt Essentials. A few examples of these type of modules are Qt 3D, Qt Print Support, Qt WebEngine, Qt Bluetooth, and many more. You can always refer to the Qt documentation for a complete list of these modules, and in fact, they are too many to be just listed here. For the most part, you can get a brief idea of what a module is used for by just looking.

For more information on this you can refer to `http://doc.qt.io/qt-5/qtmodules.html`.

# Value-Add Modules

These modules offer additional capabilities and are offered with a commercial license from Qt. Yes, you guessed it right, these are the modules that are only available in a paid version of Qt and are not offered in the open source and free version of the Qt, but they're mostly aimed to help with very specific tasks that we don't need at all for the purpose of this book. You can get a list using the Qt documentation pages.

For more information on this you can refer to `http://doc.qt.io/qt-5/qtmodules.html`.

# Technology Preview Modules

Exactly as their name implies, these modules are the ones that are usually offered in a state that is not guaranteed to work for all cases; they may or may not contain bugs or other issues, and they are simply still in development and are offered as a preview for test and feedback purposes. As soon as a module is developed and becomes mature enough, it becomes available in other categories mentioned before, and it's taken out of the technology preview category. An example of these types of modules, at the moment of writing this book, is Qt Speech, which is a module that is aimed to add support for text-to-speech in Qt applications. It's always a good idea to keep an eye on these modules if you are looking forward to becoming a fully-fledged Qt developer.

For more information on this, you can refer to `http://doc.qt.io/qt-5/qtmodules.html`.

# Platforms supported by Qt

When we are talking about developing applications, the platform can have many different meanings, including the OS type, OS version, Compiler type, Compiler version, and Architecture of the processor (32-bit, 64-bit, Arm, and more). Qt supports many (if not all) of the well-known platforms and is usually quick enough to catch up with new platforms when they are released. The following is the list of platforms supported by Qt at the moment of writing this book (Qt 5.9). Note that you will probably not use all of the platforms mentioned here, but it gives you a sense of how powerful and cross-platform Qt really is:

| Platform | Compiler | Notes |
| --- | --- | --- |
| **Windows** | | |
| Windows 10 (64-bit) | MSVC 2017, MSVC 2015, MSVC 2013, MinGW 5.3 | |
| Windows 10 (32-bit) | MSVC 2017, MSVC 2015, MSVC 2013, MinGW 5.3 | |
| Windows 8.1 (64-bit) | MSVC 2017, MSVC 2015, MSVC 2013, MinGW 5.3 | |
| Windows 8.1 (32-bit) | MSVC 2017, MSVC 2015, MSVC 2013, MinGW 5.3 | |
| Windows 7 (64-bit) | MSVC 2017, MSVC 2015, MSVC 2013, MinGW 5.3 | |
| Windows 7 (32-bit) | MSVC 2017, MSVC 2015, MSVC 2013, MinGW 5.3 | MinGW-builds gcc 5.3.0 (32-bit) |
| **Linux/X11** | | |
| openSUSE 42.1 (64-bit) | GCC 4.8.5 | |
| Red Hat Enterprise Linux 6.6 (64-bit) | GCC 4.9.1 | devtoolset-3 |
| Red Hat Enterprise Linux 7.2 (64-bit) | GCC 5.3.1 | devtoolset-4 |
| Ubuntu 16.04 (64-bit) | GCC as provided by Canonical | |
| (Linux 32/64-bit) | GCC 4.8, GCC 4.9, GCC 5.3 | |

| macOS | | |
|---|---|---|
| macOS 10.10, 10.11, 10.12 | Clang as provided by Apple | |
| **Embedded Platforms: Embedded Linux, QNX, INTEGRITY** | | |
| Embedded Linux | GCC | ARM Cortex-A, Intel boards with GCC-based toolchains |
| QNX 6.6.0, 7.0 (armv7le and x86) | GCC as provided by QNX | Hosts: RHEL 6.6 (64-bit), RHEL 7.2 (64-bit), Windows 10 (64-bit), Windows 7 (32-bit) |
| INTEGRITY 11.4.x | As provided by Green Hills INTEGRITY | Hosts: 64-bit Linux |
| **Mobile Platforms: Android, iOS, Universal Windows Platform (UWP)** | | |
| Universal Windows Platform (UWP) (x86, x86_64, armv7) | MSVC 2017, MSVC 2015 | Hosts: Windows 10 |
| iOS 8, 9, 10 (armv7, arm64) | Clang as provided by Apple | macOS 10.10 host |
| Android (API Level: 16) | GCC as provided by Google, MinGW 5.3 | Hosts: RHEL 7.2 (64-bit), macOS 10.12, Windows 7 (64-bit) |

Reference: `http://doc.qt.io/qt-5/supported-platforms.html`

As you'll see in the next sections, we'll use the Microsoft Visual C++ 2015 (or from here on, simply MSVC 2015) compiler on Windows since both Qt and OpenCV (which you'll learn about later) highly support it. We'll also use GCC on Linux and Clang on macOS operating systems. All of which are tools that are either free and open source, or they are provided by the operating system provider. Although our main development system will be Windows, we'll cover Linux and macOS operating systems whenever there is a difference between Windows and other versions. So, the default screenshots throughout the book will be that of Windows, with Linux and macOS screenshots provided wherever there's any serious difference between them and not just simply a slight difference between paths, coloring of buttons, and so on.

# Qt Creator

**Qt Creator** is the name of the **IDE (Integrated Development Environment)** used to develop Qt applications. It's also the IDE that we will use throughout this book to create and build our projects. It is worth noting that Qt applications can be created using any other IDE (such as Visual Studio or Xcode), and Qt Creator is not a requirement to build Qt applications, but it's a lightweight and powerful IDE that comes with the Qt Framework installer by default. So, the biggest advantage it has is easy integration with the Qt framework.

The following is a screenshot of the Qt Creator, which shows the IDE in code editing mode. Details on how to use the Qt Creator will be covered in the next chapter, although we'll give it a try for a couple of tests later on in this chapter too, without going into too much detail about it:

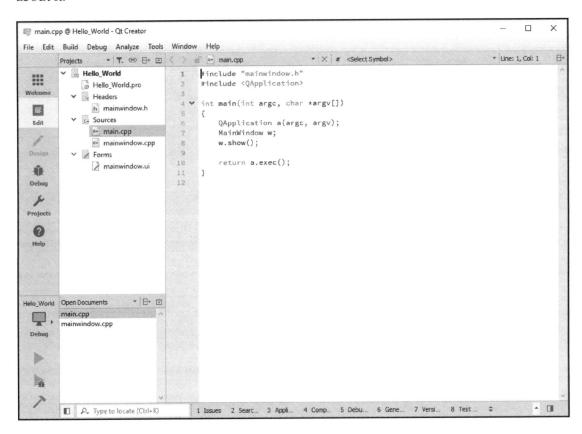

# Introduction to OpenCV

Now, it's time to introduce OpenCV, or Open Source Computer Vision library, or framework if you will, since OpenCV itself uses them interchangeably and that may also happen throughout this book. However, for the most part we'll simply stick to OpenCV. Well, let's first hear what it really is and then break it down where needed.

OpenCV is an open source and cross-platform library that is used to develop computer vision applications. With a focus on speed and performance, it includes hundreds of algorithms within a variety of modules. These modules are also categorized into two types: the `Main` and `Extra` modules. Main OpenCV modules are simply all modules that are built and maintained within OpenCV community, and they are a part of the default package provided by OpenCV.

This is in contrast to the Extra modules of OpenCV, which are more or less wrappers for third-party libraries and interfaces required to integrate them into an OpenCV build. The following are some examples of different module types with a brief description for each. It is worth noting that the number of (and sometimes even the order of) modules within OpenCV can be changed over time, so the best thing to keep in mind about this is to just pay a visit to the OpenCV documentation pages whenever something seems to be out of place, or if something is not where it used to be.

# Main modules

Here are some examples of OpenCV main modules. Note that they're just a few (and probably the most widely used) of modules within OpenCV, and covering all of them is out of the scope of this book, but it makes sense to have an idea of what OpenCV contains, just like what we saw with Qt earlier in this chapter. Here they are:

- Core functionality or simply `core` module contains all basic structures, constants, and functions used by all other OpenCV modules. For instance, the infamous OpenCV `Mat` class, which we'll use almost in every OpenCV example for the rest of the book, is defined in this module. `Chapter 4`, *Mat and QImage*, will cover this and closely-related OpenCV modules along with corresponding parts of the Qt framework.

- Image processing or `imgproc` module contains many different algorithms for image filtering, image transformation, and as the name implies, it's used for general image processing use. We'll be introduced to this module and its functions in `Chapter 6`, *Image Processing in OpenCV*.

- The 2D Features Framework module or `features2d` includes classes and methods used for feature extraction and matching. They'll be covered in more detail in `Chapter 7`, *Features and Descriptors*.

- The video module contains algorithms that are used for topics such as motion estimation, background subtraction, and tracking. This module, along with other similar modules of OpenCV, will be covered in Chapter 9, *Video Analysis*.

# Extra modules

As it was mentioned before, **Extra modules** are mostly wrappers for third-party libraries, that means they only contain interfaces or methods needed to integrate those modules. An example Extra module would be the text module. This module contains interfaces to use Text Detection in images or **OCR (Optical Character Recognition)**, and you'll also need those third-party modules for this work, and they are not covered as a part of this book, but you can always check the OpenCV documentation for an updated list of Extra modules and how they are used.

For more information on this you can refer to http://docs.opencv.org/master/index.html.

 **Platforms Supported by OpenCV**: As it was mentioned before, Platform is not just the operating system in case of application development. So, we need to know which operating systems, processor architectures, and the compiler is supported by OpenCV. OpenCV is highly cross-platform, and, almost like Qt, you can develop OpenCV applications for all major operating systems, including Windows, Linux, macOS, Android, and iOS. As we'll see later on, we'll use the MSVC 2015 (32-bit) compiler on Windows, GCC on Linux, and Clang on macOS. It's also important to note that we'll need to build OpenCV using its source code by ourselves since at the moment, prebuilt binaries are not provided for the mentioned compilers. However, as you'll see later on, OpenCV is fairly easy to build for any operating system if you have the right tools and instructions.

# Installing Qt

In this section, we'll go through the required steps to set up the complete Qt SDK (Software Development Kit) on your computer. We'll start by setting up Qt on Windows OS and make a note for Linux (Ubuntu in our case, but it's almost the same for all Linux distributions), and macOS operating system, wherever required. So, let's start.

# Preparing for Qt installation

To be able to install and use Qt, we need to first create a Qt account. Although it is not mandatory to do this, it still is highly recommended since you can get access to everything Qt related to this single, unified and free account. For any recent version of Qt that you want to install, you will need your **Qt Account** credentials, which you will only have if you have created a **Qt account**. To do this, first, you need to go to the Qt website using your favorite browser. Here is the link:

```
https://login.qt.io/login
```

Here is the screenshot of it:

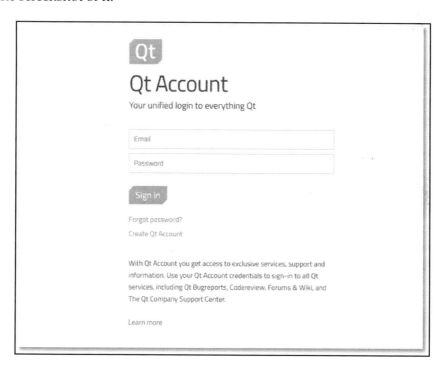

Here, you have to use your email address using the **Create Qt Account** page just under the **Sign in** button. The process is almost identical to any similar account creation on the web. You might be asked to enter captcha images to prove you are not a robot or click on an activation link in your email. After going through the procedures required by Qt, you'll have your very own Qt Account user, which is your email, and password. Make a note of that since you'll be needing it later on. We'll refer to it as your Qt Account Credentials from here on.

# Where to get it?

This is the point where we start downloading the required tools for Qt development. However, where to start? Qt maintains all officially released versions through the **Qt Downloads** web page. Here's a link: `https://download.qt.io/official_releases/`.

If you open your browser and navigate to the preceding webpage, you'll be presented with a very simple web page (similar to your file explorer program), and from there, you need to choose the right file yourself:

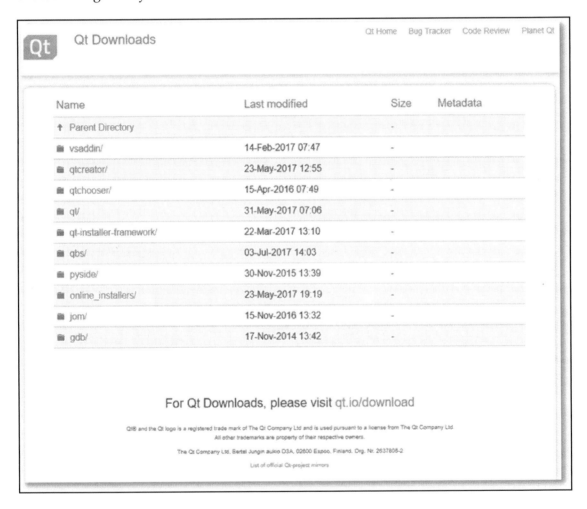

Qt releases all its official tools in here and, as you'll see, the **Last modified** column will be changing all the time. Some entries not so often, some more often. For now, we will not go into details of what each of these folders contains and what they are used for, but as you'll see later in this book, almost all of the tools required by us are in a single installer file and it's under the qt folder. So, by clicking on each entry, navigate to the following folder:
qt/5.9/5.9.1/

You'll notice the same is added to the web address in your browser:
https://download.qt.io/official_releases/qt/5.9/5.9.1/

You should note that there might be a newer version at the time when you visit this page, or this version may simply not be available anymore, so you need to start from the **Qt Download** page mentioned before, and work your way into the latest Qt version folder. Or, you can use the archive link in the **Qt Downloads** main page (https://download.qt.io/archive/) to always access previous versions of Qt.

Here are the files you need to download from the preceding folder:

**For Windows:** qt-opensource-windows-x86-5.9.1.exe

**For macOS:** qt-opensource-mac-x64-5.9.1.dmg

**For Linux:** qt-opensource-linux-x64-5.9.1.run

These are pre-built Qt libraries and contain the complete Qt SDK for each of the mentioned operating systems. This means you don't need to build Qt libraries by yourself to be able to use them. Here's what these installation files include in general and the tools we'll use:

- Qt Creator (version 4.3.1)
- Pre-Built libraries for all compilers and architecture supported on each OS:
    - Windows Desktop, Windows Mobile (on Windows)
    - Desktop (on Linux)
    - Desktop and iOS (on macOS)
    - Android (on all platforms)

**Windows users**: The Qt installation package also includes the MinGW compiler included in it, but since we will use another compiler, namely MSVC 2015, you don't really have anything to do with it. Although installing it shouldn't cause any harm.

# How to install?

You need to start the installation by executing the installation files you downloaded. If you are on a Windows or macOS operating system, then you just need to run the downloaded file. However, if you are using Linux, then you may need to make your downloaded .run file executable first before being able to actually run it. The following command can be executed on Linux to make your installer file executable:

```
chmod +x qt-opensource-linux-x64-5.9.1.run
```

Or, you can simply right-click on the .run file and make it executable using the properties dialog:

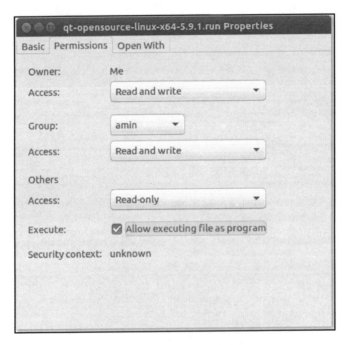

Note that you still need a working internet connection even though nothing will be downloaded and it's just to confirm your **Qt Account Credentials**. Running the installer will present you with the following series of dialogs that you need to get through. Wherever instructions on the dialog boxes are enough, just make sure you read them and provide what is required and press **Next**, **Agree**, or similar buttons to proceed forward. As you see in the following screenshots, you need to provide your **Qt Account Credentials** in order to proceed with the installation. These dialogs are identical on all operating systems:

The rest of the dialog boxes are not shown here, but they are pretty much self-explanatory, and if you have ever installed any app on any computer, then you have definitely seen similar dialogs and they need no introduction in general.

# Windows users

When installing Qt for Windows, on the **Select Components** dialog, make sure you check the checkbox next to the **msvc2015 32-bit** option. The rest is optional, but it's worth noting that installing all platforms (or Kits as they are called in Qt) usually requires too much space and can affect the Qt Creator performance in some cases. So, just make sure to select anything that you will really use. For the purpose of this book, it's just the msvc2015 32-bit option that you absolutely require.

**An important thing to note for Windows users**: You need to also install Visual Studio 2015 with at least C++ desktop development features enabled in it. Microsoft offers different types of licenses for Visual Studio. You can download the Community edition for educational purposes, which is definitely enough for this book's examples, and it's provided free of charge, but using Enterprise, Professional, or other types of Visual Studio should also be fine as long as they have the MSVC 2015 32-bit compiler.

# macOS users

When installing Qt for macOS, you will be faced with the following dialog (or a quite similar one depending on the version of macOS you are using) box if you don't have **XCode** installed on your Mac:

Unfortunately, it's not enough to follow the **Install** button, which takes a lot less time than installing Xcode, even though it might look like the obvious choice. You still need to make sure you get Xcode installed on your Mac either by pressing the **Get Xcode** button, directly getting it from **App Store**, or you'll face the following while installing Qt:

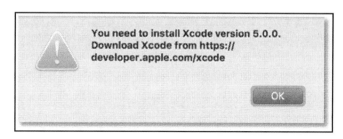

Use **App Store** to install the latest version of Xcode (at the moment of writing this book, Xcode 8.3.3 is available) then continue with Qt installation.

On the **Select Components** dialog, make sure you select at least **macOS** version. You won't need the rest of the components but installing them won't harm, other than the fact that it might take a lot of space on your computer.

## Linux users

When installing Qt for Linux, on the **Select Components** dialog, make sure you select (at least) Desktop GCC (32 bit or 64 bit, depending on your OS). You'll notice that the Qt Creator will be installed by default, and you don't need to check any options for that.

When the installation is completed, you'll have the following applications installed on your computer:

- **Qt Creator:** This is the main IDE that we'll be using throughout the book to build applications.
- **Qt Assistant:** This application is used to view Qt help files. It provides useful functionality to view Qt documentation. Nevertheless, the Qt Creator also provides a context-sensitive help, and it also has its own built-in and very handy help viewer.

- **Qt Designer:** This is used to design GUIs using Qt Widgets. Again, Qt Creator also has this designer built-in, but in case you prefer using other IDEs rather than the Qt Creator, then you can still use the Designer to help with the GUI design process.
- **Qt Linguist:** This is an excellent aid if you will be building multilingual applications. Qt Linguist helps with easier translation and integration of translated files into your build.

For Windows and macOS users, this is the end of the story for Qt installation, but Linux users still need to take care of a few more things, namely installing the application development, building tools, and some required runtime libraries for Linux. Qt always uses the compiler and build tools provided by the operating system. Linux distributions usually do not, by default, include those tools since they're only used by developers and not used by regular users. So, to install them (if they're not installed already) you can run the following command from a terminal:

```
sudo apt-get install build-essential libgl1-mesa-dev
```

You can always refer to the Qt documentation pages for required commands by all Linux distributions, but, in this book, we'll assume the distribution to be Ubuntu/Debian; however, note that usually, the commands are very similar in the pattern for all Linux distros.

For more information on this, you can refer to http://doc.qt.io/qt-5/linux.html.

# Testing Qt installation

You can now safely run Qt Creator and create wonderful applications with it. For now, let's just make sure our Qt installation is working correctly. Don't bother with the details now, since we'll be covering it all during the course of the book, and especially don't worry if you think you don't understand what's really going on behind the scenes. Just run **Qt Creator** and press the big **New Project** button seen, as follows:

In the window that appears next, choose **Application**, **Qt Widgets Application**, and then click on **Choose**, as shown in the following screenshot:

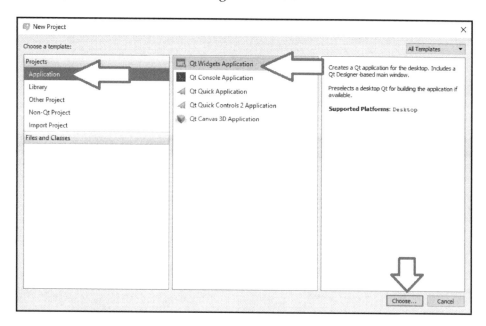

In the next window, you need to provide a name and folder (where your test project will be created) and then click **Next** to proceed forward. Make sure to check the **Use as default project location** checkbox if you want to have a dedicated folder for your Qt projects. You only need to do this once and afterward all of your projects will be created in that folder. For now, let's just put a name and path since we're only going to test our Qt installation, and click **Next**. You will see something similar to what is shown in the following screenshot:

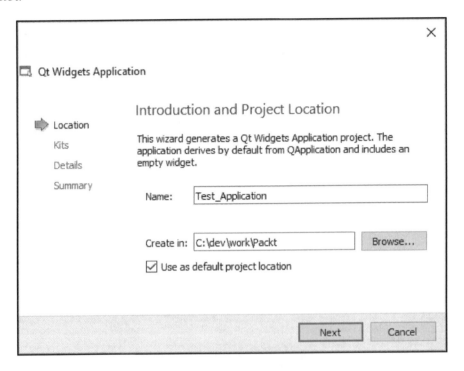

In the next window, you need to select a so-called **Kit** to build your application with. Choose the one that has a name starting with **Desktop Qt 5.9.1** and click **Next**. Depending on what components you selected during the installation of Qt, you may have more than one choice here, and depending on the operating system and compilers installed on your system, you may have more than one **Kit** with a name that starts with Desktop, so make sure you select the compilers we'll use in this book, which would be the following:

- msvc2015 32-bit on Windows
- Clang on macOS
- GCC on Linux

After you have selected the correct **Kit** according to the ones mentioned earlier, you can click on **Next** to proceed forward:

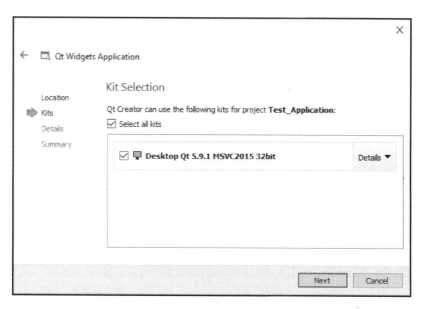

You don't really need to bother with the next two windows that appear and just clicking on **Next** should be enough for our test of Qt installation. The first window makes it easier to create a new class and the second one allows you to select a **version control** tool and track changes in your code:

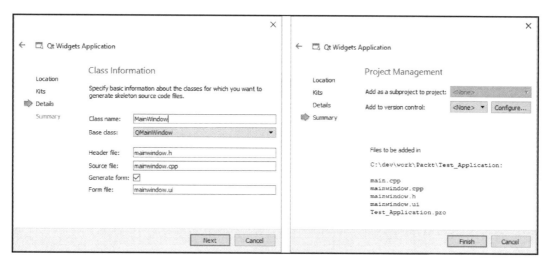

After you click on the **Finish** button on the last window, you will be taken to the **Edit** mode within Qt Creator. We'll cover different aspects of the Qt Creator in the next chapter, so for now, just click on the **Run** button (or press *Ctrl +60;R*) to start compiling your test (and empty) application, as shown here:

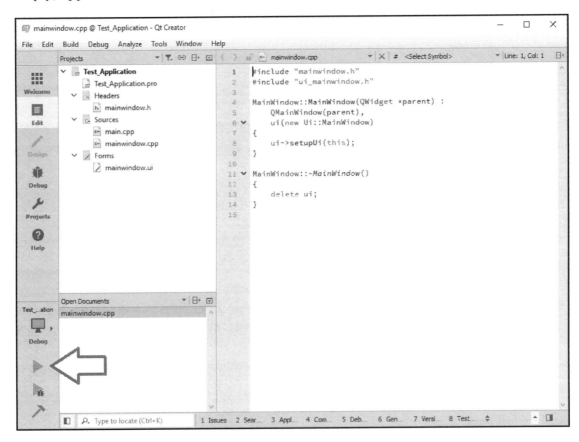

Depending on the speed of your computer, it will take some time for the build process to be finished. After a few moments, you should see your test (and first) Qt application running. It's just an empty application similar to what is seen in the following screenshot, and the purpose of doing this was to make sure our Qt installation is working as we want it to. Obviously, your empty Qt application may look a little different than this on different operating systems, and different visual options may affect the whole coloring or the way windows are displayed. Nevertheless, your newly built application should look exactly the same (or quite similar) to the window seen here:

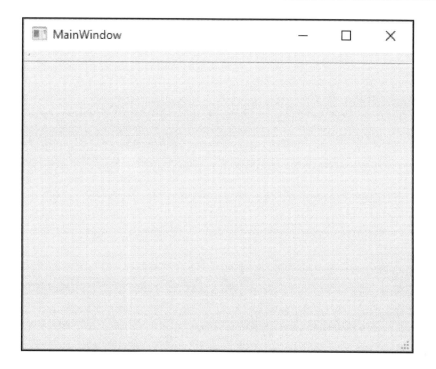

In case your application doesn't show up, make sure to go over the instructions once again. Also, make sure you don't have any conflicting installations of Qt or other settings that may interfere with Qt installation. Always refer to documentation pages and the Qt community for answers to unexpected behavior of Qt Creator or other Qt tools. Being an open source project for such a long time, Qt has grown a huge and loyal set of users who are eager to share their knowledge on the internet and answer issues faced by fellow Qt users. So, it's a good idea to keep an eye on the Qt community since you already have a unified Qt account that you can use to access Qt forums. This is the same user and password that you created to proceed with the Qt installation process.

# Installing OpenCV

In this section of the chapter, you'll learn how to build OpenCV using its source codes. As you'll see later on, and as opposed to the title of this section, we're not really *installing* OpenCV in a way similar to what we experienced with Qt installation. That's because OpenCV usually doesn't provide pre-built binaries for all compilers and platforms, and in fact it provides no pre-built binaries for macOS and Linux at all. In the most recent **Win pack** of the OpenCV, only pre-built binaries for MSVC 2015 64-bit are included, which are not compatible with the 32-bit version that we'll be using, so it's a very good idea to learn how to build OpenCV yourself. It also has the advantage of building an OpenCV framework library that is suitable for what you need. You may want to exclude some options to make your OpenCV installation lighter, or you may want to build for another compiler such as MSVC 2013. So, there are quite a lot of reasons to build OpenCV from sources by yourself.

# Preparing for an OpenCV build

Most of the open source frameworks and libraries on the internet, or at least the ones that want to remain IDE neutral (this means, a project that can be configured and built using any IDE and a project that does not depend on a specific IDE to be able to work), use CMake or similar so-called *make* systems. I guess this also answers questions such as *Why do I need CMake at all?*, *Why can't they just give the libraries and be done with it?* or any other questions like these. So, we need CMake to be able to configure and build OpenCV using sources. CMake is an open source and cross-platform application that allows for configuring and building open source projects (or apps, libraries, or so on), and you can download and use it on all operating systems that were mentioned in the previous sections. At the moment of writing this book, CMake version 3.9.1 can be downloaded from the CMake website download page (https://cmake.org/download/).

Make sure you download and install it on your computer before proceeding forward. There's nothing special about the CMake installation that needs to be taken note of, except for the fact that you should make sure you install the GUI version since that's what we'll be using in the next section and it's the default option in the link provided earlier.

# Where to get OpenCV?

OpenCV maintains its official and stable releases under the **Releases** page at their website (`http://opencv.org/releases.html`):

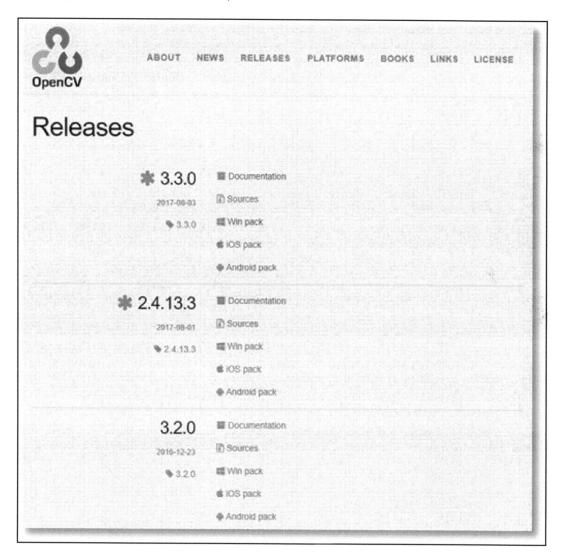

This is where you can always find the most recent release of OpenCV sources, documentation, and pre-built binaries for Windows, Android, and iOS. As new versions are released, they are added at the top of the page. At the moment of writing this book, version 3.3.0 is the most recent release of OpenCV and that's the version we'll use. So, without further ado, you should go ahead and download the Sources by clicking on the **Sources** link for version 3.3.0. Download the `source zip` file to a folder of your choice, extract it, and make a note of the extracted path since we'll use it in a few moments.

# How to build?

Now that we have all required tools and files to build OpenCV, we can start the process by running the CMake GUI application. If you've installed CMake correctly, then you should be able to run it from your desktop, start menu, or dock, depending on your operating system.

 Linux users should run the following command in a terminal before proceeding with the OpenCV build. These are basically dependencies by OpenCV itself, which need to be in place before it's configured and built:

```
sudp apt-get install libgtk2.0-dev and pkg-config
```

After you run the CMake GUI application, you need to set the following two folders:

- The **Where is the source code** folder should be set to where you downloaded and extracted OpenCV source code
- The **Where to build the binaries** folder can be set to any folder, but it's common to create a subfolder named `build` under the source codes folder and select that as the binaries folder

After these two folders are set, you can proceed forward by clicking on the
**Configure** button, as shown in the following screenshot:

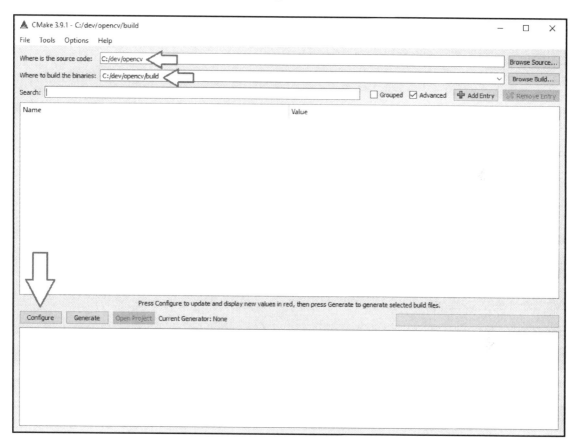

Clicking on the **Configure** button will start the configuration process. You may be asked to create the build folder if it does not already exist, to which you need to answer by clicking on the **Yes** button. Don't worry if you still feel like you're just repeating what's in the book. This will all sink in as you move forward with the book and the instructions. For now, let's just focus on getting OpenCV built and installed on your computer. Consider this an installation process that is not as easy as just clicking on a few **Next** buttons, and as soon as you start using OpenCV, it will all make sense. So, in the window that will appear next, select the correct generator and click **Finish**. See the following instructions for the correct generator type on each operating system:

 **Windows users**: You need to select **Visual Studio 14 2015**. Make sure you don't select the ARM or Win64 versions or a different Visual Studio version.

**macOS and Linux users**: You need to select **Unix Makefiles**.

You'll see a short process in CMake, and when it's finished, you'll be able to set various parameters to configure your OpenCV build. There are many parameters to configure, so we'll just bother with the ones that directly affect us.

Make sure you check the checkbox next to the **BUILD_opencv_world** option. This will allow building all OpenCV modules into a single library. So, if you're on Windows, you'll have only a single DLL file that includes all OpenCV functions. As you'll see later on, this has the advantage of bothering with only a single DLL file when you want to deploy your computer vision applications. Of course, the obvious downside to this is that your application installer size will be a little bit larger. But again, ease of deployment, will prove to be much more useful later on.

You need to click on the **Configure** button again after changing the build parameters. Wait for the reconfiguration to finish and finally click on the **Generate** button. This will make your OpenCV build ready to compile. For the next part, you'll need to execute somewhat different commands if you're using Windows, macOS, or Linux operating systems. So, here they are:

**Windows users**: Go to the OpenCV build folder that you set earlier in CMake (in our case it was `c:\dev\opencv\build`). There should be a Visual Studio 2015 Solution (that is, the type of MSVC projects) that you can easily execute and build OpenCV with. You can also immediately click on the Open Project button, which is right next to the Generate button on CMake. You can also just run Visual Studio 2015 and open the Solution file you just created for OpenCV.

After Visual Studio is opened, you need to select **Batch Build** from the Visual Studio main menu. It's right under **Build**:

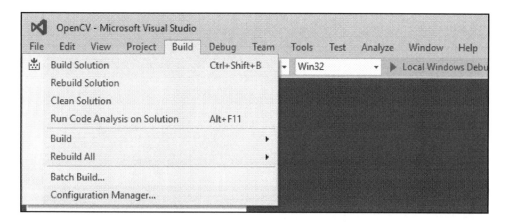

Make sure checkboxes in the **Build** column are enabled for **ALL_BUILD** and **INSTALL**, as shown in the following screenshot:

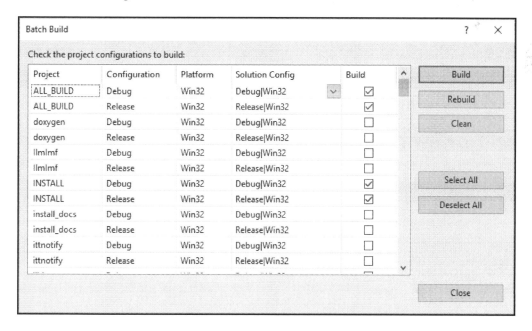

**For macOS and Linux users**: Run a terminal instance and execute the following commands after you switch to the Binaries folder you chose in CMake. To switch to a specific folder, you need to use the cd command. After you are in the OpenCV build folder (it should be the folder in your home that you chose when you opened CMake), you need to execute the following command. You'll be asked to provide the administrative password, just provide your password and press *Enter* to proceed forward with building OpenCV:

```
sudo make
```

This will trigger the build process, and depending on your computer speed this can take quite some time. Wait until building all libraries are finished and you see the progress bar reach 100%.

After the long wait, there's only one more command left to execute for macOS and Linux users. If you are on Windows, you can close Visual Studio IDE and proceed to the next step.

 **macOS and Linux users**: After the building is completed, before closing the terminal instance, execute the following command while you're still in the OpenCV `build` folder:

```
sudo make install
```

This last command for non-Windows users will make sure OpenCV is installed on your computer and is completely ready to use. You're fine to proceed forward if you didn't miss any commands in this section. You have an OpenCV framework ready to build computer vision applications with.

# Configuring OpenCV installation

Remember we mentioned that OpenCV is a framework and you will learn how to use it with Qt? Well, Qt offers a very easy-to-use method to include any third-party library, such as OpenCV, in your Qt projects. To be able to use OpenCV in Qt, you need to use a special kind of file which is called a PRI file. PRI files are files that are used to add third-party modules and include them in your Qt projects. Note that you only need to do this once, and for the rest of the book you will use this file in all your projects, so it's a very crucial (yet very easy) part of the Qt configuration.

Start by creating a text file in a folder of your choice. I recommend using the same folder you used for OpenCV build because that can help make sure you have all your OpenCV related files in a single folder. However, technically speaking, this file can be located anywhere on your computer. Rename the file to `opencv.pri` and open it using any text editor and write the following inside this PRI file:

**Windows users**: By now, your OpenCV library files should be inside the OpenCV build folder that you set on CMake previously. There should be a subfolder called `install` inside the `build` folder with all required OpenCV files inside it. In fact, now you can delete everything else and just keep these files if you need some space on your computer, but it's always a good idea to keep OpenCV sources on your computer, and we'll specifically need it in the final chapters where we'll cover more advanced OpenCV subjects. So, here's what you need inside the PRI file (be careful about path separators, you always need to use / in PRI files regardless of the operating system):

```
INCLUDEPATH += c:/dev/opencv/build/install/include
Debug: {
LIBS += -lc:/dev/opencv/build/install/x86/vc14/lib/opencv_world330d
}
Release: {
LIBS += -lc:/dev/opencv/build/install/x86/vc14/lib/opencv_world330
}
```

There is no need to say that in the preceding code, you need to replace the paths if you have used a different folder during the CMake configuration.

**macOS and Linux users**: Simply put the following inside your `opencv.pri` file:

```
INCLUDEPATH += /usr/local/include
LIBS += -L/usr/local/lib \
    -lopencv_world
```

There's one more thing left for Windows users, and that is adding OpenCV DLLs folder to the **PATH environment variable**. Simply open the **System properties** window and add a new entry in your PATH. They are usually separated by ; so just add a new one after that. Note that this path is related to the Windows operating system only, and where it can find your DLL files for OpenCV for an easier build process; users of Linux and macOS don't need to do anything regarding this.

# Testing OpenCV installation

The worst is past us, and we are now ready to dig into the world of Computer Vision and start building exciting applications using Qt and OpenCV. Although this one last step is called Testing OpenCV, it's actually the first Qt+OpenCV application that you'll write, as simple as it may seem at first. Our aim in this section is not to bother with any details of how things are working and what goes on behind the scenes, but just to make sure we have configured everything correctly and avoid wasting time with configuration-related issues later in the book. If you have followed everything as it was described and executed all instructions in the correct order, then by now, you shouldn't be worrying about anything, but it's always best to *verify*, and that is what we'll do now.

So, we'll verify our OpenCV installation with a very simple application that reads an image file from the hard disk and just displays it. Again, don't bother with any code related details since we'll cover it all in the upcoming chapters and just focus on the task at hand, that is testing our OpenCV installation. Start by running Qt Creator and creating a new Console Application. You have already done a very similar task before when you were testing your Qt installation. You need to follow exactly the same instructions, except instead of **Qt Widgets**, you have to make sure you select **Qt Console Application**. Repeat all of the similar steps like before, until you end up in Qt Creator edit mode. If you are asked about build system just select **qmake**, which should be selected by default, so you just need to move forward. Make sure to give a name such as QtCvTest to your project. This time, instead of clicking on the **Run** button, double-click on your project's PRO file, which you can find in the explorer at the left side of the Qt Creator screen, and add the following line at the end of your project's PRO file:

```
include(c:/dev/opencv/opencv.pri)
```

Note that this, in fact, is a type of *hard-coding* that should always be avoided, and as we'll see in the later chapters, we will write more sophisticated PRO files that work on all operating systems without changing a single line; however, since we're just testing our OpenCV installation, it is OK for now to go ahead with a little bit of hard-coding to simplify things a little bit and not overwhelm you with more configuration details.

So, back to what we were doing, the moment you save your PRO file by pressing *Ctrl + S,* you will notice a quick process and update in the project explorer and the `opencv.pri` file will appear in the explorer. You can always change the contents of `opencv.pri` from here, but you will probably never need to do it. Ignore the Comment-Like lines and make sure your PRO file is similar to what I have here:

```
QT += core
QT -= gui
CONFIG += c++11
TARGET = QtCvTest
CONFIG += console
CONFIG -= app_bundle
TEMPLATE = app
SOURCES += main.cpp
DEFINES += QT_DEPRECATED_WARNINGS
include(c:/dev/opencv/opencv.pri)
```

This simple line of code in our project's PRO file is basically the result of all of our efforts in this chapter. Now, we are able to add OpenCV to our Qt projects by simply including this simple piece of code in every Computer Vision project that we want to build using Qt and OpenCV.

In the upcoming chapters, we'll learn about PRO files in Qt and everything about the preceding code; however, for now let's just move on knowing that this file is responsible for our project's configurations. So, the last line, which is pretty much self-explanatory, simply means we want to add OpenCV include headers and libraries to our Qt project.

Now, you can actually write some OpenCV code. Open up your `main.cpp` file and change the contents of it to make it similar to this:

```
#include <QCoreApplication>
#include "opencv2/opencv.hpp"
int main(int argc, char *argv[])
{
    QCoreApplication a(argc, argv);
    using namespace cv;
    Mat image = imread("c:/dev/test.jpg");
    imshow("Output", image);
    return a.exec();
}
```

By default, your `main.cpp` file should already have most of what is in the preceding code, but you'll notice the include line at the top and the three lines responsible for reading and displaying a test image from my computer. You can replace the path to any other image (just make sure you stick to JPG or PNG files for now), and it's very important to make sure the image file exists and it's accessible, otherwise, our test might fail, even though our installation is still correct. The whole code is almost self-explanatory but once again, you shouldn't bother with the codes for now since we're just testing our OpenCV build, so just press the **Run** button to have your image file displayed. You should see something similar to the following screenshot on your computer:

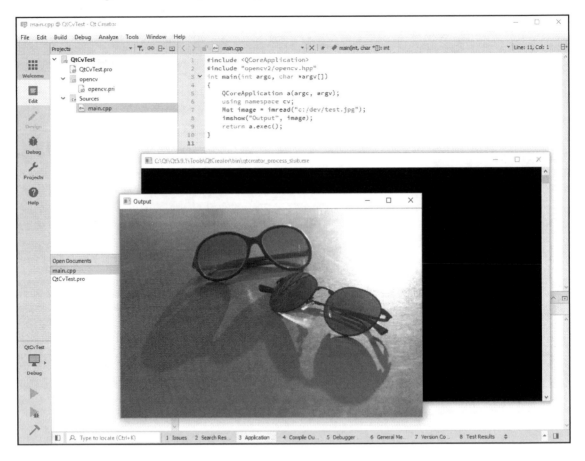

# Summary

In this chapter, you were introduced to the concept of Computer Vision in general and to the Qt and OpenCV frameworks, and you learned about their overall modular structure and also got a brief look into how seriously cross-platform they are with all the platforms they both support. You also learned how to install Qt on a computer and how to build OpenCV using its source codes. By now, you should have enough confidence to even try out a few different configurations to build OpenCV, other than the standard build mentioned in this chapter. It's always a good idea to explore some unknown and deep parts of these huge frameworks by simply taking a look in the folders and files they contain. Finally, you learned how to configure your development computer to build applications using Qt and OpenCV, and you even built your first application. In the next chapter, you'll learn more about Qt Creator by first building a console application and then moving on to building a Qt widgets application. You'll also learn about the structure of Qt projects and how to create a cross-platform integration between Qt and OpenCV frameworks. The next chapter will be the start of actual computer vision development and programming examples in this book and will lay out the foundations of our hands-on examples throughout the book.

# 2
# Creating Our First Qt and OpenCV Project

It's been a long time since the Qt and OpenCV frameworks were introduced to the open source community and the world, but it wasn't until recently that people started noticing the benefits of using the two together, and the combination became popular among computer vision experts. We're in luck since we are at a phase in the history of these two frameworks where they both have been grown enough to be combined very easily, with little or no effort. There are also no more questions about the stability of these frameworks, and they are sometimes used to build applications running on quite sensitive hardware. Even a brief search on the internet would prove this. As we'll learn in this chapter, Qt Creator has become an almost fully-grown IDE, and it provides very easy mechanisms to integrate and build computer vision applications using OpenCV. Now that we are past all installation and configurations that we faced in Chapter 1, *Introduction to OpenCV and Qt*, we will focus only on building applications using Qt and OpenCV.

In this chapter, we will start our hands-on work by learning all about Qt Creator IDE and how to create projects with it, since we are literally using Qt Creator for the rest of the book and for anything we build. You'll learn about all the benefits it offers and sees why it's a very powerful IDE in all its simplicity, look, and feel. You will learn about the Qt Creator settings and details and how to change them to fit your needs. You'll also learn about Qt Project files, source codes, user interfaces, and so on. We'll leave the gory details about everything that goes on behind the scenes when an application is built using Qt Creator for the next chapter, Chapter 3, *Creating a Comprehensive Qt+OpenCV Project*, but we'll also walk over some useful details in this chapter to get a clear understanding of the structure of a real project. These topics will all be covered in the context of creating an application so that you can have a better understanding by repeating the same tasks you learn here in this chapter.

You should note that the things you'll learn in this chapter will help you save a tremendous amount of time in the future, but this will only be the case if you really repeat it all on your computer and actually always try to use it when you do C++ programming with Qt Creator, even for non-Qt applications.

Finally, we will end the chapter by creating an actual computer vision application and applying some basic image processing algorithms to images. This chapter's goal is to prepare you for the rest of the book and familiarize you with some of the keywords that you will face all throughout the book, such as signals, slots, widgets, and so on.

In this chapter, we will cover the following topics:

- Configuring and using the Qt Creator IDE
- Creating Qt projects
- Widgets in Qt Creator
- Creating cross-platform Qt+OpenCV project files
- Using Qt Creator to design user interfaces
- Using Qt Creator to write code for user interfaces

# What is Qt Creator?

Qt Creator is not the same thing as the Qt framework. Yes, that's right; it is just an IDE created by and for the Qt framework. This is what confuses many people who are somewhat new to these terms. So, what does that really mean? In a very basic definition, it means you can use Qt Creator or any other IDE to create Qt applications. At some point, when the Qt framework became rich with classes and functions, the people responsible for Qt decided to create an IDE using the wonderful Qt framework itself, and, voila! An IDE free from the operating systems and C++ compiler types was born. Qt Creator is an IDE that supports better integration with the Qt framework, it's open source (which basically means you can use it for free), it's cross-platform, and it includes almost all the tools required from an IDE. Here's a screenshot of the **Welcome** mode in Qt Creator:

Note that we'll necessarily use all of the Qt Creator features, but it's a good idea to know what it's capable of before digging in more. Here are some of the most important features of the Qt Creator:

- Managing multiple IDE states using Sessions
- Managing multiple Qt projects
- Designing user interfaces
- Editing code
- Building and running applications on all Qt supported platforms
- Debugging applications
- Context-sensitive help

Depending on what you consider important, you may be able to extend this list with more items, but what is mentioned in the preceding list is essentially the definition of an IDE (Integrated Development Environment), which is supposed to be an application that offers all required and absolutely necessary tools of application development. Also, you can always check out the Qt documentation for additional capabilities of the Qt Creator.

# A tour of the IDE

In this section, we will take a walk around different parts and bits of Qt Creator. It's always a good idea to get a sense of your surroundings and environment when you move to a new place. You may not notice the differences at the beginning, but this is actually a very similar situation, as you'll come to realize. You are going to use the Qt Creator environment throughout the whole book, and, basically, live and work with it for the entire period of reading this book, and, later on, hopefully, for a long time in your career, personal projects, or studies. So, let's start our walk and start touching things to see what really happens.

Let's go back to the first picture in this chapter. What you see here is the initial Qt Creator screen, or as you'll see a bit later, it is the welcome mode of the Qt Creator. You may notice that the icons and colors here are slightly different than what you have on your computer, even though you installed the same version of Qt. Don't worry, as you'll see later on, it's just a theme, and you'll learn how to change it as it fits your own style and preferences. In fact, you'll see screenshots from different themes of Qt throughout the book, but keep in mind that's just the look and feel and it has nothing to do with the functionality. Qt Creator is designed in a way that it allows extremely fast and easy switching between different **Modes** in it. Switching to each mode almost totally changes what is in the main area of the Qt GUI, and serves a completely different and unique purpose of its own. Let's see which modes Qt supports and what they are used for.

# Qt Creator modes

Qt Creator has six different modes that help you open projects, edit code, design user interfaces, and more. Let's go over the following list and then try to see what they are exactly:

- Welcome
- Edit
- Design
- Debug
- Projects
- Help

Before we go over them in more detail, as I am sure you have already noticed, you can use the buttons on the left side of the Qt Creator screen to switch between different modes, as shown in the following screenshot:

For almost everything that the Qt Creator does, there is a dedicated keyboard shortcut, and that is also the case to switch between different modes. You can learn about the shortcut keys for anything on the screen by simply keeping your mouse over it without clicking for a few moments and a tip box will pop up to tell you more about this, so we won't cover an entire list of shortcut key sequences since you can easily find the most updated hotkey using the method just described. As you can see in the following screenshot, I have kept my mouse cursor over the **Design** mode button, and there it is, it tells me both the purpose of the button, which is **Switch to Design mode** and the keyboard shortcut, which is *Ctrl + 3*:

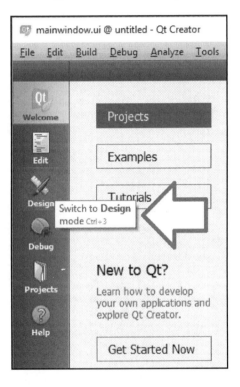

We will now learn more about different modes in Qt Creator and what they are used for. You should note that it is out of the scope of this book to just list and go over the details of each function within Qt Creator, but we'll definitely cover all aspects of Qt Creator that are used in the book. Qt Creator and almost everything regarding Qt is quickly evolving, and it's always best to keep an eye on the documentation pages and try out new or changed functionalities by yourself.

# The Welcome mode

This is the initial mode when Qt Creator is opened, and can always be switched to by using the **Welcome** button on the left:

The most important thing to note about this mode is that it, in fact, has three different sub-modes, which are mentioned as follows:

- Projects
- Examples
- Tutorials

## Projects

This screen (or sub-mode of the Welcome mode) can be used to create new Qt projects using the **New Project** button. You've already experienced how it's done very briefly in Chapter 1, *Introduction to OpenCV and Qt*. You can also open any projects saved on your computer if you click on the **Open Project** button. There's also a list containing **Recent Projects**, which is very useful and acts both as a reminder of what you were working on and a shortcut to access them. There are also **Sessions** visible on this mode, which are some of the most interesting features of Qt Creator. **Sessions** are used to store the state of the IDE and restore that state later, whenever needed. In this book, we will not bother with **Sessions**, but they are quite handy if they're used correctly, and can save you a lot of time during the development.

Understanding **Sessions** in Qt Creator would be very simple with an example. Let's say, you are working on a certain project and you have some projects opened in Qt Creator, or you have some breakpoints set in your code, and so on. All information like that is stored in the so-called **Sessions**, and can be easily restored by switching between sessions.

If you click on the **New Project** button, you will be presented with the **New Project** window, which allows you to choose a project type (or template) based on what you want to develop. As you'll see later on, we'll be using the **Applications/Qt Widgets Application** and **Library/C++ Library** options only, because it's not in the scope of this book to go through all possible Qt project templates; however, as you can see in the following screenshot, the **New Project** window consists of three sections, and you can get a very helpful description of each project type by simply choosing them. As soon as you click on any project types using the first and second lists (in the following screenshot), their description will appear in the third pane. Here's the description that appears when you select Qt Widgets Application project type (see the following image, especially pane number 3):

- Creates a Qt application for the Desktop, including a Qt Designer-based main window
- Preselects a desktop Qt for building the application if available
- Supported platforms: Desktop

As you can see, it contains a very helpful insight into what kind of project this type of template is meant for. Try going over all of the various options to familiarize yourself with the project types. It's a very good idea to be aware of the possible project types, even if you won't use them right away. The following is a screenshot of the **New Project** window:

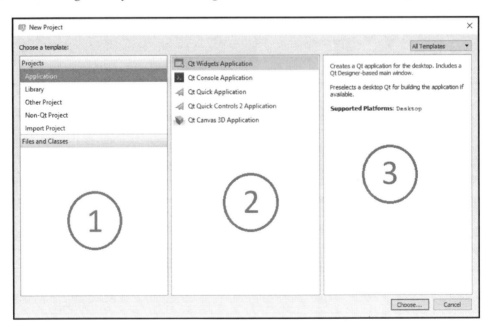

# Examples

This is one of my most favorite parts in Qt Creator, and, without a doubt, one of the most important places to learn about Qt and get an insight about what can be done with it. There are tons of examples here with explanations and are ready to build with just a click. There's also a **Search** bar in examples that you can use to search for different examples using search keywords.

# Tutorials

Currently, this part is quite similar to the examples in the sense that it is meant to train Qt Developers, but the main difference is that it contains video presentations and examples. Make sure you browse through them once in a while to get up-to-date about the new features and how to use them.

Before moving on to the next Qt Creator mode, which is the **Edit** mode, we need to create a new project. We'll use this example for the rest of this chapter, since the rest of the modes require a project for us to work with. Now that you are familiar with the Welcome mode, you can go ahead and create a new Qt Widgets Application. You already created a project in Chapter 1, *Introduction to OpenCV and Qt*, when we were testing the Qt and OpenCV installations. You need to repeat exactly the same steps. This time, just make sure you name your project Hello_Qt_OpenCV. Here are the steps you need to take:

- Click on the **New Project** button in the **Welcome** mode, or press *Ctrl + N*.
- Select **Application** and then **Qt Widgets Application** in the **New Project** window.
- Set the project name to Hello_Qt_OpenCV and choose a folder to **Create in**. If you did this previously and checked the **Use as default project location** checkbox, then you won't need to change anything regarding **Create in** here. Then, click **Next**.
- Select the only desktop kit choice that you have, depending on your operating system. Then, click **Next**.
- Leave the class information as it is. It should be **MainWindow** by default, which is OK, and then, click **Next**.
- When on the project management page, just click on **Finish**. Your project is now ready, and you can follow the rest of the examples and topics in this chapter.

# Edit mode

The **Edit** mode is probably the mode that you will spend most of your time on when working with Qt Creator. It's mainly meant for code editing and everything regarding the text-based source files of a Qt project. You can always switch to Edit mode using the **Edit** button on the right side of the screen, as shown here:

Let's first take a look at the following screenshot regarding different panes visible in the edit mode. As you can see, there are three different parts. The part highlighted with the number 1 is the main coding area, **2** is the left sidebar, and **3** is the right sidebar. By default, only the left sidebar is visible, but you can open or close each of the sidebars using the small buttons pointed using the arrows at the bottom of the screen on each side. The most important thing to note about each pane (both sidebars and main coding area in the center) is the fact that they can be split, duplicated, or their modes can be changed using the buttons pointed out using the arrows at the top on each side:

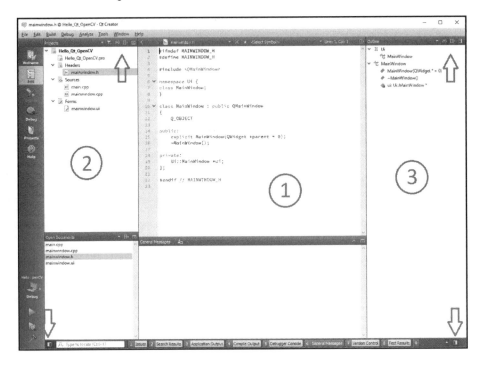

The main code editing area is a lightweight code editor that allows code completion, code highlighting, and context-sensitive help, which are basically the most important things about it that you will use. As you'll see later on, you can configure it with your preferred coloring, fonts, and more. You can also use the split button at the top to split the code editor area and work on more than one file at the same time. Try typing in some code, classes, or any C++ code that you know and play around with the code completion, and also try using context-sensitive help by pressing F1 when your mouse cursor is on a Qt class in the code editor. These tools will be your best friends for a long time to come, especially when you start working on your own projects in the future.

The following are the different modes you can select for each of the panes in both sidebars on the left and right:

- **Projects**: This contains a list of open projects and their containing files.
- **Open**: These documents simply show the files that you have already opened. You can close each one by simply clicking on the **X** button next to them.
- **Bookmarks**: This shows all the bookmarks you have made in the code. Using this pane and feature can save a lot of time during programming and later on when testing and debugging your code.
- **File System**: This is basically a file explorer pane. Note that this pane displays all files (even hidden files if you check the relevant checkbox for it in the pane) in the project folder and can also be used to explore other folders on the computer and not just the current project.
- **Class View**: This can be used to see the hierarchy of the classes in the current project.
- **Outline**: Unlike **Class View**, this shows the hierarchy of all methods and symbols in the current open source file and not the entire project. In the preceding screenshot, this pane is the one activated on the right sidebar.
- **Tests**: This displays all available tests in the project.
- **Type and Include Hierarchy**: As it can be guessed from their title, this can be used to view the hierarchy of a class and the hierarchy of the included headers.

It is important to note that, based on your programming habits, you may use some of the panes quite a lot and some other panes not so often, so make sure to have it set up to fit your own style and needs, and save a lot of time while programming.

# Design mode

This is the mode in which you will do all of your user interface design. You can switch to the **Design** mode using the **Design** button on the left part of the Qt Creator screen. Note that if this button is grayed out, which means it is inactive, then you need to select a user interface file (*.ui) first, because only ui files can be opened using the Designer. To do this, you can double-click on the mainwindow.ui file in the left pane (**Projects** pane):

The **Design** mode contains all the tools required from a powerful GUI designer. It has a **WYSIWYG (what you see is what you get)** type of GUI editor that allows adding, removing, editing, or writing code for Qt Widgets that you can add or remove from the user interface.

A Qt Widget is the most basic type of component on a Qt User Interface. Basically, anything (including the whole window itself) on the user interface, such as buttons, labels, text boxes, is a Qt Widget. Qt Widgets are all sub-classes of the QWidget class, and this allows them to receive user input events, such as mouse and keyboard events, and draw (or paint) themselves on the user interface. So, simply any Qt class that has a visual side to it and is meant to be put on the user interface must be sub-classed from the QWidget class. You will learn about many Qt Widget classes throughout the book, but a few examples would be QPushButton, QProgressBar, QLineEdit, and so on. Their purpose is almost instantly recognizable from their names.
Note that all Qt classes (without any obvious exceptions) have names starting with a Q (capital).

There's a screenshot (shown next) of the Qt Creator in the **Design** mode. As seen here, it's quite similar to what we saw with the Edit mode the screen is divided into three main parts. The main area in the middle is where you can drag and drop, resize, remove, or visually edit your user interface in any way. On the left side of the screen, there's the list of widgets that you can add to your user interface. You should try dragging and dropping some of them, any of them, basically, just to get comfortable with the designer in general and get a better sense of how it works. Later on in the book, we'll be designing quite a lot of different user interfaces, and you'll be introduced to many features gradually, but it's a very good idea to try out some designs by yourself and familiarize yourself at least with the feeling of it all. On the right side of the screen, you can view a hierarchical view of the widgets on the user interface and modify the properties of each widget. So, if you go ahead and add a few widgets to the user interface, you'll notice that whenever you choose a different widget, the properties and their values change according to that specific widget. This is where you can edit all properties of a widget that is available to the designer:

As you would do with any other IDE, most of the time, you can achieve the same goal through many different routes. For instance, you can set a widget size from the code using the editor, or even with the unrecommended way of modifying its UI file in a text editor. You should be able to decide this based on your specific needs, since no method is the best, and they all just simply apply in different situations. Usually, you are better off setting the initial properties in the user interface editor and update their values as needed throughout the code. You'll learn about this later on in this chapter.

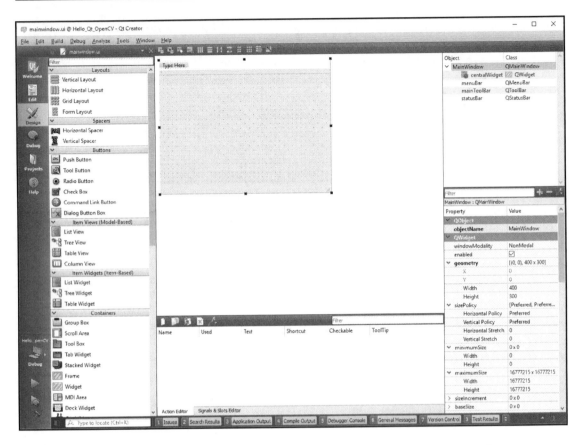

At the bottom of the central part of the user interface designer, you can see **Action Editor** and **Signals & Slots Editor**. To understand how they work, and, in fact, how Qt works in general, we need to first learn about the signals and slots in Qt. So, it's a very good idea to start with a definition of our first encounter with the concept of signals and slots, and then later experience it with a real example.

The most important addition of the Qt Framework to the standard C++ programming is the signals and slots mechanism, and it's also what makes Qt so easy to learn and powerful at the same time. It's definitely the most important difference between Qt and other frameworks too. Think of it as a method for messaging (or simply as the name implies, signaling) between Qt objects and classes. Every Qt object can emit a signal that can be connected to a slot in another (or the same) object. Let's break it down even more with a simple example. QPushButton is a Qt Widget class that can be added to a Qt user interface to create a button, as you would easily guess. It contains many signals, including an obvious pressed signal. On the other hand, MainWindow (and all Qt windows, for that matter) that was created automatically when we created our Hello_Qt_OpenCV project contains a slot named close that can be used to simply close the main window of our project. I'm sure you can imagine what would happen if we were to connect the pressed signal of a push button to the close slot of a window. There are quite a lot of ways to connect a signal to a slot, so we will learn each one of them whenever we need to use them in our examples from now on for the rest of the book.

## Designing user interfaces

This is where you start to learn how to add Qt Widgets to the user interface and make them react to user inputs and other events. Qt Creator offers extremely easy tools to design user interfaces and write code for them. You have already seen the different panes and tools available in the **Design** mode, so we can start with our example already. Make sure you switch to the **Design** mode first (if you are not already there) by selecting the mainwindow.ui file, which is the user interface file for our main window from the **Edit** mode.

When in **Design** mode, you can see a list of Qt Widgets available for use on your user interface. The purpose for most of these widgets is instantly recognizable from their icons and names, but there are still a few widgets that are specific to Qt. Here's a screenshot representing all available layouts and widgets by default in Qt Creator:

The following is a brief description of the available widgets in the Qt Creator **Design** mode (or simply the Designer from now on), as seen in the preceding screenshot. In the Designer mode, widgets are grouped based on similarities in their behavior. Try out each one of them in the designer by yourself as you proceed with the list to have a feeling of what they look like when they are put on a user interface. To do this, you can just drag and drop each widget onto your window in the Designer mode using your mouse:

- **Layouts**: These are used to manage how widgets are displayed. Visually, they are invisible (since they are not a QWidget subclass), and they only affect the widgets that are added to them. Note that layouts are simply not widgets, and they are meant as logical classes to manage how widgets are displayed. Try putting any of the Layout widgets on your user interface, and then add some of the Buttons or Display Widgets in them to see how their layout changes according to the layout type. See example images for each to get an idea of how they behave.
    - **Vertical Layout**: These are used to have a vertical layout, or, in other words, a column of widgets. (Equivalent Qt class for this layout is called QVBoxLayout). The following is a screenshot of it:

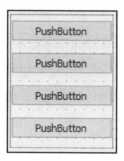

    - **Horizontal Layout**: These are used to have a horizontal layout, or, in other words, a row of widgets (Equivalent Qt class for this layout is called QHBoxLayout). The following is a screenshot of it:

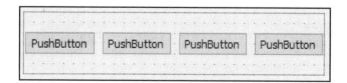

- **Grid Layout**: These can be used to have a grid of widgets with any number of rows and columns (Equivalent Qt class for this layout is called `QGridLayout`). The following is a screenshot of it:

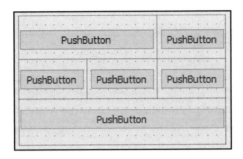

- **Form Layout**: As it can be guessed from its name, these can be used to have a form-like look with some labels and their corresponding input widgets. Think about filling a form, for example, and you'll get the idea (Equivalent Qt class for this layout is called `QFormLayout`). The following is a screenshot of it:

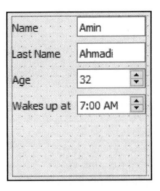

- **Spacers**: Similar to layouts, these are not visually visible, but they affect the way other widgets are displayed when they are added to a layout. See the example images, and also make sure to try a couple of spacers in between widgets by yourself. Spacers are of type `QSpacerItem`, but, normally, they should never be used directly within a code.
  - **Horizontal Spacer**: These can be used to insert a space between two widgets in a row:

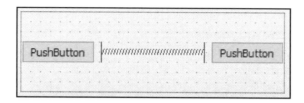

- **Vertical Spacer**: These can be used to insert a space between two widgets in a column:

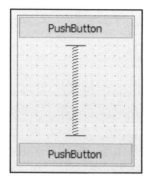

- **Buttons**: These are simply buttons. They are used to prompt an action. You may notice that radio buttons and checkboxes are also in this group, and that is because they all inherit from the QAbstractButton class, which is an abstract class that provides all interfaces required by button-like widgets.
- **Push Button**: These can be used to add a simple push button to the user interface with a text and/or icon on it (Equivalent Qt class for this widget is called QPushButton).
- **Tool Button**: These are quite similar to push buttons, but they are usually added to Toolbars

There are three different types of bars common to Qt windows (and, in fact, to Windows in general) that are not available in the widget toolbox, but they can be created, added, or removed simply by right-clicking on the window in the Designer mode and selecting relevant items from the right-click menu. Here they are:

1. Menu bar (QMenuBar)
2. Tool bar (QToolBar)
3. Status bar (QStatusBar)

A Menu bar is a typical horizontal main menu bar that appears on top of the window. There can be any number of items and sub-items in a menu and each one can trigger an action (QAction). You will learn more about actions in the upcoming chapters. The following is an example Menu bar:

A Toolbar is a movable panel that can contain Tool Buttons corresponding to specific tasks. Here's an example Toolbar. Note that they can be moved inside and even out of Qt windows:

A Status bar is a simple, horizontal information bar at the bottom that is common to most window-based applications. Whenever a new main window is created in Qt, these three types of bars are all added to the window. Note that there can be only one Menu bar and one status bar on a window, but there can be any number of status bars. If you don't need any of them, you need to remove them from the object hierarchy at the right side of the Designer window. Now that you are familiar with the three different bars in Qt, you can search for Application Example in the examples from the Qt Welcome mode to learn even more about them, and if they can be customized further.

- **Radio Button**: This can be checked or unchecked to set one choice among any number of choices, all defined by radio buttons (Equivalent Qt class for this widget is called QRadioButton).
- **Check Box**: This can be used to enable/disable an option (Equivalent Qt class for this widget is called QCheckBox).

- **Command Link Button**: This is a Windows Vista-Style command link button. They are basically push buttons that are intended to be used in place of radio buttons in wizards, so, when a command link button is pressed, it would be similar to selecting an option using a radio box and then clicking on **Next** on a wizard dialog (Equivalent Qt class for this widget is called QCommandLinkButton).

- **Dialog Button Box**: This is very useful if you want your buttons to adapt to the operating system styling in dialogs. It helps present buttons on a dialog in a fashion that is more appropriate to the current style of the system (Equivalent Qt class for this widget is called QDialogButtonBox).

- **Item Views (Model-based)**: This is based on the Model-view-controller (MVC) design pattern; they can be used to represent data from models in different types of containers.

  If you are not familiar with the MVC design pattern at all, then I suggest you should pause here and first make sure you have at least a basic understanding of what it is and how to use MVC, especially in Qt, by reading through a comprehensive article from the Qt documentation called Model/View Programming, which you can access from the **Help** mode in the Qt Creator. For the purpose of this book, we won't need very detailed information and an understanding of the MVC pattern; however, since it's a very important architecture that you will definitely come across in your future projects, I suggest you spend some time learning about it. Nevertheless, in Chapter 3, *Creating a Comprehensive Qt+OpenCV Project*, we will cover different design patterns used in Qt and OpenCV, but we will mainly focus on what we will need for the purpose of this book, since it's a very comprehensive topic and it would be completely useless to go over all possible design patterns in this book.

  - **List View**: This displays items from a model in a simple list without any hierarchy (Equivalent Qt class for this widget is called QListView).
  - **Tree View**: This displays items from a model in a hierarchical tree view.(Equivalent Qt class for this widget is called QTreeView).
  - **Table View**: This is used to display data from a model in a table with any number of rows and columns. This is especially useful with displaying tables from an SQL database or queries (Equivalent Qt class for this widget is called QTableView).

- **Column View**: This is similar to the List View with the difference being that Column View also displays hierarchical data stored in a model (Equivalent Qt class for this widget is called `QColumnView`).
- **Item Widgets (Item-Based)**: This is similar to model-based Item Views, with the difference that they are not based on the MVC design pattern, and they provide simple APIs to add, remove, or modify their items
  - **List Widget**: This is similar to List View, but with an item-based API to add, remove, and modify its items (Equivalent Qt class for this widget is called `QListWidget`)
  - **Tree Widget**: This is similar to Tree View, but with an item-based API to add, remove, and modify its items (Equivalent Qt class for this widget is called `QTreeWidget`)
  - **Table Widget**: This is similar to Table View, but with an item-based API to add, remove, and modify its items (Equivalent Qt class for this widget is called `QTableWidget`)
- **Containers**: These are used to group widgets on the user interface. Containers can contain widgets as it can be guessed from their title
  - **Group Box**: This is a simple group box with a title and borders (Equivalent Qt class for this widget is called `QGroupBox`).
  - **Scroll Area**: This provides a scrollable area, ideal for displaying content that cannot be visible completely due to a small screen size or a huge amount of viewable data (Equivalent Qt class for this widget is called `QScrollArea`).
  - **Tool Box**: This can be used to group widgets in a column of different tabs. Selecting each tab will display (expand) its containing widgets and hide (collapse) the content of other tabs. (Equivalent Qt class for this widget is called `QToolBox`).
  - **Tab Widget**: This can be used to display different groups of widgets in tabbed pages. Each page (or group of widgets) can be switched to by clicking on their relevant tab (Equivalent Qt class for this widget is called `QTabWidget`).
  - **Stacked Widget**: This is similar to Tab Widget, but only one page (or group of widgets) is visible at all times. This is especially useful when you want to have different user interfaces designed into a single file and switch between them (using the code) depending on user actions (Equivalent Qt class for this widget is called `QStackedWidget`).

- **Frame**: This can be used as a placeholder for a widget that we want to have a frame for. This widget is also the base class of all widgets that have a frame (Equivalent Qt class for this widget is called QFrame).
- **Widget**: This is the same as the QWidget class, which is the base type for all Qt Widgets. This widget contains practically nothing by itself, and it's useful when we want to create our own type of Widgets (in addition to existing Qt Widgets).
- **MDI Area**: This can be used to create a so-called Multi-Document-Interface within a window or Qt widget (Equivalent Qt class for this widget is called QMdiArea).

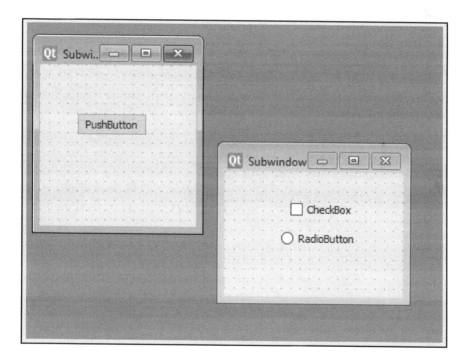

To create new windows inside an MDI Area using the Designer, you can simply right-click on an empty space and choose **Add Subwindow** from the menu. Similarly, **Next Subwindow**, **Previous Subwindow**, **Cascade**, **Tile**, and **Subwindow / Delete** are all options that are only valid when you right-click on an MDI Area widget.

- **Dock Widget**: This can be used as a placeholder for widgets that are capable of being docked inside a window or moved outside of it as a separate top window (Equivalent Qt class for this widget is called QDockWidget).
- **QAxWidget**: This widget can be used as a wrapper for an Active-X control (Equivalent Qt class for this widget is called QAxWidget).

 QAxWidget is only available for users on Windows OS. However, even on Windows, it's not enough to just add QAxWidget to your window to make it work, as it depends on a Qt Module called axcontainer. For the moment, you can skip adding this widget to your window, but you can try it again later, after we have covered how to add different Qt modules to your Qt projects later in this chapter.

- **Input Widgets**: This is exactly as it sounds; you can use the following widgets to get user input data.
    - **Combo Box**: This is sometimes referred to as a drop-down list; it can be used to select an option in a list with very little space used on the screen. Only the selected option is visible at any time. Users may even enter their own input values, depending on its configuration. (Equivalent Qt class for this widget is called QComboBox):
    - **Font Combo Box**: This is similar to Combo Box, but it can be used to select a font family. The list of fonts is created using available fonts on the computer.
    - **Line Edit**: This can be used to enter and display a single line of text (Equivalent Qt class for this widget is called QLineEdit).
    - **Text Edit**: This can be used to enter and display multiple lines of rich text. It's important to note that this widget is, in fact, a full-fledged WYIWYG rich-text editor (Equivalent Qt class for this widget is called QTextEdit).
    - **Plain Text Edit**: This can be used to view and edit multiple lines of text. Think of it as a simple notepad-like widget (Equivalent Qt class for this widget is called QPlainTextEdit).
    - **Spin Box**: This is used to enter an integer or discrete sets of values such as month names (Equivalent Qt class for this widget is called QSpinBox).

- **Double Spin Box**: This is similar to the spin box, but it accepts double values (Equivalent Qt class for this widget is called QDoubleSpinBox).
- **Time Edit**: This can be used to enter time values.(Equivalent Qt class for this widget is called QTimeEdit).
- **Date Edit**: This can be used to enter date values (Equivalent Qt class for this widget is called QDateEdit).
- **Date/Time Edit**: This can be used to enter date and time values (Equivalent Qt class for this widget is called QDateTimeEdit).
- **Dial**: This is similar to a slider, but with a round and dial-like shape. It can be used to enter integer values within a specified range (Equivalent Qt class for this widget is called QDial).
- **Horizontal/Vertical Bar**: This can be used to add scrolling functionality, both horizontally and vertically (Equivalent Qt class for this widget is called QScrollBar).
- **Horizontal/Vertical Slider**: This can be used to enter an integer value within a specified range (Equivalent Qt class for this widget is called QSlider).
- **Key Sequence Edit**: This can be used to enter a keyboard shortcut (Equivalent Qt class for this widget is called QKeySequenceEdit).

 This shouldn't be confused with the QKeySequence class, which is not a widget at all. QKeySequenceEdit is used to get QKeySequence from the user. After we have QKeySequence, we can use it in conjunction with the QShortcut or QAction classes to trigger different functions/slots. An introduction to signals/slots will be covered later on in this chapter.

- **Display Widgets**: This can be used to display output data such as numbers, text, images, date, and so on:
  - **Label**: This can be used to display numbers, text, images, or movies (Equivalent Qt class for this widget is called QLabel).
  - **Text Browser**: This is almost identical to the Text Edit widget, but with added functionality to navigate between links (Equivalent Qt class for this widget is called QTextBrowser).
  - **Graphics View**: This can be used to display the contents of a Graphics Scene (Equivalent Qt class for this widget is called QGraphicsView).

Probably the most important widget that we'll be using throughout the book is Graphics Scene (or `QGraphicsScene`), and it will be covered in `Chapter 5`, *The Graphics View Framework*.

- **Calendar Widget**: This can be used to view and select a date from a monthly calendar (Equivalent Qt class for this widget is called `QCalendarWidget`).
- **LCD Number**: This can be used to display a number in a LCD-like display. (Equivalent Qt class for this widget is called `QLCDNumber`)
- **Progress Bar**: This can be used to display a vertical or horizontal progress indicator (Equivalent Qt class for this widget is called `QProgressBar`).
- **Horizontal/Vertical Line**: This can be used to draw a simple vertical or horizontal line. Especially useful as a separator between different groups of widgets.
- **OpenGL Widget**: This class can be used as a surface for rendering the OpenGL output (Equivalent Qt class for this widget is called `QOpenGLWidget`).

Note that OpenGL is a completely separate and advanced topic in computer graphics, and it is totally out of the scope of this book; however, as it was mentioned before, it's a good idea to know the tools and widgets present within Qt for your possible further studies.

- **QQuickWidget**: This widget can be used to display the Qt Quick user interfaces. Qt Quick interfaces use the QML language to design user interfaces (Equivalent Qt class for this widget is called `QQuickWidget`).

An introduction to QML will be presented in `Chapter 12`, *Qt Quick Applications*. For now, let's make sure we don't add any QQuickWidget widgets to our user interface since we need to add additional modules to our project in order for it to work. Adding modules to Qt projects will be presented in this chapter.

# Hello Qt and OpenCV

Now, we can start designing the user interface for our `Hello_Qt_OpenCV` project. It's always a good idea to have a clear list of specifications for a project and then devise a user-friendly UI according to the requirements, then draw the user interface on a piece of paper (or in your mind if it's not a big project), and finally start creating it using the Designer. Of course, this process requires experience with the existing Qt widgets and also enough experience in creating your own widgets, but that is something that will happen eventually, and you just need to keep practicing for it.

So, to start, let's go over the specifications of the application we need to develop. Let's say:

- This application must be able to take an image as an input (the accepted image types must at least include the `*.jpg`, `*.png`, and `*.bmp` files).
- This application must be able to apply a blur filter. The user must be able to choose the Median Blur or the Gaussian Blur type to filter the input image (use a default set of parameters).
- This application must be able to save the output image and the file type (or extension, in other words) of the output image and it must be selectable by the user (`*.jpg`, `*.png`, or `*.bmp`).
- The user should be able to optionally view the output image while saving it.
- All options set on the user interface, including the blur filter type and the last opened and save image files, should be preserved and reloaded when the application is restarted.
- The users should be prompted when they want to close the application.

That should be enough for our case. Usually, you shouldn't over-deliver or under-deliver the requirements. That's an important rule when designing user interfaces. It means that you should make sure all requirements are successfully met, and, at the same time, you haven't added anything that is not wanted (or needed) in the list of requirements.

There can be countless user interface designs for such a list of requirements (or specifications); however, here's the one we'll create. Note that it is how our program will look when it is executed. Obviously, the title bar and styling may be different, depending on the operating system, but this is basically it:

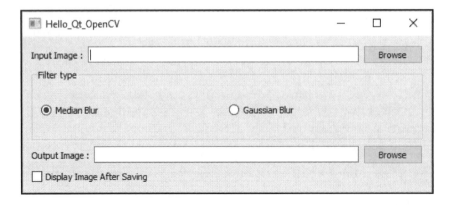

As simple as it may look, it contains all required components for such a task, and the interface is almost self-explanatory. So, someone who's going to use this application doesn't really need to know a lot about what it does and they can simply guess what is the purpose of all of the input boxes, radio buttons, checkboxes, and so on.

Here's the same UI when it's viewed on the Designer:

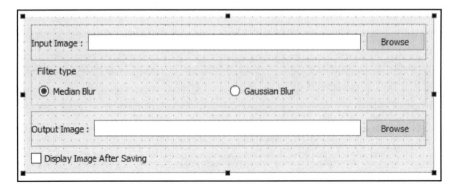

It's time to create the user interface for our project:

1. To create this user interface, you need to start by first removing the menu bar, status bar, and toolbar from your main window, since we won't need them. Right-click on the menu bar at the top and select **Remove Menu Bar**. Next, right-click anywhere on the window and select **Remove Status Bar**. Finally, right-click on the toolbar at the top and click on **Remove Toolbar**.

2. Now, add a Horizontal Layout to your window; this is the layout that is visible at the top of the preceding image. Then, add a **Label**, **Line Edit**, and **Push Button** inside it, as shown in the previous image.

3. Change the text of the Label by double-clicking on it and typing `Input Image :.` (This is the same as selecting the label and setting the text property value to `Input Image :` using the property editor at the right side of the screen.)

 Almost all Qt widgets that have a text property allows this type of editing with their text. So, from now on, when we say `Change the text of the widget X to Y`, that means either double-click and set the text or use the property editor in the designer. We can very easily expand this rule to all properties of the widgets visible in the property editor and say `Change the W of X to Y`. Here, obviously, W is the property name in the property editor of the designer, X is the widget name, and Y is the value that needs to be set. This will save us a lot of time while designing UIs.

4. Add a group box and then two radio buttons, similar to what is seen in the preceding image.
5. Next, add another Horizontal Layout, then add a `Label`, `Line Edit`, and `Push Button` in it. This will be the layout seen at the bottom, right above the checkbox.
6. Finally, add a checkbox to the window. This is the checkbox at the bottom.
7. Now, change the text for all of the widgets on the window, according to the preceding image. Your UI is almost ready. You can now try running it by clicking on the **Run** button at the bottom-left part of the screen. Make sure you don't press the **Run** button with a bug on it. Here's the one:

This will produce the same user interface you saw earlier. Now, if you try resizing the window, you will notice that everything stays where it is when you resize the window or maximize it, and it doesn't respond to changes in the application size. To make your application window respond to size changes, you need to set a layout for `centralWidget`. This also needs to be done for the group box you have on the screen.

Qt widgets all have a `centralWidget` property. This is something that is used especially with windows and container widgets in Qt designer. Using it, you can set a layout for the container or window without dragging and dropping a layout widget on central widgets, and by simply using the toolbar at the top of the designer:

You may have noticed the four small buttons here in the toolbar (as shown in the preceding screenshot), which look exactly like Layouts in the widget toolbox on the left (as shown here):

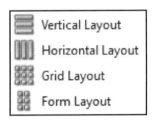

 So, let's agree on another rule for simple and quick explanations throughout the book. Whenever we say `Set the Layout of X to Y`, what we mean is to select the widget (container widget or window, in fact) first, and then, using the layout buttons at the top toolbar, choose the correct type of layout.

8. Based on what was described in the preceding information box, select the window (this means, click on an empty space on the window and not on any widgets) and set its layout to **Vertical**.

9. Do the same with group box; however, this time, set the layout to horizontal. Now, you can try running your program again. As you can see now, it resizes all of its widgets and moves them if needed in case the window size is changed. The same is happening with the group box inside the window.

10. The next thing that needs to be changed is the `objectName` property for the widgets. These names are very important, since they are used in the C++ code to access widgets on the window and interact with them. Use the names seen in the following screenshot for each one of the widgets. Note that the image shows the object hierarchy. You can also change the `objectName` property by double-clicking on widgets in the object hierarchy pane:

 Theoretically, you can use any C++ valid variable name for the `objectName` property, but, in practice, it's always best to use meaningful names. Consider following the same or a similar naming convention for your variables or widget names with the one used throughout this book. It's basically the naming convention followed by Qt developers, and it also helps increase the readability of your code.

## Writing the code for a Qt project

Now that our user interface is completely designed, we can start by writing code for our application. Right now, our application is basically nothing more than a user interface and it literally does nothing. We need to start by adding OpenCV to our project. In Chapter 1, *Introduction to OpenCV and Qt*, you already saw a brief introduction about adding OpenCV to Qt projects. We'll now take that one step further and make sure our project can be compiled and built on all three major operating systems without changing anything, provided that OpenCV is correctly installed and configured using the instructions in Chapter 1, *Introduction to OpenCV and Qt*.

So, start by opening the project's PRO file in the code editor, which will be the **Edit** mode in Qt Creator. It's called Hello_Qt_OpenCV.pro, as you may have already noticed. You need to add the following codes to the end of this file:

```
win32: {
    include("c:/dev/opencv/opencv.pri")
}

unix: !macx {
    CONFIG += link_pkgconfig
    PKGCONFIG += opencv
}
unix: macx {
    INCLUDEPATH += "/usr/local/include"
    LIBS += -L"/usr/local/lib" \
    -lopencv_world
}
```

Notice the code right before the opening curly brackets; win32 means Windows operating systems (this only applies to desktop applications and not Windows 8, 8.1, or 10 specific applications), unix: !macx means Linux operating systems, and unix: macx means macOS operating system.

This piece of code in your PRO file allows OpenCV to be included and become usable in your Qt projects. Remember, we created a PRI file in Chapter 1, *Introduction to OpenCV and Qt*? Linux and macOS users can remove it since there's no need for that file anymore in those operating systems. Only Windows users may keep it.

Note that in Windows OS, you can replace the preceding include line with the contents of the PRI file, but it's not common in practice. Also, it's worth reminding that you need to have OpenCV DLLs folder in your PATH, or your application will crash when you try to run it; however, it will still compile and build correctly. To become familiar even more with the contents of the Qt PRO files, you can search for QMAKE in Qt documentation and read about it; although, we will also cover a brief introduction in Chapter 3, *Creating a Comprehensive Qt+OpenCV Project*.

We'll not discuss what exactly those lines of code mean on each and every operating system, since that's not in the scope of our book, but it's worth noting and enough to know that when an application is built (in other words, compiled and linked), those lines are translated to all OpenCV header files, libraries, and binary files, and included in your projects so that you can easily use OpenCV functions in your code.

Now that we've taken care of configurations, let's start by writing code for each and every requirement and their relevant widgets on the user interface. Let's start with inputPushButton.

 From now on, we will refer to any widget on the user interface with its unique objectName property value. Think of them as the variable names that we can use in the code to access those widgets.

Here are the steps required for the coding part of our project:

1. Switch to the Designer again and right-click on inputPushButton. Then, select **Go to slot ...** from the menu that appears. The window that will show up includes all signals emitted by this widget. Select **pressed()** and click on **OK**:

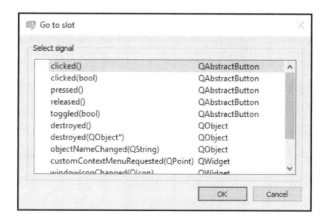

2. As you'll notice, you were taken from the Designer to Code Editor automatically. Also, now, there's a new function added to the `mainwindow.h` and `mainwindow.cpp` files.

3. In `mainwindow.h`, the following was added:

```
private slots:
    void on_inputPushButton_pressed();
```

And here's the code automatically added to `mainwindow.cpp`:

```
void MainWindow::on_inputPushButton_pressed()
{

}
```

So, the code responsible for `inputPushButton` obviously needs to be written in the `on_inputPushButton_pressed()` function that was just created. This is one of the many ways to connect a signal from a widget to a slot on another widget as it was mentioned previously in this chapter. Let's take a step back and see what just happened; in the meantime, keep an eye on the name of the function that was just created.

The `inputPushButton` widget has a signal called pressed (since it's a button) which is only emitted when it is pressed. A new slot was created inside our single window widget (MainWindow), and it's called `on_inputPushButton_pressed`. Pretty convenient, and the first question that comes to mind is, what would have happened if I had written those lines of code myself in `mainwindow.h` and `mainwindow.cpp` instead of right-clicking on the widget and selecting **Go to slot ...**, and the answer is that, it is exactly the same thing. So, to summarize, Qt automatically understands that it needs to execute the code inside `on_inputPushButton_pressed()` whenever the `inputPushButton` widget emits the pressed signal. In Qt development, this is called **Connecting Slots by Name** and it simply follows the following convention to connect signals to slots automatically `on_objectName_signal(parameters)`.

Here, `objectName` should be replaced with the value of the `objectName` property of the widget sending the signal, `signal` with the signal name, and `parameters` with the exact number and types of parameters of the signal.

Now that we know how to connect signals of widgets on the window to slots on the window itself, or, in other words, now that we know have to add a function and write code for a signal of a widget, we can save some time and avoid repetitive instructions using sentences such as The code for the signal X of the widget Y, and it would mean adding a slot responsible for a signal using the method we just learned. So, in our case, and as a first example, let's write the code for the pressed signal of the inputPushButton widget.

According to the requirements of the application, we need to make sure users can open an image file. After the image file is successfully opened, we'll write the path to the inputLineEdit widget's text property so that the user can see the complete file name and path they have selected. Let's first see what the code should look like, and then walk over it step by step:

```
void MainWindow::on_inputPushButton_pressed()
{
  QString fileName = QFileDialog::getOpenFileName(this,
    "Open Input Image",
    QDir::currentPath(),
    "Images (*.jpg *.png *.bmp)");
  if(QFile::exists(fileName))
  {
    ui->inputLineEdit->setText(fileName);
  }
}
```

To access the widgets or other elements on the user interface, just use the ui object. For example, the inputLineEdit widget from the user interface can be simply accessed via the ui class and by writing the following line:

```
ui-> inputLineEdit
```

The first line is actually a shortened version of a large code. As you'll learn over the course of this book, Qt offers many convenient functions and classes to achieve daily programming needs, such as these wrapped up into very short functions. Let's first see what Qt classes we just used:

- QString: This is probably one of the most important and widely used classes of Qt. It represents a Unicode character string. You can use it to store, convert, modify, and do countless other operations on strings with it. In this example, we just used it to store the file name read by the QFileDialog class.
- QFileDialog: This can be used to select a file or folder on the computer. It uses the underlying operating system APIs so the dialog can look different, depending on the OS.
- QDir: This class can be used to access folders on a computer and get various types of information about them.
- QFile: This can be used to access files and read from or write into them.

What's previously mentioned would be a very brief description of each of these classes, and as you can see from the preceding code, each one of them provides much more than that. For example, we just used a static function in QFile to check if the file exists or not. We also used the QDir class to get the current path (usually, that would be the path the application is running from). The only thing in the code that might need more explanation is the getOpenFileName function. The first parameter should be the parent widget. This is very important in Qt, and it is used to take care of automatic memory cleaning and, in case of dialogs and windows, to determine the parent window. This means that each object is responsible for cleaning up its children objects too when it is destroyed, and also, in case of windows, they are opened by their parent window. So, by setting this as the first parameter, we are telling the compiler (and Qt, of course) that this class is responsible for taking care of the QFileDialog class instance. The second parameter of the getOpenFileName function is obviously the title of the file selection dialog window, and the next parameter is the current path. The last parameter that we provided makes sure that only the three file types from our application requirement are shown: the *.jpg, *.png, and *.bmp files.

Using any Qt class is only possible if first, their modules are added to your project, and then their header files are included in your source files. To add a Qt module to a Qt project, you need to add a line similar to the following to your project's PRO file:

```
QT += module_name1 module_name2 module_name3 ...
```

The module_name1 and so on can be replaced by actual Qt module names for each class that can be found in the Qt documentation.
You have probably noticed the following line of code already existing in your project's PRO file:

```
QT += core gui
greaterThan(QT_MAJOR_VERSION, 4): QT += widgets
```

This simply means the core and gui modules should be included in your project. They are two of the most basic Qt modules and include many of the foundation classes of Qt. The second line means if you are using a Qt framework with a major version number of higher than four, then the widgets module also should be included. This is because of the fact that before Qt 5, the widgets module was part of the gui module, so there was no need to include it in the PRO files.
As for the include file, it's always the same as the class name itself. So, in our case, we need to add the following classes to our source code in order for the preceding code to work. The best place is usually the top of the header file, so that would be the mainwindow.h file in our case. Make sure that, at the top, you have the following classes included:

```
#include <QMainWindow>
#include <QFileDialog>
#include <QDir>
#include <QFile>
```

Give it a try and run the program to see the results until now. Then, close it and return to the Designer again. Now, we need to add the code to the outputPushButton widget. Simply repeat the same process you did with inputPushButton, but, this time, do it on outputPushButton and write the following piece of code for it:

```
void MainWindow::on_outputPushButton_pressed()
{
    QString fileName = QFileDialog::getSaveFileName(this,
```

```
"Select Output Image",
QDir::currentPath(),
"*.jpg;;*.png;;*.bmp");
if(!fileName.isEmpty())
{
   ui->outputLineEdit->setText(fileName);
   using namespace cv;
   Mat inpImg, outImg;
   inpImg = imread(ui->inputLineEdit->text().toStdString());
   if(ui->medianBlurRadioButton->isChecked())
       cv::medianBlur(inpImg, outImg, 5);
   else if(ui->gaussianBlurRadioButton->isChecked())
       cv::GaussianBlur(inpImg, outImg, Size(5, 5), 1.25);
   imwrite(fileName.toStdString(), outImg);
   if(ui->displayImageCheckBox->isChecked())
       imshow("Output Image", outImg);
}
}
```

You also need to add the OpenCV header includes to your project. Add them where you added the Qt class headers, at the top section of the mainwindow.h file, which is shown as follows:

```
#include "opencv2/opencv.hpp"
```

Now, let's review the code we just wrote and see what it really does. As you can see, this time, we used the getSaveFileName function in the QFileDialog class and the title, and also the filter is different. This is required in order for the user to choose each image types individually when they want to save output images, as opposed to seeing all images when they are opening them. This time, we also didn't check for the file's existence, since that would be done automatically by QFileDialog, so it's enough if we just check that the user did really select something or not. In the following lines, we have written some OpenCV specific code, and in the upcoming chapters, we'll learn more and more about those functions. You also used it in a very small dosage in Chapter 1, *Introduction to OpenCV and Qt*, so they're not completely foreign to you by now. But again, we will just briefly discuss them and move on with our tour of the IDE and Hello_Qt_OpenCV application.

All OpenCV functions are contained in the cv namespace, so we made sure we are using the OpenCV namespace cv. Then, to read the input image, we used the imread function. The important thing to note here is that OpenCV uses C++ std::string classes and Qt's QString should be converted to that format, otherwise, you will face errors when you try to run the program. That is done by simply using the toStdString function of QString. Note that, in this case, QString is the value returned by the text() function of the inputLineEdit widget.

Next, depending on the selected filter type, we do a simple OpenCV filtering using the `medianBlur` or `gaussianBlur` functions.

 Note that, in this case, we have used some default parameters for these OpenCV functions, but it would be even better if we got them from the user using a Spin widget, maybe? Or a Slider widget, perhaps? Maybe a nice Dial widget? Give this a try for yourself after you finish this chapter. The idea is quite simple, and it's meant to help you learn how to discover new possibilities in these frameworks by yourself. Nevertheless, you will learn how to use many widgets and even create your own in `Chapter 3`, *Creating a Comprehensive Qt+OpenCV Project*, so this will be a piece of cake over time.

Finally, `outImg`, which is the filtered output image, is written to the selected file. It's also displayed depending on the condition set by the `displayImageCheckBox` widget.

By this time, we have just two more requirements to go. First is, saving the state of all widgets on the window when the program is closed and loading them back when the program is reopened. And the other requirement, the last requirement, is to prompt the users when they want to close the program. Let's start with the last one since this means we need to know how we can write a code that needs to be executed when a window is closed. This is very simple since Qt's `QMainWindow` class (which our window is based on) is `QWidget`, and it already has a virtual C++ function that we can override and use. Simply add the following line of code to your `MainWindow` class:

```
protected:
  void closeEvent(QCloseEvent *event);
```

This should go into the class definition in the `mainwindow.h` file. The line right before the private slots seems like a good place. Now, switch to `mainwindow.cpp` and add the following piece of code to the end of the file:

```
void MainWindow::closeEvent(QCloseEvent *event)
{
  int result = QMessageBox::warning(this,
    "Exit",
    "Are you sure you want to close this program?",
    QMessageBox::Yes,
    QMessageBox::No);
  if(result == QMessageBox::Yes)
  {
    event->accept();
  }
  else
```

```
        {
          event->ignore();
        }
    }
```

I assume you've already noticed that we are now introduced to two more Qt classes, and that means we need to add their include headers to `mainwindow.h` too. Consider the following:

- `QMessageBox`: This can be used to display messages with a simple icon, text, and buttons, depending on what the purpose of the message is
- `QCloseEvent`: This is one of many Qt's event (`QEvent`) classes, and its purpose is to pass on parameters about the close event of a window

The code is almost self-explanatory, as you already know what the first parameter of the warning function is. This is used to tell Qt that our `MainWindow` class is responsible for this message box. The result of the user's choice is recorded, and then, based on that, the close event is either accepted or ignored, quite simple. Except, we still need to save the settings (text on the widgets and status of checkboxes and radio boxes) and load them. As you just learned, the best place to save settings is the `closeEvent` function. How about right before the `event->accept();` line of the code? Let's add two private functions to our `MainWindow` class, one to load the settings called `loadSettings` and the other to save the settings called `saveSettings`. We'll learn about one last Qt class in this chapter, and it's called `QSettings`. So, first add its include line to `mainwindow.h`, then add the following two function definitions to the `MainWindow` class, again, in `mainwindow.h`, right under the `Ui::MainWindow *ui;` line, in private members:

```
        void loadSettings();
        void saveSettings();
```

Here's the code required for the `loadSettings` function:

```
    void MainWindow::loadSettings()
    {
      QSettings settings("Packt",
        "Hello_OpenCV_Qt",
        this);
      ui->inputLineEdit->setText(settings.value("inputLineEdit",
        "").toString());
      ui->outputLineEdit->setText(settings.value("outputLineEdit",
        "").toString());
      ui->medianBlurRadioButton
        ->setChecked(settings.value("medianBlurRadioButton",
        true).toBool());
```

```
    ui->gaussianBlurRadioButton
      ->setChecked(settings.value("gaussianBlurRadioButton",
      false).toBool());
    ui->displayImageCheckBox
      ->setChecked(settings.value("displayImageCheckBox",
      false).toBool());
}
```

And this one is for `saveSettings`:

```
void MainWindow::saveSettings()
{
  QSettings settings("Packt",
    "Hello_OpenCV_Qt",
    this);
  settings.setValue("inputLineEdit",
    ui->inputLineEdit->text());
  settings.setValue("outputLineEdit",
    ui->outputLineEdit->text());
  settings.setValue("medianBlurRadioButton",
    ui->medianBlurRadioButton->isChecked());
  settings.setValue("gaussianBlurRadioButton",
    ui->gaussianBlurRadioButton->isChecked());
  settings.setValue("displayImageCheckBox",
    ui->displayImageCheckBox->isChecked());
}
```

You need to provide the `QSettings` class with an organization name (just as an example, we used `"Packt"`) and an application name (in our case, `"Hello_Qt_OpenCV"`) when you construct it. Then, it simply records whatever you pass to the `setValue` function and returns it with the `value` function. What we did was we simply passed everything that we want to save to the `setValue` function, such as the text in Line Edit widgets and so on, and just reloaded it when needed. Note that `QSettings`, when used like this, takes care of the storage location by itself and uses each operating system's default location to keep application-specific configurations.

Now, simply add the `loadSettings` function to the `MainWindow` class's constructor. You should have a constructor function that looks like this:

```
  ui->setupUi(this);
  loadSettings();
```

Add the `saveSettings` function to `closeEvent`, right before `event->accept()`, and that's it. We can now give our first application a try. Let's try running and filtering an image. Select each of the two filters and see what their difference is. Try playing around with the application and find its issues. Try improving it by adding more parameters to it, and so on. The following is a screenshot of the application while it's running:

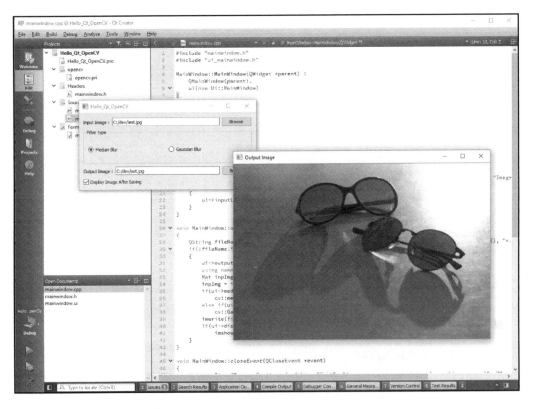

Try closing it and see if everything's alright with our exit confirmation code.

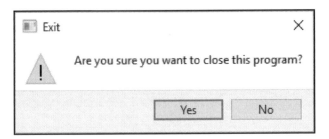

What we programmed is obviously not perfect, but it lays out almost everything that you need to know about starting with Qt Creator IDE and our advance through the chapters of this book. There are three more `Modes` in Qt Creator that we still haven't seen, and we will leave the Debug mode and the Projects mode to `Chapter 12`, *Qt Quick Applications*, where we'll dig deep into the concept of building, testing, and debugging our computer vision applications. So, let's finish our tour around the IDE by briefly going through Qt Creator's very important **Help** mode, and, after that, the `Options`.

# Help mode

Use the **Help** button on the left to switch to the **Help** mode of Qt Creator:

The most important thing about the Qt Creator **Help** mode, other than the fact that you can literally search for everything related to Qt and see countless examples for every class and module, is the fact that you must use it in order to find out the correct module required for each class. To do it, just switch to the index mode and search for a Qt class that you want to use in your applications. Here's an example:

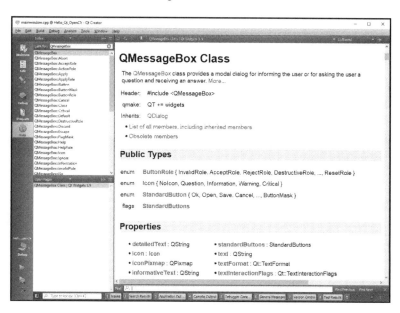

As you can see, `QMessageBox` class's documentation page can be easily accessed using the index and searching for it. Note the first two lines right after the description:

```
#include <QMessageBox>
QT += widgets
```

This basically means, in order to use `QMessageBox` in your project, you have to include the `QMessageBox` header in your source files and add the widgets module to your `PRO` file. Try searching for all the classes you used in this chapter and see their examples in the documentation. Qt Creator also offers a very powerful context-sensitive help. You can just click on *F1* with your mouse over any Qt class and its documentation page will be fetched right inside the code editor, in **Edit** mode:

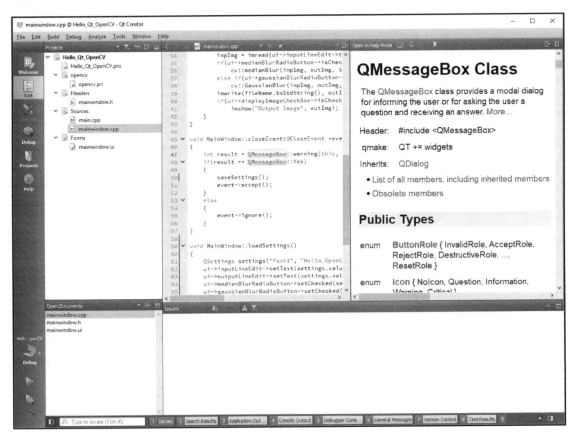

# The Qt Creator Options window

You can access Qt Creator **Options** from its main menu by clicking on **Tools** and then **Options**. Qt Creator allows a very high level of customization, so you'll find that its **Options** pages and tabs have quite a lot of parameters to configure. For most people (myself included), Qt Creator's default options would suffice for almost everything they need to do, but there are tasks that, without knowing how to configure the IDE, you won't be able to complete. Consider the following screenshot:

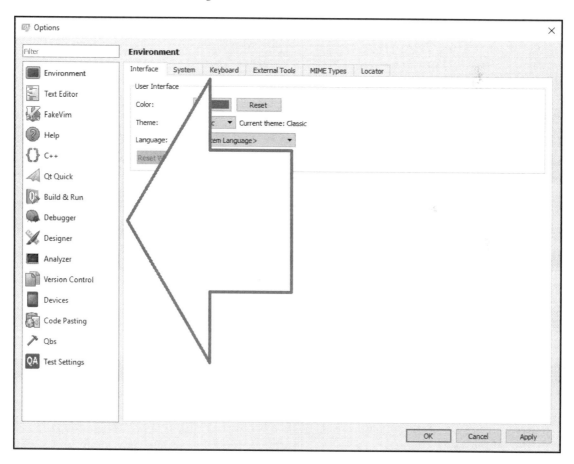

You can switch between pages using the buttons on the left. Each page contains a number of tabs, but they are all related to the same group. Here is what each group of **Options** is mainly used for:

- **Environment**: This contains settings related to the look and feel of Qt Creator in general. Here you can change the theme (which was mentioned in the beginning of this chapter), fonts and text size, language, and all settings for them.
- **Text Editor**: This group of settings includes everything related to the code editor. Here you can change settings such as **Code Highlight**, **Code Completion**, and so on.
- **FakeVim**: This is for people familiar with the Vim editor. Here, they can enable Vim-style code editing in Qt Creator and configure it.
- **Help**: As it can be guessed, this contains all options related to Qt Creator's **Help** mode and context-sensitive help feature.
- **C++**: Here, you can find settings relevant to C++ coding and code editing.
- **Qt Quick**: Options that affect Qt Quick designer and QML code editing can be found here. We'll learn more about QML in Chapter 12, *Qt Quick Applications*.
- **Build & Run**: This is probably the most important options page in Qt Creator. Settings here directly affect your application build and run experience. We'll configure some settings in Chapter 11, *Linking and Deployment*, where you'll learn about static linking in Qt.
- **Debugger**: This contains settings related to the **Debug** mode in Qt Creator. You'll learn more about this in Chapter 10, *Debugging and Testing*.
- **Designer**: This can be used to configure Qt Creator template projects and other settings related to the **Design** mode.
- **Analyzer**: This includes settings related to the Clang code analyzer, QML profiler, and so on. Covering them is out of the scope of this book.
- **Version Control**: Qt offers a very reliable integration with many version control systems, such as Git and SVN. Here, you can configure all settings related to version control in Qt Creator.
- **Devices**: As you'll see in Chapter 12, *Qt Quick Applications*, where you'll use it to configure Qt Creator for Android Development, including all settings relevant to devices.
- **Code Pasting**: This can be used to configure some of the third-party services that can be used by Qt Creator for tasks such as code sharing.

- **Qbs**: Covering Qbs is totally out of the scope of our book and we won't be needing it.
- **Test Settings**: This contains settings related to Qt Test, and so on. We'll be introduced to Qt Test in `Chapter 10`, Debugging and Testing, where you'll learn how to write unit tests for our Qt applications.

Apart from this, you can always use Qt Creator's **Filter** tool to immediately locate the settings in the **Options** window that you need:

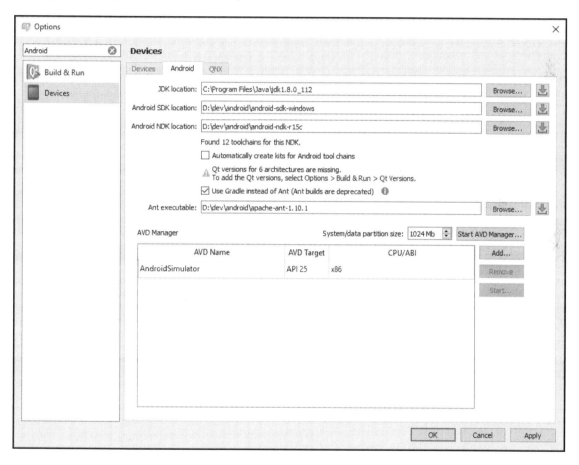

# Summary

This chapter was an introduction to Qt Creator more than it was anything else, and that is exactly what we need in order to comfortably proceed with the next chapters, concentrating on building things instead of repetitive instructions and configuration tips and hints. We learned how to use Qt Creator to design user interfaces and write code for the user interfaces. We were introduced to some of the most widely used Qt classes and how they are packed in different modules. By learning about different Qt Creator modes and building an application at the same time, we can now practice more by ourselves and even improve the application we wrote. The next chapter will be the chapter where we build the skeleton of an extendable plugin-based computer vision application that will continue almost for the rest of the book, until the very last chapters. In the next chapter, we'll learn about different design patterns in Qt and OpenCV and how we can use similar patterns to build applications that are easily maintainable and extendable.

# 3

# Creating a Comprehensive
# Qt+OpenCV Project

Professional applications never end up being professional because of some random circumstances. They are designed like this from the very beginning. Of course, it is easier said than done, but it's still quite easy if you already know the golden rule of how to create applications that can be easily extended, maintained, scaled, and customized. The golden rule here is just one simple concept, which fortunately Qt framework already has the means to implement, and that is building applications in a modular fashion. Note that modular in this sense doesn't just mean libraries or different source code modules, but modular in the sense that each of the responsibilities and capabilities of the application is created and built independently of the others. This is, in fact, exactly the way Qt and OpenCV themselves are created. An application that is modularized can be extended very easily, even by different developers from different backgrounds. An application that is modularized can be extended to support many different languages, themes (styles or looks), or better yet, many different capabilities and functions.

In this chapter, we will take on a very important and crucial task, which is building an infrastructure (or architecture) for a comprehensive computer vision application that uses the Qt and OpenCV frameworks. You'll learn how to create Qt applications that can be extended even after they are deployed (shipped to the users). This actually means many things, including how to add new languages to applications, how to add new styles to applications, and most importantly, how to build a plugin-based Qt application that can be extended by adding new plugins to it.

We will start by learning about what goes behind the scenes in general when a Qt application is built, by going through a Qt project's structure and included files. Then, we'll learn about some of the most widely used design patterns in Qt and OpenCV, and how both these frameworks enjoy the advantages of using those design patterns. Then, we will learn how to create an application that can be extended with plugins. We'll also learn about adding new styles and new languages to our applications. By the end of this chapter, we will be able to create the base of a comprehensive computer vision application that is cross-platform, multi-language, plugin-based, and with a customizable look and feel. This base application will be extended in the next two chapters, Chapter 4, *Mat and QImage*, and Chapter 5, *The Graphics View Framework*, and later on using plugins for the rest of the book, especially after Chapter 6, *Image Processing in OpenCV*, when we'll start to really dig into computer vision subjects and OpenCV libraries.

In this chapter, we will cover the following topics:

- Structure of a Qt project and Qt build process
- Design patterns in Qt and OpenCV
- Styling in Qt applications
- Languages in Qt applications
- How to use Qt Linguist tool
- How to Create and Use plugins in Qt

# Behind the scenes

In Chapter 2, *Creating Our First Qt and OpenCV Project*, you learned how to create a simple Qt+OpenCV application called Hello_Qt_OpenCV. This project included almost all of the basic features provided by Qt, although we didn't go into too much detail on how our project was built into an application with a user interface and an (almost acceptable) behavior. In this section, you will learn about what went on behind the scenes when we clicked on the **Run** button. This will help us with a better understanding of the structure of a Qt project and what the purpose of each file in the project folder is. Let's start by opening the project folder and going through the few files one by one. So, we have the following in the Hello_Qt_OpenCV folder:

```
Hello_Qt_OpenCV.pro
Hello_Qt_OpenCV.pro.user
main.cpp
mainwindow.cpp
mainwindow.h
mainwindow.ui
```

The first file in the `Hello_Qt_OpenCV.pro` list is basically the first file that is processed by Qt when our project is built. This is called a **Qt Project file** and an internal Qt program called `qmake` is responsible for processing it. Let's see what it is.

# The qmake tool

The qmake tool is a program that helps with creating makefiles using the information inside the `*.pro` files. This simply means, using a very simple syntax (as opposed to more complex syntax in other make systems), `qmake` generates all the necessary commands for correctly compiling and building an application, and puts all those generated files inside the `Build` folder.

When a Qt project is built, it first creates a new build folder, which by default, is on the same level as the project folder. In our case, this folder should have a name similar to `build-Hello_Qt_OpenCV-Desktop_Qt_5_9_1_*-Debug`, where * can be different, depending on the platform, and you can find it in the same folder where your project folder is located. All files generated by Qt (using `qmake` and some other tools that you'll learn about in this chapter) and C++ compilers are located in this folder and its subfolders. This is called the `Build` folder of your project. This is also the place where your application is created and executed from. For example, if you are on Windows, you can find the `Hello_Qt_OpenCV.exe` file (among many other files) inside the `debug` or `release` subfolders in the `Build` folder. So, from now on we will refer to this folder (and its subfolders) as the Build folder.

For instance, we already know that including the following line in our Qt Project file causes the addition of Qt's `core` and `gui` modules to our application:

```
QT += core gui
```

Let's look even further inside the `Hello_Qt_OpenCV.pro` file; the following lines are immediately noticeable:

```
TARGET = Hello_Qt_OpenCV
TEMPLATE = app
```

These lines simply mean the TARGET name is Hello_Qt_OpenCV, which is the name of our project and the TEMPLATE type app means that our project is an application. We also have the following:

```
SOURCES += \
    main.cpp \
    mainwindow.cpp
HEADERS += \
    mainwindow.h
FORMS += \
    mainwindow.ui
```

Quite obviously, this is how header files, source files, and user interface files (forms) are included in our project. We even added our own code to the Project file, as follows:

```
win32: {
   include("c:/dev/opencv/opencv.pri")
}
unix: !macx{
   CONFIG += link_pkgconfig
   PKGCONFIG += opencv
}
unix: macx{
   INCLUDEPATH += "/usr/local/include"
   LIBS += -L"/usr/local/lib" \
 -lopencv_world
}
```

You already learned that this is how Qt can see OpenCV and use it in a Qt project. Search for the qmake Manual in the **Qt help index** for more information about all possible commands and functions in qmake and more detailed information about how it works.

After qmake has processed our Qt project file, it starts looking for the source files mentioned in the project. Naturally, every C++ program has a main function (a single and unique main function) in one of its source files (not in the header files), and our application is no exception. Our main function for the application is automatically generated by Qt Creator, and it's inside the main.cpp file. Let's open the main.cpp file and see what it contains:

```
#include "mainwindow.h"
#include <QApplication>
int main(int argc, char *argv[])
{
   QApplication a(argc, argv);
   MainWindow w;
   w.show();
```

```
    return a.exec();
}
```

The first two lines are used to include our current `mainwindow.h` header and `QApplication` header files. The `QApplication` class is the main class responsible for controlling the application's control flow, settings, and so on. What you see here, inside the main function, is the basis of how Qt creates an `Event Loop` and how its underlying signal/slot mechanism and event handling system works:

```
QApplication a(argc, argv);
MainWindow w;
w.show();
return a.exec();
```

To describe it most simply, an instance of `QApplication` class is created and the application arguments (usually passed through the command line or terminal) are passed to the new instance named `a`. Then, an instance of our `MainWindow` class is created, and then it's shown. Finally, the `exec()` function of the `QApplication` class is called so that the application is entered into the main loop, and stays on until the window is closed.

 To understand how the event loop really works, try removing the last line and see what happens. When you run your application, you may notice that the window is actually shown for a very brief moment, and then it's immediately closed. This is because our application no longer has an event loop and it immediately reaches the end of the application and everything is cleared out from the memory, thus the window is closed. Now, write that line back, and as you would expect, the window stays open because the `exec()` function only returns when the `exit()` function is called somewhere (anywhere) in the code, and it returns the value set by `exit()`.

Now, let's move on to the next three files, which have the same name but different extensions. They are the `mainwindow` header, source, and user interface files. You will now learn about the actual files responsible for both the code and the user interface of the application we created in `Chapter 2`, *Creating Our First Qt and OpenCV Project*. This brings us to two more Qt internal tools called the **MetaObject Compiler** and the **User Interface Compiler**.

# Meta-Object Compiler (moc)

We already know that there are no such things as signals and slots in standard C++ code. So, how is it that by using Qt, we can have those additional capabilities in the C++ code? And that is not all. As you'll learn later on, you can even add new properties to Qt objects (called **dynamic properties**) and perform many other actions like that, which are not capabilities of standard C++ programming. Well, these are made available by using a Qt internal compiler called `moc`. Before your Qt code is actually passed on to the real C++ compiler, the `moc` tool processes your class headers (in our case, the `mainwindow.h` file) to generate the code required for enabling the Qt specific capabilities that were just mentioned. You can find these generated source files in the `Build` folder. Their name starts with `moc_`.

You can read all about the `moc` tool in the Qt documentation, but what is worth mentioning here is that `moc` searches for all header files with Qt class definitions that contain the `Q_OBJECT` macro. This macro must always be included in Qt classes that want support for signals, slots, and other Qt supported features.

Here's what we had in our `mainwindow.h` file:

```
...
class MainWindow : public QMainWindow
{
  Q_OBJECT
  public:
    explicit MainWindow(QWidget *parent = 0);
  ~MainWindow();
...
```

As you can see, our automatically generated class header file already had the `Q_OBJECT` macro in its private section. So, this is basically the standard way of creating classes (not just Window classes but any Qt classes in general) that are subclasses of `QObject` (or any other Qt object for that matter) that will support Qt supported functionalities such as signals and slots.

Now, let's move on to see how is it that we are able to access widgets in a Qt user interface file through C++ codes. If you try to view the `mainwindow.ui` file in the `Edit` mode or any other text editor, you'll notice that they are, in fact, XML files that only include the properties and some other information that is only relevant to the way widgets are shown. The answer lies in one final Qt internal compiler that you will learn about in this chapter.

# User Interface Compiler (uic)

Whenever a Qt application with a user interface is built, a Qt internal tool called `uic` is executed to process and convert the `*.ui` files into classes and source code usable in C++ code. In our case, `mainwindow.h` is converted to the `ui_mainwindow.h` file, which again, you can find in the `Build` folder. You may have already noticed this, but let's mention that your `mainwindow.cpp` file already included this header file. Check the topmost part of the file, and you'll find the following two include lines:

```
#include "mainwindow.h"
#include "ui_mainwindow.h"
```

You already knew what and where the `mainwindow.h` file is (in your `Project` folder), and you just learned that `ui_mainwindow.h` is, in fact, a generated source file that is located inside the `Build` folder.

If you take a look at the contents of the `ui_mainwindow.h` file, you'll notice a class called `Ui_MainWindow` with two functions: `setupUi` and `retranslateUi`. The `setupUi` function was automatically added to our `MainWindow` class constructor in the `mainwindow.h` function. This function is simply responsible for setting everything on the user interface according to what was set in the `mainwindow.ui` file. You'll learn about the `retranslateUi` function and how it is used while making multi-language Qt applications later on in this chapter.

After all of the Qt generated files are in the `Build` folder, they are passed over to the C++ compiler, like any other C++ program, to be compiled and later linked to create our application in the `Build` folder. Windows users should note that when you run your application using Qt Creator, all DLL file paths are resolved by the Qt Creator, but if you try to run your program from inside the `Build` folder, you will face multiple error messages and your application will crash or simply just not start at all. You will learn how to get past this issue in `Chapter 10`, *Debugging and Testing*, where you'll learn how to correctly ship your applications to your users.

# Design patterns

Even though we assume that the reader of this book is not a Design Pattern Denier, it's still a very good idea to remind ourselves why design patterns exist and why a successful framework such as Qt makes extensive use of different design patterns. Well, first of all, a design pattern is just one of many solutions to a software development task and it is not the only solution; and in fact, most of the times it's not even the fastest solution. However, a design pattern is definitely the most structured way of solving a software development problem, and it helps make sure you use some predefined template-like structures for everything you add to your program.

Design patterns have names applied to different kinds of problems such as creating objects, how they run, how they handle data, and so on. Eric Gamma, Richard Helm, Ralph E. Johnson, and John Vlissides (referred to as the *Gang of Four*) describe many of the most widely used design patterns in their book titled *Design Patterns: Elements of Reusable Object-Oriented Software*, which is considered the de-facto reference book for design patterns in computer science. If you are not familiar with design patterns, you should definitely spend some time learning about the subject before continuing with this chapter. It's also a good idea to learn about anti-patterns in software development. If you are new to the topic, you may be surprised by finding out how common some of the anti-patterns are, and it's crucial to make sure you always avoid them.

The following are some of the most important design patterns used in the Qt and OpenCV framework (ordered alphabetically), along with a brief description and a few examples of the classes or functions that implement those design patterns. Pay close attention to the example cases column in the following table to have an overview of some of the classes or functions relevant to each design pattern. Nevertheless, during the course of the book, and in various examples, you'll learn about the classes used with hands-on experience:

Because of the nature of the OpenCV framework, and the fact that it is not a general-purpose framework used to build daily-life applications, complex user interfaces, and more, it doesn't implement all of the design patterns that Qt uses, and, in comparison only a very small subset of these patterns are implemented in OpenCV. Especially because of OpenCV's aim of speed and efficiency, global functions and low-level like implementations are preferred most of the time. Nevertheless, there are OpenCV classes that implement design patterns such as Abstract Factory whenever speed and efficiency is not the goal. See the *Example cases* column next for examples:

| Design pattern | Description | Example cases |
| --- | --- | --- |
| Abstract Factory | This can be used to create so-called factory classes that are capable of creating objects and control the creation of new objects in every possible way, such as preventing an object having more than a defined number instance. | In this chapter, we will learn how to use this design pattern to write plugin-based Qt applications. The `create()` function in the `DescriptorMatcher` abstract class is an example of this design pattern in OpenCV. |
| Command | Using this design pattern, actions can be represented with objects. This allows capabilities such as organizing the order of actions, logging them, reverting them, and so on. | **QAction**: This class allows creating specific actions and assigning them to widgets. For example, a `QAction` class can be used to create an `Open File` action with an icon and text, and then it can be assigned to the main menu item and a keyboard shortcut (like *Ctrl + O*) and so on. |
| Composite | This is used to create objects that consist of child objects. This is especially useful when making complex objects that can consist of many simpler objects. | **QObject**: This is the base of all Qt classes. **QWidget**: This is the base of all Qt widgets. Any Qt class with a tree-like design architecture is an example of the Composite pattern. |

| | | |
|---|---|---|
| Facade (or Façade) | This can be used to encapsulate lower-level capabilities of an operating system (or any system for that matter) by providing a simpler interface. Wrapper and Adaptor design patterns are considered to be quite similar in definition. | **QFile**: These can be used to read/write files. Basically, all Qt classes that are wrappers around low-level APIs of operating systems are examples of the Façade design pattern. |
| Flyweight (or Bridge or Private-Implementation) | The goal of this design pattern is to avoid data copying and use shared data between related objects (unless otherwise is needed). | **QString**: This can be used to store and manipulate Unicode strings. In fact, many Qt classes enjoy these design patterns that help to pass a pointer to a shared data space whenever a copy of an object is needed, which consequently leads to faster object copying and less memory space usage. Of course, with a more complex code. |
| Memento | This can be used to save and (later on) load the state of objects. | This design pattern would be the equivalent of writing a class that is capable of storing all properties of a Qt object and restoring them to create a new one. |
| MetaObject (or Reflection) | In this design pattern, a so-called metaobject is used to describe the details of the object for a more robust access to that object. | **QMetaObject**: This simply contains meta-information about Qt classes. Covering the details of Qt's meta-object system is out of the scope of this book, but simply put, each Qt program is first compiled with the Qt MetaObject compiler (MOC) to generate the required meta objects and then compiled by the actual C++ compiler. |

| | | |
|---|---|---|
| Monostate | This allows multiple instances of the same class to behave the same way. (Usually, by accessing the same data or executing the same functions.) | **QSettings**: This is used to provide application settings save/load. We already used the QSettings class in Chapter 2, *Creating Our First Qt and OpenCV Project*, to load and save with two different instances of the same class. |
| MVC (Model-view-controller) | This is a widely-used design pattern, and it is used to separate the implementation of the application or data storage mechanism (Model) from the user interface or data representation (view) and the data manipulation (controller). | **QTreeView**: This is a tree-like implementation of model-view. **QFileSystemModel**: This is used to get a data model based on the contents of the local file system. A combination of QFileSystemModel (or any other QAbstractItemModel, for that matter) with QTreeView (or any other QAbstractItemView) can result in an MVC design pattern implementation. |
| Observer (or Publish/Subscribe) | This design pattern is used to make objects that can listen (or observe) to changes in other objects and respond accordingly. | **QEvent**: This is the base of all Qt's event classes. Think of QEvent (and all of its numerous subclasses) as a low-level implementation of the observer design pattern. On the other hand, Qt supports signal and slot mechanism, which is a more convenient and high-level method of using the Observer design pattern. We already used QCloseEvent (a subclass of QEvent) in Chapter 2, *Creating Our First Qt and OpenCV Project*. |

| | | |
|---|---|---|
| Serializer | This pattern is used when creating classes (or objects) that can be used to read or write other objects. | **QTextStream**: This can be used to read and write text into files or other IO devices.<br>**QDataStream**: This can be used to read or write binary data from IO devices and files. |
| Singleton | This can be used to restrict a class to only a single instance. | **QApplication:** This can be used to handle a Qt widgets application in various ways.<br>To be precise, the `instance()` function in `QApplication` (or the global `qApp` pointer) is an example of the Singleton design pattern. The `cv::theRNG()` function in OpenCV (used to get the default **Random Number Generator (RNG)**) is an example of Singleton implementation. Note that the RNG class itself is not a Singleton. |

References:

- *Design Patterns: Elements of Reusable Object-Oriented Software*, by Eric Gamma, Richard Helm, Ralph E. Johnson and John Vlissides (referred to as the Gang of Four)
- *An Introduction to Design Patterns in C++ with Qt, second Edition*, by Alan Ezust and Paul Ezust

 The preceding list should not be considered a complete list of design patterns in general, as it only focuses on Qt and OpenCV design patterns, and just the ones that are enough for the purpose of this book. Consider reading the mentioned reference books if you are interested in the subject, but as it was mentioned, you won't need any more than the preceding list for the purpose of this book.

It's a very good idea to check out the documentation page for each one of the classes mentioned in the preceding list. You can use the **Qt Creator Help** mode for this purpose and search for each class in the index, check out the code examples for each class and even try to use them by yourself. This is one of the best methods of learning not only about Qt but also the real implementation and behavior of different design patterns.

# Qt Resource System

In the next sections, you will learn how to add styling and multi-language support to our applications, but, before that, we must be familiar with the Qt Resource System. Simply put, it is the means in Qt to add resource files such as fonts, icons, images, translation files, style sheet files, and so on into our applications (and libraries).

Qt supports resource management using the `*.qrc` files (Resource Collection Files), which are simply XML files that include information about resource files that need to be included in our applications. Let's go through a simple example and include an icon in our `Hello_Qt_openCV` application to better understand how the Qt Resource System works:

1. Make sure you have the `Hello_Qt_OpenCV` project opened in Qt Creator. Select **File** and then **New File or Project**. In the new file window, make sure you select **Qt** from the second list on the left and then **Qt Resource File**. Consider the following screenshot:

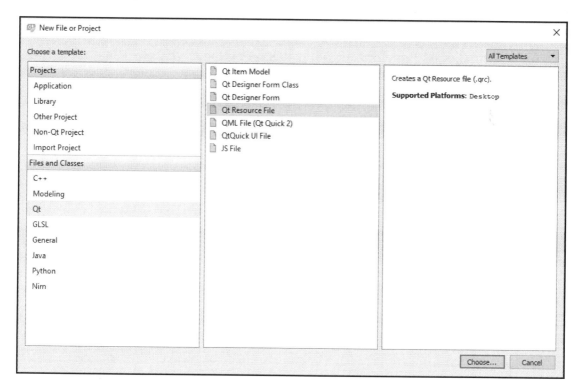

2. Click on the **Choose...** button, and in the next screen, set the name to `resources`. The path should be set to your project folder by default, so leave it as it is. Click **Next** and then **Finish**. You will end up with a new file called `resources.qrc` added to your project. If you open this file in Qt Creator (by right-clicking and selecting **Open in Editor**), you will be presented with the resource editor in Qt Creator.

3. Here, you can use the **Add** button to open up the following two options:

   **Add Files**

   **Add Prefix**

   Here, a file is just any file that you want to add to your project. However, a prefix is basically a pseudo-folder (or a container if you will) that holds a number of files. Note that this doesn't necessarily represent the folders or subfolders on your project folder, but it's merely a representation and a way to group your resource files.

4. Start by clicking on **Add Prefix** and then enter `images` in the **Prefix** field.

5. Then, click on **Add Files** and select an image file of your choice (Any `*.jpg` file on your computer would be okay for the purpose of our example.):

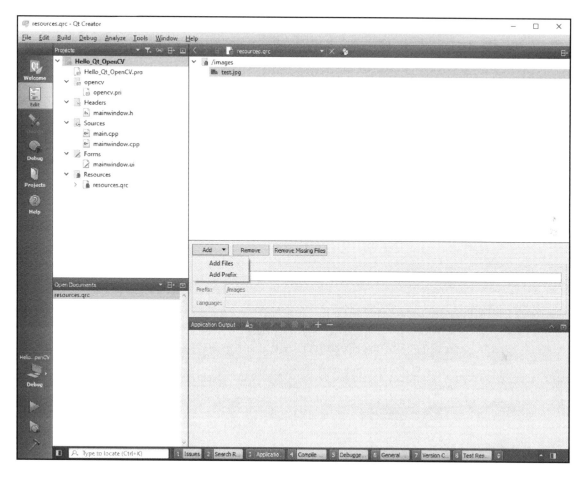

In this example, we have used the same example `test.jpg` file that was used in `Chapter 1`, *Introduction to Qt and OpenCV,* and `Chapter 2`, *Creating Our First Qt and OpenCV Project.* Note that your resource files should be in your project folder or a subfolder inside it. Otherwise, you'll get a confirmation as shown in the following screenshot; click on **Copy** if that is the case and save the resource file in your project folder:

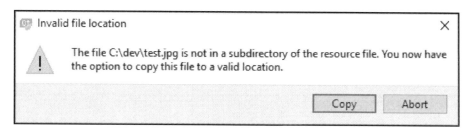

That's it. Now, when you build and run your `Hello_Qt_OpenCV` application, the image file is included in your application and can be accessed like a file that exists on the operating system. The path is a little bit different than a regular file path though. In our example, the path to the `test.jpg` file would be as follows:

```
:/images/test.jpg
```

You can expand your `*.qrc` files in Qt Creator and right-click on each resource file and then choose the **Copy Path \*\*\*** or **Copy URL \*\*\*** options to copy the path or URL of each one. The path can be used whenever a regular path is required and URL is useful whenever a URL (QUrl class in Qt) of the resource file is required. It is important to note that OpenCV may not be able to use these paths and access files in the resources because Qt Resource System is an internal Qt capability. However, these files are only meant for use by the application itself (usually in user interface related tasks), so you probably will never need to use them with OpenCV anyway.

Now you can try out the new image file by setting it as the icon of a button for example. Try selecting any of the buttons on the user interface, then find the **icon** property in the property editor, then select **Choose Resource** by pressing the small drop-down button right next to it. Now you can simply choose the image you added as the icon for the button:

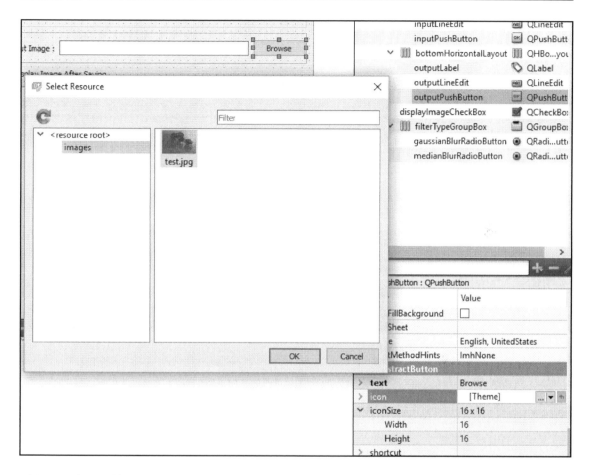

This was basically a tutorial on how to set icons to Qt widgets that support having icons. The logic is exactly the same when you want to include any other type of resource in your application and use it at runtime. You just have to assume that Qt Resource System is some kind of a secondary file system and use the files inside it, just like you would use a regular file on the file system.

# Styling applications

Qt supports styling in applications using the `QStyle` class and Qt Style Sheets. `QStyle` is the base class for all styles in Qt, and it encapsulates the styling of the Qt user interfaces. Covering the `QStyle` class is out of the scope of this book, but it should still be noted that creating a sub-class of `QStyle` and implementing different styling capabilities in it is ultimately the most powerful method of changing the look and feel of a Qt application. However, Qt also offers Style Sheets to style applications. Qt Style Sheets are almost identical in syntax to HTML **CSS (Cascading Style Sheets)**, which is an inseparable part of styling in web pages.

 CSS is a styling language that can be used to define the way objects on a user interface look. In general, using CSS files helps separate the styling of web pages from the underlying implementation. Qt uses a very similar method in its Style Sheets to describe the way widgets look. If you are familiar with CSS files, then Qt Style Sheets will be a piece of cake for you; however, even if you are introduced to the concept for the first time, rest assured that this is a method that is meant to be easy, simple, and learned quickly.

Let's see what is a Style Sheet exactly and how it is used in Qt with a simple example. Let's go back to our `Hello_Qt_OpenCV` project once again. Open the project and go to the **Designer**. Select any of the widgets on the window, or click on an empty place to select the window widget itself, and you can find a property called `styleSheet`. Basically, every Qt Widget (or `QWidget` subclass, in other words) contains a `styleSheet` property that can be set to define the look and feel of each widget.

Click on the `inputPushButton` widget and set its `styleSheet` property to the following:

```
border: 2px solid #222222;
border-radius: 10px;
background-color: #9999ff;
min-width: 80px;
min-height: 35px;
```

Do the same with `outputPushButton`; however, this time, use the following in the `styleSheet` property:

```
border: 2px solid #222222;
border-radius: 10px;
background-color: #99ff99;
min-width: 80px;
min-height: 35px;
```

As you set these style sheets in the Designer, you will see the new look of the two buttons. This is how simple styling is in Qt. The only thing needed is to know what kind of styling changes can be applied to any specific widget type. In our preceding example, we were able to change the look of the border, background color, and minimum accepted size of QPushButton. To get an overview of what kind of stylings can be applied to any widget, you can read the **Qt Style Sheets Reference** in the Qt Help mode. It should be already on your computer and you can access it offline from the **Help** index anytime. There, you will find all possible stylings for Qt widgets, with clear examples that you can copy and modify to fit your own needs and what kind of look and feel you want to have in your application. Here is the result of the two simple style sheets we just used. As you can see, we now have a different look for our browse buttons:

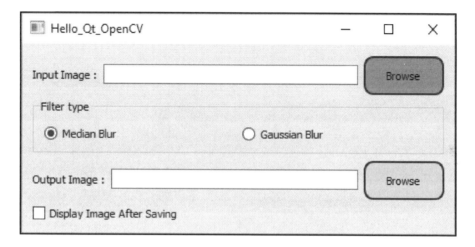

In the preceding example, we also avoided setting a proper Style Rule in the style sheet. A style rule in the Qt style sheet consists of a **Selector** and **Declaration**. The **Selector** specifies the widgets that will use the style, and declaration is simply the style itself. Again, in our preceding example, we only used a declaration and the selector was (implicitly) the widget that got the style sheet. Here's an example:

```
QPushButton
{
  border: 2px solid #222222;
  border-radius: 10px;
  background-color: #99ff99;
  min-width: 80px;
  min-height: 35px;
}
```

Here, `QPushButton` (or, in fact, everything that comes before {) is the selector and the part of the code between { and } is the declaration.

Now, let's go through some of the important concepts when setting style sheets in Qt.

# Selector types

The following are the selector types you can use in Qt style sheets. Using them wisely and efficiently can tremendously reduce the amount of code needed for style sheets and changing the look and feel of a Qt application:

| Selector Type | Example | Description |
| --- | --- | --- |
| Universal | * | These all are widgets |
| Type | `QPushButton` | These are widgets of the specified type and its subclasses |
| Property | `QPushButton[text='Browse']` | These are widgets with a specified property set to a specified value |
| Class | `.QPushButton` | These are widgets with a specified type, but not its subclasses |
| ID | `QPushButton# inputPushButton` | These are widgets with a specified type and `objectName` |
| Descendant | `QDialog QPushButton` | These are widgets that are descendants (children) of another widget |
| Child | `QDialog > QPushButton` | These are widgets that are direct children of another widget |

# Sub-controls

Or better yet, sub-widgets are the child widgets inside the complex widget. An example would be the down and up arrow buttons on a `QPinBox` widget. They can be selected with the : : operator, as seen in the following example:

```
QSpinBox::down-button
```

Always remember to refer to the Qt Style Sheets Reference article available in the **Qt Creator Help** mode for a (more or less) complete list of sub controls for each widget. Qt is an evolving framework and new functionalities are added on a regular basis so there's no better reference than its own documentation.

## Pseudo-states

Each widget can have some pseudo-states, such as hover, pressed, and more. They can be selected in style sheets using the : operator, as seen in the following example:

```
QRadioButton:!hover { color: black }
```

Just like with sub-controls, always refer to Qt Style Sheets Reference in the Qt Creator Help mode for a list of applicable pseudo-states for each widget.

## Cascading

You can set style sheets for the whole application, parent widgets, or child widgets. In our preceding examples, we simply set the style sheets for two child widgets. The styling of each widget will be decided on the cascading rule, which simply means that each widget will also get the style rules set in parent widget or the application if there are any style sheets set for them. We can use this fact to avoid redundantly setting the style rules that are common to the entire application or a specific window in each widget over and over again.

Now, let's try the following style sheet in `MainWindow`, which combines all you've learned in a single and simple example. Make sure you delete all previously set style sheets (for the two **Browse** buttons) and simply use the following in the stylesheet property of the window widget:

```
*
{
  font: 75 11pt;
  background-color: rgb(220, 220, 220);
}
QPushButton, QLineEdit, QGroupBox
{
  border: 2px solid rgb(0, 0, 0);
  border-radius: 10px;
  min-width: 80px;
  min-height: 35px;
}
QPushButton
```

```
{
    background-color: rgb(0, 255, 0);
}
QLineEdit
{
    background-color: rgb(0, 170, 255);
}
    QPushButton:hover, QRadioButton:hover, QCheckBox:hover
{
    color: red;
}
QPushButton:!hover, QRadioButton:!hover, QCheckBox:!hover
{
    color: black;
}
```

If you run your application now, you can see the change in the look. You will also notice that even the style for the **Close** confirmation dialog widgets have changed and the reason is simply the fact that we set the style sheet in its parent window. Here's a screenshot:

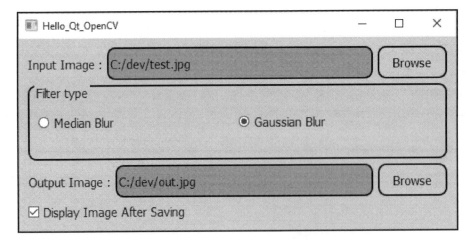

Needless to say, you can do the same by saving the style sheet in a text file and loading and setting it on runtime, as we'll do later on in this chapter when we build the foundation of our comprehensive computer vision application. You can even store a default style sheet inside the application, as you learned earlier in this chapter (refer to Qt Resource System), and load it by default, and maybe skip it if there is a custom file stored on a specific location in the computer. This way, you can easily have customizable applications. You can even split the tasks and ask a professional designer to simply provide you with a Style Sheet so that you can use it in your application. That's essentially how easy styling is in Qt applications.

For even more Style Sheet specific syntax and help, it's always best to keep an eye on the Style Sheet Syntax article in Qt Creator **Help** mode, since Qt Style Sheets are basically specific to Qt and somehow differ from the standard CSS in some cases.

# Multi-language support

In this section, you will learn how to create applications that support multiple languages using the Qt framework. In fact, it all comes down to a single class that is extremely easy to use. The `QTranslator` class is the main Qt class responsible for handling internationalization of output (displayed) text. You simply need to make sure of the following:

1. Use a default language (English, for instance) while you are building your project. This means, simply use sentences and words in the default language for everything that is displayed.
2. Make sure all literal sentences in your code, or to be specific, all literal sentences that need to be translated when a different language is selected are embraced in a `tr()` function.

> For example, in the code, if you need to write a literal sentence such as `Open Input Image` (as we did in the `Hello_Qt_OpenCV` example), simply pass it to a `tr` function and write `tr("Open Input Image")` instead. This is not the case with the Designer and only applies to the in-code literal strings. When setting a property in the designer, simply use the literal string.

3. Make sure to specify your translation files in the project file. To do this, you need to specify them with `TRANSLATIONS`, just like `SOURCES` and `HEADERS` in the project file.

> For example, if you want to have German and Turkish language translations in your application, add the following to your project (`*.PRO`) file:

```
TRANSLATIONS = translation_de.ts translation_tr.ts
```

Make sure you always use clear names for each one of the translation files. Even though you can name them as you like, it is always a good idea to name them with the language codes included (tr for Turkish, de for German, and so on), as seen in the preceding example. This also helps the Qt Linguist tool (as you'll learn later on) to know the target language for translation.

4. Create TS files (or Update them if they already exist) using the Qt's `lupdate` tool. `lupdate` is a Qt tool that searches all of the source codes and UI files for translatable text, and then creates or updates the TS files mentioned in the previous step. The person responsible for translating an application can simply open TS files using the Qt Linguist tool and simply focus on translating the application with a simple user interface.

`lupdate` is located inside the `bin` folder of the Qt installation. For example, on Windows OS, it would be a path similar to this:

```
C:\Qt\Qt5.9.1\5.9.1\msvc2015\bin
```

You can execute `lupdate` in your project from Qt Creator by simply clicking on **Tools / External / Linguist / Update Translations (lupdate)** from the main menu. Important note for Windows users: if you face any issues after running `lupdate`, it can be because of a malfunctioning Qt installation. To work around it, simply run `lupdate` using the Command Prompt of your development environment. If you followed the instructions in this book, then you can execute the `Developer Command Prompt for VS2015` from the start menu, then switch to your project folder using the CD command and then run `lupdate`, as seen here (example case is the `Hello_Qt_OpenCV` project we created earlier):

```
C:\Qt\Qt5.9.1\5.9.1\msvc2015\bin\lrelease.exe Hello_Qt_OpenCV.pro
```

After running this command, if you go into your project folder, you will notice that the TS files previously specified in the project file are now created. It's important to run `lupdate` regularly as your application grows bigger and bigger to extract new strings that require translation, and further expand multilanguage support.

5. Translate all required strings using the Qt Linguist tool. It is already installed on your computer since it's part of the default Qt installation. Simply select **File / Open** and choose all TS files (that were just created) from your `Project` folder and open them. If you have followed all instructions regarding the `Hello_Qt_OpenCV` project until now, then you should see the following screen after opening the TS files in Qt Linguist:

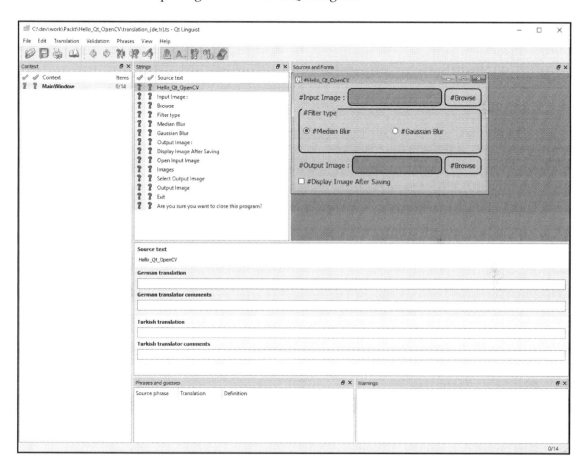

Qt Linguist allows quick and easy translation of all translatable elements in your project. Simply write the translation for each item in all of the languages shown, and mark them as `Done` using the toolbar at the top. Make sure to save before you exit the Qt Linguist tool.

6. Create QM files that are compressed and binary Qt language files using the translated TS files. To do this, you need to use the Qt `lrelease` tool.

Using `lrelease` is identical to `lupdate`, which you learned in the earlier steps. Simply replace all `lupdate` commands with `lrelease` and you'll be fine.

7. Add QM files (binary language files) to your application resources.

 You already learned how to use the Qt Resource System. Simply create a new prefix called translations and add the newly created QM files under that prefix. If correctly done, you should have the following in your project:

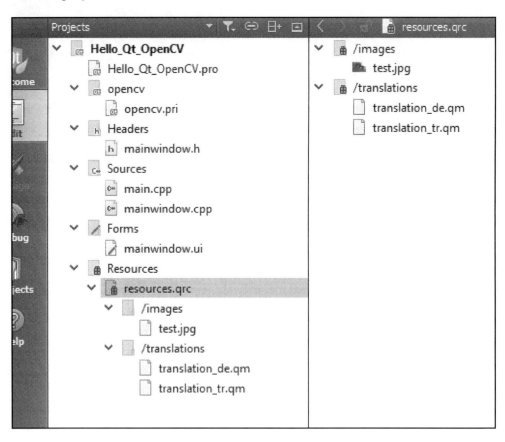

8. You can now start using the QTranslator class to have multiple languages in your application and also switch between languages at runtime. Let's go back once again to our example project, Hello_Qt_OpenCV. There are different approaches to having translators in an application, but, for now we will start with the simplest one. Start by adding the QTranslator include file to your mainwindow.h file and define two private QTranslator objects in the MainWindow class as follows:

```
QTranslator *turkishTranslator;
QTranslator *germanTranslator;
```

9. Add the following to the MainWindow constructor code, right after the call to loadSettings function:

```
turkishTranslator = new QTranslator(this);
turkishTranslator
    ->load(":/translations/translation_tr.qm");
germanTranslator = new QTranslator(this);
germanTranslator
    ->load(":/translations/translation_de.qm");
```

10. Now, it's time to add a main menu to our Hello_Qt_OpenCV project and allow the users to switch between the languages. You can do this by simply right-clicking on the window in the **Qt Creator Design** mode and selecting **Create a Menu Bar**. Then, add an item called **Language** to the top menu bar. Add three sub-items to it by simply clicking and typing the following:

- English
- German
- Turkish

Now, you should have a main menu that looks similar to this:

At the bottom of the Designer, you can find the action editor. Obviously enough, you now have three entries here, which were automatically created when you created the main menu. Each of them corresponds to each one of the language names you entered in the main menu.

11. Right-click on **Turkish** and select **Go to Slot**, then choose **triggered()** from the list and click on **OK**. In other words (as you learned in Chapter 2, *Creating Our First Qt and OpenCV Project*), write the following lines of code for the triggered slot of the `actionTurkish` object:

```
void MainWindow::on_actionTurkish_triggered()
{
    qApp->installTranslator(turkishTranslator);
}
```

12. Add the following lines for the `actionGerman` object. Basically, repeat the instructions but adapt them for the `actionTurkish` object:

```
void MainWindow::on_actionGerman_triggered()
{
    qApp->installTranslator(germanTranslator);
}
```

13. And do the same with the `actionEnglish` object. This time, you need to remove the translators from your application, since English is the default language for our application:

```
void MainWindow::on_actionEnglish_triggered()
{
    qApp->removeTranslator(turkishTranslator);
    qApp->removeTranslator(germanTranslator);
}
```

14. Well, we now have everything regarding the translation in our Qt application in place, except we need to make sure items on the screen are retranslated and basically reloaded. To do this, we need to use `changeEvent` of the `QMainWindow` class. Every time a translator is installed or removed using the preceding `installTranslator` and `removeTranslator` functions, a `Language Change` event is sent to all windows in the application. To catch this event, and make sure our window reloads on language change, we need to override the `changeEvent` function in our program. Simply add the following line of code to the protected members of the `MainWindow` class in the `mainwindow.h` file, right after the point where you previously defined `closeEvent`:

```
void changeEvent(QEvent *event);
```

15. Now add the following code snippet to your `mainwindow.cpp` file:

```cpp
void MainWindow::changeEvent(QEvent *event)
{
  if(event->type() == QEvent::LanguageChange)
  {
    ui->retranslateUi(this);
  }
  else
  {
    QMainWindow::changeEvent(event);
  }
}
```

The preceding code simply means that if the change event is a `Language Change`, then retranslate the window, otherwise, everything should proceed as it normally would. The `retranslateUi` function is generated using UIC (refer to the UIC section in this chapter), and it simply takes care of setting the correctly translated string according to the latest installed `QTranslator` object in the application.

That's it. You can now run your application and try switching between the languages. We have made our first real multi-language application. It's important to note that what you learned in this section basically applies to every Qt application and is the standard way of making multi-language applications. The more customized way of having different languages in an application would follow almost the same set of instructions, but instead of having language files built into the application using resource files, it would be much better if the languages are loaded from a location on the disk. This has the advantage of updating translations and even adding new languages (with a little bit more code) without having to rebuild the application itself.

# Creating and using plugins

Using plugins in an application is one of the most powerful methods of extending an application, and many of the applications that people use in their daily lives benefit from the power of plugins. A plugin is simply a library (`*.dll` on Windows, `*.so` on Linux, and so on) that can be loaded and used at runtime to take care of a specific task, but of course, it cannot be executed like a standalone application, and it depends on the application using it. We will also use plugins throughout this book to extend our computer vision application.

In this section, we will learn how to create an example application (called `Image_Filter`) that simply loads and uses plugins in a specified folder on the computer. However, before that we will learn how to create a plugin in Qt that uses both Qt and OpenCV frameworks, since our plugin will most probably need to do some computer vision magic using the OpenCV library. So, let's start.

First things first, we need to define a set of interfaces that are needed in order for our application to talk to the plugin. The equivalent of interfaces in C++ are classes with pure virtual functions. So, we basically need an interface with all of the functions that we expect to be present in a plugin. This is how plugins are created in general, and this is how third-party developers can write plugins for applications developed by someone else. Yes, they know about the interface of the plugin, and they just need to fill it with actual code that really does something.

# The interface

The interface is much more important than it would seem at first sight. Yes, it's basically a class that does nothing, but, it lays out the sketch of all plugins needed by our application for all time to come. So, we need to make sure all required functions are included in the plugin interface from the beginning, otherwise, it may be close to impossible to add, remove, or modify a function later on. Since at the moment we are dealing with an example project, it may not seem that serious, but in a real-life project these are usually some of the key factors that decide the extendibility of an application. So, now that we know about the importance of interfaces, we can start creating one for the purpose of our example project.

Open Qt Creator and make sure no projects are opened. Now, from the main menu, select **File /New File or Project**. From the window that appears, select C++ from the list on the left side (the one at the bottom), and then choose **C++ Header File**. Enter `cvplugininterface`, as the name of the file and proceed until you are in the code editor mode. Change the code to the following:

```
#ifndef CVPLUGININTERFACE_H
#define CVPLUGININTERFACE_H
#include <QObject>
#include <QString>
#include "opencv2/opencv.hpp"
class CvPluginInterface
{
  public:
  virtual ~CvPluginInterface() {}
  virtual QString description() = 0;
  virtual void processImage(const cv::Mat &inputImage,
```

```
            cv::Mat &outputImage) = 0;
    };
    #define CVPLUGININTERFACE_IID "com.amin.cvplugininterface"
    Q_DECLARE_INTERFACE(CvPluginInterface, CVPLUGININTERFACE_IID)
    #endif // CVPLUGININTERFACE_H
```

You probably have noticed lines similar to the following code are automatically added to any header file you create using Qt Creator:

```
    #ifndef CVPLUGININTERFACE_H
    #define CVPLUGININTERFACE_H
    ...
    #endif // CVPLUGININTERFACE_H
```

These simply ensure that each header file is included (and therefore processed) only once during application compilation. There are basically many other methods to achieve the same goal in C++, but this is the most widely accepted and used, especially by both the Qt and OpenCV frameworks to achieve the highest degree of cross-platform support. When working with Qt Creator, it is always automatically added to header files and there's no extra work needed.

The preceding codes are basically everything that is needed for a plugin interface in Qt. In our example interface, we only have two simple types of functions that we need the plugin to support, but as we'll see later on, to support parameters, languages, and so on, we need much more than this. However, for our example, this should be enough.

 A very important note for C++ developers in general, the first public member in the preceding interface, which is called a virtual destructor in C++, is one of the most important methods that many people forget to include and don't pay much attention to, so it's a good idea to see what it really is and keep it in mind to avoid memory leak, especially when using Qt Plugins:

```
    virtual ~CvPluginInterface() {}
```

Basically, any C++ base class that has a virtual method and is meant to be used polymorphically must include a virtual destructor. This helps make sure that destructors in child classes are called even when a pointer of the base class is used to access them (polymorphism). Unfortunately, with most of the C++ compilers, you won't even get a warning when making this common C++ programming mistake.

So, our plugin interface includes a function called description(), which is meant to return the description of any plugin and useful information about it. It also includes a function called processImage, which takes an OpenCV Mat class as the input and returns one as the output. Obviously, in this function, we expect each plugin to perform some kind of image processing, filter, and so on and give us the result.

After that, we define our class as an interface using the Q_DECLARE_INTERFACE macro. Without including this macro, Qt won't be able to recognize our class as a plugin interface. CVPLUGININTERFACE_IID should be a unique string in a similar package name format, but you can basically change it according to your own preferences.

Make sure you save the cvplugininterface.h file to any location of your choice and then close it. We will now create a plugin that uses this interface. Let's use one of the OpenCV functions that we previously saw in Chapter 2, *Creating Our First Qt and OpenCV Project*: medianBlur.

# The plugin

We will now create a plugin called median_filter_plugin that uses our CvPluginInterface interface class. Start by selecting **File** from the main menu and then **New File or Project**. Then, choose **Library** and **C++ Library**, as seen in the following screenshot:

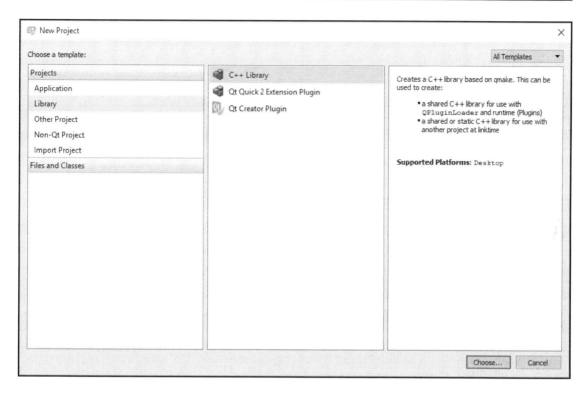

Make sure **Shared Library** is selected as **Type**, then enter `median_filter_plugin` as the name and click **Next**. Choose the kit type as **desktop** and click on **forward**. In the **Select Required Modules** page, make sure only **QtCore** is checked and continue clicking on **Next** (and eventually **Finish**) without changing any of the options until you end up in the code editor of the Qt Creator.

> We basically created a Qt Plugin project, and as you may have already noticed, the structure of the plugin project is quite similar to all application projects that we tried so far (except that it doesn't have a UI file), and that is because a plugin is really no different than an application, except that it can't run by itself.

Now, copy the `cvplugininterface.h` file that we created in the previous step to the folder of the newly created plugin project. Then, add it to the project by simply right-clicking on the project folder in the **Projects** pane and selecting **Add Existing Files** from the popup menu, as shown here:

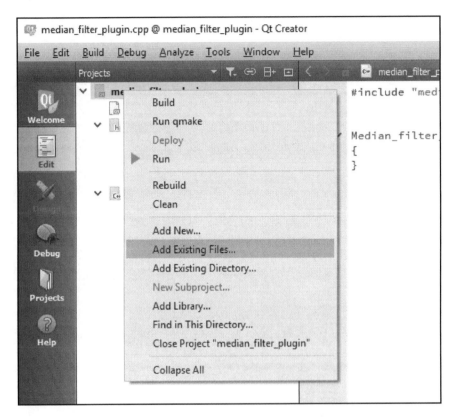

We need to tell Qt that this is a plugin and not just any library. To do that, we need to add the following to our `*.PRO` file. You can add it anywhere in the project, but it's good practice to add it to the `TEMPLATE = lib` line:

```
CONFIG += plugin
```

Now, we need to add OpenCV to our plugin project. By now, this should be a piece of cake to you. Simply add the following to your plugin's `*.PRO` file, as you did previously with the `Hello_Qt_OpenCV` project:

```
win32: {
    include("c:/dev/opencv/opencv.pri")
}
```

```
unix: !macx{
  CONFIG += link_pkgconfig
  PKGCONFIG += opencv
}
unix: macx{
 INCLUDEPATH += "/usr/local/include"
 LIBS += -L"/usr/local/lib" \
 -lopencv_world
}
```

It is a very good habit to run qmake manually when you add some code to your *.PRO file, or when you add a new class or Qt resource file using the **Qt Creator Main Menu** (and other user interface shortcuts), especially if you notice that Qt Creator is not synchronized with the content of your project. You can do this easily by selecting **Run qmake** from the right-click menu of the **Projects** pane, as shown in the following screenshot:

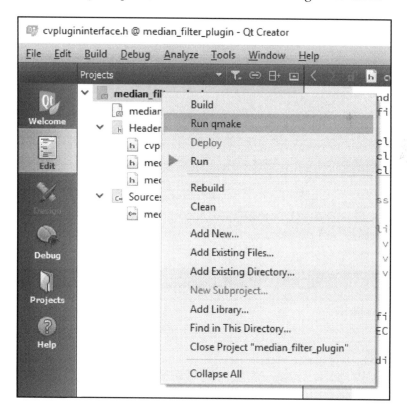

Alright, the scene is set and we can start writing the code for our first Qt+OpenCV plugin. As you'll see in the upcoming chapters, we'll add similar functionalities to our application using plugins; that way, we will only be concerned with developing plugins instead of modifying the whole application for every single feature that we add. So, it's very important to be familiar and comfortable with this step of the process.

Start by opening the `median_filter_plugin.h` file and modifying it as follows:

```
#ifndef MEDIAN_FILTER_PLUGIN_H
#define MEDIAN_FILTER_PLUGIN_H
#include "median_filter_plugin_global.h"
#include "cvplugininterface.h"
class MEDIAN_FILTER_PLUGINSHARED_EXPORT Median_filter_plugin:
  public QObject, public CvPluginInterface
{
  Q_OBJECT
  Q_PLUGIN_METADATA(IID "com.amin.cvplugininterface")
  Q_INTERFACES(CvPluginInterface)
  public:
  Median_filter_plugin();
  ~Median_filter_plugin();
  QString description();
  void processImage(const cv::Mat &inputImage,
      cv::Mat &outputImage);
};
#endif // MEDIAN_FILTER_PLUGIN_H
```

Most of the preceding code was automatically generated when you created the `median_filter_plugin` project. That is how a basic Qt library class definition looks. However, it is our additions that turn it into an interesting plugin. Let's review the preceding code to see what was really added to the class:

1. First, we included the `cvplugininterface.h` header file.
2. Then, we made sure the `Median_filter_plugin` class inherits `QObject` and `CvPluginInterface`.

3. After that, we added the macros required by Qt so that our library is recognized as a plugin. This simply means the following three lines of code that correspond to, first Q_OBJECT macro, which you learned about previously in this chapter, and should exist in any Qt class by default to allow Qt specific capabilities (such as signals and slots). Next one is Q_PLUGIN_METADATA, which needs to appear exactly once in the source codes of a plugin and is used to add meta-data about the plugin; and the last one, Q_INTERFACES, is needed to declare the interfaces implemented in the plugin. Here are the required macros:

```
Q_OBJECT
Q_PLUGIN_METADATA
Q_INTERFACES
```

4. Then, we added the definitions of description and processImage function to our class. This is where we will really define what the plugin does, as opposed to the interface class where we just had a declaration and not an implementation.

5. Finally, we can add the required changes and the actual implementation to the median_filter_plugin.cpp file. Make sure you add the following three functions to the bottom of the median_filter_plugin.cpp file:

```
Median_filter_plugin::~Median_filter_plugin()
{}

QString Median_filter_plugin::description()
{
    return "This plugin applies median blur filters to any image."
    " This plugin's goal is to make us more familiar with the"
    " concept of plugins in general.";
}
void Median_filter_plugin::processImage(const cv::Mat &inputImage,
    cv::Mat &outputImage)
{
    cv::medianBlur(inputImage, outputImage, 5);
}
```

We just added the implementation of the class destructor: the description and processImage functions. As you can see, the description function returns useful information about the plugin, in this case no complicated help page, but just a couple of sentences; and the processImage function simply applies medianBlur to the image, which you already (briefly) used in Chapter 2, *Creating Our First Qt and OpenCV Project*.

Now you can click on **Rebuild** after right-clicking on the project, or from the **Build** entry on the main menu. This will create a plugin file, which we'll use in the next section, usually under a folder in the same level with the project. This is the `Build` folder, which you got introduced to in `Chapter 2`, *Creating Our First Qt and OpenCV Project*.

 Extension of the plugin file can be different, depending on the operating system. For example, it should be `.dll` on Windows, `.dylib` or `.so` on macOS and Linux, and so on.

# The plugin loader and user

Now, we will use the plugin that we created in the previous section of the book. Let's start by creating a new Qt Widgets Application Project. Let's name it `Plugin_User`. When the project is created, add the OpenCV framework to the `*.PRO` file first (you have seen enough of this already) and then go on to create a user interface similar to this:

1. Obviously, you need to modify the `mainwindow.ui` file, design it to make it look like this, and set all object names as seen in the following screenshot:

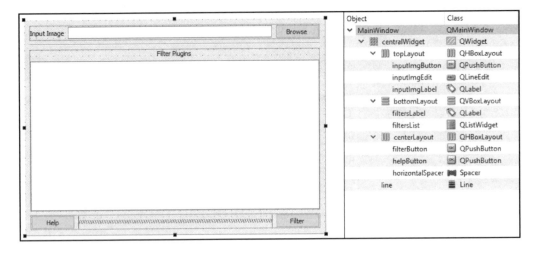

Make sure to use the same types of Layouts as seen in the preceding picture.

2. Next, add the `cvplugininterface.h` file to this project's folder, and then, using the **Add Existing Files** option, add it to the project as you did when you were creating the plugin.

3. Now, we can start writing the code for our user interface along with the code required to load, check, and use plugins. First thing's first, add the required headers to the `mainwindow.h` file as follows:

```
#include <QDir>
#include <QFileDialog>
#include <QMessageBox>
#include <QPluginLoader>
#include <QFileInfoList>
#include "opencv2/opencv.hpp"
#include "cvplugininterface.h"
```

4. Then, add a single function to the private members of the `MainWindow` class, right before `};`, which seems like a good place:

```
void getPluginsList();
```

5. Now, switch to `mainwindow.cpp` and add the following definition to the top of the file, right after any existing `#include` lines:

```
#define FILTERS_SUBFOLDER "/filter_plugins/"
```

6. Then, add the following function to `mainwindow.cpp`, which is basically the implementation of the `getPluginsList` function:

```
void MainWindow::getPluginsList()
{
  QDir filtersDir(qApp->applicationDirPath() +
    FILTERS_SUBFOLDER);
  QFileInfoList filters = filtersDir.entryInfoList(
  QDir::NoDotAndDotDot |
  QDir::Files, QDir::Name);
  foreach(QFileInfo filter, filters)
  {
    if(QLibrary::isLibrary(filter.absoluteFilePath()))
    {
    QPluginLoader pluginLoader(
        filter.absoluteFilePath(),
        this);
    if(dynamic_cast<CvPluginInterface*>(
        pluginLoader.instance()))
      {
        ui->filtersList->addItem(
            filter.fileName());
        pluginLoader
            .unload(); // we can unload for now
```

```
        }
        else
        {
            QMessageBox::warning(
                this, tr("Warning"),
                QString(tr("Make sure %1 is a correct"
                " plugin for this application<br>"
                "and it's not in use by some other"
                " application!"))
                .arg(filter.fileName()));
        }
    }
    else
    {
      QMessageBox::warning(this, tr("Warning"),
            QString(tr("Make sure only plugins"
                " exist in plugins folder.<br>"
                "%1 is not a plugin."))
                .arg(filter.fileName()));
    }
    }

    if(ui->filtersList->count() <= 0)
    {
      QMessageBox::critical(this, tr("No Plugins"),
      tr("This application cannot work without plugins!"
      "<br>Make sure that filter_plugins folder exists "
      "in the same folder as the application<br>and that "
      "there are some filter plugins inside it"));
      this->setEnabled(false);
    }
}
```

Let's first see what this function does. The preceding function, which we will call in the constructor of the MainWindow class:

- First of all, assumes that there are plugins existing in a subfolder called filter_plugins, and this subfolder is in the same folder with the application executable. (Later on, we'll need to manually create this folder inside the build folder of this project and then copy the plugin we built in the previous step into this newly created folder.) Following is used to get a direct path to the filters plugin subfolder:

```
    qApp->applicationDirPath() + FILTERS_SUBFOLDER
```

- Next, it uses the `entryInfoList` function of the `QDir` class to extract `QFileInfoList` from the folder. The `QFileInfoList` class itself is basically a `QList` class that contains `QFileInfo` items (`QList<QFileInfo>`), and each `QFileInfo` item provides information about a file on the disk. In this case, each file will be a plugin.
- After that, by iterating over the list of files in a `foreach` loop, it checks each file in the plugins folder to make sure only plugin (library) files are accepted, use the following function:

```
QLibrary::isLibrary
```

- Each library file that passes the previous step then is checked to make sure that it is compatible with our plugin interface. We will not just let any library file be accepted as a plugin, so we use the following code for this purpose.

```
dynamic_cast<CvPluginInterface*>(pluginLoader.instance())
```

- If a library passes the test in the previous step, then it is considered to be a correct plugin (compatible with `CvPluginInterface`), added to the list widget in our window, and then unloaded. We can simply reload and use it whenever we need.
- At each step, if there is a problem, `QMessageBox` is used to show useful information to the user. Also, in the end if the list is empty, meaning there are no plugins to be used, the widgets on the window are disabled and the application is not usable.

7. Don't forget to call this function from the `MainWindow` constructor, right after the `setupUi` call.

8. We also need to write the code for `inputImgButton`, which is used to open an image file. Here it is:

```
void MainWindow::on_inputImgButton_pressed()
{
  QString fileName =
    QFileDialog::getOpenFileName(
    this,
    tr("Open Input Image"),
    QDir::currentPath(),
    tr("Images") + " (*.jpg *.png *.bmp)");
    if(QFile::exists(fileName))
    {
    ui->inputImgEdit->setText(fileName);
    }
}
```

We have seen this code before and it needs no explanations. It simply allows you to open an image file and make sure it is correctly selected.

9. Now, we will write the code for `helpButton`, which will display the result of description function in the plugin:

```
void MainWindow::on_helpButton_pressed()
{
  if(ui->filtersList->currentRow() >= 0)
  {
   QPluginLoader pluginLoader(
     qApp->applicationDirPath() +
     FILTERS_SUBFOLDER +
     ui->filtersList->currentItem()->text());
     CvPluginInterface *plugin =
       dynamic_cast<CvPluginInterface*>(
     pluginLoader.instance());
     if(plugin)
     {
       QMessageBox::information(this, tr("Plugin Description"),
         plugin->description());
     }
     else
     {
      QMessageBox::warning(this, tr("Warning"),
      QString(tr("Make sure plugin %1" " exists and is usable."))
      .arg(ui->filtersList->currentItem()->text()));
     }
   }
   else
   {
     QMessageBox::warning(this, tr("Warning"), QString(tr("First
       select a filter" " plugin from the list."))); 
   }
 }
```

We use the `QPluginLoader` class to correctly load a plugin from the list, then get an instance of it using the instance function, and finally, we will call the function in the plugin via the interface.

10. The same logic also applies to `filterButton`. The only difference is that this time, we will call the actual filtering function, which is shown here:

```
void MainWindow::on_filterButton_pressed()
{
   if(ui->filtersList->currentRow() >= 0 &&
```

```
      !ui->inputImgEdit->text().isEmpty())
  {
    QPluginLoader pluginLoader(qApp->applicationDirPath() +
      FILTERS_SUBFOLDER +
      ui->filtersList->currentItem()->text());
    CvPluginInterface *plugin =
      dynamic_cast<CvPluginInterface*>(
        pluginLoader.instance());
      if(plugin)
      {
        if(QFile::exists(ui->inputImgEdit->text()))
        {
        using namespace cv;
        Mat inputImage, outputImage;
        inputImage = imread(ui->inputImgEdit->
        text().toStdString());
        plugin->processImage(inputImage, outputImage);
        imshow(tr("Filtered Image").toStdString(),
            outputImage);
        }
        else
        {
          QMessageBox::warning(this,
            tr("Warning"),
            QString(tr("Make sure %1 exists."))
            .arg(ui->inputImgEdit->text()));
        }
      }
      else
      {
       QMessageBox::warning(this, tr("Warning"),
       QString(tr(
       "Make sure plugin %1 exists and is usable." ))
       .arg(ui->filtersList->currentItem()->text()));
      }
    }
    else
    {
     QMessageBox::warning(this, tr("Warning"),
     QString(tr( "First select a filter plugin from the list." )));
  }
}
```

It is important to always keep the user informed about what's going on and the issues that might happen using QMessageBox or other types of information providing capabilities. As you see, they usually even take much more code than the actual task that is being done, but this is crucial in order to avoid crashes in your application. By default, Qt does not support exception handling and trusts that the developer will take care of all possible crash scenarios using enough dosage of the if and else instructions. Another important note about the preceding code examples is the tr function. Remember to always use it for literal strings. This way, you can easily make your application multi-language later on. Even if you are not aiming at having multiple languages supported, it is good practice to get used to adding the tr function in literal strings; it won't do any harm.

Now, we are ready to run our Plugin_User application. If we run it now, we will see an error message (which we put there ourselves), and we will be warned that there are no plugins in place. To be able to use our Plugin_User application, we need to do the following:

1. Create a folder called filter_plugins inside the build folder of the Plugin_User project. This is the folder where the executable of the project is created.

2. Copy the plugin file that we built (which would be the library file inside the build folder of the median_filter_plugin project) and paste it into the filter_plugins folder in the first step. As described earlier, a plugin file like an executable program will have an extension depending on the operating system.

Now, try running Plugin_User and everything should be fine. You should be able to see the single plugin in the list, select it, click on the help button to get information about it and click on the **filter** button to apply the filter in the plugin on an image. As seen in the following screenshot:

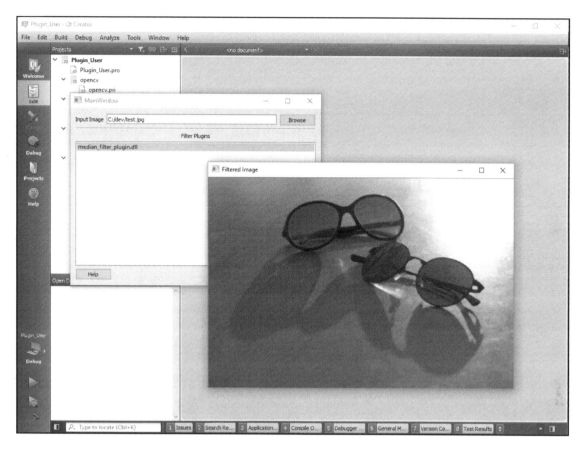

Try creating another plugin called `gaussian_filter_plugin` and follow the exact same set of instructions for `median_filter_plugin`, only this time, use the `gaussianBlur` function that you saw in `Chapter 2`, *Creating Our First Qt and OpenCV Project*. And then build it and put it in the `filter_plugins` folder and run the `Plugin_User` application again. Also, try putting some random library files (and other non-library files) to test the application we wrote in those scenarios.

One very important thing to note here is that you must make sure not to use plugins that are built in Debug mode with an application that is built in Release mode and vice versa. There are other important rules that apply to loading plugins such as a plugin that is built with a higher version of Qt can't be used with an application that is built with a lower version of Qt. A plugin that is built with a lower major version number of Qt can't be used with an application that is built with a higher major version number of Qt. Always refer to the *Deploying Plugins* article in the Qt documentation or Qt Creator Help mode for updated information about plugins and their usage.

# Creating the foundations

Everything you learned in this chapter was meant to make you ready to start building a comprehensive computer vision application that will do the following:

- Use plugins to extend its capabilities
- Use Qt style sheets to customize its look and feel
- Support multiple languages

So, starting from now we will create the foundations of our application by taking into consideration all the facts that you learned in this chapter and the previous chapters, such as the following:

- Our application will be able to save and load all user preferences and settings. We will make it happen by using the QSettings class, which you already learned how to use.
- It's best to have a centralized and single Qt style sheet that takes care of our application's overall look and feel, and better yet, loaded from the disk instead of embedding it into the application itself.

To achieve this, we will simply assume that our application has a native look unless the user manually selects a theme from the settings page of our application. Themes will be Qt Style Sheets saved in a folder called themes in the same folder where our application executable resides and the extension of the Style Sheet files will be thm. Selected theme (or Style Sheet, to be precise) will be loaded from the disk at runtime.

- Supporting multiple languages is crucial. We will create an application that allows extending the supported languages without the need to rebuild the application.

> This can be done by having Qt binary language files put inside a folder called `languages` in the same folder where our application executable resides. We can use the system default language and load the language of the user (if we have its translations and binary language files); otherwise, we can load a default language, say English. We can also allow the user to change the language of the application at runtime by selecting it from the settings page.

- We will build a computer vision application that supports processing single images and video frames.

> To be able to achieve this, we need to have a plugin interface quite similar to what we saw in this chapter (`CvPluginInterface`) that takes an image as the input and produces an output. Then, we will need to load and use those plugins almost in the exact manner that we saw in this chapter. We will assume that the plugins are located in a folder called `cvplugins`, which will exist in the same folder where our application executable resides.

Apart from this, we need to take into consideration some of the upcoming obstacles of our computer vision application. It is important to always look far up ahead when building an application; otherwise, you'll just land in an awkward situation with no way out. So, here they are:

- In our application, we will constantly deal with images and videos. Not just from files, but also input from a camera or a feed channel from a network (the internet, for instance). We will cover all of that in Chapter 4, *Mat and QImage*.
- An application involving computer vision is nothing without the proper tools to view and play around with the images. This and all related topics will be covered in Chapter 5, *The Graphics View Framework*.

- Later on, in Chapter 9, *Video Analysis,* our computer vision application will need to work with and process videos, meaning not only single images, but a consecutive set of images (or frames) will affect the result of the process. This obviously cannot be achieved with the plugin interface that we saw in this chapter, and we will need to create plugins that work in separate threads. We will leave this subject for Chapter 8, *Multithreading,* where you will learn about parallel processing mechanisms in Qt. After that, we will be able to create a new plugin interface suitable for video processing and then use it in our application.

You can now start by creating a Qt Widgets Application using Qt Creator and name it Computer_Vision. We will expand this application until the end of Chapter 9, *Video Analysis,* and we'll cover every new concept along the way. From what you learned in this and the previous chapters, you should be able to create the first three items in the list of foundations above (support for themes, languages, and plugins) by yourself, and it's strongly recommended that you at least try to do so; however, we will expand this base application during the course of the next two chapters. Later on, by the end of Chapter 5, *The Graphics View Framework,* you will be provided with a link to download the complete base project of Computer_Vision. This base project will include a MainWindow class capable of loading and displaying plugins that include a GUI within them. In this project, you will also find a plugin interface (similar to what you saw in this chapter), but with a few more functions that will allow the following:

- Getting the title of the plugin
- Getting the description (help) information of the plugin
- Getting the GUI (a Qt container widget) unique to the plugin
- Getting the type of the plugin, whether it processes and returns any image or simply displays information in its GUI
- Passing images to the plugin and getting the result

This base project source code will contain functions similar to what you saw in this chapter to set styles, change languages, and so on.

# Summary

Throughout your career as a developer or your studies and research, you will come across the word, *sustainable* a lot. This chapter's goal was to introduce you to the basic concepts of creating a sustainable application in general, and a computer vision application using Qt and OpenCV in particular. You are now familiar with creating plugins, which consequently means you can create an application that can be extended by reusable libraries created by third-party developers (or yourself, of course) and without the need to rebuild the core application. In this chapter, you also learned about customizing the look and feel of a Qt application and creating multi-language Qt applications.

It was a long, but hopefully rewarding chapter. If you have followed through every example and step-by-step instruction, then by now you should be familiar with some of the most crucial techniques of cross-platform application development using the Qt framework. In this chapter, you learned about styling and style sheets in Qt and some of the important capabilities it offers to develop good-looking applications. Then, we moved on to learn about creating multi-language applications. In a global community, and in a time where our applications are reachable to every corner of the world (thanks to online application stores and so on), building applications to support multiple languages is a must-do, and not simply a preference in most cases. After learning about multi-language application development, we moved on to the subject of plugins and learned all of its basics with a hands-on example and experience. The project we created, as simple as it may look, contains all important aspects of building plugins, and applications that use them.

In Chapter 4, *Mat and Qimage*, you will learn about OpenCV Mat and the Qt QImage class (along with the relevant classes), which are the main classes used in both frameworks to deal with image data. You will learn about all different methods to read (from file, camera, and so on) and write images, convert them to each other, and finally display them in a Qt application. Up until now, we used the imshow function in OpenCV to simply display the result images in a default window. That's going to become history in Chapter 4, *Mat and Qimage*, as you'll learn how to convert OpenCV Mat to a QImage class and then display it properly on a Qt widget.

# 4
# Mat and QImage

In `Chapter 3`, *Creating a Comprehensive Qt+OpenCV Project*, we learned about the basic rules of creating a comprehensive and sustainable application that can look appealing, support multiple languages, and be easily extendable by using the plugins system in Qt. We're now going to expand our knowledge base regarding the foundations of a computer vision application even more by learning about the classes and structures responsible for handling computer vision data types. Learning about the basic structures and data types required by both the OpenCV and Qt frameworks is the first step in understanding how the underlying computer vision functions that process them perform when executed in an application. OpenCV is a computer vision framework that aims for speed and performance. Qt on the other hand, is a growing application development framework with a massive number of classes and capabilities. That's why they both need a well-defined set of classes and structures to take care of image data that is going to be processed, displayed, and maybe even saved or printed in computer vision applications. It's always a good practice to keep ourselves familiar with a useful dosage of details about the existing structures in both Qt and OpenCV.

You have already used OpenCV's `Mat` class to briefly read and process images. As you'll learn in this chapter, even though `Mat` is the main class responsible for handling image data in OpenCV (at least traditionally that was the case), there are a few variations of the `Mat` class that will be quite useful, and some of them are even required for specific functions that you will learn about in the upcoming chapters. In case of the Qt framework, it's not too different, even though `QImage` is the main class in Qt intended for handling image data, there are a few more classes, sometimes with strikingly similar names, that are used in order to support computer vision and work with image data, videos, and so on.

In this chapter, we are going to start with the most crucial OpenCV class, named Mat, then move on to different variations (some of them subclasses of Mat), and finally introduce you to the new UMat class, which is an OpenCV 3 addition to the framework. We'll learn about the advantages of using the new UMat class (which is, in fact, Mat-compatible) instead of the Mat class. We will then move on to Qt's QImage class and learn how to pass image data between OpenCV and Qt by converting these two data types to each other. We'll also learn about QPixmap, QPainter, and a number of other Qt classes, all of which are must-know classes for anyone who is going to take on the field of computer vision.

Finally, we will learn about the numerous ways in which both OpenCV and Qt frameworks read, write, and display images and video from files, cameras, network feed sources, and so on. As you'll learn by the end of this chapter, it's always best to decide which class suits us the most depending on the required computer vision task, so we should know enough about the different options at hand when dealing with image data input or output.

The topics we will cover in this chapter include:

- An introduction to the Mat class, its subclasses, and the new UMat class
- An introduction to QImage and the main Qt classes used in computer vision
- How to read, write, and display images and video
- How to pass image data between the Qt and OpenCV frameworks
- How to create a custom widget in Qt and paint it using QPainter

# All about the Mat class

In the previous chapters, you experienced using the Mat class of the OpenCV framework very briefly, but we're going to dig a little bit deeper now. The Mat class, which borrows its name from the matrix, is an *n*-dimensional array capable of storing and handling different mathematical data types in single or multiple channels. To simplify this further, let's take a look at what an image is in terms of computer vision. An image in computer vision is a matrix (therefore a two-dimensional array) of pixels, with a specified width (number of columns in the matrix) and height (number of rows in the matrix). Furthermore, a pixel in a grayscale image can be represented with a single number (therefore a single channel), with a minimum value (usually 0) representing the black and a maximum value (usually 255, which is the highest number possible with one byte) representing the white, and all values in between corresponding to different gray intensities accordingly. Look at the following example images, which are simply zoomed-in parts of a bigger grayscale image. Each pixel is labeled with the intensity value we just mentioned:

| 63 | 53 | 35 | 48 | 107 | 210 | 183 | 179 |
|----|----|----|----|-----|-----|-----|-----|
| 67 | 63 | 46 | 28 | 54 | 127 | 199 | 182 |
| 63 | 69 | 60 | 45 | 41 | 66 | 162 | 187 |
| 71 | 75 | 74 | 59 | 39 | 50 | 96 | 186 |
| 68 | 68 | 73 | 65 | 42 | 41 | 64 | 166 |
| 66 | 61 | 64 | 63 | 52 | 41 | 47 | 116 |
| 66 | 62 | 59 | 58 | 57 | 40 | 42 | 82 |
| 61 | 61 | 59 | 56 | 56 | 44 | 44 | 59 |

| 31 | 34 | 33 | 33 | 34 | 33 | 40 | 43 |
|----|----|----|----|-----|-----|-----|-----|
| 38 | 37 | 34 | 28 | 26 | 28 | 26 | 27 |
| 26 | 29 | 26 | 20 | 26 | 29 | 30 | 31 |
| 28 | 23 | 25 | 43 | 105 | 147 | 148 | 123 |
| 23 | 31 | 67 | 126 | 183 | 180 | 190 | 198 |
| 50 | 134 | 168 | 174 | 176 | 173 | 192 | 202 |
| 115 | 166 | 177 | 180 | 185 | 188 | 185 | 179 |
| 179 | 174 | 170 | 175 | 170 | 174 | 182 | 190 |

Quite similarly, a pixel in a standard RGB color image has three different elements instead of one (therefore it has three channels), corresponding to red, blue, and green color values. Take a look at the following image for example:

As seen in the preceding image, a magnified (zoomed) image in a simple image viewer program can reveal the pixels responsible for an image. Consider each one a single element in the Mat class that can be directly accessed, modified, and worked with. This matrix-like representation of an image is what allows some of the most powerful computer vision algorithms to easily process images, measure required values, or even produce new images.

Here's another representation of the area zoomed in on in the previous example picture. Each pixel is labeled with the underlying red, green, and blue color values:

Considering the image data and pixels case helps with understanding the Mat class, and as we'll see later on, most of the functionalities in the Mat class, and OpenCV in general, assume that Mat is an image, however it is important to note that Mat can contain any data (not just images), and in fact there are cases in OpenCV where Mat is used to pass arrays of data other than images. We'll learn about some related examples in Chapter 6, *Image Processing in OpenCV*.

Since covering the mathematical details of the Mat class and OpenCV functions, in general, is not in our topmost interest at the moment, we're going to suffice with the given introduction and move on to focus more on the usage of the Mat class and its underlying methods in OpenCV.

# Constructors, properties, and methods

Constructing a `Mat` class can be done in numerous ways. At the time of writing this book, the `Mat` class has over twenty different constructors. Some of them are just convenient constructor functions, but some others are required in order to create three and more dimensional arrays for instance. Here are some of the most widely used constructors and examples of how to use them:

Create a 10x10 matrix, with each element a single channel 8-bit unsigned integer (or byte):

```
Mat matrix(10, 10, CV_8UC(1));
```

Create the same matrix and initialize all of its elements with the value of 0:

```
Mat matrix(10, 10, CV_8UC(1), Scalar(0);
```

The first parameter in the constructors shown in the preceding code is the number of rows, and the second parameter is the number of columns in the matrix. The third parameter though, which is a very important one, mixes the type, bit count, and the number of channels into a single macro. Here is the pattern of the macro and values that can be used:

```
CV_<bits><type>C(<channels>)
```

Let's see what each and every part of the macro is used for:

`<bits>` can be replaced by:

- **8**: It is used for unsigned and signed integer numbers
- **16**: It is used for unsigned and signed integer numbers
- **32**: It is used for unsigned and signed integer and floating-point numbers
- **64**: It is used for unsigned and signed floating-point numbers

`<type>` can be replaced by:

- **U**: It is used for unsigned integer
- **S**: It is used for signed integer
- **F**: It is used for signed floating-point number

Theoretically speaking, `<channels>` can be replaced by any value, but for general computer vision functions and algorithms, it won't be higher than four.

You can omit the opening and closing parentheses for the `<channels>` parameter if you use a channel count no greater than four. You can also omit `<channels>` and the preceding `C` altogether if the number of channels is just one. For better readability and consistency, it's better to use the standard pattern used in the preceding and following examples, and it's also a good programming practice to be consistent in the way you use such a widely used macro.

Create a cube (three-dimensional array) with the side length of 10 and with two channel elements of type double (64-bit), and initialize all values with the value of `1.0`. This is shown as follows:

```
int sizes[] = {10, 10, 10};
Mat cube(3,  sizes, CV_64FC(2), Scalar::all(1.0));
```

You can also use the `create` method of the `Mat` class to change the size and type of it later on. Here's an example:

```
Mat matrix;
// ...
matrix.create(10, 10, CV_8UC(1));
```

The previous contents of the `Mat` class don't matter. Basically, they all will be removed (safely cleaned up, and the allocated memory is given back to the operating system), and a new `Mat` class will be created.

You can create a `Mat` class that is part of another `Mat` class. This is called **region of interest** (**ROI**), and is especially useful when we need to access part of an image as if it was an independent image. For example, when we want to filter just part of an image. Here's how you create an ROI `Mat` class containing a 50x50 pixel wide square starting in the position 25,25 (X,Y) in an image:

```
Mat roi(image, Rect(25,25,50,50));
```

When specifying the size of `Mat` in `OpenCV`, it is usually in terms of rows and columns (cols), (height and width), which sometimes confuses people who are accustomed to seeing width first, since that's the case with many other frameworks. The reason is simply the matrix approach to images in `OpenCV`. If you feel more comfortable with the latter, you can simply use the `Size` class in OpenCV when creating `Mat` classes.

In the examples for this section, unless explicitly stated otherwise, assume that the image variable of type Mat is acquired using our test image from the previous chapters by using the imread function. This will help us with getting the information needed for the Mat class, however, we will see more about imread and similar functions later on in this chapter.

Let's take a look at the following image to better understand the concept of ROI, sizes, and positions in the Mat class of OpenCV. As seen in the following image, the top-left corner of the image is considered to be the origin of the coordinate system in an image. So, the position of the origin is (0,0). Similarly, the top-right corner of the image has the location value of (width is 1,0), in which width can be replaced by the number of columns. Considering this, the right-bottom corner of the image will have the location value of (width-1, height-1), and so on. Now, let's consider that we want to create a Mat class based on the region shown as follows. We can use the method we saw previously, but we need to provide the top-left corner of the ROI plus its width and height, using a Rect class:

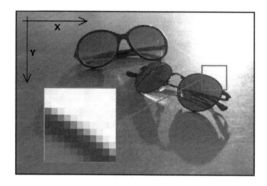

It's important to note that when creating an ROI Mat class using the previous method, all changes to the ROI pixels will affect the original image, since creating an ROI does not perform a deep copy of the contents of the original Mat class. If for any reason you want to copy a Mat class into a new (and completely independent) Mat, then you need to use the clone function, as seen in this example:

```
Mat imageCopy = image.clone();
```

Assuming that the Mat image contains the previous image (from the previous chapters), you can use the following example code to select the ROI seen in the image and make all pixels in the highlighted region have a black color:

```
4: Mat roi(image, Rect(500, 138, 65, 65));
roi = Scalar(0);
```

You can also select one or more rows, or columns in a `Mat`, in a way quite similar to the way we did with ROI, except we need to use the `row`, `rowRange`, `column`, or `colRange` functions in a `Mat` class. Here's how:

```
Mat  r = image.row(0); // first row
Mat  c = image.row(0); // first column
```

Here's another example of using the `rowRange` and `colRange` functions that can be used to select a range of rows and columns instead of only a single row. The following example code will result in a + sign with a thickness of 20 pixels, in the center of the image:

```
Mat centralRows = image.rowRange(image.rows/2 - 10,
    image.rows/2 + 10);
Mat centralColumns = image.colRange(image.cols/2 - 10,
    image.cols/2 + 10);
centralRows = Scalar(0);
centralColumns = Scalar(0);
```

And here's the result, executed on our test image:

When you extract an ROI using the methods mentioned previously, and store it in a new `Mat` class, you can use the `locateROI` function to get the size of the parent image and the top-left position of the ROI inside the parent image. Here's an example:

```
Mat centralRows = image.rowRange(image.rows/2 - 10,
    image.rows/2 + 10);
Size parentSize;
```

```
Point offset;
centralRows.locateROI(parentSize, offset);
int parentWidth = parentSize.width;
int parentHeight = parentSize.height;
int x = offset.x;
int y = offset.y;
```

After executing this code, `parentWidth` will contain the width of the image, `parentHeight` will contain the height of the image, and `x` and `y` will contain the top-left position of the `centralRows` in the parent `Mat`, or in other words, the image.

The `Mat` class also contains a number of informative properties and functions that can be used in order to get information about any individual `Mat` class instance. By informative, we mean members that provide detailed information about each and every pixel, channels, color depth, width, and height and many more members like that. Those members include:

- `depth`: This contains the depth of the `Mat` class. A depth value corresponds to the type and bit count of the `Mat` class; thus, it can be one of the following values:
    - `CV_8U`: 8-bit unsigned integers
    - `CV_8S`: 8-bit signed integers
    - `CV_16U`: 16-bit unsigned integers
    - `CV_16S`: 16-bit signed integers
    - `CV_32S`: 32-bit signed integers
    - `CV_32F`: 32-bit floating-point numbers
    - `CV_64F`: 64-bit floating-point numbers
- `channels`: This simply contains the number of channels in every element of the `Mat` class. For a standard image, this value is usually three channels.
- `type`: This will contain the type of the `Mat` class. This is the same type constant we used to create a `Mat` class earlier in this chapter.
- `cols`: This corresponds to the number of columns in the `Mat` class or image width in other words.
- `rows`: This corresponds to the number of rows in the `Mat` class or image height in other words.
- `elemSize`: This can be used to get the size of each element (in bytes) in the `Mat` class.

- `elemSize1`: This can be used to get the size of each element (in bytes) in the `Mat` class, regardless of the channel count. For example, in a three-channel image, `elemSize1` will contain the value of `elemSize` divided by three.

- `empty`: This returns true if there are no elements in the `Mat` class, otherwise it returns false.

- `isContinuous`: This can be used to check if the elements of a `Mat` are stored in a continuous fashion. For example, a `Mat` class that has only one single row is always continuous.

 A `Mat` class created using the create function is always continuous. It's important to note that the two-dimensional representation of the `Mat` class is handled using the step value in this case. This means in a continuous array of elements, every step number of elements corresponds to a single row in a two-dimensional representation.

- `isSubmatrix`: This returns `true` if the `Mat` class is a submatrix of another `Mat` class. In our previous examples, in all of the cases where we created an ROI using another image, this property will return `true` and it will be `false` in the parent `Mat` classes.

- `total`: This returns the total number of elements in a `Mat` class. For example, in an image, this value is the same as width multiplied by the height of the image.

- `step`: This returns the number of elements that correspond to one step in the `Mat` class. For example, in a standard image (a non-continuously stored one), `step` contains the width (or `cols`) of the `Mat` class.

Apart from the informative members, the `Mat` class contains a number of functions used to access (and perform actions on) its individual elements (or pixels). They include:

- `at`: This is a template function that can be used to access an element in the `Mat` class. It's especially useful to access elements (pixels) in an image. Here's an example. Let's assume we have a standard three-channel color image loaded in a `Mat` class called `image`. This means the `image` is of type `CV_8UC(3)`, then we can simply write the following to access the pixel at position `X`, `Y`, and set its color value to `C`:

```
image.at<Vec3b>(X,Y) = C;
```

OpenCV provides the Vec (vector) class and its variants for easier data access and processing. You can create and name your own Vec types using the following typedef:

```
typedef Vec<Type, C> NewType;
```

For example, in the previous code you could have defined your own 3-byte vector (such as QCvVec3B) and used it instead of Vec3b, with the following code:

```
typedef Vec<quint8,3> QCvVec3B;
```

Nevertheless, you can use the following already-present Vec types in OpenCV when you use the at function:

```
typedef Vec<uchar,  2> Vec2b;
typedef Vec<uchar,  3> Vec3b;
typedef Vec<uchar,  4> Vec4b;
typedef Vec<short,  2> Vec2s;
typedef Vec<short,  3> Vec3s;
typedef Vec<short,  4> Vec4s;
typedef Vec<ushort, 2> Vec2w;
typedef Vec<ushort, 3> Vec3w;
typedef Vec<ushort, 4> Vec4w;
typedef Vec<int,    2> Vec2i;
typedef Vec<int,    3> Vec3i;
typedef Vec<int,    4> Vec4i;
typedef Vec<int,    6> Vec6i;
typedef Vec<int,    8> Vec8i;
typedef Vec<float,  2> Vec2f;
typedef Vec<float,  3> Vec3f;
typedef Vec<float,  4> Vec4f;
typedef Vec<float,  6> Vec6f;
typedef Vec<double, 2> Vec2d;
typedef Vec<double, 3> Vec3d;
typedef Vec<double, 4> Vec4d;
typedef Vec<double, 6> Vec6d;
```

- `begin` and `end`: These can be used to retrieve and access elements in a `Mat` class using C++ STL-like iterators.
- `forEach`: This can be used to run a function in parallel on all elements of the `Mat` class. This function needs to be provided with a function object, function pointer, or a lambda.

 Lambdas are only available on C++11 and later, and they are a big reason to switch to C++11 and later if you haven't done so already.

The following three example codes achieve the same goal using the access methods mentioned in the preceding codes, they all make the image darker by dividing every pixel value by 5. First, using the `at` function:

```
for(int i=0; i<image.rows; i++)
{
  for(int j=0; j<image.cols; j++)
  {
    image.at<Vec3b>(i, j) /= 5;
  }
}
```

Next, using STL-like iterators with `begin` and `end` functions:

```
MatIterator_<Vec3b> it_begin = image.begin<Vec3b>();
MatIterator_<Vec3b> it_end = image.end<Vec3b>();
for( ; it_begin != it_end; it_begin++)
{
  *it_begin /= 5;
}
```

And finally, using the `forEach` function, provided with a lambda:

```
image.forEach<Vec3b>([](Vec3b &p, const int *)
{
  p /= 5;
});
```

Here is the resulting darker image that would be the same for all of the three preceding codes:

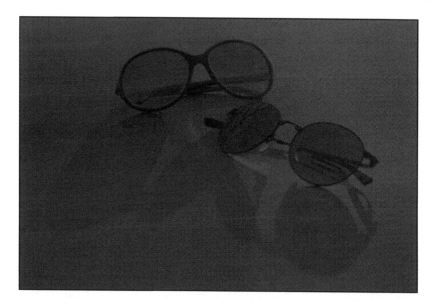

As you have already noticed, Mat is a class with many methods, and quite obviously, since it's the basic building block when working with OpenCV and images. Apart from the functions and properties, you saw previously, there are a few more functions that we need to learn about before moving on to the next section. Here they are:

- adjustROI: This function can be used to easily change the size of a submatrix (or ROI matrix to be precise).
- clone: This is a widely used function to create deep copies of a Mat class. An example case is that you might want to filter or process an image and still have a copy of the original for comparison later on.
- convertTo: This can be used to change the data type of the Mat class. This function can also scale the image optionally.
- copyTo: This function can be used to copy all (or part of an image) to another Mat.
- ptr: This can be used to get a pointer and access image data in a Mat. Depending on the overloaded version, you can get a pointer to a specific row or any other position in an image.
- release: This function is called in the Mat destructor and it basically takes care of the memory cleanup tasks required by a Mat class.
- reserve: This can be used to reserve memory space for a number of specified rows.

- `reserveBuffer`: This is similar to `reserve`, but it reserves memory space for a number of specified bytes.
- `reshape`: This can be useful when we need to change the number of channels to get a different representation of matrix data. An example case would be to convert `Mat` that has a single channel and three bytes in each one of its elements (such as `Vec3b`) to a three-channel `Mat` that has 1 byte in each one of its elements. Obviously, such a conversion (or reshape to be precise) would lead to a row count multiplied by three in the destination `Mat`. A transpose of the resulting matrix can be used to switch between rows and columns after that. You'll learn about the `t`, or transpose function, later on.
- `resize`: This can be used to change the number of rows in a `Mat` class.
- `setTo`: This can be used to set all or some of the elements in the matrix to a specified value.

Last but not least, the `Mat` class provides some convenience methods to work with matrix operations, such as:

- `cross`: To compute a cross-product of two three-element matrices.
- `diag`: To extract a diagonal from the matrix.
- `dot`: To compute a dot-product of two matrices.
- `eye`: This is a static function that can be used to create an identity matrix.
- `inv`: To create an inverse matrix.
- `mul`: To compute an element-wise multiplication or division of two matrices.
- `ones`: This is another static function that can be used to create a matrix in which all of its elements hold the value `1`.
- `t`: This is the function that can be used to get the transposed matrix of a `Mat` class. It is interesting to note that this same function is the equivalent of a mirror and 90 degrees rotate of an image. See the proceeding image for more information on this.
- `zeroes`: This can be used to create a matrix with all of its elements holding the value of zero. This is equal to a completely black image of the given width, height, and type.

In the following screenshot, the image on the left is the original image and the one on the right is the resulting transposed image. Since transpose of a transposed matrix is the same as the original matrix, we can also say that the image on the left is the transposed result of the one on the right. This is an example result of performing the `t` function of the `Mat` class on an image:

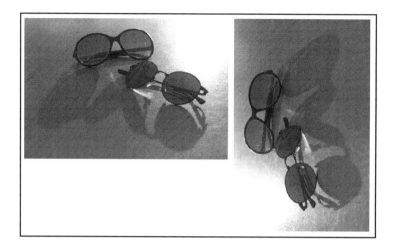

It's also important to note that all standard arithmetic operations are also possible with the Mat class. For example, instead of dividing all of the pixels one by one as we did in a previous example to discuss access methods in a Mat class, we could have simply written the following:

```
Mat darkerImage = image / 5; // or image * 0.2
```

In this case, every element in the matrix (or image if you will) will undergo the exact same operation.

# The Mat_<_Tp> class

The Mat_<_Tp> class is a subclass of the Mat class (and a template class) with identical members, but it can be quite helpful when the type of the matrix (or elements in an image) is known at <indexentry content="Mat class:Mat_ class" dbid="256603" state="mod"> compile time. It also provides a better access method (more readable, so to speak) than the at function of the Mat class. Here's a short example:

```
Mat_<Vec3b> imageCopy(image); // image is a Mat class
imageCopy(10, 10) = Vec3b(0,0,0); // imageCopy can use ()
```

Provided that you are careful about the types, you can pass a Mat_<_Tp> class to any function that accepts a Mat class, without any issues.

# Matx< _Tp, m, n >

The Matx class is only used in case of <indexentry content="Mat class:Matx class" dbid="256603" state="mod"> small matrices which have a known type, width, and height at compile time. It has methods similar to Mat and provides matrix operations, again like Mat. In general, you can use the same Mat class that you just learned about instead of Matx, since it provides more flexibility and functions to work with.

# The UMat class

The UMat class is a newly introduced Mat-like class and is not available on OpenCV versions prior to version 3.0. The advantage of using the new UMat class (or Unified Mat class) depends mostly on the presence of an OpenCL layer on the platform it is running on. We're not going to go through the gory details of that, but it should be enough to note that OpenCL (with an L, not to be confused with our own OpenCV) is a framework that allows the use of CPUs, GPUs, and other computing resources on a system to work together (sometimes even in parallel) to achieve a common computing goal. So, simply put, if it exists on a platform, then passing the UMat class to an OpenCV function will cause the underlying OpenCL instructions to be called (given that they are implemented in the specific function), thus achieving a higher performance with computer vision applications. Otherwise, UMat is simply converted to a Mat class and the standard CPU-only implementations are invoked. This allows for a unified abstraction (that's where the U is coming from) and makes it easier to use faster OpenCL implementations, unlike the previous versions of OpenCV where all OpenCL implementations were in the ocl namespace and completely separate from the standard implementations.

So, it's always best to use the UMat class instead of Mat especially in CPU-intensive functions with an underlying OpenCL implementation. As long as we are not going to use older OpenCV versions, there will be no problems. Just note that in cases when an explicit conversion between a Mat and UMat is required (and as you'll see later on, there are cases where it's required), each class provides a function that can be used to convert it to the other:

```
Mat::getUMat
UMat::getMat
```

For both of these functions an access flag is required, which can be:

- ACCESS_READ
- ACCESS_WRITE

- `ACCESS_RW`
- `ACCESS_FAST`

Throughout the course of the book, we'll try to use the `Mat` and `UMat` classes interchangeably wherever possible. `UMat` and the `OpenCL` implementations is a growing OpenCV phenomenon, and there's a huge advantage in getting used to using it.

# InputArray, OutputArry, InputOutputArray

You'll notice that most OpenCV functions accept these types of parameters instead of `Mat` and its similar data types. These are proxy data types used for better readability and data type support. That simply means you can pass any of the following data types to OpenCV functions that except InputArray, OutputArray or InutOutputArray data types:

- `Mat`
- `Mat_<T>`
- `Matx<T, m, n>`
- `std::vector<T>`
- `std::vector<std::vector<T> >`
- `std::vector<Mat>`
- `std::vector<Mat_<T> >`
- `UMat`
- `std::vector<UMat>`
- `double`

Notice that OpenCV treats standard C++ vectors (`std::vector`) just like a `Mat` or a similar class. The more or less obvious reason is that their underlying data structure is more or less the same.

You should never explicitly create an `InputArray`, `OutputArry`, or `InputOutputArray`. Simply pass one of the types mentioned previously and everything will be fine.

# Reading images using OpenCV

Now that we have learned all about the `Mat` class in OpenCV, we can move on to learn how to read images and fill a `Mat` class with an image to further process it. As you have seen briefly in the previous chapters, the `imread` function can be used to read images from the disk. Here's an example:

```
Mat image = imread("c:/dev/test.jpg", IMREAD_GRAYSCALE |
    IMREAD_IGNORE_ORIENTATION);
```

`imread` simply takes a C++ `std::string` class as the first parameter and an `ImreadModes` flag as the second parameter. If for any reason the image cannot be read, then it returns an empty `Mat` class (`data == NULL`), otherwise, it returns a `Mat` class filled with the image pixels with the type and color specified in the second parameter. Depending on the availability of some image types in the platform, `imread` can read the following image types:

- Windows bitmaps: \*.bmp, \*.dib
- JPEG files: \*.jpeg, \*.jpg, \*.jpe
- JPEG 2000 files: \*.jp2
- Portable Network Graphics: \*.png
- WebP: \*.webp
- Portable image format: \*.pbm, \*.pgm, \*.ppm, \*.pxm, \*.pnm
- Sun rasters: \*.sr, \*.ras
- TIFF files: \*.tiff, \*.tif
- OpenEXR Image files: \*.exr
- Radiance HDR: \*.hdr, \*.pic
- Raster and Vector geospatial data supported by Gdal

You can see, `ImreadModes` enum for possible flags that can be passed to the `imread` function. In our example, we used the following:

```
IMREAD_GRAYSCALE | IMREAD_IGNORE_ORIENTATION
```

This means we want the image to be loaded as grayscale and we also want to ignore the orientation information stored in the EXIF data part of the image file.

OpenCV also supports reading multi-page image files. You need to use the `imreadmulti` function for this reason. Here's a simple example:

```
std::vector<Mat> multiplePages;
```

```
bool success = imreadmulti("c:/dev/multi-page.tif", multiplePages,
    IMREAD_COLOR);
```

Apart from `imread` and `imreadmulti`, OpenCV also supports reading images from a memory buffer using the `imdecode` function. This is especially useful in case the image is not stored on disk or needs to be read in a data stream from a network. The usage is almost identical to the `imread` function except that you need to provide it with the data buffer instead of the filename.

# Writing images using OpenCV

The `imwrite` function in OpenCV can be used to write images into files on disk. It uses the extension of the filename to decide the format of the image. To customize the compression rate and similar settings in an `imwrite` function, you need to use `ImwriteFlags`, `ImwritePNGFlags`, and so on. Here's a simple example demonstrating how to write an image into a JPG file with a progressive mode set on and a relatively low quality (higher compression rate):

```
std::vector<int> params;
params.push_back(IMWRITE_JPEG_QUALITY);
params.push_back(20);
params.push_back(IMWRITE_JPEG_PROGRESSIVE);
params.push_back(1); // 1 = true, 0 = false
imwrite("c:/dev/output.jpg", image, params);
```

You can omit the `params` altogether if you want to use the default settings and simply write:

```
imwrite("c:/dev/output.jpg", image, params);
```

See the `imread` function in the previous section for the same list of supported file types in the `imwrite` function.

Apart from `imwrite`, OpenCV also supports writing images into a memory buffer using the `imencode` function. Similar to `imdecode`, this is especially useful in case the image needs to be passed on to a data stream instead of being saved into a file. The usage is almost identical to the `imwrite` function, except that you need to provide it with the data buffer instead of the filename. In this case, since there is no filename specified, `imdecode` also needs the extension of the image to decide the output format.

# Reading and writing videos in OpenCV

OpenCV provides a single and extremely easy-to-use class called `VideoCapture` for reading videos (or image sequences) from files saved on disk, or from capture devices, cameras, or a network video stream (for instance an RTSP address on the internet). You can simply use the `open` function to try opening a video from any of the mentioned source types and then use the `read` function to grab incoming video frames into images. Here's an example:

```
VideoCapture video;
video.open("c:/dev/test.avi");
if(video.isOpened())
{
  Mat frame;
  while(true)
  {
    if(video.read(frame))
    {
        // Process the frame ...
    }
    else
    {
        break;
    }
  }
}
video.release();
```

If you want to load an image sequence, you simply need to replace the filename with the file path pattern. For instance, `image_%02d.png` will read images with filenames like `image_00.png`, `image_01.png`, `image_02.png`, and so on.

In case of video streams from a network URL, simply provide the URL as the filename.

Another important thing to note about our example is that it is not a complete and ready-to-use example. As you'll notice if you give it a try, whenever your program enters the `while` loop it will keep the GUI from being updated and your application might even crash. When working with Qt, a quick fix for this is to make sure GUI (and other) threads are also processed by adding the following code inside the loop:

```
qApp->processEvents();
```

We'll learn about more correct workarounds for this issue later on in `Chapter 8`, *Multithreading* and `Chapter 9`, *Video Analysis*.

Apart from what we learned, the `VideoCapture` class provides two important functions, namely `set` and `get`. These can be used to configure numerous parameters of the class. For a complete list of configurable parameters, you can refer to the `VideoCaptureProperties` enum.

Here's a tip that never gets old. You can also use Qt Creator code completion and simply write `CAP_PROP_` since all relevant parameters start with that. This same trick is basically applicable to find out about any function, enum, and so on. Using such tricks in different IDEs are usually not covered in books, but can mean saving a whole lot of time in some cases. Take what was just said in the previous point, for example, you can write `VideoCaptureProperties` in the Qt Creator code editor, then hold on the *Ctrl* button and simply click on it. This will take you to the source of the enum and you can review all possible enums, and if you're lucky, documentation inside the source code is waiting for you.

Here's a simple example that reads the number of frames in the video:

```
double frameCount = video.get(CAP_PROP_FRAME_COUNT);
```

Here's another example that sets the current position of the frame grabber in the video to frame number `100`:

```
video.set(CAP_PROP_POS_FRAMES, 100);
```

Almost identical to the `VideoCapture` class in terms of using it, you can use the `VideoWriter` class to write videos and image sequences to disk. However, when writing videos with the `VideoWriter` class you need a few more parameters. Here's an example:

```
VideoWriter video;
video.open("c:/dev/output.avi", CAP_ANY, CV_FOURCC('M','P', 'G',
    '4'), 30.0, Size(640, 480), true);
if(video.isOpened())
{
  while(framesRemain())
  {
    video.write(getFrame());
  }
}
video.release();
```

In this example, the `framesRemain` and `getFrame` functions are imaginary functions that check if there are remaining functions to be written, and also get the frame (`Mat`). As seen in the example, a capture API needs to be provided in this case (we omitted it in `VideoCapture` since it's optional). Also, a `FourCC` code, **FPS (frames per second)**, and frame size are mandatory when opening a video file for writing. `FourCC` codes can be entered using the `CV_FOURCC` macro defined in `OpenCV`.

Refer to `http://www.fourcc.org/codecs.php` for a list of possible `FourCC` codes. It's important to note that some `FourCC` codes and their corresponding video formats might not be available on a platform. This is important when deploying your application to your customers. You need to make sure your application can read and write the video formats it needs to support.

# The HighGUI module in OpenCV

The HighGUI module in OpenCV is responsible for making quick and simple GUIs. We already used one of the widely used functions within this module, `imshow`, to quickly display images in Chapter 3, *Creating a Comprehensive Qt+OpenCV Project*, of this book. But, as we are going to learn about Qt and a more sophisticated framework for dealing with GUI creation, we are going to skip this module completely and move on to Qt subjects. However, just before that, it's worth quoting the current introduction of the HighGUI module in the OpenCV documentation:

> *"While OpenCV was designed for use in full-scale applications and can be used within functionally rich UI frameworks (such as Qt\\*, WinForms\\*, or Cocoa\\*) or without any UI at all, sometimes there it is required to try functionality quickly and visualize the results. This is what the HighGUI module has been designed for."*

As you'll learn later on in this chapter, we'll also stop using the `imshow` function and stick to Qt capabilities for a proper and consistent image display.

# Image and video handling in Qt

Qt uses several different classes to work with image data, videos, cameras, and related computer vision subjects. In this section, we are going to learn about them and also learn how to link between OpenCV and Qt classes, for a more flexible computer vision application development experience.

# The QImage class

Perhaps the most important computer vision-related class in Qt, `QImage` is the main Qt class for handling image data and it provides pixel-level access to images, along with many other functions for working with image data. We are going to cover the most important subset of its constructors and functionalities, especially the ones important when working with `OpenCV`.

`QImage` contains many different constructors which allow the creation of a `QImage` from files or raw image data, or an empty image to work with and manipulate its pixels. We can create an empty `QImage` class with a given size and format, as seen in the following example:

```
QImage image(320, 240, QImage::Format_RGB888);
```

This creates a standard RGB color image that is 320x240 pixels (width and height). You can refer to the `QImage::Format` enum (using QImage class documentation) for a complete list of supported formats. We can also pass a `QSize` class instead of the values and write the following:

```
QImage image(QSize(320, 240), QImage::Format_RGB888);
```

The next constructor is also one of the methods for creating a `QImage` from an OpenCV `Mat` class. The important thing to note here is that the format of the data in the OpenCV `Mat` class should be compatible with that of the `QImage` class. By default, OpenCV loads color images in the BGR format (not RGB), so if we try to construct a `QImage` using that, we'll have wrong channel data in place. So, we first need to convert it to RGB. Here's an example:

```
Mat mat = imread("c:/dev/test.jpg");
cvtColor(mat, mat, CV_BGR2RGB);
QImage image(mat.data,
             mat.cols,
             mat.rows,
             QImage::Format_RGB888);
```

The `cvtColor` function in this example is an OpenCV function that can be used to change the color space of a `Mat` class. If we omit that line, we'll get a `QImage` that has its blue and red channels swapped.

A correct version of the previous code (and the recommended way of converting a `Mat` to a `QImage`) can be created with the next `QImage` constructor that we're going to see. It also requires a `bytesPerLine` parameter, which is the `step` parameter we learned about in the `Mat` class. Here's an example:

```
Mat mat = imread("c:/dev/test.jpg");
cvtColor(mat, mat, CV_BGR2RGB);
QImage image(mat.data,
             mat.cols,
             mat.rows,
             mat.step,
             QImage::Format_RGB888);
```

The advantage of using this constructor and the `bytesPerLine` parameter is that we can also convert image data which is continuously stored in memory.

The next constructor is also a method of reading `QImage` from files saved on disk. Here's an example:

```
QImage image("c:/dev/test.jpg");
```

Note that the files types supported by Qt and OpenCV are independent of each other. This simply means that a file type might simply not be supported in one of the mentioned frameworks, and in that case, you need to choose the other framework when reading that specific file type. By default, Qt supports reading the following image file types:

| Format | Description | Support |
|--------|-------------|---------|
| BMP | Windows Bitmap | Read/write |
| GIF | Graphic Interchange Format (optional) | Read |
| JPG | Joint Photographic Experts Group | Read/write |
| JPEG | Joint Photographic Experts Group | Read/write |
| PNG | Portable Network Graphics | Read/write |
| PBM | Portable Bitmap | Read |
| PGM | Portable Graymap | Read |
| PPM | Portable Pixmap | Read/write |
| XBM | X11 Bitmap | Read/write |
| XPM | X11 Pixmap | Read/write |

Table source for reference: QImage class documentation at `http://doc.qt.io/qt-5/qimage.html`.

Apart from all of the constructors, a `QImage` includes the following members, which are extremely handy when working with images:

- `allGray`: This can be used to check if all pixels in the image are shades of gray. This basically checks if all pixels have the same RGB values in their respective channels.
- `bits` and `constBits` (which is simply the `const` version of `bits`): These can be used to access the underlying image data in a `QImage`. This can be used to convert a `QImage` to a `Mat` for further processing in `OpenCV`. The same as what we saw when converting a `Mat` to a `QImage`, here too we need to make sure they are compatible with the format. To be sure of that, we can add a `convertToFormat` function that makes sure our `QImage` is a standard three-channel RGB image. Here's an example:

  ```
  QImage image("c:/dev/test.jpg");
  image = image.convertToFormat(QImage::Format_RGB888);
  Mat mat = Mat(image.height(),
                image.width(),
                CV_8UC(3),
                image.bits(),
                image.bytesPerLine());
  ```

   It's extremely important to note that when passing data like this, and like what we saw when converting a `Mat` to a `QImage`, the same space in memory is passed between classes in Qt and OpenCV. This means that if you modify the `Mat` class in the previous example, you'll be in fact modifying the image class, since you just passed its data pointer to the `Mat` class. This can be both extremely useful (easier manipulation of images) and dangerous (application crashes) at the same time, and you need to be careful when working with Qt and OpenCV like this. If you want to make sure your `QImage` and `Mat` class have completely separate data, you can use the `clone` function in the `Mat` class or the `copy` function in `QImage`.

- `byteCount`: This returns the number of bytes occupied by the image data.
- `bytesPerLine`: This is similar to the `step` parameter in the `Mat` class. It provides bytes per each scanline in an image. This is basically the same as `width`, or better yet, `byteCount/height`.

- `convertToFormat`: This can be used to convert the image to another format. We already saw an example of this in the previous example for the `bits` function.
- `copy`: This can be used to copy part (or all) of the image to another `QImage` class.
- `depth`: This returns the depth (or bits per pixel) of the image.
- `fill`: This function can be used to fill all of the pixels in an image with the same color.

 Functions like these, and many other similar functions in the Qt framework, work with three color types, `QColor`, `Qt::GlobalColor`, and finally an integer value corresponding to the bits in a pixel. Even though they are very easy to use, it would be wise to spend a few minutes reading their documentation page in Qt Creator `Help` mode, before continuing.

- `format`: This can be used to get the current format of the image data in `QImage`. As we saw in previous examples, `QImage::Format_RGB888` is the format that is most compatible when passing image data between Qt and `OpenCV`.
- `hasAlphaChannel`: This returns true if the image has an Alpha channel. The Alpha channel is used for determining the transparency level of a pixel.
- `height`, `width`, and `size`: These can be used to get the height, width, and size of the image.
- `isNull`: This returns `true` if there is no image data, otherwise it returns `false`.
- `load`, `loadFromData`, and `fromData`: These can be used to retrieve an image from the disk or from data stored in a buffer (similar to `imdecode` in `OpenCV`).
- `mirrored`: This is actually an image processing function that can be used to mirror (flip) an image vertically, horizontally or both.
- `pixel`: Similar to the `at` function in the `Mat` class, `pixel` can be used to retrieve the pixel data.
- `pixelColor`: This is similar to `pixel`, but this one returns a `QColor`.
- `rect`: This returns a `QRect` class that contains the bounding rectangle of the image.
- `rgbSwapped`: This is an extremely handy function, especially when working with OpenCV and displaying images. It swaps the blue and red channels without changing the actual image data. As we'll see later on in this chapter, this is required for correctly displaying `Mat` classes in Qt and avoiding an OpenCV `cvtColor` function call.
- `save`: These can be used to save the contents of the image to a file.

- `scaled`, `scaledToHeight`, and `scaledToWidth`: All of the three mentioned functions can be used to resize an image to fit a given size. Optionally, you can use one of the following constants when calling this function to take care of any aspect ratio issues. We'll see more about this in the upcoming chapters.
    - `Qt::IgnoreAspectRatio`
    - `Qt::KeepAspectRatio`
    - `Qt::KeepAspectRatioByExpanding`
- `setPixel` and `setPixelColor`: These can be used to set the contents of an individual pixel in the image.
- `setText`: This can be used to set a text value in the image formats that support it.
- `text`: This can be used to retrieve the text value set to an image.
- `transformed`: This function, as its name suggests, is used for transforming an image. It takes a `QMatrix` or `QTransform` class and returns the transformed image. Here's a simple example:

```
QImage image("c:/dev/test.jpg");
QTransform trans;
trans.rotate(45);
image = image.transformed(trans);
```

- `trueMatrix`: This can be used to retrieve the transformation matrix used for transforming the image.
- `valid`: This takes a point (X, Y) and returns true if the given point is a valid position inside the image, otherwise it returns false.

# The QPixmap class

The `QPixmap` class is in some ways similar to `QImage`, but `QPixmap` is intended to be used when we need to display images on the screen. `QPixmap` can be used to load and save an image (just like `QImage`) but it doesn't provide the flexibility to manipulate image data, and we'll also use it only when we need to display any images after we're done with all our modifications, processing, and manipulation. Most `QPixmap` methods have the same name as `QImage` methods and they are basically used in an identical manner. Two functions that are important for us and don't exist in `QImage` are as follows:

- `convertFromImage`: This function can be used to fill the `QPixmap` data with image data from a `QImage`

- `fromImage`: This is a static function that basically does the same thing as `convertFromImage`

We are now going to create an example project to practice with what we've learned so far. Without a real hands-on project, all the exciting techniques learned in this chapter would go to waste, so let's start with our image viewing example application:

1. Start by creating a new **Qt Widgets Application** in Qt Creator and name it `ImageViewer`.

2. Then choose `mainwindow.ui` and, using the **Designer**, remove the menu bar, status bar, and toolbar, and drop a single label widget (`QLabel`) on the window. Click on an empty space on the window and press *Ctrl + G* to lay out everything (your only widget which is a label) as a grid. This will make sure everything is always resized to fit the window.

3. Now change the `alignment/Horizontal` property of the `label` to `AlignHCenter`. Then change both of its `Horizontal` and `VerticalsizePolicy` properties to `Ignored`. Next, add the following `include` statements to your `mainwindow.h` file:

    ```
    #include <QPixmap>
    #include <QDragEnterEvent>
    #include <QDropEvent>
    #include <QMimeData>
    #include <QFileInfo>
    #include <QMessageBox>
    #include <QResizeEvent>
    ```

4. Now, add the following protected functions to the `MainWindow` class definition in `mainwindow.h` using the code editor:

    ```
    protected:
    void dragEnterEvent(QDragEnterEvent *event);
    void dropEvent(QDropEvent *event);
    void resizeEvent(QResizeEvent *event);
    ```

5. Also, add a private `QPixmap` to your `mainwindow.h`:

    ```
    QPixmap pixmap;
    ```

6. Now, switch to `mainwindow.cpp` and add the following into the `MainWindow` constructor function so that it's called right at the beginning of the program:

    ```
    setAcceptDrops(true);
    ```

7. Next, add the following function in the `mainwindow.cpp` file:

```cpp
void MainWindow::dragEnterEvent(QDragEnterEvent *event)
{
  QStringList acceptedFileTypes;
  acceptedFileTypes.append("jpg");
  acceptedFileTypes.append("png");
  acceptedFileTypes.append("bmp");

  if (event->mimeData()->hasUrls() &&
    event->mimeData()->urls().count() == 1)
  {
    QFileInfo file(event->mimeData()->urls().at(0).toLocalFile());
    if(acceptedFileTypes.contains(file.suffix().toLower()))
    {
      event->acceptProposedAction();
    }
  }
}
```

8. Another function that should be added to `mainwindow.cpp` is the following:

```cpp
void MainWindow::dropEvent(QDropEvent *event)
{
  QFileInfo file(event->mimeData()->urls().at(0).toLocalFile());
  if(pixmap.load(file.absoluteFilePath()))
  {
   ui->label->setPixmap(pixmap.scaled(ui->label->size(),
       Qt::KeepAspectRatio,
       Qt::SmoothTransformation));
  }
  else
  {
    QMessageBox::critical(this,
        tr("Error"),
        tr("The image file cannot be read!"));
  }
}
```

9. Finally, add the following function to `mainwindow.cpp`, and we're ready to execute our application:

```cpp
void MainWindow::resizeEvent(QResizeEvent *event)
{
  Q_UNUSED(event);
  if(!pixmap.isNull())
  {
```

```
ui->label->setPixmap(pixmap.scaled(ui->label->width()-5,
                                    ui->label->height()-5,
                                    Qt::KeepAspectRatio,
                                    Qt::SmoothTransformation));
        }
    }
```

You've guessed it right, we just wrote an application that displays images that are dragged and dropped inside it. By adding a `dragEnterEvent` function to `MainWindow` we were able to check if the dragged object is a file, and especially if it's a single file. Then we checked for the image type to make sure it's supported.

In the `dropEvent` function, we simply loaded the `QPixmap` with the image file that is dragged and dropped into the window of our application. Then we set the `pixmap` property of the `QLabel` class to our `pixmap`.

Finally, in the `resizeEvent` function we made sure that no matter the size of the window, our image is always scaled to fit the window with a correct aspect ratio.

 Forget one simple step in what was described and you'll face issues with the drag and drop programming techniques in Qt. For example, without the following line, that was in the constructor of our `MainWindow` class, no drops will be accepted, no matter what functions are added to the `MainWindow` class:

```
setAcceptDrops(true);
```

Here's a screenshot of the resulting application. Try dragging and dropping different images into the application window to see what happens. You can even try dragging and dropping non-image files to make sure they're not accepted:

This was basically a tutorial on how to display an image in Qt and also how to add drag and drop functionality into a Qt application. As we saw in the preceding example, `QPixmap` can be easily displayed in conjunction with a `QLabel` widget. A `QLabel` widget name can be misleading sometimes, but in fact, it can be used to display not only plain text, but also rich text, pixmaps, and even movies (using the `QMovie` class). Since we already know how to convert a `Mat` to a `QImage` (and vice versa), and also how to convert a `QImage` to a `QPixmap`, we can write something like the following to load an image using `OpenCV`, process it using some computer vision algorithms (we'll learn more about this in `Chapter 6`, *Image Processing in OpenCV* and later), then convert it to a `QImage` and consequently to a `QPixmap`, and finally display the result on a `QLabel` as seen in this example code:

```
cv::Mat mat = cv::imread("c:/dev/test.jpg");
QImage image(mat.data,
             mat.cols,
             mat.rows,
             mat.step,
             QImage::Format_RGB888);
ui->label->setPixmap(QPixmap::fromImage(image.rgbSwapped()));
```

# The QImageReader and QImageWriter classes

The `QImageReader` and `QImageWriter` classes can be used to have more control over the image read and write process. They support the same file types as `QImage` and `QPixmap`, but offer a lot more flexibility, provide error messages when something is wrong with the image reading or writing process, and you can also set and get a lot more image properties if you use the `QImageReader` and `QImageWriter` classes. As you'll see later in the upcoming chapters, we'll use these same classes in our comprehensive computer vision application to have better control over the reading and writing of images. For now, we'll suffice with this short introduction and move on to the next section.

# The QPainter class

The QPainter class can be used to draw (and basically paint) on any Qt class that is a subclass of the QPaintDevice class. What does that mean? It means basically anything including Qt widgets, that have a visual side and something can be drawn on them. So to name a few, QPainter can be used to draw on a QWidget class (which means basically all existing and custom made Qt widgets), QImage, QPixmap, and many other Qt classes. You can see the QPaintDevice class documentation page in Qt Creator **Help** mode for a full list of Qt classes that inherit QPaintDevice. QPainter has numerous functions, a lot of which have names starting with draw, and covering all of them would need a whole chapter by itself, but we are going to see a basic example of how it's used with QWidget and then with QImage. Basically, the same logic applies to all classes that can be used with QPainter.

So, as it was said, you can create a custom Qt widget by yourself and use QPainter to create (or paint) its visual side. This is, in fact, one of the methods (and a popular one) for creating a new Qt widget. Let's do this with an example to help it sink in. We are going to create a new Qt widget that simply shows a blinking circle:

1. Start by creating a Qt Widgets Application called Painter_Test.
2. Then select **File / New File or Project** from the main menu.
3. In **the New File or Project** window, select **C++** and **C++ Class** then press **Choose**.
4. In the window that appears, make sure **Class name** is set to QBlinkingWidget and **Base class** is selected as **QWidget**. Make sure the **Include QWidget** checkbox is checked and leave the rest of the options as seen in the following screenshot:

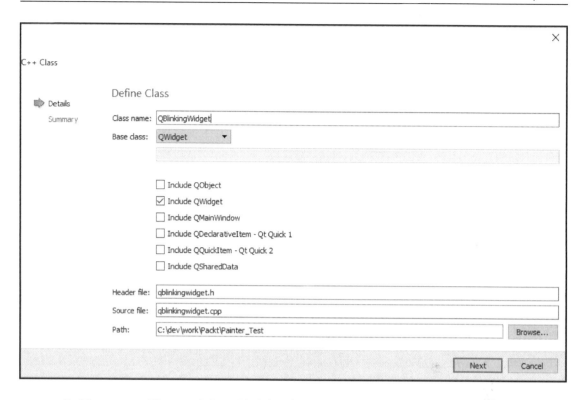

5. Now press **Next** and then **Finish**. This will create and add a new class with a header and a source file to your project.

6. Now you need to override the `paintEvent` method of the `QBlinkingWidget` and do some drawing with `QPainter`. So, start by adding the following `include` statements to the `qblinkingwidget.h` file:

```
#include <QPaintEvent>
#include <QPainter>
#include <QTimer>
```

7. Now, add the following protected member to the `QBlinkingWidget` class (add it after the existing public members for instance):

```
protected:
  void paintEvent(QPaintEvent *event);
```

8. You also need to add a private slot to this class. So, add the following after the previous protected `paintEvent` function:

```
private slots:
  void onBlink();
```

9. There's one last thing to add to the `qblinkingwidget.h` file, add the following private members we are going to use in our widget:

```
private:
  QTimer blinkTimer;
  bool blink;
```

10. Now, switch to `qblinkingwidget.cpp` and add the following code inside the constructor function that is automatically created:

```
blink  = false;
connect(&blinkTimer,
  SIGNAL(timeout()),
  this,
  SLOT(onBlink()));
blinkTimer.start(500);
```

11. Next, add the following two methods to `qblinkingwidget.cpp`:

```
void QBlinkingWidget::paintEvent(QPaintEvent *event)
{
  Q_UNUSED(event);
  QPainter painter(this);
  if(blink)
      painter.fillRect(this->rect(),
          QBrush(Qt::red));
  else
      painter.fillRect(this->rect(),
          QBrush(Qt::white));
}

void QBlinkingWidget::onBlink()
{
  blink = !blink;
  this->update();
}
```

12. Now, switch to the **Design** mode by opening `mainwindow.ui`, and then add a widget to your `MainWindow` class. By `Widget`, we mean exactly `Widget`, which is an empty one, as you'll notice when you add it to your `MainWindow`. See the following screenshot:

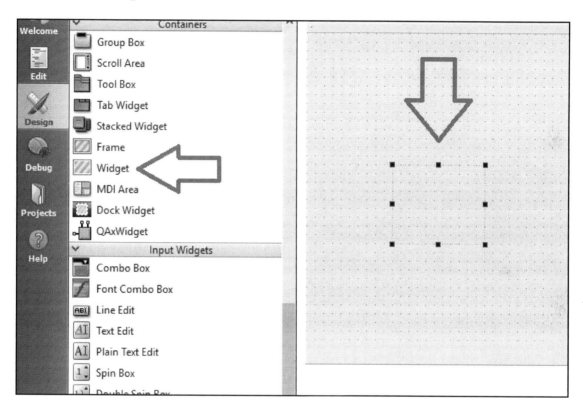

13. Now, right click on the added empty widget, which is a `QWidget` class, and choose **Promote to** from the pop-up menu:

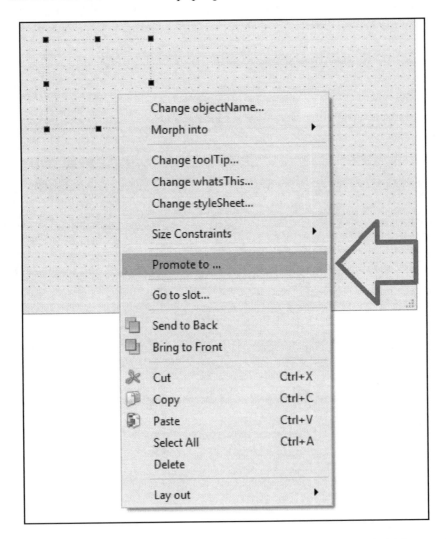

14. In the new window that will be opened, called the **Promoted Widgets** window, set **Promoted class name** to `QBlinkingWidget` and press the **Add** button:

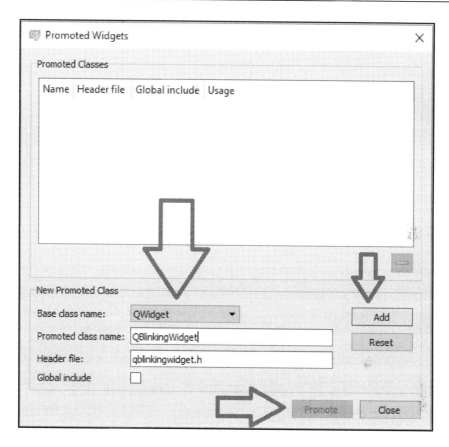

15. Finally, press **Promote**. Your application and custom widget are ready to run. As soon as your application starts you will see it blinking every 500 milliseconds (half a second).

This is, in fact, the general method of creating custom widgets in Qt. To create a new custom Qt widget and use it in your Qt Widgets Application, you need to:

1. Create a new class that inherits `QWidget`.
2. Override its `paintEvent` function.
3. Draw on it using a `QPainter` class.
4. Add a `QWidget` (widget) to your window.
5. Promote it to your newly created widget.

Promoting a `QWidget` to a custom-made widget is in fact also the method used when you get a widget made by a third-party developer (or from the internet perhaps) and want to use it in your application window.

In the preceding example, we used the `fillRect` function of `QPainter` to simply fill it with red and white colors every second, depending on the blink variable status. Similarly, you can use `drawArc`, `drawEllipse`, `drawImage`, and many more functions in `QPainter` to draw almost anything on a widget. The important thing to note here is that we passed `this` to the `QPainter` instance when we wanted to draw on the widget. In case we want to draw on a `QImage`, we just need to make sure we construct the `QPainter` by passing the `QImage` to it or using the `begin` function. Here's an example:

```
QImage image(320, 240, QImage::Format_RGB888);
QPainter painter;
painter.begin(&image);
painter.fillRect(image.rect(), Qt::white);
painter.drawLine(0, 0, this->width()-1, this->height()-1);
painter.end();
```

All drawing functions, in this case, need to be enclosed in a `begin` and `end` function call.

# Camera and video handling in Qt

Since we are going to use OpenCV interfaces for handling images, cameras, and videos, we are not going to cover all of the possibilities that the Qt framework provides in order to read, view and process videos. But sometimes, especially when one of the two frameworks provides a better or simpler implementation of a feature, it really becomes too tempting to avoid it. For example, even though OpenCV provides very powerful methods for working with cameras, as we'll see in Chapter 12, *Qt Quick Applications*, Qt still has a lot to say when it comes to handling cameras on Android, iOS, and mobile platforms in general. So, let's see a brief introduction to some of the important and existing Qt classes for the camera and video handling, and leave them until we use them in Chapter 12, *Qt Quick Applications*.

Search the Qt Creator **Help** index for Qt Multimedia C++ classes to get a complete and updated list of available classes under the Qt Multimedia module, along with documentation and examples.

Here they are:

- QCamera: This provides access to cameras available on a platform.
- QCameraInfo: This can be used to get information about the available cameras on a platform.
- QMediaPlayer: This can be used to play video files and other types of recorded media.
- QMediaRecorder: This class is useful when recording videos or other media types.
- QVideoFrame: This class can be used to access individual frames grabbed by the camera.
- QVideoProbe: This can be used to monitor frames from a camera or video source. This class can also be used to process frames further in Qt.
- QVideoWidget: This can be used to display incoming frames from a camera or video source.

Note that all of the classes mentioned exist in the multimedia module of Qt, so to be able to use them, you need to first make sure the multimedia module is exposed to your project by adding the following line to your Qt Project PRO file:

```
QT += multimedia
```

Apart from the classes mentioned previously, the Qt multimedia module offers numerous other classes for working with video data. You can always check out each class's documentation page in Qt Creator **Help** mode by searching for it in the help index. Usually, a new Qt version introduces new classes or updates to the existing classes, so, to be a real Qt developer means keeping an eye on the documentation pages and updates, and maybe even reporting bugs or issues when you find any, since Qt is still an open source framework that relies on support from its community of open source users.

# Summary

This chapter was an important milestone since it introduced the concepts required for linking OpenCV and Qt frameworks together. In this chapter, we learned all about the Mat class and its variants. We learned about the new Transparent API in OpenCV and how using the UMat class can improve the performance of our computer vision applications. We also learned about reading and writing images and videos, and also capturing video frames from cameras and network-based video feeds. Later, we moved on to learning about the Qt capabilities and classes that are related to computer vision and working with images. The QImage class in Qt, which is the equivalent of the Mat class in OpenCV, was introduced in this chapter. We also learned about the QPixmap and QPainter classes, and several other Qt classes. While doing just that, we also learned how to create a custom Qt widget and use the QPainter class to draw on a QImage class. Finally, we ended the chapter with an introduction to Qt classes related to video and camera handling.

In Chapter 5, *The Graphics View Framework*, we will complete the puzzle of computer vision in Qt and OpenCV, by introducing a very powerful class called QGraphicsScene, and the Graphics View Framework, that can be used to view and manipulate image data in an extremely flexible way. Chapter 5, *The Graphics View Framework* will be the last chapter before a complete dive into the world of computer vision and image processing, since our comprehensive computer vision application will be completed with one of its most important features, that is its image viewer and manipulator, and we'll continue with learning new computer vision tricks, each time adding a new plugin to it, as we learned in the previous chapters.

# 5
# The Graphics View Framework

Now that we are familiar with the basic building blocks of computer vision applications in both Qt and OpenCV frameworks, we can move on to learn more about the development of the visualization part in computer vision applications. Talk about computer vision and every user immediately looks for some preview image or video. Take any image editor that you want, for example, they all contain an area on their user interface that is immediately noticeable and can be easily recognized from the rest of the components on the GUI, by some border or even simple lines. The same can be said about the video editing software and literally anything that needs to work with visual concepts and media input sources. Also, the exact same reasoning is true for computer vision applications that we will create. Of course, there are cases where the result of the process is simply displayed as numerical values or sent over the network to some other party involved with the process. However, fortunately for us, we will see both of the cases, so we need something similar to have in our applications so that the users can preview the files that they have opened or view the resulting transformed (or filtered or so on) images on the screen. Or even better, see the result of some object detection algorithm in a real-time video output preview panel. This panel is basically a Scene, or even better, it's a Graphics Scene and it's the subject that is going to be covered in this chapter of the book.

Beneath the many modules, classes and sub-frameworks within the Qt framework, there's a jewel dedicated to easier graphics handling, called the **Graphics View Framework**. It contains numerous classes, almost all of them with names starting with QGraphics, and all of which can be used to handle most of the graphical tasks one can encounter when building a computer vision application. The Graphics View Framework simply divides all possible objects into three major categories, and with that comes the architecture that allows easily adding, removing, modifying, and of course, displaying the graphical objects.

- The Scene (QGraphicsScene class)
- The View (QGraphicsView widget)
- Graphical Items (QGraphicsItem and its subclasses)

In the previous chapters, we used the simplest means of visualizing images using both OpenCV (imshow function) and Qt label widgets, which provide almost no flexibility at all in terms of handling the displayed images, such as selecting them, modifying them, scaling them, and so on. Even for the simplest task such as selecting a graphical item and dragging it to some other position, we have to write tons of code and go through confusing mouse event handling. The same goes for zooming in and out of images. However, by using the classes in the Graphics View Framework, all this can be handled with much more ease, and with much more performance, since the Graphics View Framework classes are meant to deal with many graphical objects and in a performant way.

In this chapter, we will start learning about the most important classes in the Graphics View Framework of the Qt, and, by important, we obviously mean the classes most relevant to what we require in order to build a comprehensive computer vision application. The subjects learned in this chapter will complete the foundation of our Computer_Vision project, which we created at the end of Chapter 3, *Creating a Comprehensive Qt+OpenCV project*. By the end of this chapter, you'll be able to create a scene similar to what you have seen in image editing software, where you will be able to add new images to the scene, select them, remove them, zoom in and out of the scene, and so on. You will also find a link to the foundation and base version of the Computer_Vision project at the end of this chapter, with which we will continue working until the final chapters of this book.

In this chapter, we will cover the following chapters:

- How to use QGraphicsScene to draw graphics on a scene
- How to use QGraphicsItem and its subclasses to manage graphical items
- How to view a QGraphicsScene using a QGraphicsView
- How to develop zoom in, zoom out, and other image editing and viewing capabilities

# The Scene-View-Item architecture

As it was mentioned in the introduction, the Graphics View Framework in Qt (or simply Qt from now on) divides possible graphics-related objects that you need to deal with into three major categories, which are Scene, View, and Items. Qt includes classes with quite noticeable names to handle each part of this architecture. Even though in theory it's easy to separate them from each other, in practice, they are very much intertwined. This means we cannot really dig deep into one of them without mentioning the others. Clear out one part of the architecture and you'll have no graphics at all. Also, taking another look at the architecture, we can see the model-view design pattern where the model (in this case, the scene) is totally unaware of how, or which part of it is displayed. As it's called in Qt, this is an Item-based approach to Model-View programming and we'll keep that in mind while also get, a brief idea of what each one of them is in practice:

- The Scene or QGraphicsScene manages the Items or instances of QGraphicsItem (its subclasses), contains them, and propagates events (such as mouse clicks and so on) into the items.
- The View or the QGraphicsView widget is used to visualize and display the contents of QGraphicsScene. It's also responsible for propagating events to QGraphicsScene. The important thing to note here is the different coordinate systems that both QGraphicsScene and QGraphicsView have. As you can guess, a location on a scene will not be the same if it's zoomed in, zoomed out, or undergoes different similar transformations. QGraphicsScene and QGraphicsView both provide functions to convert a location value suitable for each other.
- The Items, or instances of the QGraphicsItem subclasses, are the items contained within QGraphicsScene. They can be lines, rectangles, images, text, and so on.

Let's start with a simple introductory example, and then move on to discuss each one of the preceding classes in detail:

1. Create a Qt Widgets Application named Graphics_Viewer, similar to the project you created in Chapter 4, *Mat and Qimage*, to learn about displaying images in Qt. However, this time simply add a **Graphics View** widget into it without any labels, menus, status bars, and so on. Leave its objectName property as graphicsView.

2. Also, add the same drag and drop functionality you did as before. As you learned previously, you need to add `dragEnterEvent` and `dropEvent` to your `MainWindow` class. And don't forget to add `setAcceptDrops` to the constructor of the `MainWindow` class. This time, obviously, you need to remove the code to set `QPixmap` on `QLabel`, since we don't have any labels in this project.

3. Now, add the required variables to the private members section of the `MainWindow` class in `mainwindow.h`, seen as follows:

```
QGraphicsScene scene;
```

`scene` is basically the Scene that we will use and display in the `QGraphicsView` widget that we added to our `MainWindow` class. Most probably, you'll need to add an `#include` statement for every class that is used which is not recognizable by the code editor. You'll also get compiler errors regarding this, which are usually a good reminder of the classes we forget to include in our source codes. So from now on, just make sure to add a `#include` directive similar to the one as follows, for every Qt class you use. However, if any special action is required for a class to be usable, it will be explicitly stated in the book:

```
#include <QGraphicsScene>
```

4. Next, we need to make sure our `graphicsView` object can access the scene. You can do this by adding the following line to the `MainWindow` constructor function. (The lines after step 5.)

5. Also, you need to disable `acceptDrops` for `graphicsView` since we want to be able to get a hold of images dropped everywhere on the window. So, make sure your `MainWindow` constructor only contains the following function calls:

```
ui->setupUi(this);
this->setAcceptDrops(true);
ui->graphicsView->setAcceptDrops(false);
ui->graphicsView->setScene(&scene);
```

6. Next, in the `dropEvent` function wherein the previous example project we set the `pixmaps` property of the label, this time we need to make sure `QGraphicsItem` is created and added to the scene, or `QGraphicsPixmapItem` to be precise. This can be done in two ways, let's see the first one:

```
QFileInfo file(event
        ->mimeData()
        ->urls()
        .at(0)
```

```
        .toLocalFile());
QPixmap pixmap;
if(pixmap.load(file
        .absoluteFilePath()))
{
  scene.addPixmap(pixmap);
}
else
{
 // Display an error message
}
```

In this case, we simply used the `addPixmap` function of `QGraphicsScene`. Alternatively, we can create `QGraphicsPixmapItem` and add it to the scene using the `addItem` method, seen as follows:

```
QGraphicsPixmapItem *item =
    new QGraphicsPixmapItem(pixmap);
scene.addItem(item);
```

In both cases, there is no need to be worried about the item pointer since the scene will take ownership of it when `addItem` is called, and it will be cleaned up from memory automatically. Of course, in case we want to remove the item manually from the scene and the memory completely, we can write a simple delete statement to get rid of the item, as shown here:

```
delete item;
```

Our simple code has a big issue, not seen at first sight, but in case we continue dragging and dropping images into window, each time the latest image is added to the top of the previous images and previous images are not cleaned up. In fact, it's a good idea if you try and see this for yourself. But, first add the following line after the line where `addItem` is written:

```
qDebug() << scene.items().count();
```

You'll need to add the following header file to your `mainwindow.h` file for this to work:

```
#include <QDebug>
```

Now, if you run the application and try adding images by dragging and dropping them on the window, you'll notice that in the **Application Output** pane at the bottom of the Qt Creator code editor screen, each time an image is dropped the number shown is increased, that is the `count` of `items` in the `scene`:

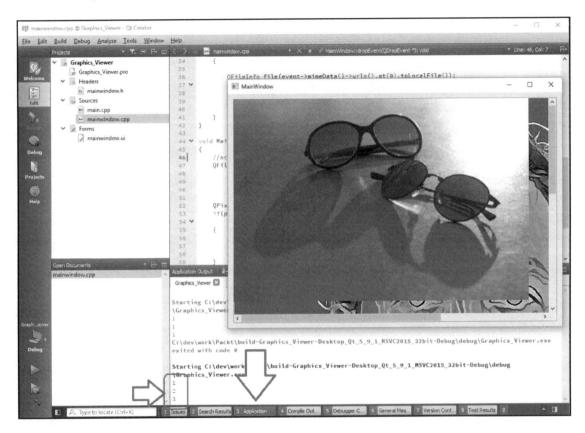

 Using `qDebug()` as shown in the preceding example is a trick many Qt developers use for quickly viewing the value of some variables during development. `qDebug()` in Qt is a similar toy with `std::cout` in the way that it's used to output to the console (or terminal). We will learn much more about testing and debugging in `Chapter 10`, *Debugging and Testing*, but for now, let's make a note of `qDebug()` and use it to quickly fix minor issues in our code when we are developing using Qt and C++.

7. So, to fix the issue mentioned in the preceding example, we obviously need to `clear` the `scene` before we add anything to it. So simply add the following before any `addItem` (or `addPixmap` and so on) is called:

```
scene.clear();
```

Try running your application again and see the result. Now, only one image should exist after it's dropped into the window of our application. Also, make a note of the application output and you'll see the value shown is always `1`, that is because only one image remains in `scene` at all times. In the example project that we just saw, we used all existing main parts in the Graphics View Framework of Qt, namely a Scene, an Item, and a View. We will now learn about these classes in detail, and in the meantime, create a powerful graphics viewer and editor for our comprehensive computer vision application, namely the `Computer_Vision` project.

# The Scene, QGraphicsScene

This class provides almost all methods required for manipulating multiple graphics items (`QGraphicsItem`), even though we only used it with a single `QGraphicxPixmapItem` in the previous example. In this section, we will review some of the most important functions in this class. As it was mentioned before, we'll mainly focus on the properties and methods required for our use case, since covering all methods, although they are all important, would be fruitless for the purpose of our book. We will skip the constructor functions of `QGraphicsScene` since they are simply used to take the dimensions of the scene and create a scene accordingly. As for the rest of the methods and properties, here they are, and for some of them that may not be too obvious, you can find a simple example code that you can try out with the `Graphics_Viewer` project we created earlier in this chapter:

- The `addEllipse`, `addLine`, `addRect`, and `addPolygon` functions, as it can be guessed from their names, can be used to add generic geometric shapes to the scene. Some of them provide overloaded functions for easier parameter input. Each one of the mentioned functions returns their corresponding `QGraphicsItem` subclass instance (shown as follows) when it is created and added to the scene. The returned pointer can be kept and later used to modify, remove, or otherwise work with the item:
  - `QGraphicsEllipseItem`
  - `QGraphicsLineItem`
  - `QGraphicsRectItem`
  - `QGraphicsPolygonItem`

Here's an example:

```
scene.addEllipse(-100.0, 100.0, 200.0, 100.0,
        QPen(QBrush(Qt::SolidPattern), 2.0),
        QBrush(Qt::Dense2Pattern));

scene.addLine(-200.0, 200, +200, 200,
        QPen(QBrush(Qt::SolidPattern), 5.0));

scene.addRect(-150, 150, 300, 140);

QVector<QPoint> points;
points.append(QPoint(150, 250));
points.append(QPoint(250, 250));
points.append(QPoint(165, 280));
points.append(QPoint(150, 250));
scene.addPolygon(QPolygon(points));
```

Here's the result of the preceding code:

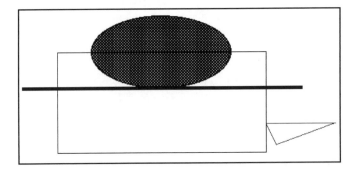

- The addPath function can be used to add QPainterPath to the scene with a given QPen and QBrush. The QPainterPath class can be used to record paint operations similar to what we saw with QPainter and use them later on. The QPen and QBrush classes on the other hand have quite self-explanatory titles, but we'll also get to use them in the example cases later on in this chapter. The addPath function returns a pointer to the newly created QGraphicsPathItem instance.
- The addSimpleText and addText functions can be used to add plain text and formatted text into the scene. They return a pointer to QGraphicsSimpleTextItem or QGraphicsTextItem respectively.

- The addPixmap function, which we already used in the preceding example, can be used to add images to the scene and it returns a pointer to a QGraphicsPixmapItem class.
- The addItem function simply accepts any of the QGraphicsItem subclasses and adds it to the scene. We also used this function in the preceding example.
- The addWidget function can be used to add Qt widgets to the scene. Except for some special widgets (namely, widgets with Qt::WA_PaintOnScreen flag set or widgets that are drawn with external libraries such as OpenGL or Active-X), you can add any other widget to the scene just like you would add it to a window. This provides immense powers for creating a scene with interactive graphical items. You can definitely use it to create simple games, add buttons that perform some action on images, and so many other things. We'll use this to a great extent in our Computer_Vision projects with enough examples to get you started, but here's a short example for now:

```
QPushButton *button = new QPushButton(Q_NULLPTR);
connect(button, SIGNAL(pressed()), this, SLOT(onAction()));
button->setText(tr("Do it!"));
QGraphicsProxyWidget* proxy = scene.addWidget(button);
proxy->setGeometry(QRectF(-200.0, -200, 400, 100.0));
```

The preceding code simply adds a button with the caption Do it! and connects it to a slot named onAction. Whenever this button on the scene is pressed, the onAction function is called. Exactly the same as when you add a button to a window:

- The setBackgroundBrush, backgroundBrush, setForegroundBrush, and foregroundBrush functions allow access to the QBrush class responsible for brushing the background and the foreground of the scene.
- The font and setFont functions can be used to get or set a QFont class to determine the font used in the scene.
- The minimumRenderSize and setMinimumRenderSize functions are useful when we want to define a minimum size to decide if an item is eligible for being drawn (rendered) or not.

- The `sceneRect` and `setSceneRect` functions can be used to specify the bounding rectangle of the scene. This basically means the width and height of the scene, plus its place on the coordinate system. It's important to note that if `setSceneRect` is not called, or a rectangle is not set in the constructor of `QGraphicsScene`, then calling `sceneRect` will always return the biggest rectangle that can cover all of the items added to the scene. It's always best to set a scene rectangle and basically set it again manually (using `setSceneRect`) if needed, because of any changes in the scene and so on.

- The `stickyFocus` and `setStickyFocus` functions can be used to enable or disable the **Sticky Focus** mode for the scene. If **Sticky Focus** is enabled, clicking on an empty space in the scene will not have any effect on the focused item; otherwise, the focus will be simply cleared and the selected items will not be selected anymore.

- The `collidingItems` is a very interesting function that can be used to simply find out if an item shares some part of its area (or in other words collides) with any other items. You need to pass a `QGraphicsItem` pointer along with `Qt::ItemSelectionMode`, and you'll get a `QList` of `QGraphicsItem` instances that your item collides with.

- The `createItemGroup` and `destroyItemGroup` functions can be used to create and remove `QGraphicsItemGroup` class instances. `QGraphicsItemGroup` is basically another `QGraphicsItem` subclass (like `QGraphicsLineItem` and so on) that can be used to group, and consequently represent, a set of graphical items as a single item.

- The `hasFocus`, `setFocus`, `focusItem`, and `setFocusItem` functions are all used to deal with the currently focused item in the graphics scene.

- The `width` and `height`, which returns the same value as `sceneRect.width()` and `sceneRect.height()`, can be used to get the width and height of the scene. It's important to note that the values returned by these functions are of type `qreal` (which is the same as `double`, by default) and not `integer` since the scene coordinates don't work in terms of pixels. Unless a scene is drawn using a view, everything on it is treated as logical and non-visual as opposed to visual, which is the domain of the `QGraphicsView` class.

- The `invalidate`, which is the same as `update()` in certain cases, can be used to request a redraw of the scene wholly or partially. Similar to a refresh functionality.

- The `itemAt` function is useful to find a pointer to the `QGraphicItem` at a certain position in the scene.
- The `item` returns the list of items added to the scene. Basically, `QList` of `QGraphicsItem`.
- The `itemsBoundingRect` can be used to get a `QRectF` class, or simply the smallest rectangle that can contain all of the items on the scene. This function is especially useful in case we need to have all of the items in view or perform similar actions.
- The `mouseGrabberItem` can be used to get the item that is currently clicked on without the mouse button being released. This function returns a `QGraphicsItem` pointer and using that we can easily add "Drag and Move" or similar functionalities to the scene.
- The `removeItem` function can be used to remove an item from the scene. This function does not delete the item and the caller is responsible for any required cleanups.
- The `render` can be used to Render the scene on `QPaintDevice`. This simply means you can use a `QPainter` class (as you learned in Chapter 4, *Mat and Qimage*) to draw the scene on a `QImage`, `QPrinter` and similar classes by passing the pointer of the painter class to this function. Optionally, you can render a portion of the scene on a portion of the `QPaintDevice` render target class, and also take care of aspect ratio handling.
- The `selectedItems`, `selectionArea`, and `setSelectionArea` functions, when used in conjunction, can help with handling one or multiple item selections. By providing a `Qt::ItemSelectionMode` enum, we can select an item based on either completely selecting the item in a box, or just part of it and so on. We can also provide a `Qt::ItemSelectionOperation` enum entry to this function to make the selection additive or replacing all previously selected items.
- The `sendEvent` function can be used to send `QEvent` classes (or subclasses) to items on the scene.
- The `style` and `setStyle` functions are used to set and get the styling of the scene.
- The `update` function can be used to redraw part or all of the scene. This function is best used in conjunction with the change signal emitted by the `QGraphicsScene` class when there is a change in the visual parts of the scene.
- The `views` function can be used to get a `QList` class containing `QGraphicsView` widgets that are being used to display (or view) this scene.

Apart from the preceding existing methods, `QGraphicsScene` provides a number of virtual functions that can be used to further customize and enhance the behavior and also looks of the `QGraphicsScene` class. For this reason, like any other similar C++ class, you need to create a subclass of `QGraphicsScene` and simply add the implementations for these virtual functions. This is, in fact, the best way to use the `QGraphicsScene` class and it allows a tremendous amount of flexibility added to the newly created subclass:

- The `dragEnterEvent`, `dragLeaveEvent`, `dragMoveEvent`, and `dropEvent` functions can be overridden to add drag and drop functionality to the scene. Note that this is quite similar to what we did in the previous examples to have an image dragged and dropped to the window. Each of these events provides enough information and parameters to take care of the whole drag and drop process.
- The `drawBackground` and `drawForeground` functions should be overridden if we need to add a custom background or foreground to the whole scene. Of course, for simple background or foreground painting or coloring tasks, we can simply call the `setBackgroundBrush` and `setForegroundBrush` functions and skip overriding these functions.
- The `mouseDoubleClickEvent`, `mouseMoveEvent`, `mousePressEvent`, `mouseReleaseEvent`, and `wheelEvent` functions can be used to take care of different mouse events in the scene. For example, we will use `wheelEvent` later on in this chapter when we will add zoom in and zoom out capability to our scene in the `Computer_Vision` project.
- The `event` can be overridden to process all events received by the scene. This function is basically responsible for dispatching events to their corresponding handlers, but it can also be used to take care of custom events or events that do not have a convenience function, such as all of the preceding mentioned events.

 Just like all of the classes you learned about so far, whether it's in Qt or OpenCV, the list of methods, properties, and capabilities provided in this book should not be considered a full list of every possible aspect of a class. It's always best to learn about new functions and properties using the documentation of the framework. However, the descriptions in this book aim to be simpler, and especially with a computer vision developer point of view.

# The Items, QGraphicsItem

This is the base class of all items drawn on the scene. It contains various methods and properties to deal with drawing each item, collision detection (with other items), handling mouse clicks and other events, and much more. Even though you can subclass it and create your own graphical items, Qt provides a set of subclasses too, which can be used for most (if not all) of the daily graphical tasks. Here are those subclasses, some of which we already used in the previous examples, directly or indirectly:

- QGraphicsEllipseItem
- QGraphicsLineItem
- QGraphicsPathItem
- QGraphicsPixmapItem
- QGraphicsPolygonItem
- QGraphicsRectItem
- QGraphicsSimpleTextItem
- QGraphicsTextItem

As it was previously mentioned, QGraphicsItem provides numerous functions and properties to deal with the problems and tasks in a graphical application. In this section, we'll go through some of the most important members in QGraphicsItem that consequently help us by getting familiar with its subclasses previously mentioned:

- The acceptDrops and setAcceptDrops functions can be used to make an item accept drag and drop events. Note that this is very similar to the drag and drop event we already saw in the previous examples, but the main difference here is that the item itself becomes aware of drag and drop events.
- The acceptHoverEvents, setAcceptHoverEvents, acceptTouchEvents, setAcceptTouchEvents, acceptedMouseButtons, and setAcceptedMouseButtons functions all deal with the item interaction and its response to mouse clicks and so on. The important thing to note here is that an item can respond or ignore different mouse buttons depending on the Qt::MouseButtons enum setting. Here's a simple example:

```
QGraphicsRectItem *item =
    new QGraphicsRectItem(0,
                          0,
                          100,
                          100,
                          this);
```

```
item->setAcceptDrops(true);
item->setAcceptHoverEvents(true);
item->setAcceptedMouseButtons(
        Qt::LeftButton |
        Qt::RightButton |
        Qt::MidButton);
```

- The `boundingRegion` function can be used to get a `QRegion` class describing the region of the graphical item. This is a very important function since it can be used to get the exact area where the item needs to be drawn (or redrawn), and unlike the bounding rectangle of an item, since simply put, an item may only cover part of its bounding rectangle, like a line and so on. See the following example for more information on this.

- The `boundingRegionGranularity` and `setBoundingRegionGranularity` functions can be used to set and get the level of granularity when calculating the `boundingRegion` function of an item. Granularity in this sense is a real number between 0 and 1, which corresponds to the expected level of details when calculating:

```
QGraphicsEllipseItem *item =
    new QGraphicsEllipseItem(0,
                             0,
                             100,
                             100);
scene.addItem(item);
item->setBoundingRegionGranularity(g); // 0 , 0.1 , 0.75 and 1.0
QTransform transform;
QRegion region = item->boundingRegion(transform);
QPainterPath painterPath;
painterPath.addRegion(region);
QGraphicsPathItem *path = new QGraphicsPathItem(painterPath);
scene.addItem(path);
```

In the preceding code, if you replace g with $0.0$, $0.1$, $0.75$, and $1.0$, you'll get the following results. Obviously, a value of 0 (which is the default granularity) results in a single rectangle (the bounding rectangle), which is not an accurate estimation. As we increase the level a granularity, we get more accurate regions (set of rectangles basically) that cover our graphical shape and item:

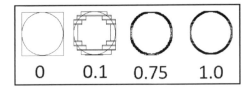

- The `childItems` function can be used to get a `QList` filled with the `QGraphicsItem` classes that are children of this item. Think of them as the sub-items of a more complex item.
- The `childrenBoundingRect`, `boundingRect`, and `sceneBoundingRect` functions can be used to retrieve a `QRectF` class containing the `bounding rect` of the children of this item, the item itself, and the scene.
- The `clearFocus`, `setFocus` and `hasFocus` functions can be used to remove, set, and get the focus status of this item. An item that has focus, receives keyboard events.
- The `collidesWithItem`, `collidesWithPath`, and `collidingItems` functions can be used to check if this item is in a collision with any given item and also a list of items that this item is colliding with.
- The `contains` function takes a point location (`QPointF` class to be precise) and checks if this item contains that point.
- The `cursor`, `setCursor`, `unsetCursor`, and `hasCursor` functions are useful for setting, getting, and unsetting a specific mouse cursor type for this item. You can also check if the item has any set cursor before unsetting it. When set, if the mouse cursor is over this item, the cursor shape changes to the one set.
- The `hide`, `show`, `setVisible`, `isVisible`, `opacity`, `setOpacity`, and `effectiveOpacity` functions are all related to the visibility (and opacity) of the item. All of these functions have self-explanatory names and the only one worth noting is `effectiveOpacity`, which might be different than this item's opacity since it's calculated based on this item and its parent item's opacity level. Ultimately, `effectiveOpacity` is the opacity level used for drawing this item on the screen.

- The `flags`, `setFlags`, and `setFlag` functions can be used to get or set the flags for this item. By flags, what we basically mean is a combination of items from the `QGraphicsItem::GraphicsItemFlag` enum. Here's an example code:

```
item->setFlag(QGraphicsItem::ItemIsFocusable, true);
item->setFlag(QGraphicsItem::ItemIsMovable, false);
```

 It's important to note that when we use the `setFlag` function, all of the previous flag states are preserved and only the one flag in this function is affected. However, when we use `setFlags`, basically all flags are reset according to the given flags combination.

- The `grabMouse`, `grabKeyboard`, `ungrabMouse`, and `ungrabKeyboard` methods are useful when we want to change the item that gets mouse and keyboard events from the scene. Obviously, and with the default implementation, only one item at a time can grab mouse or keyboard and unless another one grabs or the item itself ungrabs or is deleted or hidden, the grabber remains the same. We can always use the `mouseGrabberItem` function in the `QGraphicsScene` class to get the grabber item, as you saw earlier in this chapter.
- The `setGraphicsEffect` and `graphicsEffect` functions can be used to set and get a `QGraphicsEffect` class. This is a very interesting and easy to use, yet powerful function that can be used to add filters or effects to the items on the scene. `QGraphicsEffect` is the base class of all graphical effects in Qt. You can subclass it and create your own graphical effects or filters or simply use one of the provided Qt graphics effects. At the moment, there are a few graphics effects class in Qt that you can try out for yourself:
    - `QGraphicsBlurEffect`
    - `QGraphicsColorizeEffect`
    - `QGraphicsDropShadowEffect`
    - `QGraphicsOpacityEffect`

Let's see an example custom graphics effect and also use Qt's own graphics effects to familiarize ourselves even more with the concept:

1. You can use the same `Graphics_Viewer` project we created earlier on in this chapter. Simply open it in Qt Creator and using **New File or Project** from the main menu, choose **C++** and **C++ Class** and click on the **Choose** button.

2. Next, make sure you enter `QCustomGraphicsEffect` as the class name. Choose **QObject** as **Base class** and finally check the **Include QObject** checkbox (if it's not checked by default). Click on **Next**, and then the **Finish** button.

3. Then, add the following include statements to the newly created `qcustomgraphicseffect.h` file:

```
#include <QGraphicsEffect>
#include <QPainter>
```

4. After that, you need to make sure our `QCustomGraphicsEffect` class inherits `QGraphicsEffect` instead of `QObject`. Make sure you first change the class definition line in the `qcustomgraphicseffect.h` file as seen here:

```
class QCustomGraphicsEffect : public QGraphicsEffect
```

5. We also need to update the constructor of the class and make sure the QGraphicsEffect constructor is called in our class constructor, otherwise we'll get a compiler error. So, change the class constructor in the qcustomgraphics.cpp file as seen here:

```
QCustomGraphicsEffect::QCustomGraphicsEffect(QObject *parent)
    : QGraphicsEffect(parent)
```

6. Next, we need to implement the draw function. This is basically how all QGraphicsEffect classes are made--by implementing the draw function. So, add the following line of code to our QCustomGraphicsEffect class definition in the qcustomgraphicseffect.h file:

```
protected:
    void draw(QPainter *painter);
```

7. And then, we need to write the actual effect code. In this example, we will write a simple threshold filter, which, depending on the grayscale value of a pixel, either sets it to complete black or completely white. Even though the code may look a bit tricky at first, it simply uses the lessons we have already learned in the previous chapters. And, it's also a simple example of how easy it is to write new effects and filters using the QGraphicsEffect class. As you can see, the pointer to the QPainter class passed into the draw function can be used to simply modify and draw it after the changes required by the effect:

```
void QCustomGraphicsEffect::draw(QPainter *painter)
{
  QImage image;
  image = sourcePixmap().toImage();
  image = image.convertToFormat(
        QImage::Format_Grayscale8);
  for(int i=0; i<image.byteCount(); i++)
  image.bits()[i] =
        image.bits()[i] < 100 ?
            0
          :
            255;
  painter->drawPixmap(0,0,QPixmap::fromImage(image));
}
```

8. Finally, we can use our new effect class. Just make sure it's included in the `mainwindow.h` file:

```
#include "qcustomgraphicseffect.h"
```

9. And then, use it by calling the `setGraphicsEffect` function of the item. In our `Graphics_Viewer` project, we implemented `dropEvent`. You can simply add the following code snippet to the `dropEvent` function, so you'd have the following:

```
QGraphicsPixmapItem *item = new QGraphicsPixmapItem(pixmap);
item->setGraphicsEffect(new QCustomGraphicsEffect(this));
scene.addItem(item);
```

If all is done correctly when you run the application and drop an image on it, you'll notice the result of our threshold effect:

Try replacing `QCustomGraphicsEffect` in the final step where we used our custom graphics effect, with any of the Qt provided effect's class names and check the result for yourself. As you can see, they provide a tremendous amount of flexibility when it comes to the graphics effects and similar concepts.

Now, let's move on to the remaining functions and properties in the QGraphicsItem class:

- The group and setGroup functions are useful when we want to add an item to a group or get the group class containing the item, provided that this item belongs to any groups. QGraphicsItemGroup is the class responsible to handle groups like you learned earlier in this chapter.

- The isAncestorOf function can be used to check if this item is a parent (or parent of a parent and so on) of any given other item.

- The setParentItem and parentItem and be set and retrieve the parent item of the current item. An item may simply not have any parents at all, in which case, the parentItem function returns zero.

- The isSelected and setSelected functions can be used to change the selected mode of an item. These functions are closely related to setSelectionArea and similar functions you learned about in the QGraphicsScene class.

- The mapFromItem, mapToItem, mapFromParent, mapToParent, mapFromScene, mapToScene, mapRectFromItem, mapRectToScene, mapRectFromParent, mapRectToParent, mapRectFromScene, and mapRectToScene functions, all of which have even more convenience overloaded functions, make up a long list of functions used to basically map from or to, or in other words, can be used to convert the coordinates from or to the scene, another item, or the parent. This is, in fact, quite simple to grasp if you consider the fact that each individual item and the scene work in their own coordinate system if they have nothing to do with other items. First, take a look at the following diagram, and then let's discuss this in even more detail:

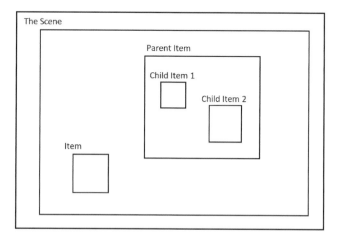

Since **The Scene** contains all items, let's assume that the main coordinate system (or the world coordinate system) is the coordinate system of **The Scene**. This is, in fact, quite a valid assumption. So, **Item** would have a position value of (A, B) in the scene. Similarly, **Parent Item** has a position of (D, E) in the scene. Now, this is where it gets a little tricky, **Child Item 1** has a position value of (F, G) in the **Parent Item**. Similarly, **Child Item 2** has a position value of (H, I) in the **Parent Item**. Obviously, if the number of parents and children increase, we'll have a maze of different coordinate systems, and that's where the mapping functions mentioned can be useful. Here are a few example cases. You can test it for yourself using the following piece of code to create a scene with items similar to the one mentioned earlier:

```
QGraphicsRectItem *item =
new QGraphicsRectItem(0,
                        0,
                        100,
                        100);
item->setPos(50,400);
scene.addItem(item);
QGraphicsRectItem *parentItem =
    new QGraphicsRectItem(0,
                            0,
                            320,
                            240);
parentItem->setPos(300, 50);
scene.addItem(parentItem);

QGraphicsRectItem *childItem1 =
    new QGraphicsRectItem(0,
                            0,
                            50,
                            50,
                            parentItem);
childItem1->setPos(50,50);
QGraphicsRectItem *childItem2 =
    new QGraphicsRectItem(0,
                            0,
                            75,
                            75,
                            parentItem);
childItem2->setPos(150,75);

qDebug() << item->mapFromItem(childItem1, 0,0);
qDebug() << item->mapToItem(childItem1, 0,0);
qDebug() << childItem1->mapFromScene(0,0);
qDebug() << childItem1->mapToScene(0,0);
qDebug() << childItem2->mapFromParent(0,0);
```

```
qDebug() << childItem2->mapToParent(0,0);
qDebug() << item->mapRectFromItem(childItem1,
                                  childItem1->rect());
qDebug() << item->mapRectToItem(childItem1,
                                childItem1->rect());
qDebug() << childItem1->mapRectFromScene(0,0, 25, 25);
qDebug() << childItem1->mapRectToScene(0,0, 25, 25);
qDebug() << childItem2->mapRectFromParent(0,0, 30, 30);
qDebug() << childItem2->mapRectToParent(0,0, 25, 25);
```

Try running the preceding code in Qt Creator and in a Qt Widgets Project and you'll see the following in the application output pane of the Qt Creator, which is basically the result of the qDebug() statements:

```
QPointF(300,-300)
QPointF(-300,300)
QPointF(-350,-100)
QPointF(350,100)
QPointF(-150,-75)
QPointF(150,75)
QRectF(300,-300 50x50)
QRectF(-300,300 50x50)
QRectF(-350,-100 25x25)
QRectF(350,100 25x25)
QRectF(-150,-75 30x30)
QRectF(150,75 25x25)
```

Let's try seeing the instruction that produced the first result:

```
item->mapFromItem(childItem1, 0,0);
```

item has a position of (50,400) in the scene and childItem1 has a position of (50,50) in parentItem. This statement takes the position (0,0) in the childItem1 coordinate system and converts it to the coordinate system of the item. Check the other instructions by yourself one by one. It's very simple yet extremely handy when we want to move around items in the scene or do similar transformations on items in the scene:

- The moveBy, pos, setPos, x, setX, y, setY, rotation, setRotation, scale, and setScale functions can be used to get or set different geometric properties of the item. It's interesting to note that pos and mapToParent(0,0) return the same values. Check the preceding example and try this out by adding it in the example code.

- The `transform`, `setTransform`, `setTransformOriginPoint`, and `resetTransform` functions can be used to apply or retrieve any geometric transformation to the item. It's important to note that all transformations assume an origin point (usually 0,0), which can be changed using `setTransformOriginPoint`.

- The `scenePos` function can be used to get the position of the item in the scene. It's the same as calling `mapToScene(0,0)`. You can try this out in the preceding example by yourself and compare the results.

- The `data` and `setData` functions can be used to set and retrieve any custom data in and from an item. For example, we can use this to store the path of the image set to `QGraphicsPixmapItem`, or literally any other type of information associated with the specific item.

- The `zValue` and `setZValue` functions can be used to modify and retrieve the `z` value of an item. `z` value decides which items should be drawn in front of the other items and so on. An item with a higher `z` value will always be drawn on an item with a lower `z` value.

Similar to what we saw in the `QGraphicsScene` class, the `QGraphicsItem` class also contains many protected and virtual functions that can be reimplemented mostly for handling different kinds of events passed on to items from the scene. A few important and very useful examples would be the following:

- `contextMenuEvent`
- `dragEnterEvent, dragLeaveEvent, dragMoveEvent, dropEvent`
- `focusInEvent, focusOutEvent`
- `hoverEnterEvent, hoverLeaveEvent, hoverMoveEvent`
- `keyPressEvent, keyReleaseEvent`
- `mouseDoubleClickEvent, mouseMoveEvent, mousePressEvent, mouseReleaseEvent, wheelEvent`

# The View, QGraphicsView

We're down to the last part of The Graphics View Framework in Qt. The QGraphicsView class is a Qt Widget class that can be placed on a window to display QGraphicsScene, which itself contains a number of QGraphicsItem subclasses and/or widgets. Similar to the QGraphicsScene class, this class also provides tons of capabilities, methods, and properties to deal with the visualization part of the graphics. We'll review some of the most important ones in the following list, and then we'll learn how to subclass QGraphicsView and extend it to have several important capabilities in our comprehensive computer vision application, such as zoom in, zoom out, item selection, and so on. So, here are the methods and members of the QGraphicsView class that we'll need in a computer vision project:

- The alignment and setAlignment functions can be used to set the alignment of the scene in the view. It's important to note that this will only have a visible effect when the view can completely display the scene and still has enough space, and no scroll bars are needed by the view.

- The dragMode and setDragMode functions can be used to get and set the drag mode of the view. This is one of the most important capabilities of the view that can decide what happens when the left button on the mouse is clicked and dragged on the view. We'll make use of it in the following example and learn all about it. We'll make use of the QGraphicsView::DragMode enum to set different drag modes.

- The isInteractive and setInteractive functions allow retrieving and modifying the interactive behavior of the view. An interactive view reacts to mouse and keyboard (if implemented), otherwise, all mouse and keyboard events will be ignored and the view can only be used for viewing and not interacting with the items in the scene.

- The optimizationFlags, setOptimizationFlags, renderHints, setRenderHints, viewportUpdateMode, and setViewportUpdateMode functions are used respectively to get and set parameters related to both performance and render quality of the view. In the following example project, we'll see use cases of these functions in practice.

- The `rubberBandSelectionMode` and `setRubberBandSelectionMode` functions can be used to set the item selection mode of the view in case `dragMode` are set to `RubberBandDrag` mode. The following can be set, which are entries in the `Qt::ItemSelectionMode` enum:
    - `Qt::ContainsItemShape`
    - `Qt::IntersectsItemShape`
    - `Qt::ContainsItemBoundingRect`
    - `Qt::IntersectsItemBoundingRect`
- The `sceneRect` and `setSceneRect` functions are useful for getting and setting the visualized area of the scene in the view. Obviously, this value is not necessarily the same as `sceneRect` of the `QGraphicsScene` class.
- The `centerOn` function can be used to make sure a specific point or item is in the center of the view.
- The `ensureVisible` function can be used to scroll the view to a specific area (with given margins) to make sure it's in the view. This function works on a point, rectangle, and graphics item.
- The `fitInView` function, quite similar to `centerOn` and `ensureVisible` but with the major difference that this function also scales the contents of the view to fit in the view, with a given aspect ratio handling parameter, which can be one of the following:
    - `Qt::IgnoreAspectRatio`
    - `Qt::KeepAspectRatio`
    - `Qt::KeepAspectRatioByExpanding`
- The `itemAt` function can be used to retrieve the item at a specific position in the view.

We already learned that each item in the scene and the scene have their own coordinate systems, and we need to use the mapping functions to convert positions from one to the other and vice versa. That's also the case with the view. **The View** also has its own coordinate system, with the major difference being the fact that positions and rectangles and so on in the view are actually measured in terms of pixels so they are integer numbers, but the scene and items use real numbers for their positions and so on. This is due to the fact that **The Scene** and items are all logical entities until they are viewed on a view, thus all real numbers are converted to the integers while the whole (or part of) the scene is prepared to be displayed on the screen. The following image can help you understand this better:

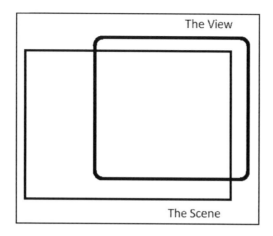

In the preceding diagram, the center point in the view is actually somewhere in the top-right quarter of the scene. **The View** provides similar mapping functions (to the ones we saw in items) to convert a position from the scene coordinate system to view coordinate system and vice versa. Here they are, plus a few more remaining functions and methods of **The View** we need to learn about before moving on:

- The `mapFromScene` and `mapToScene` functions can be used to convert a position from and to the scene coordinate system. Quite consistently with what was mentioned before, the `mapFromScene` functions accept real values and return integer values, whereas the `mapToScene` functions accept integers and return real numbers. We'll make use of these functions when we develop the zoom capability of the view later on.
- The `items` functions can be used to get a list of items in the scene.
- The `render` function is useful for performing a render of the whole view or part of it. This function is used exactly like render in `QGraphicsScene`, except this one performs the same on the view.
- The `rubberBandRect` function can be used to get the rubber band selected rectangle. As it was mentioned before, this is only relevant in case drag mode is set to `rubberBandSelectionMode`.
- The `setScene` and `scene` functions can be used to set and get a scene for the view.
- The `setMatrix`, `setTransform`, `transform`, `rotate`, `scale`, `shear`, and `translate` functions can all be used to modify or retrieve the mentioned geometric properties of the view.

Just the same as the `QGraphicsScene` and `QGraphicsItem` classes, `QGraphicsView` also provides a number of identical protected virtual members that can be used to further extend the capabilities of the view. We will now extend our `Graphics_Viewer` example project to support even more items, item selection, item removal, and zoom in and zoom out capabilities, and during this process, we'll get an overview of some of the most important use cases of the view, scene, and items as we learned in this chapter. So, let's get it done already:

1. Start by opening the `Graphics_Viewer` project in Qt Creator; then, from the main menu select **New File or Project**, and then in the **New File or Project** window choose **C++** and **C++ Class**, then click on the **Choose** button.

2. Make sure you enter `QEnhancedGraphicsView` as the class name and choose `QWidget` as the base class. Also, check the checkbox next to `Include QWidget`, if it's not checked already. Then, click **Next**, and then **Finish**.

3. Add the following to include the `qenhancedgraphicsview.h` header file:

   ```
   #include <QGraphicsView>
   ```

4. Make sure the `QEnhancedGraphicsView` class inherits `QGraphicsView` instead of `QWidget` in the `qenhancedgraphicsview.h` file, as shown here:

   ```
   class QEnhancedGraphicsView : public QGraphicsView
   ```

5. You have to correct the constructor implementation of the `QEnhancedGraphicsView` class as seen here. This is obviously done in the `qenhancedgraphicsview.cpp` file as follows:

   ```
   QEnhancedGraphicsView::QEnhancedGraphicsView(QWidget
      *parent)
    : QGraphicsView(parent)
   {
   }
   ```

6. Now, add the following protected member to our enhanced view class definition in the `qenhancedgraphicsview.h` file:

   ```
   protected:
     void wheelEvent(QWheelEvent *event);
   ```

7. And add its implementation to the `qenhancedgraphicsview.cpp` file, as mentioned in the following code block:

```
void QEnhancedGraphicsView::wheelEvent(QWheelEvent *event)
{
  if (event->orientation() == Qt::Vertical)
  {
    double angleDeltaY = event->angleDelta().y();
    double zoomFactor = qPow(1.0015, angleDeltaY);
    scale(zoomFactor, zoomFactor);
    this->viewport()->update();
    event->accept();
  }
  else
  {
    event->ignore();
  }
}
```

You need to make sure `QWheelEvent` and `QtMath` are included in our class source files, otherwise, you'll get compiler errors for the `qPow` function and the `QWheelEvent` class. The preceding code is mostly self-explanatory—it starts by checking the mouse wheel event orientation, and then, based on the amount of movement in the wheel, applies a scale to both X and Y axes. Then, it updates the viewport to make sure everything is redrawn as needed.

8. Now, we need to promote the `graphicsView` object on the window (as we saw earlier) by going into the **Design** mode in Qt Creator. We need to right-click and choose **Promote To** from the context menu. Then, enter `QEnhancedGraphicsView` as the promoted class name and click on the **Add** button, and finally click on the **Promote** button. (You already learned about promoting in previous examples and this one is no exception.) Since the `QGraphicsView` and `QEnhancedGraphicsView` classes are compatible (first is the parent class of the latter), we can promote the parent to child, and/or demote it if we don't need it. Promoting is like converting a widget to its child widget to support and add more functionalities.

9. You need to add one small piece of code to the top of the `dropEvent` function in `mainwindow.cpp` to ensure that zoom level (scale transform to be precise) is reset when a new image is loaded:

```
ui->graphicsView->resetTransform();
```

Now you can start the application and try scrolling using your mouse wheel. You can see the scale-level changes as you turn the wheel upwards or downwards. Here's a screenshot of the result application while zoomed in and out of an image:

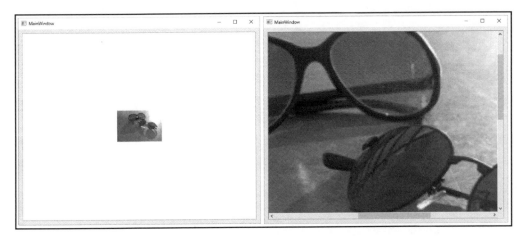

If you try a little bit more, one thing is quickly noticed, the zoom function always works toward the center of the image, which is very odd and uncomfortable. To be able to fix this issue, we need to make use of a few more tips, tricks, and functions we learned about in this chapter:

1. Start by adding another private protected function to our enhanced view class. We'll make use of `mouseMoveEvent` in addition to `wheelEvent`, which we used earlier on. So, add the following line of code to the protected members section in the `qenhancedgraphicsview.h` file:

   ```
   void mouseMoveEvent(QMouseEvent *event);
   ```

2. Also, add a private member as seen here:

   ```
   private:
     QPointF sceneMousePos;
   ```

3. Now, move on to the implementation part of it and add the following code lines to the `qenhancedgraphicsview.cpp` file:

   ```
   void QEnhancedGraphicsView::mouseMoveEvent(QMouseEvent
       *event)
   {
     sceneMousePos = this->mapToScene(event->pos());
   }
   ```

4. You also need to adjust the `wheelEvent` function a little bit. Make sure it looks like the following:

```
if (event->orientation() == Qt::Vertical)
{
  double angleDeltaY = event->angleDelta().y();
  double zoomFactor = qPow(1.0015, angleDeltaY);
  scale(zoomFactor, zoomFactor);
  if(angleDeltaY > 0)
  {
    this->centerOn(sceneMousePos);
    sceneMousePos = this->mapToScene(event->pos());
  }
  this->viewport()->update();
  event->accept();
}
else
{
  event->ignore();
}
```

You can see what's happening here quite easily just by paying attention to the function names. We implemented `mouseMoveEvent` to pick up the position of the mouse (in scene coordinates, this is very important); then we made sure that after zooming in (not zooming out), the view makes sure the collected point is at the center of the screen. Finally, it updates the position for further comfortable zooming experiences. It's important to note that sometimes small defects or capabilities, such as this, can mean how comfortably a user can use your application and ultimately this is an important parameter in the growth (or worst, the fall) of your applications.

Now, we'll add yet a few more capabilities to the `Graphics_Viewer` application. Let's start by making sure our `Graphics_Viewer` application is capable of handling an unlimited number of images:

1. First of all, we need to ensure that the scene is not cleared after each image is dropped in the view (and consequently, the scene), so start by removing the following line from `dropEvent` in `mainwindow.cpp`:

   ```
   scene.clear();
   ```

2. Also, remove the following code line from `dropEvent`, which we added earlier to reset the zoom and scale:

   ```
   ui->graphicsView->resetTransform();
   ```

3. Now, add the following two lines of code instead to the starting point of the `dropEvent` in `mainwindow.cpp` file:

```
QPoint viewPos = ui->graphicsView->mapFromParent
    (event->pos());
QPointF sceneDropPos = ui->graphicsView->mapToScene
    (viewPos);
```

4. Then, make sure the item's position is set to `sceneDropPos` shown as follows:

```
item->setPos(sceneDropPos);
```

That's it, nothing else is needed for now. Start the `Graphics_Viewer` application and try dropping images inside it. After the first image, try zooming out and adding even more images. (Try not to fill up the memory by exaggerating this test, because if you try adding lots and lots of images, your application will start consuming too much memory and thus causing issues for the operating system. Needless to say, your application may simply crash.) Here's a screenshot of a few images dragged and dropped in various locations on the scene:

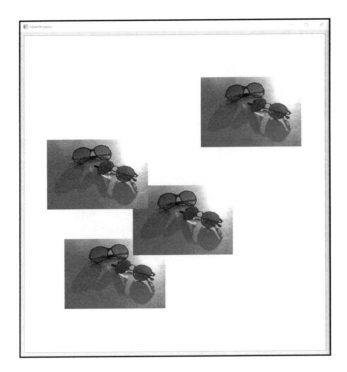

It's obvious that this application still misses a lot, but there are some very crucial capabilities that we'll cover in this chapter before leaving the rest for you to figure out and discover by yourself. Some very important missing features are that we are not able to select items, remove them, or apply some effect to them. Let's do it all at once for a simple yet capable `Graphics_Viewer` application. As you already know, later on, we will use all of the techniques we learned in our comprehensive computer vision application (named `Computer_Vision` project). So, let's get started with these final additions to the `Graphics_Viewer` project:

1. Start by adding yet another protected member to the enhanced graphics view class, as seen here:

   ```
   void mousePressEvent(QMouseEvent *event);
   ```

2. Then, add the following private slots to the same class definition:

   ```
   private slots:
      void clearAll(bool);
      void clearSelected(bool);
      void noEffect(bool);
      void blurEffect(bool);
      void dropShadowEffect(bool);
      void colorizeEffect(bool);
      void customEffect(bool);
   ```

3. Now, add all required implementations to the view class source file, which is the `qenhancedgraphicsview.cpp` file. Start by adding the implementation for `mousePressEvent` as follows:

   ```
   void QEnhancedGraphicsView::mousePressEvent(QMouseEvent
     *event)
   {
    if(event->button() == Qt::RightButton)
    {
     QMenu menu;
     QAction *clearAllAction = menu.addAction("Clear All");
     connect(clearAllAction,
           SIGNAL(triggered(bool)),
           this,
           SLOT(clearAll(bool)));
     QAction *clearSelectedAction = menu.addAction("Clear Selected");
     connect(clearSelectedAction,
           SIGNAL(triggered(bool)),
           this,
           SLOT(clearSelected(bool)));
   ```

```
QAction *noEffectAction = menu.addAction("No Effect");
connect(noEffectAction,
        SIGNAL(triggered(bool)),
        this,
        SLOT(noEffect(bool)));
QAction *blurEffectAction = menu.addAction("Blur Effect");
connect(blurEffectAction,
        SIGNAL(triggered(bool)),
        this,
        SLOT(blurEffect(bool)));
// ***
menu.exec(event->globalPos());
event->accept();
}
else
{
  QGraphicsView::mousePressEvent(event);
}
}
```

In the preceding code, `//***` is basically repeated in the same pattern for the `dropShadowEffect`, `colorizeEffect`, and `customEffect` function slots. What we did in the preceding code is simply create and open a **Context** (right-click) menu, and we connect each action to a slot we will add in the next step.

4. Now, add the implementations for slots as seen here:

```
void QEnhancedGraphicsView::clearAll(bool)
{
  scene()->clear();
}
void QEnhancedGraphicsView::clearSelected(bool)
{
  while(scene()->selectedItems().count() > 0)
  {
   delete scene()->selectedItems().at(0);
   scene()->selectedItems().removeAt(0);
  }
}
void QEnhancedGraphicsView::noEffect(bool)
{
  foreach(QGraphicsItem *item, scene()->selectedItems())
  {
   item->setGraphicsEffect(Q_NULLPTR);
  }
}
```

```
void QEnhancedGraphicsView::blurEffect(bool)
{
  foreach(QGraphicsItem *item, scene()->selectedItems())
  {
    item->setGraphicsEffect(new QGraphicsBlurEffect(this));
  }
}

//***
```

Same as the previous code, the same pattern follows for the remaining slots.

5. There are some final things we need to take care of before our application is ready for a test run. First, we need to make sure our enhanced graphics view class is interactive and allows selection of items by clicking and dragging. You can do it by adding the following piece of code to the mainwindow.cpp file. Right after setting the scene and so in the initialization function (constructor function):

```
ui->graphicsView->setInteractive(true);
ui->graphicsView->setDragMode(QGraphicsView::RubberBandDrag);
ui->graphicsView->setRubberBandSelectionMode(
    Qt::ContainsItemShape);
```

6. And, last but not least, add the following code lines in the dropEvent function of mainwindow.cpp to make sure items are selectable. Add them right after the item creation code and before the line where they are added to the scene:

```
item->setFlag(QGraphicsItem::ItemIsSelectable);
item->setAcceptedMouseButtons(Qt::LeftButton);
```

That's it. We are ready to start and test our `Graphics_Viewer` application, which can now also add effects and has even more capabilities. Here is a screenshot displaying the behavior of the so-called **Rubber Band** selection mode:

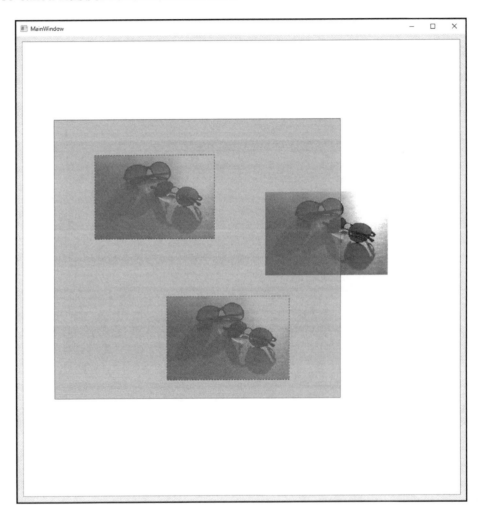

And finally, here's a screenshot of the `Graphics_Viewer` application in action while adding different effects to the images in the scene:

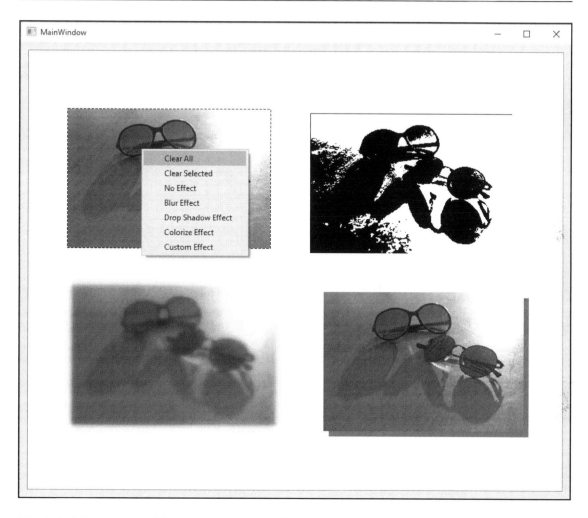

That's it. We are now able to create a powerful graphics viewer and also add it to the Computer_Vision project, which we will use in the upcoming chapters while learning new and more OpenCV and Qt skills and techniques. As it was promised, you can download the complete version of the Computer_Vision project from the following link:

https://github.com/PacktPublishing/Computer-Vision-with-OpenCV-3-and-Qt5/tree/
master/ch05/computer_vision

As we have repeatedly mentioned this over and over again during the course of the previous chapters, the goal of this project is to help us focus solely on the computer vision subjects by taking care of every required GUI capability, languages, themes, and so on. This project is a complete example of everything you learned so far. It's an application that can be customized with styles, can support new languages, and can be extended using plugins. It also packs everything you learned in this chapter in a nice and powerful graphics viewer that we will use for the rest of the book. Make sure you download it before continuing with the following chapters.

The `Computer_Vision` project contains two projects in a Qt multi-project, or to be precise, a `subdirs` project type. First is `mainapp`, and the second is the `template_plugin` project. You can copy (clone) and replace the code and GUI files in this project to create new plugins compatible with the `Computer_Vision` project. That's exactly what we'll do in `Chapter 6`, *Image Processing in OpenCV*), and for most of the OpenCV skills that you learn, we will create a plugin for `Computer_Vision`. This project also contains an example additional language, and an example additional theme, which can again be simply copied and modified to create new languages and themes for the application. Make sure you review the entire downloaded source code and make sure there's no mystery in it and that you completely understand everything in the `Computer_Vision` project source codes. Again, this is meant to summarize and pack all you've learned into a single, comprehensive, and reusable example project.

# Summary

We've come a long way since the starting chapters of the book, and by now, we are fully equipped with lots of useful techniques to take on the task of computer vision application development. In all of the previous chapters, including the one we just finished, you learned more about the required skills to create a powerful and comprehensive application (in general, for the most part) rather than just focusing on the computer vision (OpenCV skills to be precise) aspect of it. You learned how to create applications that support multiple languages, themes and styles, plugins; and in this chapter, you learned how to visualize images and graphical items in a scene and on a view. We are now armed with almost everything we need to dig deeper into the world of computer vision application development.

In Chapter 6, *Image Processing in OpenCV*, you will learn more about OpenCV and possible image processing techniques in it. For each learned subject, we'll simply assume that we're creating a plugin compatible with the Computer_Vision project. This means that we'll use the **Template Plugin** within the Computer_Vision project, copy it, and simply make a new plugin that is capable of a specific computer vision task, transform filter, or calculation. This, of course, does not mean that you can't create a standalone application that does the same, and as you'll see in the upcoming chapters, our plugins have GUIs, which is essentially nothing different than creating an application, or a Qt Widgets Application to be precise, which you learned all about in the previous chapters. Nevertheless, from now on we'll move on to more advanced subjects and our focus will be mostly on the computer vision aspects of our application. You'll learn how to use the numerous filtering and other image processing capabilities in OpenCV, color spaces supported by it, many transformation techniques, and even more.

# 6
# Image Processing in OpenCV

It always starts with an unprocessed and raw image, taken with a smartphone, webcam, DSLR camera, or, in short, any device that is capable of shooting and recording image data. However, it usually ends with sharp or blurred; bright, dark, or balanced; black and white or colored; and many other different representations of the same image data. This is probably the initial step (and one of the most important steps) in computer vision algorithms, and it's usually referred to as **Image Processing** (for now, let's forget about the fact that, sometimes, computer vision and Image Processing are used interchangeably; this is a discussion for history experts). Of course, you can have image processing in between or in the final phases of any computer vision process, but, in general, any photo or video recorded with most of the existing devices undergoes some kind of image processing algorithm before anything else. Some of these algorithms are just meant to convert the image format, some are meant to adjust colors, remove noise, and so much more we can't begin to name. The OpenCV framework offers plenty of capabilities to deal with different kinds of image processing tasks, such as image filtering, geometric transformation, drawing, dealing with different color spaces, image histograms, and so on, which will be the main focus of this chapter.

In this chapter, you'll learn about many different functions and classes, especially from the `imgproc` module in the OpenCV framework. We will start with image filtering, and, during the process, you'll learn how to create GUIs that allow proper usage of the existing algorithms. After that, we'll move on to learn about geometric transformation capabilities provided by OpenCV. We will then briefly go through what color spaces are, how they are converted to each other, and so on. After that, we'll move on to learn about drawing functions in OpenCV. As we saw in the previous chapters, Qt framework also provides quite flexible functions for drawing, and it even allows easier handling of different graphical items on the screen by using the scene-view-item architecture; however, we will also use OpenCV drawing functions in some situations that are usually quite fast and provide enough capabilities for daily graphical tasks. We will end the chapter with one of the most powerful, yet easy-to-use matching and detection methods in OpenCV, namely the **template matching** method.

This chapter will be full of interesting examples and hands-on learning material, and it's important to make sure that you try all of them in order to see them at work, and learn about them based on a first-hand experience and not just by following the screenshots and example source code provided in the chapter and at the end of some sections.

In this chapter, we will cover the following topics:

- How to create a new plugin for the `Computer_Vision` project and each learned OpenCV skill
- How to filter images
- How to perform an image transformation
- Color spaces, how to convert them to each other, and how to apply color mappings
- Image thresholding
- Drawing functions available in OpenCV
- Template matching and how to use it for object detection and counting

# Image filtering

In this starting section, you will learn about different linear and non-linear image filtering methods available in OpenCV. It's important to note that all of the functions discussed in this section take a Mat image as an input and produce a Mat image of the same size and the same number of channels. In fact, the filters are applied to each channel independently. In general, filtering methods take a pixel and its neighboring pixels from the input image and calculate the value of the corresponding pixel in the resulting image based on a function response from those pixels.

This usually requires an assumption to be made about the pixels that do not exist, while calculating the filtered pixel result. OpenCV provides a number of methods to overcome this issue, and they can be specified in almost all of the OpenCV functions that need to deal with this phenomenon using the cv::BorderTypes enum. We will see how it is used in our first example in this chapter a bit later, but, before that, let's make sure we completely understand it using the following diagram:

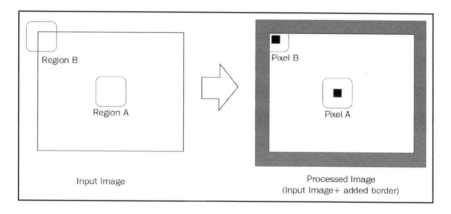

As seen in the preceding diagram, a calculation (or, in this case, a filtering function) takes the pixels in **Region A** and gives us the **Pixel A** in the resulting **Processed Image** (or filtered image in this case). There's no issue in this case since all pixels in the neighborhood of **Pixel A** in the **Input Image** are all inside of the image, that is **Region A**. But what about the pixels near the edges of the image, or as it is referred to in OpenCV, the Border Pixels? As you can see, not all of the neighboring pixels of **Pixel B** fall into the input image, that is, **Region B**. And that is where we need to make an assumption to consider the value of the pixels outside an image as zeros, same as the border pixels and so on. That is exactly what the cv::BorderTypes enum is about, and we'll need to specify it in our examples with a suitable value.

Now, let's demonstrate the usage of `cv::BorderTypes` with our first example before we start with image filtering functions. We'll take this opportunity to also learn how we can create new plugins (or clone existing plugins) for the `Computer_Vision` project that we started in the previous chapters. So, let's start:

1. In case you have followed the examples in the book completely until now, you should be able to easily create a new plugin for the `Computer_Vision` project if you have already downloaded it at the end of Chapter 5, *The Graphics View Framework*. To do this, start by duplicating (or copy and paste in the same folder, this simply depends on the OS that you are using) the `template_plugin` folder inside the `Computer_Vision` project folder. Then, rename the new folder to `copymakeborder_plugin`. We will create our first real plugin for the `Computer_Vision` project and see how `cv::BorderTypes` works with a real example.

2. Go to the `copymakeborder_plugin` folder, and rename all files here to match the plugin folder name. Simply replace all `template` words in file names with `copymakeborder`.

3. You can guess that now we also need to update the project file for `copymakeborder_plugin`. To do this, you can simply open the `copymakeborder_plugin.pro` file in a standard text editor, or drag and drop it in into the **Qt Creator Code Editor** area (not the **Projects** pane). Then, set `TARGET` to `CopyMakeBorder_Plugin`, as seen here. Obviously, you need to update the already existing similar line seen here:

```
TARGET = CopyMakeBorder_Plugin
```

4. Similar to the previous step, we need to also update `DEFINES` accordingly:

```
DEFINES += COPYMAKEBORDER_PLUGIN_LIBRARY
```

5. And, finally, make sure the `HEADERS` and `SOURCES` entries in the `pro` file are also updated, as seen here, and then save and close the `pro` file:

```
SOURCES += \
    copymakeborder_plugin.cpp
HEADERS += \
    copymakeborder_plugin.h \
    copymakeborder_plugin_global.h
```

6. Now, open the `computer_vision.pro` file using Qt Creator. This will open up the entire `Computer_Vision` project, which is `Qt Multi-Project`. Qt allows the handling of multiple projects in a single container project, or as it is called by Qt itself, a `subdirs` project type. Unlike a regular Qt Widgets application project, `subdirs` projects usually (not necessarily) have a very simple and short `*.pro` file. A single line mentioning the `TEMPLATE` type as `subdirs` and a `SUBDIRS` entry that lists all the project folders within the `subdirs` project folder. Let's open the `computer_vision.pro` file in **Qt Creator Code Editor** to see this for ourselves:

```
TEMPLATE = subdirs
SUBDIRS += \
mainapp \
template_plugin
```

7. Now, simply add `copymakeborder_plugin` to the list of entries. Your updated `computer_vision.pro` file should look like this:

```
TEMPLATE = subdirs
SUBDIRS += \
mainapp \
template_plugin \
copymakeborder_plugin
```

 Note that in all `qmake` (and basically in all Qt project files) definitions, if an entry is divided to multiple lines, we need to add \ in all but the last line, as seen in the preceding code blocks. We can write the same thing by removing \ and simply adding white-space characters between entries. The latter is not the recommended method, but it would still be correct.

8. Lastly, for this part, we need to update the contents of `copymakeborder_plugin` source and header files, because obviously, the class names, included header files, and even some compiler directives need to be updated. It is really frustrating to deal with those kinds of programming overheads, so let's use this opportunity to learn about one of the most useful tricks in Qt Creator, that is, the **Find in This Directory...** function of Qt Creator. You can use this to literally find (and replace) anything in a Qt project folder or subfolder. You will learn and use this technique when we want to avoid manually browsing through files and replacing pieces of code, one by one. To use it, you simply need to select the right folder from the **Projects** pane, right-click on it, and choose the **Find in This Directory ...** option. Let's do it with the `copymakeborder_plugin` project, as seen in the screenshot:

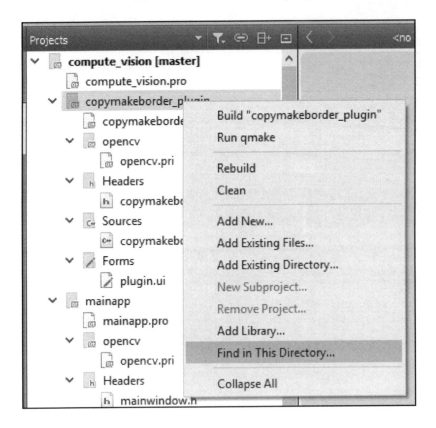

9. This will open up the **Search Results** pane at the bottom of the Qt Creator window, as seen in the following screenshot. Here, you have to enter TEMPLATE_PLUGIN in the **Search for:** field. Also, make sure the **Case sensitive** option is checked. Leave the rest of the options as they are and click on the **Search & Replace** button:

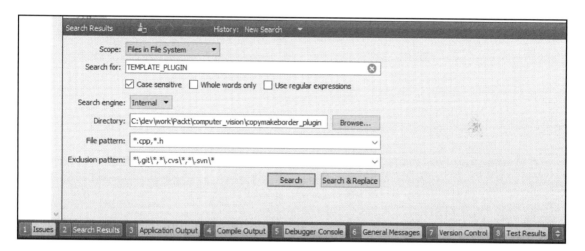

10. This will switch the **Search Results** pane to the **Replace** mode. Fill the **Replace with:** field with COPYMAKEBORDER_PLUGIN and click the **Replace** button. This is shown as follows:

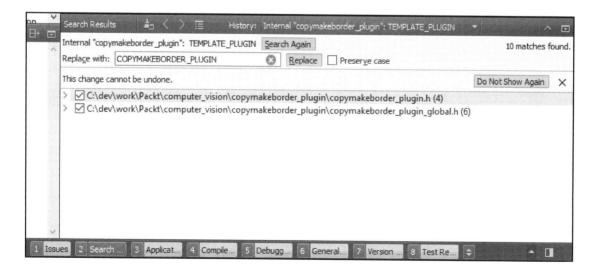

11. In the previous steps, we used the find and replace the functionality of Qt Creator to replace all `TEMPLATE_PLUGIN` entries with `COPYMAKEBORDER_PLUGIN`. Use the same skill and replace all `template_plugin` entries with `copymakeborder_plugin`, and all `Template_Plugin` entries with `CopyMakeBorder_Plugin`. With this, our new plugin project is ready to be programmed and finally used in the `Computer_Vision` project.

All of the preceding steps in our first example project in this chapter were meant only for preparing a plugin project, and, from now on, if and whenever it is needed, we will refer to these same steps as **Cloning or (Copying) the Template Plugin** to create the X plugin, whereas X in this example was simply `copymakeborder_plugin`. This will help us avoid a lot of repetitive instructions, and, at the same time, will allow us to focus more on learning new OpenCV and Qt skills. By going through the preceding steps, as long and exhausting as they may seem, we will avoid dealing with reading images, displaying images, choosing the right language, choosing the right theme and style, and so many other tasks since they are all in a single sub-project of the `Computer_Vision` project, called `mainapp`, which is simply a **Qt Widgets Application** responsible for taking care of all tasks that should not concern a plugin performing a specific computer vision task. In the following steps, we will simply fill in the existing functions of the plugin and create its required GUI. Then, we can copy the built plugin library files to the `cvplugins` folder beside the `Computer_Vision` executable, and when we run `mainapp` in the `Computer_Vision` project, each plugin will be displayed as an entry in `Plugins` from the main menu, including the newly added ones. The same pattern will be followed in all examples for the rest of the book, for the most part at least, meaning that unless we need to specifically change part of the plugin or the main app, all instructions regarding the clone and creating of the new plugin (preceding steps) will be omitted.

As it was mentioned in the previous chapters, it's always a good idea to run `qmake` manually after changing the `*.pro` file (or files). Simply right-click on the project from the **Projects** pane in Qt Creator and click on **Run qmake**.

12. It's time to write the codes for our plugin and create its GUI accordingly. Open the `plugin.ui` file and make sure its user interface includes the following widgets. Also, pay attention to the `objectName` values of the widgets. Notice that the layout of the entire `PluginGui` file is set to a grid layout, shown as follows:

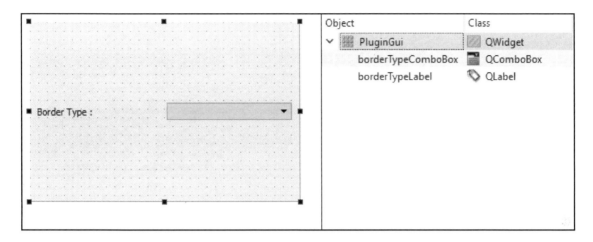

13. Set the `size Policy/Horizontal Policy` property of `borderTypeLabel` to `Fixed`. This will ensure that the label occupies a fixed horizontal space according to its width.

14. Add a method for the `currentIndexChanged(int)` signal of the `borderTypeComboBox` widget by right-clicking on it, selecting **Go to slot ...**, choosing the mentioned signal, and clicking on the **OK** button. Then, write the following line of code in the newly created function (or slot, to be precise) for this signal:

```
emit updateNeeded();
```

The purpose of this signal is to tell `mainapp` that, after a change in the combo box's selected item, the plugin may produce different results and that `mainapp` may want to update its GUI based on this signal. You can check the source code for the `mainapp` project and you'll notice that this signal from all plugins is connected to a relevant slot in `mainapp`, which simply calls the `processImage` function of the plugin.

15. Now, in the `copymakeborder_plugin.cpp` file, add the following piece of code to its `setupUi` function. The contents of the `setupUi` function should look like this:

```
ui = new Ui::PluginGui;
ui->setupUi(parent);
QStringList items;
items.append("BORDER_CONSTANT");
items.append("BORDER_REPLICATE");
items.append("BORDER_REFLECT");
```

```
items.append("BORDER_WRAP");
items.append("BORDER_REFLECT_101");
ui->borderTypeComboBox->addItems(items);
connect(ui->borderTypeComboBox,
SIGNAL(currentIndexChanged(int)),
this,
SLOT(on_borderTypeComboBox_currentIndexChanged(int)));
```

We are already familiar with the starting UI-related calls, which are almost identical to the same calls in every **Qt Widgets Application**, as we learned about them in the previous chapters. After that, we fill our combo box with relevant items that are simply the entries in the `cv::BorderTypes` enum. Each item index value will be the same as their corresponding enum values if inserted in this order. Finally, we will manually connect all of the signals to their relevant slots in the plugin. Note that this is slightly different from a regular **Qt Widgets Application**, in which you don't need to connect signals and slots that are name-compatible with each other, since they are connected automatically via a call to `QMetaObject::connectSlotsByName` in the code files automatically generated by UIC (refer to `Chapter 3`, *Creating a Comprehensive Qt+OpenCV Project*, about UIC).

16. Finally, update the `processImage` function in the plugin, as seen here:

```
int top, bot, left, right;
top = bot = inputImage.rows/2;
left = right = inputImage.cols/2;
cv::copyMakeBorder(inputImage,
    outputImage,
    top,
    bot,
    left,
    right,
ui->borderTypeComboBox->currentIndex());
```

Here, we will call the `copyMakeBorder` function that is similarly called inside functions that need to deal with an assumption about the non-existing pixels outside of an image. We will simply assume that the added border to the top and bottom of the image is half the image height, and the added border to the left and right of the image is half the image width. As for the `borderType` parameter, we will simply get it from the selected item on the plugin GUI.

Everything is completed and we are ready to test our plugin. Make sure that you build the entire `Computer_Vision` multi-project by right-clicking on it from the **Projects** pane and selecting **Rebuild** (to make sure all is cleaned and rebuilt) from the menu. Then, go to the plugin `Build` folder, copy the library file from there and paste it into the `cvplugins` folder beside the `mainapp` executable file (in the main app `Build` folder), and finally run `mainapp` from Qt Creator.

As soon as `mainapp` is started, you'll be faced with an error message (if the plugins are not copied or have a wrong format) or you will end up in the `Computer_Vision` application main window. You can then choose the plugin we just built from the **Plugins** menu of `mainapp` if it's not already selected. You can see the GUI we designed for the plugin inside the group box in the main window of `mainapp`. Then, you can open or save the contents of the graphics scene using the main menu. Try opening a file and then switching between different choices in the plugin combo box. You can also view the original image by checking the **View Original Image** checkbox. Here's a screenshot:

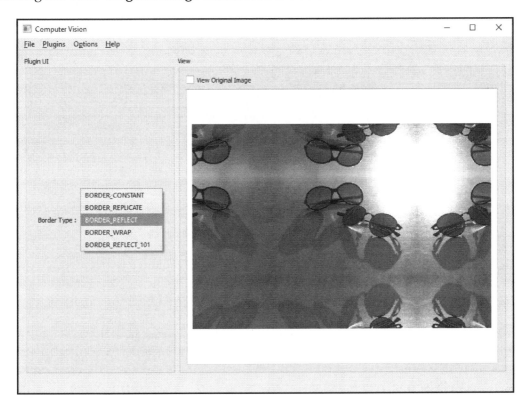

Choose any other **Border Type** from the combo box and you'll immediately notice how the resulting image changes. It's important to note that BORDER_REFLECT_101, which is also the default border type (if you don't specify one in OpenCV filtering and similar functions), is quite similar to BORDER_REFLECT, but it does not repeat the last pixel before the border. See the OpenCV documentation pages of cv::BorderTypes for more information about this. Here are the results, which are, as it was mentioned before, the same for each and every OpenCV function that needs to deal with similar kinds of interpolation of external (non-existent) pixels:

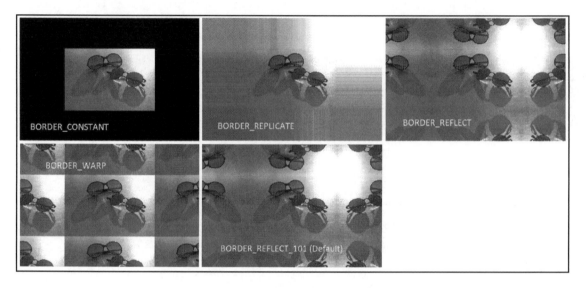

That's it. We are now ready to start with the filtering functions available in OpenCV.

# Filtering functions in OpenCV

All filtering functions in OpenCV take an image and produce an image of the exact same size and channels. As it was mentioned before, they all take a borderType parameter too, which we just finished experimenting with and learning about. Other than that, each filtering function has its own required parameters that configure its behavior. Here is a list of available OpenCV filtering functions with their descriptions and how they are used. At the end of the list, you can get a link to a single example plugin (called filter_plugin) and its source code, which includes most of the filters mentioned in the following list, with GUI controls to experiment with different parameters and settings for each one:

- `bilateralFilter`: This can be used to get a `Bilateral Filtered` copy of an image. Depending on the sigma values and diameter, you can get an image that may not look too different from the original, or a cartoonish looking image (if sigma values are high enough). Here's an example code of the `bilateralFilter` function at work as a plugin for our application:

```
bilateralFilter(inpMat,outMat,15,200,200);
```

This is the screenshot of the `bilateralFilter` function:

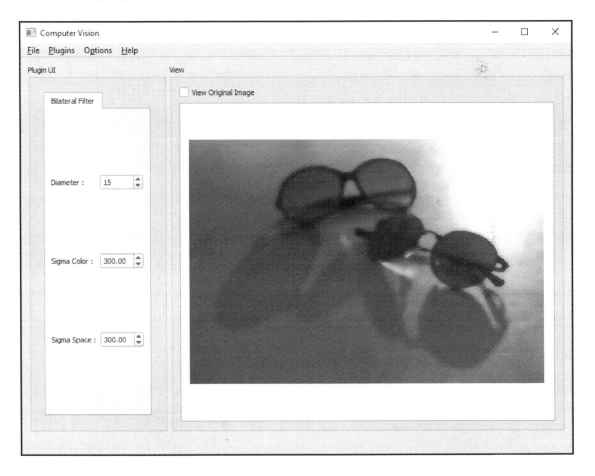

- blur, boxFilter, sqrBoxFilter, GaussianBlur, and medianBlur: These are all used for getting a smoothed version of the input image. All of these functions use a kernel size parameter, which is basically the same as a diameter parameter, and it's used to decide the diameter of the neighboring pixels from which the filtered pixel will be calculated. (These are some of the same filter functions we used in the earlier chapters of the book, although we didn't learn about their details.) GaussianBlur function needs to be provided with the Gaussian kernel standard deviation (sigma) parameters, both in the X and Y direction. (See OpenCV documentation for enough information about the mathematical source of these parameters.) Practically speaking, it's worth noting that the kernel size in the Gaussian filter must be an odd and positive number. Also, a higher sigma value would only have a significant effect on the result if the kernel size is also high enough. Here are a couple of examples of the smoothing filters mentioned (at left, GaussianBlur, at right, medianBlur), along with example function calls:

```
Size kernelSize(5,5);
blur(inpMat,outMat,kernelSize);
int depth = -1; // output depth same as source
Size kernelSizeB(10,10);
Point anchorPoint(-1,-1);
bool normalized = true;
boxFilter(inutMat,outMat,depth,
    kernelSizeB,anchorPoint, normalized);
double sigma = 10;
GaussianBlur(inpMat,outMat,kernelSize,sigma,sigma);
int apertureSize = 10;
medianBlur(inpMat,outMat,apertureSize);
```

Following screenshots depict the result of Gaussian and Median blur along with a GUI used to set their parameters:

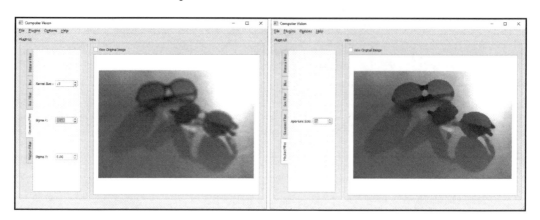

- `filter2D`: This function can be used to apply a custom filter to an image. The one important parameter that you need to provide to this function is the kernel matrix. This function is very powerful and it can produce a lot of different results including the same result as the blur functions we saw earlier on, and many other filters, depending on the provided kernel. Here are a couple of example kernels and how they are used, along with the resulting images. Make sure to try different kernels (you can search on the internet for tons of useful kernel matrices) and experiment with this function for yourself:

```
// Sharpening image
Matx33f f2dkernel(0, -1, 0,
                  -1, 5, -1,
                  0, -1, 0);
int depth = -1; // output depth same as source
filter2D(inpMat,outMat,depth,f2dkernel);

*****

// Edge detection
Matx33f f2dkernel(0, +1.5, 0,
                  +1.5, -6, +1.5,
                  0, +1.5, 0);
int depth = -1; // output depth same as source
   filter2D(inpMat,outMat,depth,f2dkernel);
```

The resulting image of the first kernel in the preceding code is seen on the left (which is a sharpened version of our image), while the second kernel, which produces an edge detection of the image, is visible on the right:

- Laplacian, Scharr, Sobel, and spatialGradient: These functions deal with image derivatives. Image derivatives are very important in computer vision since they can be used to detect regions with changes, or, better yet, significant changes (since that's one of the use cases of derivatives) in an image. Without going into too much of their theoretical and mathematical details, it can be mentioned that, in practice, they are used to deal with an edge or corner detection and are widely used by key point extraction methods in the OpenCV framework. In the preceding example and image, we also used a derivative calculation kernel. Here are a few examples of how they are used, and their resulting images. The screenshots are from the Computer_Vision project and filter_plugin, which there is a link for shortly after this list. You can always use Qt Widgets such as spin boxes, dials, and sliders to get different parameter values of OpenCV functions for better control over the function's behavior:

```
int depth = -1;
int dx = 1; int dy = 1;
int kernelSize = 3;
double scale = 5; double delta = 220;
Sobel(inpMat, outMat, depth,dx,dy,kernelSize,scale,delta);
```

The following is the output screenshot of the preceding code:

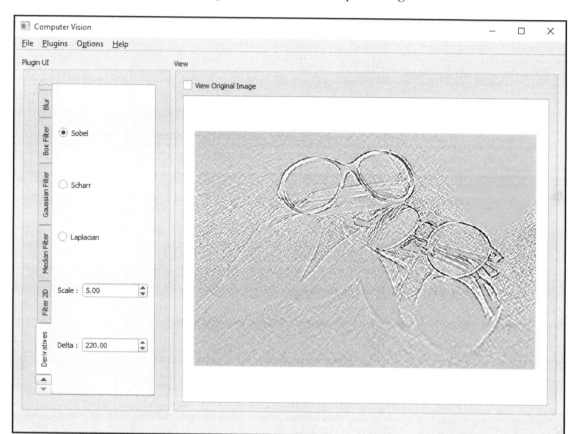

If we use the following code:

```
int depth = -1;
int dx = 1; int dy = 0;
double scale = 1.0; double delta = 100.0;
Scharr(inpMat,outMat,depth,dx,dy,scale,delta);
```

We'll end up with something similar to this:

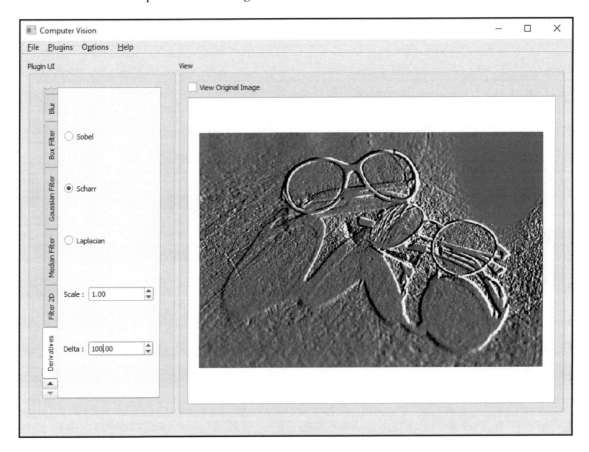

And for the following code:

```
int depth = -1; int kernelSize = 3;
double scale = 1.0; double delta = 0.0;
Laplacian(inpMat,outMat,depth, kernelSize,scale,delta);
```

Something similar to the following will be produced:

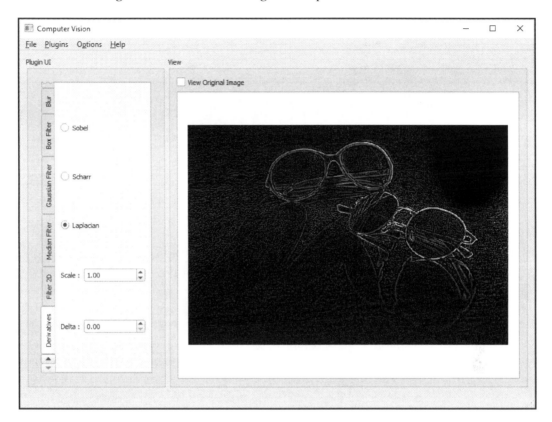

- `erode` and `dilate`: These functions, as it can be guessed from their names, are useful for getting an erosion and dilation effect. Both functions take a structuring element matrix that can be constructed by simply calling the `getStructuringElement` function. Optionally, you can choose to run the function (or iterate it) more than once to get a more and more eroded or dilated image. Here are examples of how both of these functions are used and their resulting images:

```
erode(inputImage,
outputImage,
getStructuringElement(shapeComboBox->currentIndex(),
Size(5,5)), // Kernel size
Point(-1,-1), // Anchor point (-1,-1) for default
iterationsSpinBox->value());
```

The following are the resulting images:

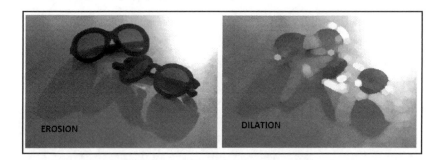

You can pass exactly the same parameters to the `dilate` function. In the preceding code, it is assumed that the shape of the structuring element is acquired by using a **Combo Box** widget, which can be `MORPH_RECT`, `MORPH_CROSS`, or `MORPH_ELLIPSE`. Also, the iteration count is set by using a **Spin Box** widget, which can be a number greater than zero.

Let's continue with the next function:

- `morphologyEx`: This function can be used to perform various morphological operations. It takes an operation type parameter along with identical parameters we used in the `dilate` and `erode` functions. Here are the parameters that can be passed to the `morphologyEx` function, along with their meanings:
    - `MORPH_ERODE`: This produces the same results as the `erode` function.
    - `MORPH_DILATE`: This produces the same results as the `dilate` function.
    - `MORPH_OPEN`: This can be used to perform an opening operation. It is the same as dilating an eroded image and is useful for removing small artifacts in the image.
    - `MORPH_CLOSE`: This can be used to perform a closing operation. It is the same as eroding a dilated image and is useful for removing small disconnections in lines and so on.
    - `MORPH_GRADIENT`: This function provides the outline of an image, and it's the same as the difference of an eroded and dilated version of the same image.
    - `MORPH_TOPHAT`: This can be used to get the difference between an image and its opening morph.

- `MORPH_BLACKHAT`: This can be used to get the difference between the closing of an image and the image itself.

Here is an example code, and, as you can see, the function call is very similar to that of dilating and erode. Again, we will assume that the morphology type and shape is selected using **Combo Box** widgets and iteration count using a `SpinBox`:

```
morphologyEx(inputImage,
    outputImage,
    morphTypeComboBox->currentIndex(),
    getStructuringElement(shapeComboBox->currentIndex(),
    Size(5,5)), // kernel size
    Point(-1,-1), // default anchor point
iterationsSpinBox->value());
```

And here are the resulting images of different morphology operations:

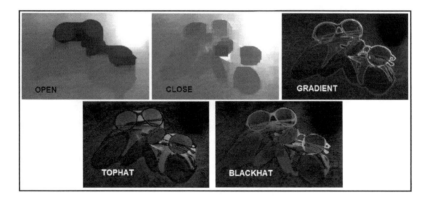

You can use the following link to get a copy of the source codes for `filter_plugin`, which is compatible with the `Computer_Vision` project and includes most of the image filtering functions you learned in this section. You can use this same plugin to test with and produce most of the images seen in this section. Try extending the plugin to control even more parameters or try adding, even more, functions to the plugin. Here is the link to  filter_plugin source codes: You can use the following link

```
https://github.com/PacktPublishing/Computer-Vision-with-OpenCV-3-and-Qt5/tree/
master/ch06/filter_plugin
```

# Image transformation capabilities

In this section, you will learn about the image transformation capabilities available in OpenCV. In general, there are two image transformation categories in OpenCV, called geometric and miscellaneous (which simply means everything else) transformations if you take a look at the OpenCV documentation. The reason for this is explained here.

**Geometric transformations**, as it can be guessed from their name, deal mostly with geometric properties of images, such as their size, orientation, shape, and so on. Note that a geometric transformation does not change the contents of the image, but it merely changes the form and shape of it by moving around the pixels of an image depending on the geometric transformation type. Same as what we saw with filtering images in the beginning of the previous section, geometric transformation functions also need to deal with the extrapolation of pixels outside of an image, or, simply put, making an assumption about the non-existing pixels when calculating the transformed image. For this, you can use the same `cv::BorderTypes` enum you learned about previously in this chapter, when we worked on the first example, `copymakeborder_plugin`.

Apart from that, and in addition to the required extrapolation, geometric transformation functions also need to deal with an interpolation of pixels, since the calculated position of pixels in a transformed image will be of type `float` (or `double`) and not `integer`, and since each pixel can only have a single color and its location must be specified with integer numbers, a decision needs to be made about the value of the pixel. To better understand this, let's consider one of the simplest geometric transformations, that is, resizing an image, which is done using the `resize` function in OpenCV. For instance, you can resize an image to half its size, and when this is done, the calculated new position of at least half of the pixels in the image will contain non-integer values. The pixel in location (2,2) will be in location (1,1) in the resized image, but the pixel in location (3,2) will need to be in the location (1.5,1) and so on. OpenCV provides a number of interpolation methods, which are defined in the `cv::InterpolationFlags` enum, and they include the following:

- `INTER_NEAREST`: This is for the nearest neighbor interpolation
- `INTER_LINEAR`: This is for bilinear interpolation
- `INTER_CUBIC`: This is for bicubic interpolation
- `INTER_AREA`: This is for a pixel area relation resampling
- `INTER_LANCZOS4`: This is for the Lanczos interpolation over a neighborhood of 8x8

Almost all of the geometric transformation functions need to be provided with a
`cv::BorderType` and `cv::InterpolationFlags` parameter to deal with the required
extrapolation and interpolation parameters.

# Geometric transformations

We will now start with some of the most important geometric transformations and then
learn about color spaces and how they are converted to each other along with some of the
widely used non-geometric (or miscellaneous) transformations. So, here they are:

- `resize`: This function can be used to resize an image. Here's an example of how
  it's used:

```
// Resize to half the size of input image
resize(inMat, outMat,
Size(), // an empty Size
0.5, // width scale factor
0.5, // height scale factor
INTER_LANCZOS4); // set the interpolation mode to Lanczos

// Resize to 320x240, with default interpolation mode
resize(inMat, outMat, Size(320,240));
```

- `warpAffine`: This function can be used to perform an affine transformation. You
  need to provide this function with a proper transform matrix, which can be
  obtained using the `getAffineTransform` function.
  The `getAffineTransform` function must be provided with two triangles (source
  and transformed), or, in other words, two set of three points. Here's an example:

```
Point2f triangleA[3];
Point2f triangleB[3];

triangleA[0] = Point2f(0 , 0);
triangleA[1] = Point2f(1 , 0);
triangleA[2] = Point2f(0 , 1);

triangleB[0] = Point2f(0, 0.5);
triangleB[1] = Point2f(1, 0.5);
triangleB[2] = Point2f(0.5, 1);

Mat affineMat = getAffineTransform(triangleA, triangleB);

warpAffine(inputImage,
outputImage,
```

```
affineMat,
inputImage.size(), // output image size, same as input
INTER_CUBIC, // Interpolation method
BORDER_WRAP); // Extrapolation method
```

Here is the resulting image:

You can also use the `warpAffine` function to perform a rotation of the source image. Simply use the `getRotationMatrix2D` function to get the transform matrix we used in the preceding code and use it again with the `warpAffine` function. Note that this method can be used to perform a rotation of any degrees and not just 90 degrees and its multipliers. Here's an example code that rotates the source image −45.0 degrees around the center of the image. Optionally, you can also scale the output image; in this example, we scale the output image to half the size of the source image while rotating it:

```
Point2f center = Point(inputImage.cols/2,
    inputImage.rows/2);
double angle = -45.0;
double scale = 0.5;
Mat rotMat = getRotationMatrix2D(center, angle, scale);

warpAffine(inputImage,
           outputImage,
           rotMat,
           inputImage.size(),
           INTER_LINEAR,
           BORDER_CONSTANT);
```

The following is the resulting output screenshot:

- `warpPerspective`: This function is useful for performing a perspective transform. Similar to the `warpAffine` function, this function also requires a transform matrix that can be obtained using the `findHomography` function. The `findHomography` function can be used to calculate homography changes between two set of points. Here is an example code in which we use two sets of corner points to calculate the homography change matrix (or the transform matrix for `warpPerspective`), and then use it to perform a perspective change. In this example, we have also set the extrapolation color value (optionally) to a dark shade of gray:

```
std::vector<Point2f> cornersA(4);
std::vector<Point2f> cornersB(4);

cornersA[0] = Point2f(0, 0);
cornersA[1] = Point2f(inputImage.cols, 0);
cornersA[2] = Point2f(inputImage.cols, inputImage.rows);
cornersA[3] = Point2f(0, inputImage.rows);

cornersB[0] = Point2f(inputImage.cols*0.25, 0);
cornersB[1] = Point2f(inputImage.cols * 0.90, 0);
cornersB[2] = Point2f(inputImage.cols, inputImage.rows);
cornersB[3] = Point2f(0, inputImage.rows * 0.80);
```

```
Mat homo = findHomography(cornersA, cornersB);
warpPerspective(inputImage,
                outputImage,
                homo,
                inputImage.size(),
                INTER_LANCZOS4,
                BORDER_CONSTANT,
                Scalar(50,50,50));
```

The following is the resulting output screenshot:

- remap: This function is a very powerful geometric transformation function that can be used to perform a remapping of pixels from the source to the output image. This means that you can relocate a pixel from the source image to some other position in the destination image. You can simulate the same behavior of the previous transformations and many other transformations, provided that you create a correct mapping and pass it to this function. Here are a couple of examples that demonstrate the power of the remap function and how easily it can be used:

```
Mat mapX, mapY;
mapX.create(inputImage.size(), CV_32FC(1));
mapY.create(inputImage.size(), CV_32FC(1));
for(int i=0; i<inputImage.rows; i++)
for(int j=0; j<inputImage.cols; j++)
{
    mapX.at<float>(i,j) = j * 5;
    mapY.at<float>(i,j) = i * 5;
}
```

```
remap(inputImage,
  outputImage,
  mapX,
  mapY,
  INTER_LANCZOS4,
  BORDER_REPLICATE);
```

As seen in the preceding code, apart from the input and output images, and interpolation and extrapolation parameters, we need to provide the mapping matrices, one for the X direction and one for the Y direction. Here is the result of the remapping from the preceding code. It simply makes the image five times smaller (note that the image size stays the same in the `remap` function, but the contents are basically squeezed five times the original size). This is shown in the following screenshot:

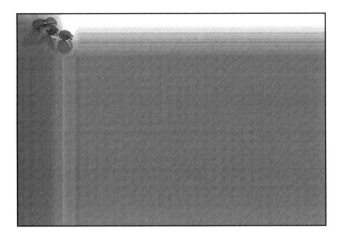

You can try a lot of different remapping of images by simply replacing the code within the two `for` loops, and fill the `mapX` and `mapY` matrices with different values. Here are a few more remapping examples:

Consider the first example:

```
// For a vertical flip of the image
mapX.at<float>(i,j) = j;
mapY.at<float>(i,j) = inputImage.rows-i;
```

Consider the following example:

```
// For a horizontal flip of the image
mapX.at<float>(i,j) = inputImage.cols - j;
mapY.at<float>(i,j) = i;
```

It's usually better to convert the OpenCV image coordinates to the standard coordinate system (Cartesian coordinate system) and deal with x and y in terms of standard coordinates, and then convert them back to the OpenCV coordinate system. The reason for this is simply the fact that the coordinate system we learn in school or in any geometry book or course uses the Cartesian coordinate system. Another reason is the fact that it also provides negative coordinates, which allow much more flexibility when dealing with transformations. Here's an example:

```
Mat mapX, mapY;
mapX.create(inputImage.size(), CV_32FC(1));
mapY.create(inputImage.size(), CV_32FC(1));

// Calculate the center point
Point2f center(inputImage.cols/2,
               inputImage.rows/2);

for(int i=0; i<inputImage.rows; i++)
  for(int j=0; j<inputImage.cols; j++)
  {
    // get i,j in standard coordinates, thus x,y
    double x = j - center.x;
    double y = i - center.y;

    // Perform a mapping for X and Y
    x = x*x/500;
    y = y;

    // convert back to image coordinates
    mapX.at<float>(i,j) = x + center.x;
    mapY.at<float>(i,j) = y + center.y;
  }

remap(inputImage,
      outputImage,
      mapX,
      mapY,
      INTER_LANCZOS4,
      BORDER_CONSTANT);
```

Here's the result of the mapping operation in the preceding code example:

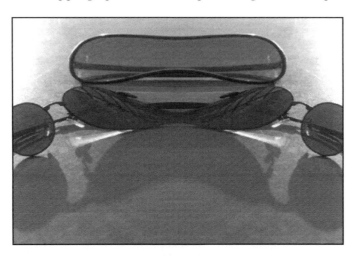

Another—and a very important—usage of the `remap` function is for correcting lens distortion in images. You can use the `initUndistortRectifyMap` and `initWideAngleProjMap` functions to get the required mappings in the X and Y direction for the distortion correction and then pass them to the `remap` function.

You can use the following link to get a copy of the source code for `transform_plugin`, which is compatible with the `Computer_Vision` project and includes the transformation functions you learned in this section. You can use this same plugin to test with and produce most of the images seen in this section. Try extending the plugin to control even more parameters, or try different mapping operations and experiment with different images for yourself. Here is the link to `transform_plugin` source codes:

`https://github.com/PacktPublishing/Computer-Vision-with-OpenCV-3-and-Qt5/tree/master/ch06/transform_plugin`

# Miscellaneous transformations

**Miscellaneous transformations** deal with a variety of other tasks that cannot be considered geometric transformations, such as color space (and format) conversion, applying color maps, Fourier transformation, and so on. Let's take a look at them.

# Colors and color spaces

Simply put, a color space is a model used to represent the color values of the pixels in an image. Strictly speaking, a color in computer vision consists of one or more numeric values, each corresponding to a channel, speaking in terms of the OpenCV `Mat` class. Thus, the color space is the model that defines how these numeric value (or values) are translated into colors. Let's take an example case to better understand this. One of the most popular color spaces (sometimes also referred to as image format, especially in Qt framework) is the RGB color space, in which a color is made out of a combination of red, green, and blue colors. RGB color space is widely used by TVs, monitors, LCDs, and similar display screens. Another example would be the CMYK (or **CMYB (Cyan, Maroon, Yellow, Black**)) color space, which, as it can be guessed, is a four channel color space, and it's mostly used in color printers. There are many other color spaces, each with their own advantages and use cases, but we'll suffice with the given examples as we'll focus mostly on the conversion of uncommon color spaces to more common ones, especially grayscale and BGR (note that B and R are swapped in BGR, otherwise it's similar to RGB) color space, which is the default color space in most OpenCV functions dealing with color images.

As we just mentioned, in computer vision science and consequently in the OpenCV framework, it is often necessary to convert color spaces to each other, since some properties of images are usually much more easily distinguished in certain color spaces. Also, as we have already learned in the previous chapters, we can easily display a BGR image using a Qt Widget, but the same cannot be said for the other color spaces.

OpenCV frameworks allow conversion between different color spaces using the `cvtColor` function. This function simply takes the input and output images along with a conversion code, which is an entry in the `cv::ColorConversionCodes` enum. Here are a couple of examples:

```
// Convert BGR to HSV color space
cvtColor(inputImage, outputImage, CV_BGR2HSV);

// Convert Grayscale to RGBA color space
cvtColor(inputImage, outputImage, CV_GRAY2RGBA);
```

OpenCV framework provides a function (similar to the `remap` function but quite different in nature) called `applyColorMap`, which can be used to map colors from the input image to other colors in the output image. You simply need to provide it with an input image, an output image, and a color mapping type from the `cv::ColormapTypes` enum. Here's a simple example:

```
applyColorMap(inputImage, outputImage, COLORMAP_JET);
```

The following is the output screenshot of the preceding code:

You can use the following link to get a copy of the source code for `color_plugin`, which is compatible with the `Computer_Vision` project and includes the color mapping function you learned in this section, controlled by a proper user interface. Using the source code provided here, try different color mapping operations and experiment with different images by yourself. Here is the link to color_plugin source codes:

```
https://github.com/PacktPublishing/Computer-Vision-with-OpenCV-3-and-Qt5/tree/
master/ch06/color_plugin
```

# Image thresholding

In computer vision science, thresholding is a method of image segmentation, which itself is the process of distinguishing between groups of related pixels, either in terms of intensity, color, or any other image properties. The OpenCV framework provides a number of functions to deal with image segmentation in general; however, in this section, you will learn about two of the most basic (although widely used) image segmentation methods in the OpenCV framework (and in computer vision): `threshold` and `adaptiveThreshold`. So, without wasting any more words, here they are:

- `threshold`: This function can be used to apply a fixed-level threshold to an image. Although it is possible to use this function with a multi-channel image, it is usually used on a single channel (or grayscale) image to create a binary image with the accepted pixels that pass the threshold level and the ones that do not. Let's explain this with an example scenario and one that you can face a lot. Let's assume we need to detect the darkest parts of an image, in other words, black colors in the image. Here's how we can use the threshold function to filter out only the pixels in the image, which have a pixel value that is almost black:

```
cvtColor(inputImage, grayScale, CV_BGR2GRAY);
threshold(grayScaleIn,
        grayScaleOut,
        45,
        255,
        THRESH_BINARY_INV);
cvtColor(grayScale, outputImage, CV_GRAY2BGR);
```

In the preceding code, first, we convert our input image to grayscale color space and then apply the threshold function, then convert back the result to BGR color space. Here is the resulting output image:

In the preceding example code, we used `THRESH_BINARY_INV` as the threshold type parameter; however, if we had used `THRESH_BINARY`, we would have gotten an inverted version of the result. The `threshold` function simply gives us all pixels with a value greater than the threshold value parameter, which is `40` in our preceding example.

Next one is `adaptiveThreshold`:

- `adaptiveThreshold`: This can be used to apply an adaptive threshold to a grayscale image. This function, depending on the adaptive method passed to it (`cv::AdaptiveThresholdTypes`), can be used to calculate the threshold value of each pixel individually, and automatically. However, you still need to pass a maximum threshold value, a block size (that can be 3, 5, 7, and so on), and a constant value that will be deducted from the calculated mean value for the blocks, which can be zero. Here's an example:

```
cvtColor(inputImage, grayScale, CV_BGR2GRAY);
adaptiveThreshold(grayScale,
                  grayScale,
                  255,
                  ADAPTIVE_THRESH_GAUSSIAN_C,
                  THRESH_BINARY_INV,
                  7,
                  0);
cvtColor(grayScale, outputImage, CV_GRAY2BGR);
```

Same as before, and what we did in the threshold function, we will convert the image color space from BGR to grayscale first, then apply the adaptive threshold, and finally convert it back. Here is the result of the preceding example code:

Use the following link to get a copy of the source codes for `segmentation_plugin`, which is compatible with the `Computer_Vision` project and includes the thresholding function you learned in this section, controlled by a proper user interface:

`https://github.com/PacktPublishing/Computer-Vision-with-OpenCV-3-and-Qt5/tree/master/ch06/segmentation_plugin`

# Discrete Fourier transform

Fourier transformation can be used to get the underlying frequencies out of a time function. **Discrete Fourier transformation** or **DFT**, on the other hand, is a method to calculate the underlying frequencies of a sampled time function (thus discrete). That is a purely mathematical definition and a very short one in that sense, so to put it in terms of computer vision and image processing, you need to first try to think about an image (a grayscale image) as a discrete distribution of points on a three dimensional space, where X and Y of each discrete element are the pixel position in the image and Z is the intensity value of the pixel. If you are able to do that, then you can also imagine that there is such a function that can produce those points in space. With such a picture in mind, Fourier transformation is the method of converting that function to its underlying frequencies. Don't worry if you still feel lost. If you are unfamiliar with the concept, you should definitely consider reading a bit about the mathematics of Fourier transformation online, or you can even consult your mathematics professor.

In mathematics, Fourier analysis is a method of deriving information based on a Fourier transformation of an input data. Again, to give this a more computer vision oriented sense of the meaning, a DFT of an image can be used to derive information not visible in the first place and in the original image itself. This highly varies, depending on the target field of a computer vision application, but we'll see an example case to better understand how DFT is used. So, to start, you can use the `dft` function in OpenCV to get a DFT of an image. Notice that since an image (grayscale) is a 2D matrix, `dft` will actually perform a 2D Discrete Fourier transformation, which produces a function of frequency with complex values. Here's how a DFT is performed in OpenCV on a grayscale (single channel) image:

1. We need to start by getting the most optimal size to calculate a DFT of an image. A DFT transform performed on an array that has a size which is a power of two (2, 4, 8, 16, and so on) is a much faster, more efficient process. A DFT transform performed on an array which has a size that is the product of 2 is also quite efficient. So, `getOptimalDFTSize`, which uses the principle we just mentioned, is used to getting the smallest size greater than our image size, which is optimal for performing DFT. Here is how it's done:

   ```
   int optH = getOptimalDFTSize( grayImg.rows );
   int optW = getOptimalDFTSize( grayImg.cols );
   ```

2. Next, we need to create an image with this optimal size, filling the pixels in the added width and height with zeros. For this reason, we can use the `copyMakeBorder` function that we learned about earlier on in this chapter:

   ```
   Mat padded;
   copyMakeBorder(grayImg,
                  padded,
                  0,
                  optH - grayImg.rows,
                  0,
                  optW - grayImg.cols,
                  BORDER_CONSTANT,
                  Scalar::all(0));
   ```

3. Now, we have our optimal sized image inside `padded`. What we need to do now is to form a two-channel `Mat` class suitable for feeding into the `dft` function. This can be done using the merge function. Note that, since `dft` needs a floating-point `Mat` class, we also need to convert our optimal sized image to a `Mat` class with floating point elements, as seen here:

   ```
   Mat channels[] = {Mat_<float>(padded),
                     Mat::zeros(padded.size(),
   ```

```
                CV_32F) };
    Mat complex;
    merge(channels, 2, complex);
```

4. Everything is ready to perform a Discrete Fourier transformation, so we will simply call it as seen here. The result is also stored in `complex`, which will be a complex value `Mat` class:

```
    dft(complex, complex);
```

5. Now, we need to split the complex result to its consisting real and complex parts. We can use the `channels` array again for this purpose, as seen here:

```
    split(complex, channels);
```

6. Now, we need to convert the complex result to its magnitude using the `magnitude` function; this will be the result suitable for displaying purposes, after a few more transformations later on. Since `channels` now contain the two channels of the complex result, we can use it in the `magnitude` function, seen as follows:

```
    Mat mag;
    magnitude(channels[0], channels[1], mag);
```

7. The `magnitude` function result (if you try to view the elements) will be quite big, so much that it is not possible to visualize with the possible scale for grayscale images. So, we will use the following lines of code to convert it to the much smaller logarithmic scale:

```
    mag += Scalar::all(1);
    log(mag, mag);
```

8. Since we calculated the DFT using the optimal size, we now need to crop the result if it has an odd number of rows or columns. This can be easily done using the following code snippet. Note that a bitwise `and` operation with $-2$ is used for removing the last bit in a positive integer number and making it an even number, or, basically, the reverse of what we did when creating the `padded` image with extra pixels:

```
    mag = mag(Rect(
                    0,
                    0,
                    mag.cols & -2,
                    mag.rows & -2));
```

9. Since the result is a spectrum displaying the waves created by the frequency functions that were obtained by the DFT, we should move the origin of the result to the center of it, which is currently at the top-left corner. We can use the following code to create four ROIs for the four quarters of the result, and then swap the quarter at the top-left of the result with the one at the bottom-right, and also swap the quarter at the top-right with the one at the bottom-left:

```
int cx = mag.cols/2;
int cy = mag.rows/2;

Mat q0(mag, Rect(0, 0, cx, cy));    // Top-Left
Mat q1(mag, Rect(cx, 0, cx, cy));   // Top-Right
Mat q2(mag, Rect(0, cy, cx, cy));   // Bottom-Left
Mat q3(mag, Rect(cx, cy, cx, cy));  // Bottom-Right

Mat tmp;
q0.copyTo(tmp);
q3.copyTo(q0);
tmp.copyTo(q3);

q1.copyTo(tmp);
q2.copyTo(q1);
tmp.copyTo(q2);
```

10. Trying to visualize the result will still not be possible, unless we scale the result into correct grayscale range (0 to 255) using the `normalize` function as seen here:

```
normalize(mag, mag, 0, 255, CV_MINMAX);
```

11. Using the `imshow` function in OpenCV, we can already view the result, but to be able to view it in Qt widgets, we need to convert it to the correct depth (8 bits) and a number of channels, so we'll need the following as the last step:

```
Mat_<uchar> mag8bit(mag);
cvtColor(mag8bit, outputImage, CV_GRAY2BGR);
```

Now you can try running this on our test image. The result will be the following:

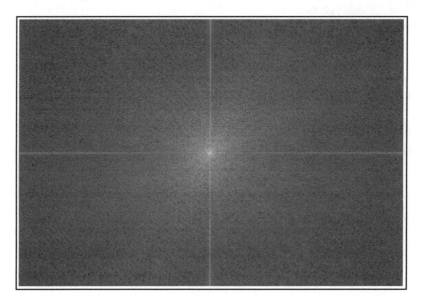

What you see here in the result should be interpreted as waves viewed directly from above, in which the brightness of each pixel is, in fact, a representation of its height. Try running the same process on different kinds of each images to see how the result changes. Apart from visually inspecting the DFT results (depending on the use case), a very special use case of DFT, which we'll leave for you to try for yourself, is to perform an inverse DFT after masking out parts of the DFT result, to get the original image back. This process can alter the original image in many ways, depending on the part of the DFT result that is filtered. This subject depends quite a lot on the contents of the original image and has deep ties to the mathematical properties of the DFT, but it is definitely worth researching and experimenting with. To conclude, you can perform an inverse DFT by calling the same `dft` function and passing an additional `DCT_INVERSE` parameter to it. Obviously, this time, the input should be a calculated DFT of an image and the output will be the image itself.

Reference: OpenCV documentation, Discrete Fourier Transform.

# Drawing in OpenCV

It's impossible to ignore drawing text and shapes on an image when the subject is OpenCV and computer vision in general. For countless reasons, you will need to draw (output) some text or shapes on the output images. For example, you may want to write a program that prints the date of the image (or images) on it. Or you may want to draw a square around faces in the image after performing a face detection. Even though Qt framework also provides quite powerful functions to deal with such tasks, it is also possible to use OpenCV itself to draw on images. In this section, you will learn about using OpenCV drawing functions one by one, which are surprisingly very easy to use, along with example codes and output results.

Drawing functions in OpenCV accept an input and output image, quite understandably, along with a few parameters which are common to most of them. Here are the mentioned common parameters of drawing functions in OpenCV along with their meaning and possible values:

- `color`: This parameter is simply the color of the object being drawn on the image. It can be created using scalar and needs to be in BGR format (for color images) as it is the default color format for most OpenCV functions.
- `thickness`: This parameter, which is set to 1 by default, is the thickness of the outlines of the object being drawn on the image. This parameter is specified in terms of pixels.
- `lineType`: This can be one of the entries in the `cv::LineTypes` enum, and it decides the detailing of the outlines of the object being drawn on the image. As seen in the following image, `LINE_AA` (antialiasing) is smoother, but it is also drawn slower than `LINE_4` and `LINE_8` (default `lineType`). Following image depicts the difference between `cv::LineTypes`:

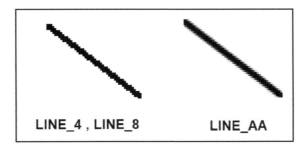

- `shift`: This parameter is used only in case the points and locations provided to drawing functions include fractional bits. In this case, the value of each point is first shifted according to the shift parameter using the following conversion function. In case of standard integer point values, the shift value will be zero, which also makes the following conversion have no effect on the result:

```
Point(X , Y) = Point( X * pow(2,-shift), Y * pow(2,-shift) )
```

Now, let's start with the actual drawing functions:

- `line`: This can be used to draw a line on an image by taking the start and end points of the line. The following sample code draws an X mark on the image (two lines connecting the corners of the image) with a thickness of 3 pixels and with red coloring:

```
cv::line(img,
         Point(0,0),
         Point(img.cols-1,img.rows-1),
         Scalar(0,0,255),
         3,
         LINE_AA);
cv::line(img,
         Point(img.cols-1,0),
         Point(0, img.rows-1),
         Scalar(0,0,255),
         3,
         LINE_AA);
```

- `arrowedLine`: This is used to draw an arrowed line. The direction of the arrow is decided by the end (or second) point, otherwise, the usage of this function is identical to `line`. Here's an example code to draw an arrowed line from the top almost toward the center of the image:

```
cv::arrowedLine(img,
                Point(img.cols/2, 0),
                Point(img.cols/2, img.rows/3),
                Scalar(255,255,255),
                5,
                LINE_AA);
```

- `rectangle`: This can be used to draw a rectangle on the image. You can either pass a rectangle (`Rect` class) to it or two points (`Point` class), first one corresponding to the top-left corner of the rectangle and second one corresponding to the bottom-right corner of the rectangle. The following is an example rectangle that is drawn at the center of the image:

```
cv::rectangle(img,
              Point(img.cols/4, img.rows/4),
              Point(img.cols/4*3, img.rows/4*3),
              Scalar(255,0,0),
              10,
              LINE_AA);
```

- `putText`: This function can be used to draw (or write or put) text on an image. Apart from the regular drawing parameters in the OpenCV drawing functions, you need to provide this function with the text that needs to be drawn on the image ,along with a font face and scale parameter. Font face can be one of the entries in the `cv::HersheyFonts` enum and scale is the font scaling which is font dependent. An example of the following code block can be used to write `Computer Vision` in an image:

```
cv::putText(img,
            "Computer Vision",
            Point(0, img.rows/2),
            FONT_HERSHEY_PLAIN,
            2,
            Scalar(255,255,255),
            2,
            LINE_AA);
```

The following screenshot is the result of all drawing examples we saw in this section when they are executed sequentially on our test image:

Apart from the drawing functions we saw in this section, OpenCV also provides functions to draw circles, polylines, ellipses, and so on. All of which are used in exactly the similar manner we saw in this chapter. Try using those functions to familiarize yourself with all drawing possibilities in OpenCV. You can always get the most updated list of drawing functions in OpenCV by referring to its documentation, which is very easily accessible from the front page of the OpenCV website (`https://opencv.org/`).

# Template matching

The OpenCV framework offers many different methods for object detection, tracking, and counting. Template matching is one of the most basic methods of object detection in OpenCV, yet, if it's used correctly and in conjunction with good threshold values, it can be used to effectively detect and count objects in an image. It is done by using a single function in OpenCV called the `matchTemplate` function.

The `matchTemplate` function takes an image as the input parameter. Consider it the image that will be searched for the object (or better yet, the scene that may contain the template) that we are interested in. It also takes a template as the second parameter. This template is also an image, but it's the one that will be searched for within the first image parameter. Another parameter required by this function, which is also the most important parameter and the one that decides the template matching method, is the `method` parameter, which can be one of the entries in the `cv::TemplateMatchModes` enum:

- TM_SQDIFF
- TM_SQDIFF_NORMED
- TM_CCORR
- TM_CCORR_NORMED
- TM_CCOEFF
- TM_CCOEFF_NORMED

If you are interested, you can visit the `matchTemplate` documentation page for the mathematical calculations done by each one of the preceding methods, but, practically speaking, you can understand the way each one of them performs by knowing how the `matchTemplate` function works in general.

The `matchTemplate` function slides the template of size `WxH` over an image of size `QxS` and compares the template with all overlapping parts of the image, using the method specified in the `method` parameter, then stores the result of the comparison in the `result Mat`. It is obvious that the image size (`QxS`) must be greater than the template size (`WxH`). It is important to note that the resulting `Mat` size is, in fact, `Q-WxS-H`, that is, the image height and width minus the template height and width. This is due to the fact that the sliding of the template happens only over the source image and not even a single pixel outside of it.

If one of the methods with `_NORMED` in their name is used for template matching, then there is no need for a normalization after the template matching function, since the result will be in the range between `0` and `1`; otherwise, we will need to normalize the result using the `normalize` function. After we have the normalized the result, we can use the `minMaxLoc` function to locate the global minimum (darkest point in the image) and global maximum (brightest point in the image) values in the resulting image. Remember, the `result Mat` class contains the result of comparison between the template and overlapping parts of the image. That means, depending on the template matching method used, either a global minimum or global maximum value location in the `result Mat` class is actually the best template match; therefore, the best candidate for our detection result. Let's assume we want to match the image seen on the left side, within the image seen on the right side of the following screenshot:

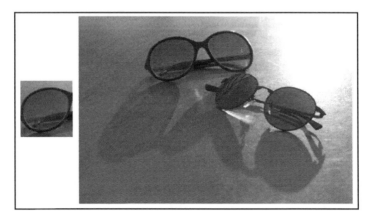

We can use the `matchTemplate` function for this reason. Here's an example case:

```
matchTemplate(img, templ, result, TM_CCORR_NORMED);
```

In the preceding function call, `img` is loaded with the image itself (image on the right) and `templ` is loaded with the template image (on the left) and `TM_CCORR_NORMED` is used as the template matching method. If we visualize `result` Mat in the preceding code (using the `imshow` function for simplicity), we'll have the following output. Notice the brightest point in the resulting image:

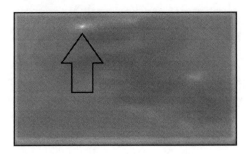

This is the best possible location for our template match. We can use the `minMaxLoc` function to find this location and draw a rectangle around it (the same size of our template) by using the drawing functions you learned about previously in this chapter. Here's an example:

```
double minVal, maxVal;
Point minLoc, maxLoc;
minMaxLoc(result, &minVal, &maxVal, &minLoc, &maxLoc);
rectangle(img,
          Rect(maxLoc.x, maxLoc.y, templ.cols, templ.rows),
          Scalar(255,255,255),
          2);
```

By visualizing `img`, we will have the following screenshot as an output:

It's worth noting that the `matchTemplate` function is not scale-invariant. This means it won't be able to match templates of various sizes inside the image, but only the same size of the one given to the function. Another use case of the `matchTemplate` function is to count the number of objects in an image. To be able to do this, you need to make sure you run the `matchTemplate` function inside a loop and remove the matched part from the source image after each successful matching so that it is not found in the next `matchTemplate` call. Try to write the code for this on your own as a very good example case for learning more about template matching and how it is used for template counting.

 Template counting is a widely used method for counting objects (or products) in a production line or flat surfaces, or counting similarly shaped and sized cells in a microscopic image, along with countless other similar use cases and applications.

# Summary

We are now familiar with some of the most widely used functions, enums, and classes in the OpenCV framework. Most of the skills you learned in this chapter are used almost in every computer vision application, one way or another. Starting from image filtering, which is one of the most initial steps in a computer vision process, up until image transformation methods and color space conversion, every computer vision application needs to have access to these methods, either to be able to perform a specific task or to optimize its performance in some way. In this chapter, you learned all about image filtering and geometric transformations. You learned how to use functions such as `remap` to perform countless image transformations. You also learned about color spaces and how to convert them to each other. Later on, we even used color mapping functions to map colors in an image to another set of colors. Then, you learned about image thresholding and how to extract parts of an image with a specific pixel value. As you'll see throughout your career or research in computer vision, thresholding is something that is required and used all the time and everywhere for countless reasons. After thresholding, you learned about drawing capabilities in the OpenCV framework. As mentioned before, Qt framework also provides tons of interfaces to deal with drawing tasks, but, still, it is inevitable that sometimes we may need to use OpenCV itself for the drawing tasks. Finally, we finished the chapter by learning about template matching and how it is used.

In `Chapter 7`, *Features and Descriptors*, we will dig deeper into the world of computer vision and the OpenCV framework by learning about key points and feature descriptors and how they can be used for object detection and matching. You will also learn about a number of key concepts such as histograms. You will learn what histograms are and how they are extracted and used in general. In `Chapter 7`, *Features and Descriptor*, we will also be the complementing chapter to the one we just finished, in which we will use most of the skills learned in this chapter along with the new set of skills related to image features and key points, to perform more sophisticated matching, comparison, and detection tasks in images.

# 7
# Features and Descriptors

In `Chapter 6`, *Image Processing in OpenCV*, we learned about image processing mostly in terms of the image content and pixels. We learned how to filter them, transform them, or play around with the pixel values in one way or another. Even to match a template, we simply used the raw pixel contents to get a result and find out if an object exists in part of an image or not. However, we still haven't learned about the algorithms that allow us to differentiate between objects of a different kind, not just based on their raw pixels, but also the collective meaning of an image based on its specific features. It is almost a trivial task for a human being to identify and recognize different types of faces, cars, written words, and almost any visible and visual object, given that they are not extremely similar. For us human beings, this happens in most cases without us even thinking about it. We can differentiate even between very similar faces, based on small and unique bits and pieces on the faces that our brain picks up, almost automatically, and again uses them to identify faces, whenever we see those faces again. Or, take, for example, brands of different cars. Most major car manufacturers have logos that are almost hacked into our brains. And our brains use that logo to differentiate car models (or manufacturers) quite easily. So, simply put, all the time that we are looking at our surrounding environment and everything in it, our brain, with the help of our eyes, searches for distinguishable pieces in any visual object (obviously, object can be anything in this context), and later on uses those pieces to identify the same, or similar visual objects. Of course, there is always a chance for error, even with the human brain and eyes, and there is also the fact that we might simply forget what a particular object (or face) looked like.

What we just described in the introduction paragraph is also the basis on which many computer vision algorithms that are used for the same purpose are created. In this chapter, you will learn about some of the most important classes and methods in the OpenCV framework, which allows us to find distinguishable pieces in images (or objects in images) called **features** (or keypoints). We will then move on to learn about descriptors, which are, as the name suggests, descriptions of the features we find. So, we will learn how to detect features in an image and then extract descriptors from features. These descriptors then can be used for many purposes in computer vision applications, including the comparison of two images, homography change detection, locating known objects inside an image, and many more. It is important to note that saving, processing, and basically performing any operation on features and descriptors of an image is usually a lot faster and easier than trying to achieve the same with the image itself, since features and descriptors are simply a bunch of numeric values that try to describe the image in one way or another, depending on the algorithm used to detect features and extract descriptors.

As you can easily guess from what we have seen so far, especially during the course of the previous chapters, both OpenCV and Qt frameworks are a huge collection of tools, classes, functions, and much more, that allow you to create powerful computer vision applications or any other type of applications for that matter. So, one thing that can be said for sure is that covering all and every piece of these frameworks in a book is impossible, and also fruitless; instead, since both of these frameworks are created in a highly structured manner, we can still have a clue about the classes or functions that we see and use for the first time, provided that we have a clear mind about the hierarchy of the underlying classes within these frameworks. This is almost completely true about classes and methods used to detect features and extract descriptors. That is why, in this chapter, we will start by going through the hierarchy of classes used in OpenCV for feature detection and descriptor extraction, and then we'll dive into the details of how they are used in practice.

In this chapter, we will cover the following topics:

- What are the algorithms in OpenCV?
- How to use existing OpenCV algorithms
- Detecting features (or keypoints) using the `FeatureDetector` classes
- Extracting descriptors using the `DescriptorExtractor` classes
- How to match descriptors and use it for detection
- How to draw a result of descriptor matching
- How to choose an algorithm for our use case

# Base of all algorithms – the Algorithm class

All algorithms in OpenCV, or better yet, at least the ones that are not too short and simple, are created as subclasses of the `cv::Algorithm` class. This class, as opposed to what you would normally expect, is not an abstract class, which means you can create instances of it, which simply do nothing. Even though this may be changed sometime in the future, it doesn't really affect the way we will access and use it. The way the `cv::Algorithm` class is used in OpenCV, and also the recommended way in case you want to create your own algorithms, is that first a subclass of `cv::Algorithm` that contains all required member functions for a specific purpose or goal gets created. Then, this newly created subclass can be again subclassed to create different implementations of the same algorithm. To better understand this, let's first see the `cv::Algorithm` class in detail. Here's (roughly) how it looks if you take a peek at the OpenCV source codes:

```
class Algorithm
{
  public:
  Algorithm();
  virtual ~Algorithm();
  virtual void clear();
  virtual void write(FileStorage& fs) const;
  virtual void read(const FileNode& fn);
  virtual bool empty() const;
  template<typename _Tp>
    static Ptr<_Tp> read(const FileNode& fn);
  template<typename _Tp>
    static Ptr<_Tp> load(const String& filename,
        const String& objname=String());
  template<typename _Tp>
    static Ptr<_Tp> loadFromString(const String& strModel,
        const String& objname=String());
  virtual void save(const String& filename) const;
  virtual String getDefaultName() const;
  protected:
  void writeFormat(FileStorage& fs) const;
};
```

First, let's see what the `FileStorage` and `FileNode` classes, which are used in the `cv::Algorithm` class are (and also many other OpenCV classes), and then go through the methods within the `cv::Algorithm` class:

- The `FileStorage` class can be used to easily write to and read from XML, YAML, and JSON files. This class is widely used in OpenCV to store various types of information produced or required by many algorithms. This class works almost like any other file reader/writer class, except the fact that it works with the mentioned file types.
- The `FileNode` class, which itself is a subclass of the `Node` class, is used to represent a single element in the `FileStorage` class. A `FileNode` class can be a single leaf in the collection of the `FileNode` elements or a container for other `FileNode` elements.

Apart from the two classes mentioned in the preceding list, OpenCV also has another class named `FileNodeIterator`, which, as the name suggests, can be used to iterate over nodes in an STL, like a loop. Let's see a small example that describes how the preceding mentioned classes are used in practice:

```
using namespace cv;
String str = "a random note";
double d = 999.001;
Matx33d mat = {1,2,3,4,5,6,7,8,9};
FileStorage fs;
fs.open("c:/dev/test.json",
    FileStorage::WRITE | FileStorage::FORMAT_JSON);
fs.write("matvalue", mat);
fs.write("doublevalue", d);
fs.write("strvalue", str);
fs.release();
```

Such a code in OpenCV will result in the creation of a JSON file, as follows:

```
{
  "matvalue": {
    "type_id": "opencv-matrix",
    "rows": 3,
    "cols": 3,
    "dt": "d",
    "data": [ 1.0, 2.0, 3.0, 4.0, 5.0, 6.0, 7.0, 8.0, 9.0 ]
  },
  "doublevalue": 9.9900099999999998e+02,
  "strvalue": "a random note"
}
```

As you can see, the `FileStorage` class almost takes care of everything in regard to making sure the structure of the JSON file is correct and everything is stored in such a way that it can be easily retrieved later on. It is usually better to check if opening a file was successful by using the `isOpened` function, which we simply skipped for the sake of simplicity. This whole process is known as **serializing a class or data structure**. Now, to read it back, we can do the following:

```
using namespace cv;
FileStorage fs;
fs.open("c:/dev/test.json",
    FileStorage::READ | FileStorage::FORMAT_JSON);
FileNode sn = fs["strvalue"];
FileNode dn = fs["doublevalue"];
FileNode mn = fs["matvalue"];
String str = sn;
Matx33d mat = mn;
double d = dn;
fs.release();
```

For the sake of readability, and also to demonstrate that the `FileStorage` class actually reads and creates instances of the `FileNode` class, we have assigned each value to `FileNode` and then to the variables themselves, but, quite obviously, you can directly assign the result of reading nodes to variables of suitable types. Both of these classes have a lot more than this to offer and they are definitely worth checking out for yourself, but it should be enough for us and the purpose of explaining how the `cv::Algorithm` class uses them. So, now that we learned that these classes can be used to easily store and retrieve a different kind of classes, and even OpenCV-specific types, we can dig deeper into the `cv::Algorithm` itself.

As you saw previously, in its declaration and also in its implementation, the `cv::Algorithm` class uses the mentioned classes to store and retrieve the state of an algorithm, meaning its underlying parameters, input or output values, and so on. And to do that, it provides methods that we'll go through very briefly.

 For now, do not worry about how they are used in detail, since, they are, in fact, reimplemented in the subclasses and the way most of them work is, in fact, dependent on the specific algorithm implementing it; so, let's only focus on the structure and how they are organized in OpenCV.

Here are the methods provided by the `cv::Algorithm` class:

- `read`: This has a few overloaded versions that can be used to read the state of an algorithm.
- `write`: This is similar to `read`, except it is used to save the state of an algorithm.
- `clear`: This can be used to clear the state of an algorithm.
- `empty`: This can be used to determine if an algorithm's state is empty. This means, for example, if it is correctly loaded (read) or not.
- `load`: This is almost the same as `read`.
- `loadFromString`: This is quite similar to `load` and `read`, except it reads and loads the state of an algorithm from a string.

Take a look at the `cv::Algorithm` documentation page (and especially its inheritance diagram) on the OpenCV website, and you'll immediately notice the huge number of classes in OpenCV that reimplement it. You can guess that they all have the functions previously mentioned. In addition to that, each one of them offers methods and functions that are specific to each and every one of them. Among the many classes that reimplement `cv::Algorithm`, there is a class named `Feature2D`, which is basically the class we will learn about in this chapter, and it is responsible for all feature detection and descriptor extraction algorithms existing in OpenCV. This class and its subclasses are known as **2D Features Framework** in OpenCV (consider it a sub-framework of OpenCV framework), and it's the subject of our next section in this chapter.

# The 2D Features Framework

As it was mentioned previously in this chapter, OpenCV provides classes to perform various feature detection and descriptor extraction algorithms created by computer vision researchers from all across the world. Just like any other complex algorithm implemented in OpenCV, feature detectors and descriptor extractors are also created by subclassing the `cv::Algorithm` class. This subclass is called `Feature2D`, and it contains various functions that are common to all feature detection and descriptor extraction classes. Basically, any class that can be used to detect features and extracts descriptors should be a subclass of `Featured2D`. OpenCV uses the following two class types for this purpose:

- `FeatureDetector`
- `DescriptorExtractor`

It's important to note that both of these classes are, in fact, just a different name for
Feature2D since they are created inside OpenCV using the following typedef statements
(we'll talk about the reason for this later on in this section):

```
typedef Feature2D FeatureDetector;
typedef Feature2D DescriptorExtractor;
```

It's also a good idea to see the declaration of the Feature2D class:

```
class Feature2D : public virtual Algorithm
{
  public:
  virtual ~Feature2D();
  virtual void detect(InputArray image,
    std::vector<KeyPoint>& keypoints,
    InputArray mask=noArray() );
  virtual void detect(InputArrayOfArrays images,
    std::vector<std::vector<KeyPoint> >& keypoints,
    InputArrayOfArrays masks=noArray() );
  virtual void compute(InputArray image,
    std::vector<KeyPoint>& keypoints,
    OutputArray descriptors );
  virtual void compute( InputArrayOfArrays images,
    std::vector<std::vector<KeyPoint> >& keypoints,
    OutputArrayOfArrays descriptors );
  virtual void detectAndCompute(InputArray image,
    InputArray mask,
    std::vector<KeyPoint>& keypoints,
    OutputArray descriptors,
    bool useProvidedKeypoints=false );
    virtual int descriptorSize() const;
    virtual int descriptorType() const;
    virtual int defaultNorm() const;
    void write( const String& fileName ) const;
    void read( const String& fileName );
    virtual void write( FileStorage&) const;
    virtual void read( const FileNode&);
    virtual bool empty() const;
};
```

Let's do a quick review of what's in the `Feature2D` class's declaration. First of all, it's a subclass of the `cv::Algorithm`, as we learned earlier. The read, write, and empty functions are simply reimplemented functions that existed in cv::Algorithm. However, the following functions are new and non-existent in cv::Algorithm, and they are basically additional functions that feature detectors and descriptor extractors will need:

- The `detect` function can be used to detect features (or keypoints) from an image or a set of images.
- The `compute` function can be used to extract (or compute) descriptors from keypoints.
- The `detectAndCompute` function can be used to perform both detect and compute with a single function.
- `descriptorSize`, `descriptorType`, and `defaultNorm` are algorithm dependent values and they are reimplemented in each `Feature2D` subclass that is capable of extracting descriptors.

As strange as this may seem, there is a good reason to categorize feature detectors and descriptors in this way, and with a single class, and that is because some algorithms (not all) provide functions for both feature detection and descriptor extraction. This will become clearer as we proceed with a number of algorithms created for this purpose. So, let's start with the existing `Feature2D` classes and algorithms in the OpenCV 2D Features Framework.

# Detecting features

OpenCV provides a number of classes to deal with detecting features (keypoints) from an image. Each class has its own implementation depending on the specific algorithm it implements and may require a different set of parameters to perform correctly, or with the best performance. However, what all of them have in common is the `detect` function (because they are all subclasses of `Feature2D`) mentioned previously, which can be used to detect a set of keypoints from an image. A keypoint or feature in OpenCV is a `KeyPoint` class instance that contains most of the information needed to be stored for a proper keypoint (these terms, namely keypoint and feature, are used interchangeably, and a lot, so just try to get used to it). Following are the members of `KeyPoint` class along with their definitions:

- `pt`, or simply point: This contains the position of the keypoint (*X* and *Y*) in the image.

- `angle`: This refers to the clockwise rotation (0 to 360 degrees) of the keypoint, that is, if the algorithm detecting the keypoint is capable of finding it; otherwise, it will be set to −1.
- `response`: This is the strength of the keypoint, and it can be used to sort or filter weak keypoints, and so on.
- `size`: This refers to a diameter specifying a neighborhood of the keypoint that can be used for further processing.
- `octave`: This is the octave level (or pyramid level) of the image, from which this specific keypoint was detected. This is a very powerful and practical concept that is widely used to achieve independence from the scale (scale invariant) when detecting keypoints, or using them to further detect an object that may have different sizes on the image. To achieve this, different scaled versions (smaller versions only) of the same image are processed with the same algorithm; each scale is basically called `octave` or a level in the pyramid.

The `KeyPoint` class provides other members and methods for convenience so that you can check for yourself, but we definitely went through all of the important properties that we need to be familiar with, in order to further use them. Now, let's see a list of the existing OpenCV feature detector classes along with a brief description of them and an example of how they are used:

- `AgastFeatureDetector`, which includes an implementation of the **AGAST** (**Adaptive and Generic Accelerated Segment Test**) algorithm, can be used to detect corners in an image. It requires three parameters (all of which can be omitted to use the default values) that configure its behavior. Here's an example:

```
Ptr<AgastFeatureDetector> agast = AgastFeatureDetector::create();
vector<KeyPoint> keypoints;
agast->detect(inputImage, keypoints);
```

As simple as that, we just used `AgastFeatureDetector` with the default set of parameters. Before digging deeper into the result of the preceding operation, let's first take a look at the code itself, since one of the most important and practical classes in OpenCV (called `Ptr`) is used in it. As seen in the previous code, we used the `Ptr` class, which is OpenCV's implementation of shared pointers (also known as **smart pointers**). One of the advantages of using smart pointers is that you don't need to worry about freeing up the memory allocated for the class after you have finished using it. Another advantage, and the reason why it's called shared pointers, is the fact that more than one `Ptr` class can use (share) a single pointer and the pointer (the memory allocated) is only kept until the last instance of `Ptr` pointing to it is destroyed. In a complex code, this can mean a huge amount of simplicity.

Next, it's important to note that you need to use the static `create` function, to create a shared pointer instance of the `AgastFeatureDetector` class. You won't be able to create an instance of this class since it is an abstract class. The rest of the code is nothing new. We simply create `std::vector` of KeyPoint and then detect keypoints in our input `Mat` image using the underlying algorithm for AGAST.

Another way, and perhaps the more flexible way, of writing the same code would be by using polymorphism and the `Feature2D` class. Since `AgastFeatureDetector` is, in fact, a subclass of `Feature2D`, we can write the same code, like this:

```
Ptr<Feature2D> fd = AgastFeatureDetector::create();
vector<KeyPoint> keypoints;
fd->detect(inputImage, keypoints);
```

Of course, this would only prove to be useful in case we would like to switch between different feature-detection algorithms without creating and passing around many instances of many classes. Here's an example, in which, depending on the value of `alg` (which can be an entry from an enum that we have defined, and that includes the names of possible algorithms), either the AGAST or AKAZE algorithm is used to detect keypoints (which we'll see later on in this chapter):

```
Ptr<Feature2D> fd;
switch(alg)
{
   case AGAST_ALG:
   fd = AgastFeatureDetector::create();
   break;

   case AKAZE_ALG:
    fd = AKAZE::create();
    break;
}
vector<KeyPoint> keypoints;
fd->detect(inputImage, keypoints);
```

One more tip before talking about the parameters of AGAST algorithm, which is, you can draw the detected keypoints by iterating over the detected keypoints and drawing points (circles in fact, but so small they will be the same as a dot) as seen here:

```
inputImage.copyTo(outputImage);
foreach(KeyPoint kp, keypoints)
circle(outputImage, kp.pt, 1, Scalar(0,0,255), 2);
```

Or, even better, by using the `drawKeypoints` function that is dedicated for this purpose in the OpenCV 2D Feature Framework. It has the advantage that you don't need to copy your image to the output image, and it also makes sure to color keypoints in a way that they are more distinguishable. Here's an example; in fact, here's the entire code to detect and draw the keypoints using AGAST algorithm in OpenCV:

```
Ptr<AgastFeatureDetector> agast = AgastFeatureDetector::create();
vector<KeyPoint> keypoints;
agast->detect(inputImage, keypoints);
drawKeypoints(inputImage, keypoints, outputImage);
```

We will be using the simple and non-polymorphic method in our examples, but, nevertheless, it is always more practical to use polymorphism as described earlier on in this chapter, and switch between different algorithms suitable for different situations.

Assuming that the image on the left side is our original test image, executing the preceding code will produce the resulting image on the right side, shown as follows:

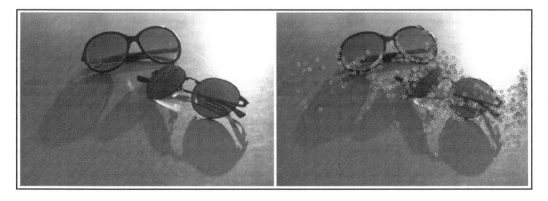

And here's a zoomed in part of the resulting image:

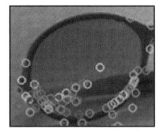

As you can see, all detected keypoints are drawn on the resulting image. Also, it's always better if we run some kind of blur filter (if images are too sharp) before running any feature detection function. This helps with reducing unwanted (and incorrect) keypoints. The reason for this is that in a sharp image, even the slightest bits and pieces of the image can be detected as edges or corner points.

In the preceding examples, we simply used the default parameters (by omitting them), but to have a better control over the behavior of the AGAST algorithm, we need to take care of the following parameters:

- The `threshold` value, which is set to `10` by default, is used to pass features based on the difference of intensity between a pixel and pixels on a circle surrounding it. The higher the threshold means the lower the number of detected features, and vice versa.
- `NonmaxSuppression` can be used to apply non-maximum suppression to detected keypoints. This parameter is set to true by default and can be used to further filter out unwanted keypoints.
- The `type` parameter can be set to one of the following values and decides the type of the AGAST algorithm:
  - `AGAST_5_8`
  - `AGAST_7_12d`
  - `AGAST_7_12s`
  - `OAST_9_16` (Default value)

You can use proper Qt widgets to fetch the value of parameters from the user interface. Here's an example user interface for the AGAST algorithm along with the underlying code for it. Also, you can download the complete `keypoint_plugin` source codes provided at the end of this section that contains this, and the following feature detection examples, all in one plugin, which is compatible with our comprehensive `computer_vision` project:

Notice the change in the number of detected keypoints when we change the threshold and choose a different type of AGAST algorithm. In the following example code, `agastThreshSpin` is `objectName` of the spin box widget, `agastNonmaxCheck` is `objectName` of the checkbox, and `agastTypeCombo` is `objectName` of the combo box that is used to select the type:

```
Ptr<AgastFeatureDetector> agast =
    AgastFeatureDetector::create();
vector<KeyPoint> keypoints;
agast->setThreshold(ui->agastThreshSpin->value());
agast->setNonmaxSuppression(ui->agastNonmaxCheck->isChecked());
agast->setType(ui->agastTypeCombo->currentIndex());
agast->detect(inputImage,
              keypoints);
drawKeypoints(inputImage,
              keypoints,
              outputImage);
```

OpenCV provides a convenience function that can be used to directly call the AGAST algorithm on grayscale images without using the `AgastFeatureDetector` class. This function is called `AGAST` (or `cv::AGAST`, if we consider the namespace), and, by using it, we can write the same code, as shown here:

```
vector<KeyPoint> keypoints;
AGAST(inputImage,
      keypoints,
      ui->agastThreshSpin->value(),
      ui->agastNonmaxCheck->isChecked(),
      ui->agastTypeCombo->currentIndex());
drawKeypoints(inputImage,
              keypoints,
              outputImage);
```

Algorithms seen in this section, and almost any other algorithm implemented in OpenCV, are usually based on research studies and published papers from all around the world. It's worth taking a look at the relevant papers for each algorithm to have a clear idea of the underlying implementation of it and also the exact effect of the parameters, and how they can be used effectively. So, at the end of each example and after going through each algorithm, its reference papers (if any) will be shared with you for further study, if you are interested. The first one, which is for the AGAST algorithm, appears right after this information box.

Reference: Elmar Mair, Gregory D. Hager, Darius Burschka, Michael Suppa, and Gerhard Hirzinger. Adaptive and generic corner detection based on the accelerated segment test. In European Conference on Computer Vision (ECCV'10), September 2010.

Let's continue with our list of feature detection algorithms.

# KAZE and AKAZE

The `KAZE` and `AKAZE` (**Accelerated KAZE**) classes can be used to detect features using the KAZE algorithm (an accelerated version of it). For more information about the details of the KAZE and AKAZE algorithms, refer to the papers mentioned in the following reference papers list. Similar to what we saw with AGAST, we can use the default set of parameters and simply call the `detect` function, or we can get the required parameters using proper Qt widgets and control the behavior of the algorithm even further. Here's an example:

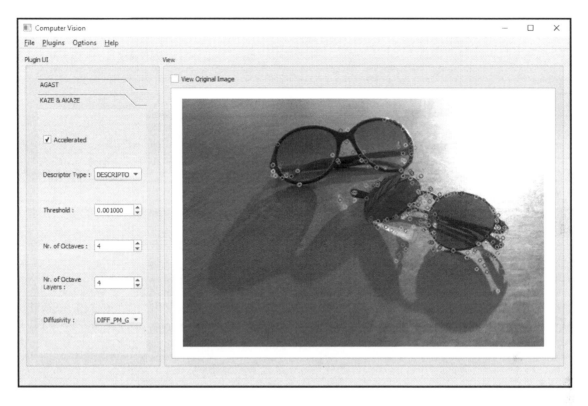

Main parameters in both AKAZE and KAZE are as follows:

- nOctaves, or **Nr. of Octaves** (**4** by default), can be used to define the maximum octave levels of an image.
- nOctaveLayers, or **Nr. of Octave Layers** (**4** by default), is the number of sub-levels per octave (or per scale level).
- **Diffusivity** can take one of the following entries, and it is the non-linear diffusion method used by the KAZE and AKAZE algorithms (as described in the reference paper for this algorithm later on):
    - DIFF_PM_G1
    - DIFF_PM_G2
    - DIFF_WEICKERT
    - DIFF_CHARBONNIER
- **Threshold** is the response value to accept a keypoint (**0.001000** by default). Lower the threshold, higher the number of detected (and accepted) keypoints, and vice versa.

- The **Descriptor Type** parameter can be one of the following values. Note that this parameter only exists in the AKAZE class:
  - `DESCRIPTOR_KAZE_UPRIGHT`
  - `DESCRIPTOR_KAZE`
  - `DESCRIPTOR_MLDB_UPRIGHT`

- The `descriptor_size` is used to define the size of the descriptor. A value of zero (which is also the default value) means a full-sized descriptor.

- The `descriptor_channels` can be used to set the number of channels in the descriptor. By default, this value is set to **3**.

For now, do not bother with the descriptor related parameters, such as **Descriptor Type** and **Size**, and number of channels, as we'll see later on. These same classes are also used to extract descriptors from features and that is where these parameters will have an effect, not necessarily with detecting keypoints and the `detect` function in particular.

Here's the source code for the preceding example user interface, in which, depending on the state of **Accelerated** checkbox in our preceding example user interface, KAZE (unchecked) or AKAZE (accelerated) is selected:

```
vector<KeyPoint> keypoints;
if(ui->kazeAcceleratedCheck->isChecked())
{
  Ptr<AKAZE> akaze = AKAZE::create();
  akaze->setDescriptorChannels(3);
  akaze->setDescriptorSize(0);
  akaze->setDescriptorType(
    ui->akazeDescriptCombo->currentIndex() + 2);
  akaze->setDiffusivity(ui->kazeDiffCombo->currentIndex());
  akaze->setNOctaves(ui->kazeOctaveSpin->value());
  akaze->setNOctaveLayers(ui->kazeLayerSpin->value());
  akaze->setThreshold(ui->kazeThreshSpin->value());
  akaze->detect(inputImage, keypoints);
}
else
{
  Ptr<KAZE> kaze = KAZE::create();
  kaze->setUpright(ui->kazeUprightCheck->isChecked());
  kaze->setExtended(ui->kazeExtendCheck->isChecked());
  kaze->setDiffusivity(ui->kazeDiffCombo->currentIndex());
  kaze->setNOctaves(ui->kazeOctaveSpin->value());
  kaze->setNOctaveLayers(ui->kazeLayerSpin->value());
  kaze->setThreshold(ui->kazeThreshSpin->value());
  kaze->detect(inputImage, keypoints);
```

```
    }
    drawKeypoints(inputImage, keypoints, outputImage);
```

Reference papers:

1. *KAZE Features*. Pablo F. Alcantarilla, Adrien Bartoli and Andrew J. Davison. In European Conference on Computer Vision (ECCV), Fiorenze, Italy, October 2012.
2. *Fast Explicit Diffusion for Accelerated Features in Nonlinear Scale Spaces*. Pablo F. Alcantarilla, Jesús Nuevo and Adrien Bartoli. In British Machine Vision Conference (BMVC), Bristol, UK, September 2013.

# The BRISK class

The BRISK class can be used to detect features in an image using the **BRISK** (**Binary Robust Invariant Scalable Keypoints**) algorithm. Make sure to refer to the following paper for details on how it works and underlying implementation in OpenCV. The usage though, is quite similar to what we saw in AGAST and KAZE, in which the class is created using the create function, then the parameters are set (if we will not for the defaults), and, finally, the detect function is called. Here's a simple example:

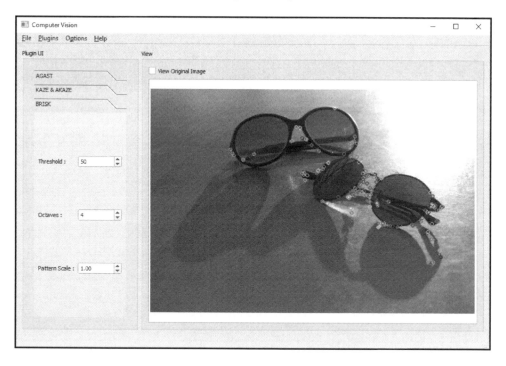

The following is the source code for such a user interface. The widget names are easy to guess, and each one corresponds to one of the three parameters needed by the BRISK algorithm, which are `thresh` (similar to threshold in the `AGAST` class, since BRISK uses a similar method internally), `octaves` (similar to the number of octaves in the KAZE and AKAZE classes), and `patternScale`, which is an optional pattern scaling parameter used by the BRISK algorithm, and it's set to one by default:

```
vector<KeyPoint> keypoints;
Ptr<BRISK> brisk =
    BRISK::create(ui->briskThreshSpin->value(),
                  ui->briskOctaveSpin->value(),
                  ui->briskScaleSpin->value());
drawKeypoints(inputImage, keypoints, outputImage);
```

Reference paper: Stefan Leutenegger, Margarita Chli, and Roland Yves Siegwart. Brisk: Binary robust invariant scalable keypoints. In Computer Vision (ICCV), 2011 IEEE International Conference on, pages 2548-2555. IEEE, 2011.

# FAST

The `FastFeatureDetector` class can be used to detect features from an image using the `FAST` method (**Features from Accelerated Segment Test**). The FAST and AGAST algorithms share a lot since both are methods that use Accelerated Segment Test, and this is obvious even in the OpenCV implementation and how this class is used. Make sure to refer to the paper for this algorithm to learn more about its details; however, we'll be focusing on how it's used with another example:

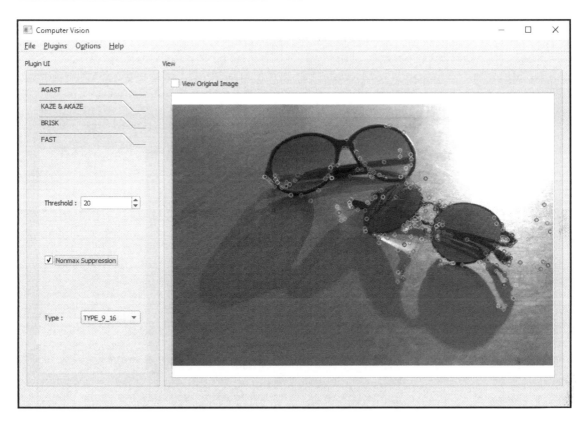

And, here is the source code for such a user interface that uses the FAST algorithm to detect keypoints from an image. All three parameters are identical in meaning to that of the AGAST algorithm, except the type can be one of the following:

- `TYPE_5_8`
- `TYPE_7_12`
- `TYPE_9_16`

Reference paper: Edward Rosten and Tom Drummond. Machine learning for high-speed corner detection. In Computer Vision-ECCV 2006, pages 430-443. Springer, 2006.

# GFTT (Good Features to Track)

GFTT is a feature detector only. GFTTDetector can be used to detect features using Harris (named after the creator) and GFTT corner detection algorithms. So, yes, this class is, in fact, two feature detection methods combined into one class and the reason is that GFTT is actually a modified version of the Harris algorithm, and which one is used will be decided by the input parameters. So, let's see how it's used with an example case and then briefly go through the parameters:

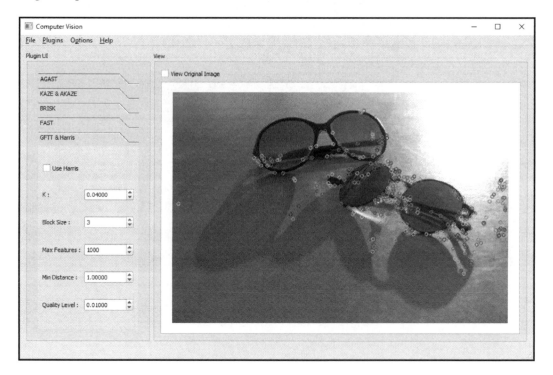

Here is the relevant source code for this user interface:

```cpp
vector<KeyPoint> keypoints;
Ptr<GFTTDetector> gftt = GFTTDetector::create();
gftt->setHarrisDetector(ui->harrisCheck->isChecked());
gftt->setK(ui->harrisKSpin->value());
gftt->setBlockSize(ui->gfttBlockSpin->value());
gftt->setMaxFeatures(ui->gfttMaxSpin->value());
gftt->setMinDistance(ui->gfttDistSpin->value());
gftt->setQualityLevel(ui->gfttQualitySpin->value());
gftt->detect(inputImage, keypoints);
drawKeypoints(inputImage, keypoints, outputImage);
```

Here are the parameter and their definitions for GFTTDetector class:

- The useHarrisDetector, if set to true, will use the Harris algorithm, otherwise GFTT. This parameter is set to false by default.
- The blockSize can be used to set the block size that will be used to calculate a derivative covariation matrix in the neighborhood of a pixel. It is 3 by default.
- K is the constant parameter value used by the Harris algorithm.
- The maxFeatures or maxCorners can be set to limit the number of keypoints detected. It is set to **1000** by default, but if the number of keypoints exceeds this number, only the strongest responses are returned.
- The minDistance is the minimum acceptable value between keypoints. This value is set to **1** by default and it is not a pixel-wise distance, but rather an Euclidean distance.
- The qualityLevel is the threshold-level value used to filter out keypoints with a quality measure below a certain level. Note that the actual threshold is calculated by multiplying this value with the best-detected keypoint quality in an image.

Reference papers:

1. Jianbo Shi and Carlo Tomasi. *Good features to track*. In Computer Vision and Pattern Recognition, 1994. Proceedings CVPR'94., 1994 IEEE Computer Society Conference on, pages 593-600. IEEE, 1994.
2. C. Harris and M. Stephens (1988). *A combined corner and edge detector*. Proceedings of the 4th Alvey Vision Conference. pp. 147-151.

# ORB

Finally, the ORB algorithm, which is the last feature-detection algorithm we'll cover in this section.

The ORB class can be used to detect keypoints in images using the ORB, or the **Oriented BRIEF (Binary Robust Independent Elementary Features)** algorithm. This class encapsulates some of the methods we have already seen such as FAST or Harris to detect the keypoints. So, some of the parameters set in the class constructor or using setter functions are related to the descriptor extraction, which we'll learn about later on; nevertheless, the ORB class can be used to detect keypoints, as seen in the following example:

Here's the source code required for such a user interface. Again, the objectName properties of the widgets are pretty much self-explanatory, as seen in the preceding image, but let's see the code first and then go through the parameters in detail:

```
vector<KeyPoint> keypoints;
Ptr<ORB> orb = ORB::create();
orb->setMaxFeatures(ui->orbFeaturesSpin->value());
orb->setScaleFactor(ui->orbScaleSpin->value());
orb->setNLevels(ui->orbLevelsSpin->value());
orb->setPatchSize(ui->orbPatchSpin->value());
```

```
orb->setEdgeThreshold(ui->orbPatchSpin->value()); // = patch size
orb->setWTA_K(ui->orbWtaSpin->value());
orb->setScoreType(ui->orbFastCheck->isChecked() ?
                    ORB::HARRIS_SCORE
                :
                    ORB::FAST_SCORE);
orb->setPatchSize(ui->orbPatchSpin->value());
orb->setFastThreshold(ui->orbFastSpin->value());
orb->detect(inputImage, keypoints);
drawKeypoints(inputImage, keypoints, outputImage);
```

The sequence is exactly the same as other algorithms we have seen so far. Let's see what are the parameters that were set:

- The MaxFeatures parameter is simply the maximum number of keypoints that should be retrieved. Note that the number of keypoints that are detected can be a lot lower than this, but never higher.
- ScaleFactor, or pyramid decimation ration, which is somewhat similar to the octave parameters we saw in the previous algorithms, is used to decide the scale value for each level of the pyramid that will be used to detect keypoints and extract descriptors from different scales of the same image. This is how scale invariance is implemented in ORB.
- NLevels is the number of levels of the pyramid.
- PatchSize is the size of the patch used by the ORB algorithm. For detailed information about this, make sure to refer to the following reference paper, but for a short description, the patch size decides the area around a keypoint where description extraction will take place. Note that the PatchSize and EdgeThreshold parameters need to be about the same value, which is also set to the same value in the preceding example.
- EdgeThreshold is the border in pixels that will be ignored during keypoint detection.
- WTA_K, or the K value for WTA hash, used internally in the ORB algorithm, is a parameter used to decide the number of points that will be used to create each element in the ORB descriptor. We'll see more about this later on in this chapter.
- ScoreType, which can be set to one of the following values, decides the keypoint detection method used by ORB algorithm:
  - ORB::HARRIS_SCORE is for the Harris corner detection algorithm
  - ORB::FAST_SCORE is for the FAST keypoint detection algorithm
- FastThreshold is simply the threshold value used in the key point detection algorithm by ORB.

Reference papers:

1. Ethan Rublee, Vincent Rabaud, Kurt Konolige, and Gary Bradski. *Orb: an efficient alternative to sift or surf.* In Computer Vision (ICCV), 2011 IEEE International Conference on, pages 2564-2571. IEEE, 2011.
2. Michael Calonder, Vincent Lepetit, Christoph Strecha, and Pascal Fua, *BRIEF: Binary Robust Independent Elementary Features,* 11th European Conference on Computer Vision (ECCV), Heraklion, Crete. LNCS Springer, September 2010.

That's it. We are now familiar with how to detect keypoints using various algorithms available in OpenCV 3. Of course, unless we extract descriptors from these keypoints, those keypoints (or features) are pretty much useless; so, in the next section, we will learn about extraction of descriptors from keypoints, which will consequently lead us to descriptor matching capabilities in OpenCV, where we can use the classes we learned about in this section, to identify, detect, track, and categorize objects and images. Note that for each of the algorithms we learned about, it's best to read the paper to be able to understand all the details about it, especially if you are aiming to build your own custom keypoint detectors, but to use them as they are, just like it was mentioned before, having a clear idea of their purpose should be enough.

# Extracting and matching descriptors

A descriptor in computer vision is a way of describing a keypoint that is completely dependent on the specific algorithm that is used for extracting it, and, unlike keypoints (which are defined in the `KeyPoint` class), descriptors do not have a common structure, except more or less the fact that each descriptor represents a keypoint. Descriptors in OpenCV are stored in `Mat` classes, where each row in the resulting descriptor `Mat` class refers to a descriptor of a keypoint. As we learned in the previous section, we can use the `detect` function of any `FeatureDetector` subclass to basically detect a set of keypoints from an image. Similarly, we can use the `compute` function of any `DescriptorExtractor` subclass to extract descriptors from keypoints.

Because of the way feature detectors and descriptor extractors are organized in OpenCV (both are `Feature2D` subclasses, as we learned earlier in this chapter), it's surprisingly easy to use both of them in conjunction, and, in fact, as you'll see in this section, we'll use exactly the same classes (or, to be precise, the ones that also offer descriptor extraction methods) to extract feature descriptors from the keypoints we found using various classes in the previous section, to locate an object inside a scene image. It is important to note that not all extracted keypoints are compatible with all descriptors, and not all algorithms (`Feature2D` subclasses, in this case) provide both the `detect` function and the `compute` function. The ones that do though, also provide a `detectAndCompute` function that does both keypoint detection and feature extraction in one go, and it is faster than calling the two functions separately. Let's start with our first example case so that this all becomes clearer. This is also an example of all the required steps to match the features of two separate images, which can be used for detection, comparison, and so on:

1. First, we'll use the AKAZE algorithm (using the `AKAZE` class we learned about in the previous section) to detect keypoints from the following images:

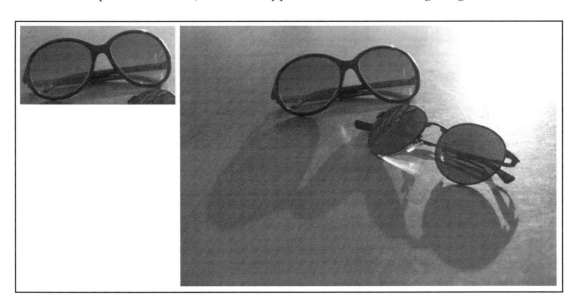

We can use the following piece of code to extract keypoints from both images:

```
using namespace cv;
using namespace std;
Mat image1 = imread("image1.jpg");
Mat image2 = imread("image2.jpg");
Ptr<AKAZE> akaze = AKAZE::create();
```

```
// set AKAZE params ...
vector<KeyPoint> keypoints1, keypoints2;
akaze->detect(image1, keypoints1);
akaze->detect(image2, keypoints2);
```

2. Now that we have the features (or keypoints) of both images, we can use the same AKAZE class instance to extract descriptors from these keypoints. Here's how it's done:

```
Mat descriptor1, descriptor2;
akaze->compute(image1, keypoints1, descriptor1);
akaze->compute(image2, keypoints2, descriptor2);
```

3. Now we have what is needed to match two images which is the descriptors of the keypoints in both images. To be able to perform a descriptor matching operation, we need to use a class called DescriptorMatcher (quite conveniently) in OpenCV. It is extremely important to note that this matcher class needs to be set to the correct type, otherwise, you won't get any results, or you may even face errors in your application on runtime. In case of the AKAZE algorithm that we used in this example to detect keypoints and extract descriptors, we can use the FLANNBASED type in DescriptorMatcher. Here's how it's done:

```
descMather = DescriptorMatcher::create(
    DescriptorMatcher::FLANNBASED);
```

Note that you can pass one of the following values to the create function of DescriptorMatcher, and this is completely dependent on an algorithm you used to extract the descriptors, obviously, because matching will be performed on the descriptors. You can always refer to each algorithm's documentation to know which ones you can use for any specific descriptor type, for example, algorithms such as AKAZE and KAZE have a floating-point type descriptor, so you can use FLANNBASED with them; however, descriptors which have a bit String type, such as ORB, will need matching methods that can work with the Hamming distance of descriptors. Following are the existing methods you can use for matching:

- FLANNBASED
- BRUTEFORCE
- BRUTEFORCE_L1
- BRUTEFORCE_HAMMING
- BRUTEFORCE_HAMMINGLUT
- BRUTEFORCE_SL2

The worst-case scenario, of course, when trying to find the correct matching algorithm for any specific descriptor type, is to just simply try each one if you are not sure.

4. Now we need to call the `match` function of `DescriptorMatcher` to try and match the keypoints found in the first image (or the object we need to detect) with the ones found in the second image (or the scene that may contain our object). The `match` function will require a vector of `DMatch` and it will fill it with all the matching results. Here is how it's done:

```
vector<DMatch> matches;
descMather->match(descriptor1, descriptor2, matches);
```

A `DMatch` class is a simple class used only as a structure to hold the matching result data:

- `queryIdx`, or query descriptor index: This is the index of the descriptor in the first image
- `trainIdx`, or train descriptor index: This is the index of the descriptor in the second image
- `imgIdxtrain`, or image index: This is the index of the second image used for matching (this parameter only makes sense when we are matching our first image against multiple different second images)
- `distance`: This is simply the distance between the compared descriptors

5. Before digging deeper into how the result of a matching operation is interpreted, we will learn about how to use the `drawMatches` function. Similar to the `drawKeypoints` function, `drawMatches` can be used to automatically create a proper output result meant for displaying. Here's how:

```
drawMatches(image1,
            keypoints1,
            image2,
            keypoints2,
            matches,
            dispImg);
```

In the preceding code, `dispImg` is obviously a `Mat` class that can be displayed. Here's the resulting image:

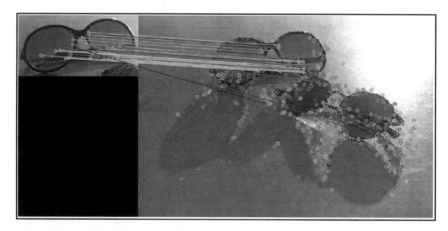

As you can see, the `drawMatches` function takes the first and second images and their keypoints along with the matching result and takes care of everything that is needed to draw a proper result. In this example, we only provided the required parameters, which leads to random colors and drawing all keypoints and matched ones (using a line that connects them together). There are, of course, a few other parameters that can be used to further modify how it works. Optionally, you can set the color of keypoints and lines and also decide to ignore the unmatched keypoints. Here's another example:

```
drawMatches(image1,
            keypoints1,
            image2,
            keypoints2,
            matches,
            dispImg,
            Scalar(0, 255, 0), // green for matched
            Scalar::all(-1), // unmatched color (default)
            vector<char>(), // empty mask
            DrawMatchesFlags::NOT_DRAW_SINGLE_POINTS);
```

This produces the following result:

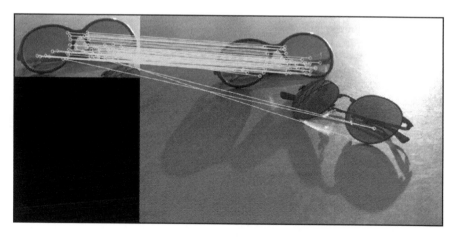

Now, the coloring is much more suitable for what we have here; also notice the few incorrect matchings that are quite normal and can be taken care of by modifying the parameters of the KAZE algorithm, or even using another algorithm. Let's now see how we can interpret the results of matching.

6. Interpreting the result of the matching is completely dependent on the use case. For example, if we are matching two images with the same size and the same content type (such as faces, objects of the same type, fingerprints, and so on), then we may want to take into consideration the number of matched keypoints that have a distance value higher than some threshold. Or, as in our current example case, we may want to use matching to detect an object in a scene. A common way of doing this is to try and find the homography change between the matched keypoints. To be able to do this, we need to perform the following three operations:

- First, we need to filter out matching results to get rid of less strong matches, or, in other words, only keep the good matches; again, this completely depends on your scene and object, but, usually, with a few trial and errors, you can find the best thresholds
- Next, we need to use the `findHomography` function to get the homography change between the good keypoints
- Finally, we need to use `perspectiveTransform` to transform the object bounding box (rectangle) to the scene

You learned about findHomography and perspectiveTransform and how they are used in Chapter 6, *Image Processing in OpenCV*.

Here's how we can filter out unwanted matching results to get the good matches. Note that the 0.1 value for the matching threshold is found using trial and error. It is also common to find the minimum and maximum distance in the matches set, and then only accept matches that have a distance less than some value related to the minimum distance, although that is not how we have done it in here:

```
vector<DMatch> goodMatches;
double matchThresh = 0.1;
for(int i=0; i<descriptor1.rows; i++)
{
    if(matches[i].distance < matchThresh)
        goodMatches.push_back(matches[i]);
}
```

 You can use the power of the Qt framework and user interfaces in such cases that you need to fine-tune a threshold value. For example, you can use the Qt slider widgets to quickly and easily fine-tune and find the threshold you need. Just make sure matchThresh is replaced with the value of your slider widget.

Now, we can use the good matches to find the homography change. To do this, we will first need to filter our keypoints according to the good matches and then feed these filtered keypoints (just the points) to the findHomography function to get the required transformation matrix or the homography change. Here it is:

```
vector<Point2f> goodP1, goodP2;
for(int i=0; i<goodMatches.size(); i++)
{
    goodP1.push_back(keypoints1[goodMatches[i].queryIdx].pt);
    goodP2.push_back(keypoints2[goodMatches[i].trainIdx].pt);
}
Mat homoChange = findHomography(goodP1, goodP2);
```

Lastly, we can apply a perspective transform to the matched points using the homography change matrix that we just found. To do this, first, we need to construct four points corresponding to the four corners of the first image, then apply the transformation, and, finally, simply draw the four lines connecting the four result points. Here's how it is done:

```
vector<Point2f> corners1(4), corners2(4);
corners1[0] = Point2f(0,0);
corners1[1] = Point2f(image1.cols-1, 0);
corners1[2] = Point2f(image1.cols-1, image1.rows-1);
corners1[3] = Point2f(0, image1.rows-1);

perspectiveTransform(corners1, corners2, homoChange);

image2.copyTo(dispImage);

line(dispImage, corners2[0], corners2[1], Scalar::all(255), 2);
line(dispImage, corners2[1], corners2[2], Scalar::all(255), 2);
line(dispImage, corners2[2], corners2[3], Scalar::all(255), 2);
line(dispImage, corners2[3], corners2[0], Scalar::all(255), 2);
```

Here's the result of this operation:

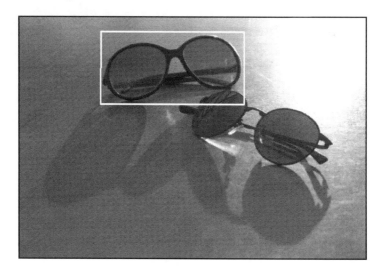

This is not really a test of how powerful this method is since the object is basically cut from the same image. Here is the result of running the same process, but this time the second image has a rotation and perspective change and even some noise (it's an image taken using a smartphone from the screen). The result is pretty much correct, even though a small part of the first image is outside of the view:

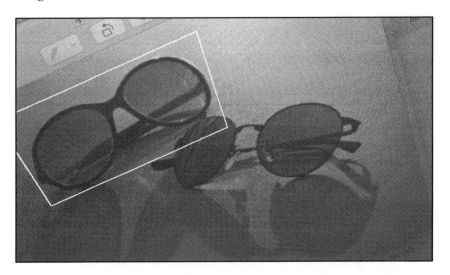

 For reference purposes, this match and detect was done using the AKAZE algorithm with the DESCRIPTOR_KAZE descriptor type, 0.0001 threshold, 4 octaves, 4 octave layers, and the DIFF_PM_G1 diffusivity arguments. Try different parameters with different lighting conditions and images for yourself.

We can also combine the drawMatches results with the detection results, which means that, we can draw the detection bounding box right over the matching result image, which may be more helpful, especially when fine-tuning parameters or for any other informational purposes. To do this, you need to make sure the drawMatches function is called first to create the output image (the dispImg variable in our example), then add all points with an offset value since drawMatches will also output the first image on the left side. This offset simply helps move our resulting bounding box to the right, or, in other words, adds the width of the first image to the X member of each point. Here's how it's done:

```
Point2f offset(image1.cols, 0);

line(dispImage, corners2[0] + offset,
   corners2[1] + offset, Scalar::all(255), 2);
line(dispImage, corners2[1] + offset,
```

```
        corners2[2] + offset, Scalar::all(255), 2);
    line(dispImage, corners2[2] + offset,
      corners2[3] + offset, Scalar::all(255), 2);
    line(dispImage, corners2[3] + offset,
      corners2[0] + offset, Scalar::all(255), 2);
```

Here is the resulting image:

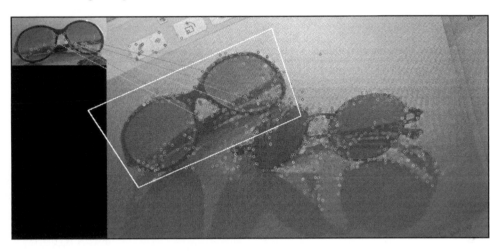

In the preceding example, as you can see in the result, the image is distorted in many ways (such as scale, orientation, and so on), but still, the algorithm can perform well with a correct set of input parameters. In theory, and ideally, we always look for an out-of-the-box algorithm, and we would like it to perform well for all possible cases; however, unfortunately, in practice, that does not happen at all or happens very rarely. In the next section, we will learn how to choose the best algorithms for our use cases.

# How to choose an algorithm

As it was mentioned, there is no algorithm that can be easily used for all out-of-the-box cases, and the main reason for this is the huge variety of software and hardware related factors. An algorithm may be highly accurate, but, at the same time, it may require lots of resources (such as memory or CPU usage).

Another algorithm may require fewer parameters (which is almost always a relief), but then again, it may not be able to achieve its highest performance. We can't even begin to name all the possible factors that affect choosing the best Feature2D (or featured detector and descriptor extractor) algorithm or the best matching algorithm, but we can still take into consideration some of the main and more well-known factors that are also the reason why OpenCV and most computer vision algorithms are created the way they are, in terms of structure. Here are those factors:

- Accuracy
- Speed
- Resource usage (memory, disk space, and so on)
- Availability

Note that the word performance usually refers to a combination of accuracy, speed, and resource usage. So, what we are looking for is essentially an algorithm that is as performant as we require it to be, and it is available for the platform (or platforms) that we need our application to work on. It is important to mention that you, as an engineer, can also affect these parameters, especially by narrowing down your use case to exactly what is needed. Let's explain this by going through the factors we just mentioned.

# Accuracy

First of all, accuracy is quite misleading, because, as soon as we see some accuracy drops, we usually tend to move away from an algorithm, but the correct way is to clarify the accuracy requirement for your use case first. Check out the data sheets of the computer vision-based machines made by very well-known companies, and immediately you'll notice things like more than 95 %, and so on. This doesn't mean that the machine is imperfect. Quite the opposite—it means the accuracy of the machine is well-defined and the user can expect a certain amount of accuracy, and, at the same time, they can live with a certain low amount of error. All being said, it is always good and recommended to aim for a 100 percent accuracy.

There is no better way to choose an accurate algorithm for your use case other than taking a peek at the papers and references of that algorithm, and, even better, trying it for yourself. Make sure to create user interfaces using the proper widgets in Qt so that you can easily experiment with existing (or maybe even your own) algorithms. Create benchmarks and make sure you are perfectly aware of the behavior of any certain algorithm when its threshold or some other parameter is changed.

Also, make sure to choose the algorithm depending on what you need in terms of scale and rotation independence. For example, using standard AKAZE descriptor types (non-upright), in AKAZE, the algorithm allows rotation independence, so your matching can even work with rotated objects. Or, use a higher octave (or pyramid level) number since that can help with the matching of images with different sizes, thus achieving scale independence.

# Speed

How fast your algorithm performs is especially important, in case you are developing a real-time application where the **FPS (frames per second**, or framerate) value must be as high as possible. So, same as the accuracy, you need to be careful with clarifying this requirement, too. If you match two images and show some matching results to the user, even a delay of half a second (500 ms) may still be acceptable, but, when working with high FPS values, half a second of delay for each frame is extremely high.

You can use the `TickMeter` class or the `getTickFrequency` and `getTickCount` functions in OpenCV to measure the execution time of a computer vision process (or any process for that matter). First, let's see how the older method works:

```
double freq = cv::getTickFrequency();
double tick = cv::getTickCount();
processImage(); // Any process
double dur = (cv::getTickCount() - tick) / freq;
```

The `getTickFrequency` function can be used to get the CPU tick count in a second (or frequency). Similarly, `getTickCount` can be used to get the numbers of CPU ticks that are passed since the startup. So, it is obvious that in the previous example code, we will get the duration of executing the `processImage` function in seconds.

The `TickMeter` class though, provides much more flexibility and it is easier to use. You simply start it before any process and stop it after the process. Here's how it's done:

```
cv::TickMeter meter;
meter.start();
processImage(); // Any process
meter.stop();
meter.getTimeMicro();
meter.getTimeMilli();
meter.getTimeSec();
meter.getTimeTicks();
```

Switch between different algorithms that meet your accuracy requirements and measure their speed using this technique, and choose the one that works best for you. Try to stay away from rules of thumb such as ORB is faster, or BRISK is more accurate, and so on. Even though descriptors that have a bit `String` type (such as ORB) are usually faster in terms of matching (since they use Hamming distance); more recent algorithms such as AKAZE can use the GPU and OpenCV `UMat` (refer to `Chapter 4`, *Mat and QImage*, to learn more about the `UMat` class) to perform faster. So, try to use your measurements or any trusted measurement reference as your source for rule of thumbs.

You can also use the `QElapsedTimer` class of Qt, in a similar way to the `TickMeter` class of OpenCV, to measure the execution time of any process.

# Resource usage

Especially with more recent and high-end devices and computers, this is usually not a big issue, but it still can be a problem with computers that have a limited amount of disk and memory space, such as embedded computers. Try to use resource monitor applications that come pre-shipped with the operating systems for this purpose. For example, on Windows, you can use the **Task Manager** application to view the used resources, such as memory. On macOS, you can use the **Activity Monitor** application to view even the amount of battery power (energy) that is used by each program, along with the memory and other resource usage information. On Linux, you can use a variety of tools, such as a **System Monitor**, for exactly the same purpose.

# Availability

Even though OpenCV and Qt are both cross-platform frameworks, an algorithm (or even a class or function) can still be dependent on the platform-specific capabilities, especially for performance reasons. It is important and quite obvious to note that you need to make sure the algorithm you use is available on the platforms you aim to release your applications in. The best source for this is usually the documentation pages of underlying classes in both OpenCV and Qt frameworks.

You can download the complete source code for keypoint detection, descriptor extraction, and descriptor matching from the following link. You can use the same plugin to compare different algorithms in terms of accuracy and speed. Needless to say, this plugin is compatible with our `computer_vision` project that we have been building throughout the book: `https://github.com/PacktPublishing/Computer-Vision-with-OpenCV-3-and-Qt5/tree/master/ch07/keypoint_plugin`.

# Summary

Feature detection, description, and matching are probably some of the most important and hot topics in computer vision that are still in intensive progress and improvement. The algorithms that were presented in this chapter are but a fraction of the existing algorithms in the world, and the reason that we chose to present them is the fact that they are all more or less free to use by the public, and also the fact that they are included in OpenCV by default, under the `feature2d` module. If you are interested in learning about more algorithms, you can also check out **Extra 2D Features Framework (xfeature2d)**, which contains non-free algorithms such as SURF and SIFT, or other algorithms still in experimental states. Of course, you need to separately download and add them to the OpenCV source code before building them to include their functions in your OpenCV installation. It is also recommended. However, also make sure to try out the algorithms you learned about in this chapter using different images and with various parameters to familiarize yourself with them.

By finishing this chapter, you can now use a feature and descriptor-related algorithms to detect keypoints and extract features and match them to detect objects or compare images with each other. Using the classes presented in this chapter, you can now properly display the result of your matching operation and also measure the performance of each process to decide which one is faster.

In `Chapter 8`, *Multithreading*, we will learn about multithreading and parallel processing in Qt (and where it applies in OpenCV) and how we can efficiently create and use threads and processes that live separately from the main thread in your application. Using the knowledge from the upcoming chapter, we will be prepared to tackle video processing and computer vision tasks that continue executing on consecutive frames from video files or camera frames.

# 8
# Multithreading

It wasn't a long time ago that computer programs were designed and built to run a series of instructions, one after another. In fact, this approach is so easy to understand and implement that, even today, we use the same approach to write scripts and simple programs that take care of the required tasks in a serial manner. However, over time and especially with the rise of more powerful processors, multitasking became the main issue. Computers were expected to perform more than one task at a time since they were quick enough to execute the instructions required by multiple programs and still had some free time. Of course, as time passed, even more complicated programs were written (games, graphical programs, and so on), and the processor had to fairly manage the time slice used by different programs so that all of them continued to operate correctly. Programs (or processes, to use the more suitable word in this context) were split into smaller pieces called **threads**. This approach, or multithreading, until now, has helped with creating responsive and fast processes that are able to run alongside similar or totally irrelevant processes, thus leading to a smooth multitasking experience.

On a computer with a single processor (and single core), each thread is given a time slice and the processor is obviously only able to attend to one thread at a time, but the switching between multiple threads is usually so fast that from the users' point of view, it seems like real parallelism. However, nowadays, even the processor inside most of the smartphones that people carry around in their pocket has the capability to process multiple threads using multiple cores in their processor.

To be sure we have a clear understanding about threads and how we can use them, and why it is impossible to write a powerful computer vision program without using threads, let's see the main difference between a process and a thread:

- Processes are similar to individual programs and they are directly executed by the operating systems
- Threads are subsets of a process, or, in other words, a process can contain multiple threads
- A process is (usually) independent from any other process, whereas threads share memory and resources with each other (note that processes can interact with each other through the means provided by the operating system)

Each process may or may not, depending on the way it is designed, create and execute different threads to achieve maximum performance and responsiveness. Each thread, on the other hand, will perform a specific task required by the process. A typical example of this in Qt and GUI programming is the progress information. When a complex and time taking process is running, it usually needs to display information about the stage and state of the progress, such as the remaining percentage of work, the remaining time to complete, and so on. This is best done by separating the actual task and GUI update tasks into separate threads. Another example of this, which is quite common in computer vision, is the video (or camera) processing. You need to make sure the video is correctly read, processed, and displayed when required. This, and such examples, will be our main focus in this chapter while we learn about multithreading capabilities in Qt framework.

In this chapter, we will cover the following topics:

- Multithreading methods in Qt
- How to use `QThread` and multithreading classes in Qt
- How to create responsive GUIs
- How to process multiple images
- How to process multiple cameras or videos

# Multithreading in Qt

The Qt framework offers many different technologies to deal with multithreading in applications. The QThread class is used to handle all sorts of multithreading functionality and, as we'll see in this chapter, using it is also the most powerful and flexible way of handling threads in Qt framework. In addition to QThread, the Qt framework offers a number of other namespaces, classes, and functions that help with various multithreading requirements. Here's a list of them, before we see examples of how they are used:

- QThread: This class is the base of all threads in the Qt framework. It can be subclassed to create new threads, in which case, you need to override the run method, or you can create new instances of it and move any Qt object (the QObject subclass) into a new thread by calling the moveToThread function.

- QThreadPool: This can be used to manage threads and help reduce thread creation costs by allowing existing threads to be reused for new purposes. Every Qt application contains a global QThreadPool instance that can be accessed by using the QThreadPool::globalInstance() static function. This class is used in conjunction with the QRunnable class instances to control, manage, and recycle runnable objects in a Qt application.

- QRunnable: This provides another way of creating threads, and it is the base of all runnable objects in Qt. Unlike QThread, QRunnable is not a QObject subclass and is used as an interface for a piece of code that needs to be run. You need to subclass and override the run function to be able to use QRunnable. As it was mentioned earlier, QRunnable instances are managed by the QThreadPool class.

- QMutex, QMutexLocker, QSemaphore, QWaitCondition, QReadLocker, QWriteLocker, and QWriteLocke: These classes are used to deal with inter-thread synchronization tasks. Depending on the situation, these classes can be used to avoid issues such as threads overriding each other's calculation, threads trying to read or write to a device that can only handle one thread at a time, and many similar issues. It is often necessary to manually take care of such issues when creating multithreaded applications.

- `QtConcurrent`: This namespace can be used to create multithreaded applications using a high-level API. It makes it easier to write multithreaded applications without the need to deal with mutexes, semaphores, and inter-thread synchronization issues.
- `QFuture`, `QFutureWatcher`, `QFututeIterator`, and `QFutureSynchronizer`: These classes are all used in conjunction with the `QtConcurrent` namespace to handle multithreaded and asynchronous operation results.

In general, there are two different approaches to multithreading in Qt. The first approach, which is based on `QThread`, is the low-level approach that provides a lot of flexibility and control over the threads but requires more coding and care in order to work flawlessly. However, there are ways to make multithreaded applications using `QThread` with much less work, and we'll learn about them in this chapter. The second approach is based on the `QtConcurrent` namespace (or the Qt Concurrency framework), which is the high-level approach to creating and running multiple tasks within an application.

# Low-level multithreading using QThread

In this section, we will learn how to use `QThread` and its affiliate classes to create multithreaded applications. We will go through this by creating an example project, which processes and displays the input and output frames from a video source using a separate thread. This helps leave the GUI thread (main thread) free and responsive while more intensive processes are handled with the second thread. As it was mentioned earlier, we will focus mostly on the use cases common to computer vision and GUI development; however, the same (or a very similar) approach can be applied to any multithreading problem.

We will use this example project to implement multithreading using two different approaches available in Qt for working with `QThread` classes. First, subclassing and overriding the run method, and second, using the `moveToThread` function available in all Qt objects, or, in other words, `QObject` subclasses.

# Subclassing QThread

Let's start by creating an example Qt Widgets application in the Qt Creator named
`MultithreadedCV`. Add the OpenCV framework to this project the same way as we
learned in the beginning chapters of this book: by including the following piece of code in
your `MultithreadedCV.pro` file (see `Chapter 2`, *Creating Our First Qt and OpenCV Project*
or `Chapter 3`, *Creating a Comprehensive Qt+OpenCV Project* for more about this):

```
win32: {
   include("c:/dev/opencv/opencv.pri")
}
unix: !macx{
  CONFIG += link_pkgconfig
  PKGCONFIG += opencv
}
unix: macx{
INCLUDEPATH += /usr/local/include
  LIBS += -L"/usr/local/lib" \
   -lopencv_world
}
```

Then, add two label widgets to your `mainwindow.ui` file, shown as follows. We will use
these labels to display the original and processed video from the default webcam on the
computer:

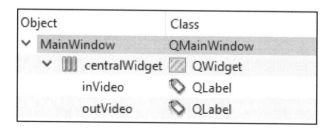

Make sure to set the `objectName` property of the label on the left to `inVideo` and the one on the right to `outVideo`. Also, set their `alignment/Horizontal` property to `AlignHCenter`. Now, create a new class called `VideoProcessorThread` by right-clicking on the project PRO file and selecting **Add New** from the menu. Then, choose **C++ Class** and make sure the combo boxes and checkboxes in the new class wizard look like the following screenshot:

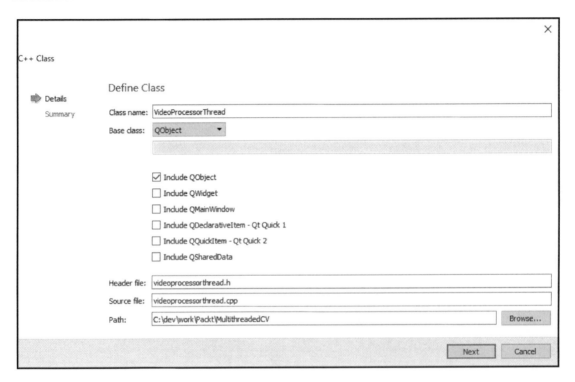

After your class is created, you'll have two new files in your project called `videoprocessorthread.h` and `videoprocessor.cpp`, in which you'll implement a video processor that works in a thread separate from the `mainwindow` files and GUI threads. First, make sure that this class inherits `QThread` by adding the relevant include line and class inheritance, as seen here (just replace `QObject` with `QThread` in the header file). Also, make sure you include OpenCV headers:

```
#include <QThread>
#include "opencv2/opencv.hpp"

class VideoProcessorThread : public QThread
```

You need to similarly update the `videoprocessor.cpp` file so that it calls the correct constructor:

```
VideoProcessorThread::VideoProcessorThread(QObject *parent)
    : QThread(parent)
```

Now, we need to add some required declarations to the `videoprocessor.h` file. Add the following line to the `private` members area of your class:

```
void run() override;
```

And then, add the following to the `signals` section:

```
void inDisplay(QPixmap pixmap);
void outDisplay(QPixmap pixmap);
```

And finally, add the following code block to the `videoprocessorthread.cpp` file:

```
void VideoProcessorThread::run()
{
  using namespace cv;
  VideoCapture camera(0);
  Mat inFrame, outFrame;
  while(camera.isOpened() && !isInterruptionRequested())
  {
    camera >> inFrame;
    if(inFrame.empty())
        continue;

    bitwise_not(inFrame, outFrame);

    emit inDisplay(
        QPixmap::fromImage(
            QImage(
              inFrame.data,
              inFrame.cols,
              inFrame.rows,
              inFrame.step,
              QImage::Format_RGB888)
                .rgbSwapped()));

    emit outDisplay(
        QPixmap::fromImage(
            QImage(
              outFrame.data,
                outFrame.cols,
                outFrame.rows,
```

```
                    outFrame.step,
                    QImage::Format_RGB888)
                        .rgbSwapped()));
        }
    }
```

The `run` function is overridden and it's implemented to do the required video processing task. If you try to do the same inside the `mainwindow.cpp` code in a loop, you'll notice that your program becomes unresponsive, and, eventually, you have to terminate it. However, with this approach, the same code is now in a separate thread. You just need to make sure you start this thread by calling the `start` function, not `run`! Note that the `run` function is meant to be called internally, so you only need to reimplement it as seen in this example; however, to control the thread and its execution behavior, you need to use the following functions:

- `start`: This can be used to start a thread if it is not already started. This function starts the execution by calling the `run` function we implemented. You can pass one of the following values to the `start` function to control the priority of the thread:
    - `QThread::IdlePriority` (this is scheduled when no other thread is running)
    - `QThread::LowestPriority`
    - `QThread::LowPriority`
    - `QThread::NormalPriority`
    - `QThread::HighPriority`
    - `QThread::HighestPriority`
    - `QThread::TimeCriticalPriority` (this is scheduled as much as possible)
    - `QThread::InheritPriority` (this is the default value, which simply inherits priority from the parent)

- `terminate`: This function, which should only be used in extreme cases (means never, hopefully), forces a thread to terminate.
- `setTerminationEnabled`: This can be used to allow or disallow the `terminate` function.
- `wait`: This function can be used to block a thread (force waiting) until the thread is finished or the timeout value (in milliseconds) is reached.

- requestInterruption and isRequestInterrupted: These functions can be used to set and get the interruption request status. Using these functions is a useful approach to make sure the thread is stopped safely in the middle of a process that can go on forever.
- isRunning and isFinished: These functions can be used to request the execution status of the thread.

Apart from the functions we mentioned here, QThread contains other functions useful for dealing with multithreading, such as quit, exit, idealThreadCount, and so on. It is a good idea to check them out for yourself and think about use cases for each one of them. QThread is a powerful class that can help maximize the efficiency of your applications.

Let's continue with our example. In the run function, we used an OpenCV VideoCapture class to read the video frames (forever) and apply a simple bitwise_not operator to the Mat frame (we can do any other image processing at this point, so bitwise_not is only an example and a fairly simple one to explain our point), then converted that to QPixmap via QImage, and then sent the original and modified frames using two signals. Notice that in our loop that will go on forever, we will always check if the camera is still open and also check if there is an interruption request to this thread.

Now, let's use our thread in MainWindow. Start by including its header file in the mainwindow.h file:

```
#include "videoprocessorthread.h"
```

Then, add the following line to the private members' section of MainWindow, in the mainwindow.h file:

```
VideoProcessorThread processor;
```

Now, add the following code to the MainWindow constructor, right after the setupUi line:

```
connect(&processor,
        SIGNAL(inDisplay(QPixmap)),
        ui->inVideo,
        SLOT(setPixmap(QPixmap)));

connect(&processor,
        SIGNAL(outDisplay(QPixmap)),
        ui->outVideo,
        SLOT(setPixmap(QPixmap)));
processor.start();
```

And then add the following lines to the `MainWindow` destructor, right before the `delete ui;` line:

```
processor.requestInterruption();
processor.wait();
```

We simply connected the two signals from the `VideoProcessorThread` class to two labels we had added to the `MainWindow` GUI, and then started the thread as soon as the program started. We also request the thread to stop as soon as `MainWindow` is closed and right before the GUI is deleted. The `wait` function call makes sure to wait for the thread to clean up and safely finish executing before continuing with the delete instruction. Try running this code to check it for yourself. You should see something similar to the following image as soon as the program starts:

The video from your default webcam on the computer should start as soon as the program starts, and it will be stopped as soon as you close the program. Try extending the `VideoProcessorThread` class by passing a camera index number or a video file path into it. You can instantiate as many `VideoProcessorThread` classes as you want. You just need to make sure to connect the signals to correct widgets on the GUI, and this way you can have multiple videos or cameras processed and displayed dynamically at runtime.

# Using the moveToThread function

As we mentioned earlier, you can also use the moveToThread function of any QObject subclass to make sure it is running in a separate thread. To see exactly how this works, let's repeat the same example by creating exactly the same GUI, and then creating a new C++ class (same as before), but, this time, naming it VideoProcessor. This time though, after the class is created, you don't need to inherit it from QThread, leave it as QObject (as it is). Just add the following members to the videoprocessor.h file:

```
signals:
    void inDisplay(QPixmap pixmap);
    void outDisplay(QPixmap pixmap);

public slots:
    void startVideo();
    void stopVideo();

private:
    bool stopped;
```

The signals are exactly the same as before. The stopped is a flag we'll use to help us stop the video so that it does not go on forever. The startVideo and stopVideo are functions we'll use to start and stop the processing of the video from the default webcam. Now, we can switch to the videoprocessor.cpp file and add the following code blocks. Quite similar to what we had before, with the obvious difference that we don't need to implement the run function since it's not a QThread subclass, and we have named our functions as we like:

```
void VideoProcessor::startVideo()
{
    using namespace cv;
    VideoCapture camera(0);
    Mat inFrame, outFrame;
    stopped = false;
    while(camera.isOpened() && !stopped)
    {
        camera >> inFrame;
        if(inFrame.empty())
            continue;

        bitwise_not(inFrame, outFrame);

        emit inDisplay(
            QPixmap::fromImage(
                QImage(
```

```
                        inFrame.data,
                        inFrame.cols,
                        inFrame.rows,
                        inFrame.step,
                        QImage::Format_RGB888)
                            .rgbSwapped()));

            emit outDisplay(
                QPixmap::fromImage(
                    QImage(
                        outFrame.data,
                        outFrame.cols,
                        outFrame.rows,
                        outFrame.step,
                        QImage::Format_RGB888)
                            .rgbSwapped()));
        }
    }

    void VideoProcessor::stopVideo()
    {
        stopped = true;
    }
```

Now we can use it in our `MainWindow` class. Make sure to add the `include` file for the `VideoProcessor` class, and then add the following to the private members' section of `MainWindow`:

```
    VideoProcessor *processor;
```

Now, add the following piece of code to the `MainWindow` constructor in the `mainwindow.cpp` file:

```
    processor = new VideoProcessor();

    processor->moveToThread(new QThread(this));

    connect(processor->thread(),
            SIGNAL(started()),
            processor,
            SLOT(startVideo()));

    connect(processor->thread(),
            SIGNAL(finished()),
            processor,
            SLOT(deleteLater()));
```

```
connect(processor,
      SIGNAL(inDisplay(QPixmap)),
      ui->inVideo,
      SLOT(setPixmap(QPixmap)));

connect(processor,
      SIGNAL(outDisplay(QPixmap)),
      ui->outVideo,
      SLOT(setPixmap(QPixmap)));

processor->thread()->start();
```

In the preceding code snippet, first, we created an instance of `VideoProcessor`. Note that we didn't assign any parents in the constructor, and we also made sure to define it as a pointer. This is extremely important when we intend to use the `moveToThread` function. An object that has a parent cannot be moved into a new thread. The second highly important lesson in this code snippet is the fact that we should not directly call the `startVideo` function of `VideoProcessor`, and it should only be invoked by connecting a proper signal to it. In this case, we have used its own thread's started signal; however, you can use any other signal that has the same signature. The rest is all about connections.

In the `MainWindow` destructor function, add the following lines:

```
processor->stopVideo();
processor->thread()->quit();
processor->thread()->wait();
```

This is quite self-explanatory, but, just to be clear, let's make another note here, and that is after a thread has been started like this, it must be stopped by calling the `quit` function, and also, there shouldn't be any running loops or pending instructions in its object. If either one of these conditions is not met, you'll face serious issues with handling your threads.

# Thread synchronization tools

Multithreaded programming usually requires maintaining inter-thread conflicts and issues that are simply produced because of parallelism and the fact that the underlying operating system is responsible for taking care of when and how long exactly a thread will run. A powerful framework that offers multithreaded capabilities, such as the Qt framework, must also provide the means to deal with such issues, and fortunately, as we'll learn in this chapter, it does.

In this section, we will learn about possible issues that can arise from multithreading programming and the existing classes in Qt that can be used to take care of those issues. These classes are called **thread synchronization tools** in general. Thread synchronization refers to handling and programming threads in such a way that they are aware of the status of other threads using simple and easy-to-use means, and, at the same time, they can continue to fulfill their own specific tasks.

# Mutexes

If this and the upcoming sections regarding the thread synchronization tools feel already familiar to you, then you'll have an easy time following the subjects that are covered, and you'll quickly learn how easy to use are the same tools implemented in Qt; otherwise, it may be a good idea to follow these sections thoroughly and carefully. So, let's start with our first thread synchronization tool. In general, if two threads try to access the same object (such as variable or class instance, and so on) at the same time, and if the order of what each thread does with the object is important, then the resulting object may sometimes be different from what we expect. Let's break it down with an example because it may still be quite confusing, even if you totally follow what was just mentioned. Assume that one thread is reading a `Mat` class instance called `image` all the time using the following lines of code (in the reimplemented `run` function of `QThread` or from a class in a different thread using the `moveToThread` function, doesn't matter):

```
forever
{
    image = imread("image.jpg");
}
```

 The `forever` macro is a Qt macro (same as `for(;;)`) that can be used to create infinite loops. Using such Qt macros can help increase the readability of your codes.

And a second different thread is modifying this image all the time. Let's assume a very simple image processing task such as this (convert the image to grayscale and then resize it):

```
forever
{
    cvtColor(image, image, CV_BGR2GRAY);
    resize(image, image, Size(), 0.5, 0.5);
}
```

If these two threads run at the same time, then, at some point, the imread function of the first thread may be called after cvtColor and before resize in the second thread. If this happens, we would not get a grayscale image that is half the size of our input image (as it is intended in the example code). There is no way we can prevent it with this code since it's all up to the operating system when switching between threads at runtime. In multithreaded programming, this is a type of race condition problem, and it is solved by making sure each thread waits for its turn before accessing and modifying an object. The solution to this problem is called **access serialization**, and, in multithreaded programming, it is usually solved using mutex objects.

A mutex is simply a means of protecting and preventing an object instance from being accessed by more than one thread at a time. Qt provides a class called QMutex (quite conveniently) to deal with access serialization and we can use it very easily in our preceding example, as seen here. We just need to make sure a QMutex instance exists for our Mat class. Since our Mat class was called image, let's call its mutex imageMutex, then we will need to lock this mutex inside each thread that is accessing the image, and unlock it after we are done with it. So, for the first thread, we'll have this:

```
forever
{
    imageMutex.lock();
    image = imread("image.jpg");
    imageMutex.unlock();
}
```

And for the second thread, we will have the following code block:

```
forever
{
    imageMutex.lock();
    cvtColor(image, image, CV_BGR2GRAY);
    resize(image, image, Size(), 0.5, 0.5);
    imageMutex.unlock();
}
```

This way, whenever each one of the two threads starts working with the image, first, it locks the mutex using the lock function. If simply, in the middle of its process, the operating system decides to switch to the other thread, one which will also try to lock the mutex, but since the mutex is already locked, the new thread that called the lock function will be blocked until the first thread (which is called the lock) calls unlock. Think of it in terms of obtaining a key to a lock. Only the thread that calls the lock function of a mutex can unlock it by calling the unlock function. This ensures that, as long as an object is being accessed by a thread, all other threads should simply wait until it's done!

It may not be obvious from our simple example, but, in practice, using mutexes can become a burden if the number of functions that need the sensitive object increases. So, when working with Qt, it is best to use the QMutexLocker class to take care of locking and unlocking the mutexes. If we go back to our previous example, we can rewrite the same code like this:

```
forever
{
  QMutexLocker locker(&imageMutex);
  image = imread("image.jpg");
}
```

```
And for the second thread:
forever
{
  QMutexLocker locker(&imageMutex);
  cvtColor(image, image, CV_BGR2GRAY);
  resize(image, image, Size(), 0.5, 0.5);
}
```

When you construct a QMutexLocker class by passing your mutex into it, the mutex gets locked, and as soon as QMutexLocker is destroyed (for an instance when it goes out of scope), the mutex is unlocked.

# Read-write locks

As powerful as mutexes are, they lack certain capabilities, such as different types of locks. So, even though they are quite useful for access serialization, they cannot be effectively used for cases such as read-write serialization, which basically rely on two different types of locks: read and write. Let's again break this down with an example. Let's assume we want various threads to be able to read from an object (such as a variable, class instance, file, and so on) at the same time, but we want to make sure only one thread can modify (or write to) that object at any given time. For such cases, we can use the Read-Write Lock mechanisms, which are basically enhanced mutexes. The Qt framework provides the QReadWriteLock class that can be used in a similar way as the QMutex class, except that it provides a lock function for reading (lockForRead) and another lock function for writing (lockForWrite). Here are the features of each lock function:

- If the lockForRead function is called in a thread, other threads can still call lockForRead and access the sensitive object for reading purposes. (By sensitive object, we mean the object that we are using the locks for it.)

- Also, if the `lockForRead` function is called in a thread, any thread that calls `lockForWrite` will be blocked until that thread calls the unlock function.
- If the `lockForWrite` function is called in a thread, all other threads (whether it is for reading or writing) will be blocked until that thread calls unlock.
- If the `lockForWrite` function is called in a thread while there is already a read lock in place by a previous thread, all new threads that call `lockForRead` will have to wait for the thread that needs a write lock. Thus, a thread that needs `lockForWrite` will be given higher priority.

To simplify the features of read-write lock mechanisms that we just mentioned, we can say, `QReadWriteLock` can be used to make sure multiple readers can access an object at the same time and writers will have to wait for readers to finish first. On the other hand, only one writer will be allowed to write to the object; and, to guarantee that writers don't wait forever if there are too many readers, they will be given higher priority.

Now, let's see an example code on how to use the `QReadWriteLock` class. Note that the `lock` variable here has the `QReadWriteLock` type and the `read_image` function is an arbitrary function that reads from an object:

```
forever
{
    lock.lockForRead();
    read_image();
    lock.unlock();
}
```

Similarly, in a thread that needs to write to the object, we will have something like this (`write_image` is an arbitrary function that writes to an object):

```
forever
{
  lock.lockForWrite();
  write_image();
  lock.unlock();
}
```

Similar to `QMutex`, where we use `QMutexLocker` for easier handling of the `lock` and `unlock` functions, we can use `QReadLocker` and `QWriteLocker` classes to lock and unlock a `QReadWriteLock` accordingly. So, for the first thread in the preceding example, we'll have the following lines of code:

```
forever
{
    QReadLocker locker(&lock);
```

```
    Read_image();
}
```

And for the second one, we will need the following lines of code:

```
forever
{
  QWriteLocker locker(&lock);
  write_image();
}
```

# Semaphores

Sometimes, in multithreaded programming, we need to make sure multiple threads can access a limited number of identical resources accordingly. For instance, a device that will be used to run a program might have a very limited amount of memory on it, so we would prefer that our threads that need an extensive amount of memory take this fact into account and act based on the available amount of memory. This and similar issues in multithreaded programming are usually taken care of by using semaphores. A semaphore is similar to an enhanced mutex, which is not only capable of locking and unlocking, but also keeping track of the number of available resources.

The Qt framework provides a class called `QSemaphore` (conveniently enough) to work with semaphores in multithreaded programming. As semaphores are used for thread synchronization based on the number of available resources, the function names are also more suitable for this purpose instead of the `lock` and `unlock` functions. Here are the available functions in the `QSemaphore` class:

- `acquire`: This can be used to acquire a specific amount of resources that are needed. If there are not enough resources, then the thread will be blocked and has to wait until there are enough resources.
- `release`: This can be used to release a specific amount of resources that are already used and not needed anymore.
- `available`: This can be used to get the number of available resources. This function can be used in case we want our threads to perform another task instead of waiting for resources.

Nothing can shed more light on this but a proper example. Let's assume we have 100 megabytes of available memory space to be used by all our threads, and each thread requires $X$ number of megabytes to perform its task, depending on the thread, so $X$ is not the same in all threads and let's say it is calculated using the size of the image that will be processed in the thread or any other method for that matter. For our current issue at hand, we can use a QSemaphore class to make sure our threads only access the available memory space and not more. So, we will create a semaphore in our program like this:

```
QSemaphore memSem(100);
```

And, inside each thread, before and after the memory intensive process itself, we will acquire and release the required memory space, like this:

```
memSem.acquire(X);
process_image(); // memory intensive process
memSem.release(X);
```

Note that in this example, if X is greater than 100 in a certain thread, then it will not be able to continue past acquire until the release function calls (released resources) become equal or greater than the acquire function calls (acquired resources). This means the number of available resources can be increased (created) by calling the release function with a value more than the acquired resources.

# Wait conditions

Another common issue in multithreaded programming can occur because a certain thread must wait for some condition other than the thread being executed by the operating system. In such cases, if quite naturally, a mutex or a read-write lock is used by the thread, it can block all other threads because it is simply the thread's turn to run and it is waiting for some specific condition. One would expect that the thread that needs to wait for a condition, goes to sleep after it releases the mutex or read-write lock so that other threads continue to operate, and when the condition is met, it is woken up by another thread.

In the Qt framework, there is a class called QWaitCondition, which is dedicated to handling such issues we just mentioned. This class can be used by any thread that may need to wait for some condition. Let's go through this with a simple example. Assume that a number of threads work with a Mat class (an image to be precise), and one thread is responsible for reading this image (only when it exists). Now, also assume that another process, program, or user is responsible for creating this image file, so it may not be available for a while. Since the image is used by multiple threads, we may have needed to use a mutex to ensure that threads access it one at a time. However, the reader thread may still need to wait if the image still does not exist; so, for the reader thread, we will have something like this:

```
forever
{
    mutex.lock();
    imageExistsCond.wait(&mutex);
    read_image();
    mutex.unlock();
}
```

Note that in the example, mutex is of type QMutex and imageExistsCond is of type QWaitCondition. The preceding code snippet simply means, lock the mutex and start your work (reading the image), but if you have to wait until the image exists, then release the mutex so that other threads can continue to work. This requires another thread that is responsible for waking up the reader thread. So, we will have something like this:

```
forever
{
    if(QFile::exists("image.jpg"))
        imageExistsCond.wakeAll();
}
```

This thread is simply checking for the existence of the image file all the time and if that exists, it tries to wake all threads that are waiting for this wait condition. We can also use the wakeOne function instead of wakeAll, which simply tries to wake one random thread that is waiting for the wait condition. This can be useful in case we would like only one thread to start working if the condition is met.

This concludes our discussion of thread synchronization tools (or primitives). The classes presented in this section are the most important classes in the Qt framework that are used in conjunction with threads to handle thread synchronization. Make sure to check out the Qt documentation to learn about other functions existing in those classes that can be used to further improve the behavior of multithreaded applications. When writing multithreaded applications like this, or, in other words, using the low-level approach, we must make sure the threads are aware of each other one way or another, using the classes we just presented in this section. Also, it is important to note that these techniques are not the only possible way to take care of thread synchronization and sometimes (as the program grows to become more complex), you will definitely need to use a mixture of these techniques, tweak them, bend them, or even invent some of your own.

# High-level multithreading using QtConcurrent

Apart from what you learned in the previous section, the Qt framework also provides a high-level API for creating multithreaded programs without the need to deal with thread synchronization tools, such as mutexes, locks, and so on. The `QtConcurrent` namespace, or the Qt Concurrent module in Qt framework, provides easy-to-use functions that can be used to create multithreaded applications, or, in other words, concurrency, by processing through lists of data using the optimal number of threads for any platform. This will become crystal clear after we go through the functions in `QtConcurrent` and classes that are used in conjunction with it. After that, we will also deal with real-life examples to learn about the power of the Qt Concurrent module and how to utilize it.

The following functions in general (and their slightly different variants) can be used to deal with multithreading using the high-level `QtConcurrent` API:

- `filter`: This can be used to filter a list. This function needs to be provided with a list containing the data to be filtered and a filtering function. The filtering function we provide will be applied to each item in the list (using the optimal or a custom number of threads), and, depending on the value returned by the filter function, the item will be removed or kept in the list.
- `filtered`: This works the same way as `filter`, except it returns the filtered list instead of updating the input list in place.
- `filteredReduced`: This works in a way similar to the `filtered` function, but it also applies a second function to each item that passes the filter.

- `map`: This can be used to apply a specific function to all items in a list (using the optimal or a custom number of threads). Quite obviously, and similar to the `filter` function, the `map` function also needs to be provided with a list and a function.
- `mapped`: This works the same way as `map`, except it returns the resulting list instead of updating the input list in place.
- `mappedReduced`: This function works similar to a `mapped` function, but it also applies a second function to each item after the first mapping function.
- `run`: This function can be used to easily execute a function in a separate thread.

Whenever we talk about return values in the Qt Concurrent module, what we actually mean is the result of asynchronous computations. The reason is simply that of the fact that Qt Concurrent starts all computations in separate threads and no matter which one of the functions in `QtConcurrent` namespace you use, they will return immediately to the caller and the result will be available only after the computations are completed. This is done by using the so-called future variables, or, as it is implemented in the Qt framework, `QFuture` and its affiliate classes.

The `QFuture` class can be used to retrieve the result of a computation started by one of the functions mentioned in the `QtConcurrent` namespace; control its work by pausing, resuming, and such methods; and monitor the progress of that computation. To be able to use Qt signals and slots for a more flexible control over the `QFuture` class, we can use a convenient class called `QFutureWatcher`, which contains signals and slots that can be used for easier monitoring of the computation by using widgets such as progress bars (`QProgressBar` or `QProgressDialog`).

Let's summarize and clarify all that was mentioned in a real-life example application. Describing how `QFuture` and its affiliate classes are used is impossible without also describing the `QtConcurrent` namespace functions, and this can only be possible by an example:

1. Let's start by creating a Qt Widgets application project using Qt Creator, and name it `ConcurrentCV`. We will create a program that uses the Qt Concurrent module to process multiple images. To focus more on the multithreading part of the program, the process will be quite simple. We will read the date and time of each image and write it over the image, at the top-left corner of each image.

2. After the project is created, add OpenCV framework to your project by adding the following lines in your `ConcurrentCV.pro` file:

```
win32: {
```

```
    include("c:/dev/opencv/opencv.pri")
}
unix: !macx{
 CONFIG += link_pkgconfig
  PKGCONFIG += opencv
}
unix: macx{
 INCLUDEPATH += /usr/local/include
 LIBS += -L"/usr/local/lib" \
 -lopencv_world
}
```

3. To be able to use Qt Concurrent module and `QtConcurrent` namespace in a Qt project, you must make sure it is specified in your `.pro` file by adding the following line:

```
QT += concurrent
```

4. Now, we need to write the code for a couple of functions we'll require in our application. First one is getting the list of images (`*.jpg` and `*.png` files are enough) in a folder selected by the user. To be able to do this, add the following line to the `mainwindow.h` private members:

```
QFileInfoList getImagesInFolder();
```

5. Needless to say, `QFileInfoList` must be in the includes list in `mainwindow.h` file. `QFileInfoList` is, in fact, a `QList` containing `QFileInfo` elements, and it can be retrieved using the `entryInfoList` function of the `QDir` class. So, add its implementation to `mainwindow.cpp`, as seen here. Note that we simply use the file creation date and don't deal with image `EXIF` data and original date or time of taking the picture using a camera, for the sole purpose of simplicity:

```
QFileInfoList MainWindow::getImagesInFolder()
{
    QDir dir(QFileDialog::getExistingDirectory(this,
    tr("Open Images Folder")));
        return dir.entryInfoList(QStringList()
        << "*.jpg"
        << "*.png",
        QDir::NoDotAndDotDot | QDir::Files,
        QDir::Name);
}
```

6. The next function we require is called `addDateTime`. We can define and implement it outside of our class, and it is the function that we will use when calling the `QtConcurrent` map function later on. Define it like this in the `mainwindow.h` file:

```
void addDateTime(QFileInfo &info);
```

7. Add its implementation to the `mainwindow.cpp` file, like this:

```cpp
void addDateTime(QFileInfo &info)
{
  using namespace cv;
  Mat image = imread(info.absoluteFilePath().toStdString());
  if(!image.empty())
  {
   QString dateTime = info.created().toString();
   putText(image,
     dateTime.toStdString(),
     Point(30,30) , // 25 pixels offset from the corner
     FONT_HERSHEY_PLAIN,
     1.0,
     Scalar(0,0,255)); // red
   imwrite(info.absoluteFilePath().toStdString(),
        image);
  }
}
```

8. Now open the `mainwindow.ui` file, and, in **Design** mode, create a UI similar to the following. As it is seen in the following, `loopBtn` widget is `QPushButton` with text **Process in a loop** and `concurrentBtn` widget is `QPushButton` with text **Process concurrently**. To be able to compare the results of doing this task using multiple threads or in a single thread with a simple loop, we will implement both of the cases and measure the time it takes to complete in each case. Also, make sure to set the value property of the `progressBar` widget to zero before proceeding with the next steps:

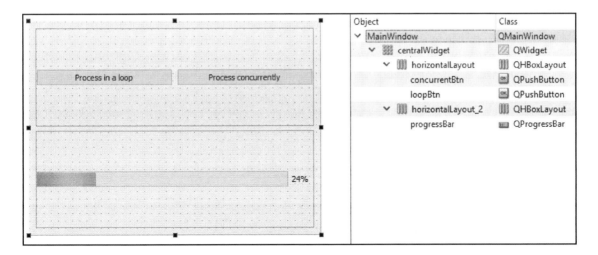

9. The only thing left to do is execute the process in a loop (with a single thread) using QtConcurrent (multithreaded). So, write the following piece of code for the pressed slot of loopBtn:

```
void MainWindow::on_loopBtn_pressed()
{
    QFileInfoList list = getImagesInFolder();

    QElapsedTimer elapsedTimer;
    elapsedTimer.start();

    ui->progressBar->setRange(0, list.count()-1);
    for(int i=0; i<list.count(); i++)
    {
     addDateTime(list[i]);
     ui->progressBar->setValue(i);
     qApp->processEvents();
    }

    qint64 e = elapsedTimer.elapsed();

    QMessageBox::information(this,
    tr("Done!"),
    QString(tr("Processed %1 images in %2 milliseconds"))
      .arg(list.count())
      .arg(e));
}
```

It's fairly simple, and definitely inefficient, as we'll learn in a few moments. This code simply loops through the files list and passes them to the `addDateTime` function, which simply reads the image and adds the date time stamp and overwrites the image.

10. Finally, add the following piece of code for the `pressed` slot of the `concurrentBtn` widget:

```cpp
void MainWindow::on_concurrentBtn_pressed()
{
    QFileInfoList list = getImagesInFolder();
    QElapsedTimer elapsedTimer;
    elapsedTimer.start();
    QFuture<void> future = QtConcurrent::map(list, addDateTime);
    QFutureWatcher<void> *watcher =
        new QFutureWatcher<void>(this);
    connect(watcher,
        SIGNAL(progressRangeChanged(int,int)),
        ui->progressBar,
        SLOT(setRange(int,int)));
    connect(watcher,
        SIGNAL(progressValueChanged(int)),
        ui->progressBar,
        SLOT(setValue(int)));
    connect(watcher,
        &QFutureWatcher<void>::finished,
        [=]()
    {
        qint64 e = elapsedTimer.elapsed();
        QMessageBox::information(this,
            tr("Done!"),
        QString(tr("Processed %1 images in %2 milliseconds"))
        .arg(list.count())
        .arg(e));
    });
    connect(watcher,
        SIGNAL(finished()),
        watcher,
        SLOT(deleteLater()));
    watcher->setFuture(future);
}
```

Before we review the preceding code and see how it works, try running the application and using both buttons with a folder of test images. The performance difference, especially on a multi-core processor, is so much that there is no need for any precise measurement. On a test machine (let's say a medium-level system nowadays) that I used with about 50 random images, the concurrent (multithreaded) version finished the job at least three times faster. There are ways to make it even more efficient, such as setting the number of threads created and used by the Qt Concurrent module, but, before that, let's see what the code does.

The starting lines are the same as before, but this time, instead of looping through the files list, we pass the list to the QtConcurrent::map function. This function then automatically starts a number of threads (using the default and ideal thread count, which is also adjustable) and applies the addDateTime function to each entry in the list. The order in which items are processed is completely undefined, but the result will be the same. The result is then passed to QFuture<void>, which is monitored by a QFutureWatcher<void> instance. As mentioned earlier, the QFutureWatcher class is a convenient way of monitoring computations from QtConcurrent, which are assigned to a QFuture class. Note that, in this case, QFutureWatcher is defined as a pointer and deleted later when the process is completed. The reason is that QFutureWatcher must remain alive for the entire time the process continues and can be deleted only after computations are finished. So, first, all required connections for QFutureWatcher are made, and then its future variable is set accordingly. It's important to make sure you set the future after all the connections are made. And it is all that is required to make a multithreaded computation using QtConcurrent that also signals the GUI in a proper way.

Note that you can also define the QFuture classwide or globally, and then use its thread control functions to easily control the computations run by QtConcurrent. QFuture contains the following (self-explanatory) functions that can be used to control the computation:

- pause
- resume
- cancel

You can also use the following functions (again, quite self-explanatory because of the naming) to retrieve the status of a computation:

- isStarted
- isPaused

- `isRunning`
- `isFinished`
- `isCanceled`

This concludes our review of the preceding code. As you can see, as long as you understand the structure and what is needed to be passed and connected, using `QtConcurrent` is fairly easy and that is the way it's supposed to be.

> Use the following function to set the maximum thread count for `QtConcurrent` functions:
>
> `QThreadPool::globalInstance()->setMaxThreadCount(n)`
>
> Try it with our example case and see how changing the number of threads affects the process time. If you play around with different numbers of threads, you'll notice that a higher number of threads don't necessarily mean a higher performance or quicker code, and that is why there is always an ideal thread count which is dependent on the processor and other system-related specs.

We can use the `QtConcurrent` filter and other functions in a similar way. For instance, for the filter function, we need to define a function that returns a Boolean for each item. Let's assume we want our preceding example application to skip images that are older than a certain date (before 2015) and remove them from the list of files, then we can define our filter function like this:

```
bool filterImage(QFileInfo &info)
{
  if(info.created().date().year() < 2015)
     true;
  else
     false;
}
```

And then call `QtConcurrent` to filter our list like this:

```
QtConcurrent::filter(list, filterImage);
```

In this case, we need to pass the filtered result to the `map` function, but there is a better way, and that is calling the `filteredReduced` function, as seen here:

```
QtConcurrent::filteredReduced(list, filterImage, addDateTime);
```

Note that the `filteredReduced` function returns a `QFuture<T>` result, where `T` is the same type as the input list. Unlike before, where we simply received `QFuture<void>` suitable to monitor the progress of the computation, `QFuture<T>` also contains the resulting list. Note that since we are not really modifying the individual elements in the list (instead we are updating the files), we will only be able to observe the change in the number of elements in the list, but if we try the same with updating a list of `Mat` classes or `QImage` classes (or any other variable for that matter), then we'll observe that the individual items are also changed according to the code in the reduce function.

# Summary

It is impossible to say that this was all there was to talk about multithreading and parallel programming, but it is fair to say that we covered some of the most important topics that can get up on your feet to write multithreaded and highly-efficient computer vision applications (or any other application). You learned how to subclass `QThread` to create new thread classes that perform a specific task or use the `moveToThread` function to move an object responsible for a complex and time-taking computation into another thread. You also learned about some of the most important low-level multithreading primitives, such as mutexes, semaphores, and so on. By now, you should be fully aware of the issues that may arise because of implementing and using multiple threads in our applications, and also the solution to those issues. If you think you still need to practice this to make sure you are familiar with all the presented concepts, then you've definitely paid good attention to all the subjects. Multithreading can be a hard and complex approach, but quite rewarding in the end if you spend a good amount of time exercising different possible multithreading scenarios. For instance, you can try dividing the tasks into some program you have written before (or seen online or in a book or anywhere else) and turn it into a multithreaded application.

In Chapter 9, *Video Analysis*, we'll combine what you learned in this chapter with the chapters before, and, by doing that, dive into video processing subjects. You'll learn about tracking moving objects in a video from camera or a file, detecting motion in videos, and more topics, all of which require handling consecutive frames and preserving what is calculated from the previous frames; in other words, calculations that depend not only on an image, but also the images before that (in time). So, we'll be using threads, using any of the methods you learned in this chapter, to implement the computer vision algorithms you'll learn in the upcoming chapter.

# 9

# Video Analysis

Apart from everything we have seen up until now throughout this book, there is another side to the computer vision story, and that is dealing with videos, cameras, and essentially real-time processing of the input frames. It is one of the most popular computer vision topics and for good reason, since it can power live machines or devices that monitor their surroundings for objects of interest, movements, patterns, colors, and so on. All of the algorithms and classes that we have learned about, especially in Chapter 6, *Image Processing in OpenCV* and Chapter 7, *Features and Descriptors*, were meant to work with a single image, and for this same reason they can be easily applied to individual video frames in the exact same way. We only need to make sure individual frames are correctly read (for instance using the `cv::VideoCapture` class) into `cv::Mat` class instances and then passed into those functions as individual images. But when dealing with videos, and by videos we mean a video feed from the network, a camera, a video file, and so on, sometimes we need results that are obtained by processing consecutive video frames from a specific time period. This means results that not only depend on the image currently fetched from a video, but also frames that were fetched before that.

In this chapter, we'll learn about some of the most important algorithms and classes in OpenCV that are meant to work with consecutive frames; thus, videos. We'll start by learning about some of the concepts used by these algorithms such as histograms and back-projection images, and then we'll dig deeper into each algorithm by using examples and gaining hands-on experience. We'll learn how to use the infamous MeanShift and CamShift algorithms for real-time object tracking, and we'll continue with motion analysis in videos. Most of what we'll learn in this chapter will be related to the video analysis module (simply called `video`) within the OpenCV framework, but we'll also make sure to go through any relevant subjects from other modules that are required in order to effectively follow the topics in this chapter, especially histograms and back-projection images that are essential to understanding the video analysis topics covered in this chapter. Background/foreground detection is also one of the most important topics we'll learn about in this chapter. By using these methods combined, you'll be able to effectively process videos to detect and analyze movements, isolate parts and pieces in video frames based on their colors, or process them in one way or another using the existing OpenCV algorithms for image processing.

Also, based on what we learned from `Chapter 8`, *Multithreading*, we'll be using threads to implement the algorithms we learn in this chapter. These threads will be independent of any project type; whether it is a stand-alone application, library, plugin, and so on, you'll be able to simply include and use them.

The following topics will be covered in this chapter:

- Histograms and how to extract, use, or visualize them
- Back-projection images
- MeanShift and CamShift algorithms
- Background/foreground detection and motion analysis

# Understanding histograms

As was mentioned in the introductory part of this chapter, there are a few concepts in computer vision that are especially important when dealing with video processing and the algorithms we'll talk about later on in this chapter. One of those concepts is histograms. Since understanding histograms is essential to understanding most of the video analysis topics, we'll go through quite a bit of information about them in this section, before moving on to the next topics. A histogram is often referred to as a way of representing the distribution of data. It is a very simple and complete description, but let's also describe what it means in terms of computer vision. In computer vision, a histogram is a graphical representation of the distribution of pixel values in an image. For example, in a grayscale image, a histogram will be a graph representing the number of pixels that contain each possible intensity in the grayscale (a value between 0 and 255). In an RGB color image, it would be three graphs, each representing the number of pixels that contain all possible red, green, or blue intensities. Note that a pixel value doesn't necessarily mean the color or intensity value. For example, in a color image converted to HSV color space, the histogram of it will contain hue, saturation, and value data.

Histograms in OpenCV are calculated using the `calcHist` function and stored in `Mat` classes, since they can be stored as an array of numbers, possibly with multiple channels. The `calcHist` function requires the following parameters to calculate a histogram:

- `images`, or the input images, are the images that we want to calculate the histograms for. It should be an array of `cv::Mat` classes.
- `nimages` is the number of images in the first parameter. Note that you can also pass an `std::vector` of `cv::Mat` classes for the first parameter, in which case you can omit this parameter.
- `channels` is an array that contains the index number of the channels that will be used to calculate the histogram.
- `mask` can be used to mask the image so that the histogram is calculated using only part of the input image. If no mask is required, we can pass an empty `Mat` class, otherwise, we need to provide a single-channel `Mat` class that contains zeros for all the pixels that should be masked and non-zero values for all the pixels that should be considered when calculating the histogram.
- `hist` is the output histogram. This should be a `Mat` class and it will be filled with the calculated histogram when the function returns.
- `dims` is the dimensionality of the histogram. It can contain a value between one and 32 (in current OpenCV 3 implementation). We need to set this depending on the number of channels we'll use to calculate the histogram.

- `histSize` is an array that contains the size of the histogram in each dimension, or the so-called *bin* size. Binning in histograms is referred to the treating of similar values as the same when calculating the histogram. We'll see what this exactly means later on with an example, but for now, let's suffice by mentioning the fact that the size of a histogram is the same as the bin count of it.
- `ranges` is an array of arrays containing the range of the values for each channel. Simply put, it should be an array that contains a pair of values for the minimum and maximum possible values for a channel.
- `uniform` is a Boolean flag that decides whether the histogram should be uniform or not.
- `accumulate` is a Boolean flag that decides whether the histogram should be cleared before it is calculated or not. This can be quite useful in case we want to update a previously calculated histogram.

Now, let's see how this function is used with a couple of examples. First, and for an easier use case, we'll calculate the histogram of a grayscale image:

```
int bins = 256;
int channels[] = {0}; // the first and the only channel
int histSize[] = { bins }; // number of bins

float rangeGray[] = {0,255}; // range of grayscale
const float* ranges[] = { rangeGray };

Mat histogram;

calcHist(&grayImg,
    1, // number of images
    channels,
    Mat(), // no masks, an empty Mat
    histogram,
    1, // dimensionality
    histSize,
    ranges,
    true, // uniform
    false // not accumulate
);
```

In the preceding code, `grayImg` is a grayscale image in a `Mat` class. The number of images is just one, and the `channels` index array parameter only includes one value (zero, for the first channel) since our input image is single-channel and grayscale. `dimensionality` is also one, and the rest of the parameters are the same as their default values (if they are omitted).

After executing the preceding code, we'll have the resulting histogram of the grayscale image inside a `histogram` variable. It's a single-channel and single-column `Mat` class with `256` rows, each row representing the number of pixels that have the pixel value the same as the row number. We can draw each of the values stored in the `Mat` class as a graph using the following code, and the output will be the visualization of our histogram in a bar chart:

```
double maxVal = 0;
minMaxLoc(histogram,
  Q_NULLPTR, // don't need min
  &maxVal,
  Q_NULLPTR, // don't need index min
  Q_NULLPTR // don't need index max
);

outputImage.create(640, // any image width
  360, // any image height
  CV_8UC(3));

outputImage = Scalar::all(128); // empty grayish image

Point p1(0,0), p2(0,outputImage.rows-1);
for(int i=0; i<bins; i++)
{
    float value = histogram.at<float>(i,0);
    value = maxVal - value; // invert
    value = value / maxVal * outputImage.rows; // scale
    p1.y = value;
    p2.x = float(i+1) * float(outputImage.cols) / float(bins);
    rectangle(outputImage,
      p1,
      p2,
      Scalar::all(0),
      CV_FILLED);
    p1.x = p2.x;
}
```

This code might look a bit tricky at first, but in fact it is quite simple, and it's based on the fact that each value in the histogram needs to be drawn as a rectangle. For each rectangle, the top-left point is calculated using the `value` variable and width of the image divided by number of bins, or in other words, `histSize`. In our example code, we simply assigned the highest possible value to the bins (which is 256), which leads to a high-resolution visualization of the histogram, since each bar in the bar chart graph will represent one-pixel intensity in the grayscale.

Note that the resolution in this sense doesn't refer to the image resolution or quality, but rather the resolution in the sense of the number of smallest pieces forming our bar chart.

We also assume that the output visualization height will be the same as the peak (highest point) of the histogram. If we run these codes on the grayscale image seen on the left side in the following picture, then the resulting histogram will be the one seen on the right:

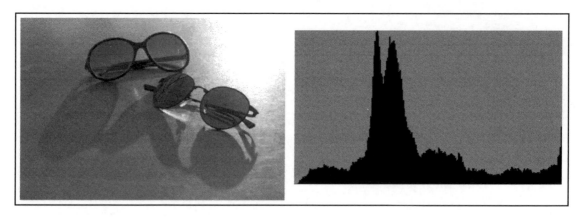

Let's interpret the output histogram visualization and shed some more light on what effect the parameters we used in the code have in general. First of all, from the left to the right, each bar refers to the number of pixels that have a specific grayscale intensity value. The leftmost bar (which is quite low) refers to absolute black (zero intensity value) and the rightmost bar refers to absolute white (255), and all of the bars in between referring to different shades of gray. Notice the small jump on the rightmost part. That is formed in fact because of the lightest part of the input image (top-left corner). The height of each bar is divided by the highest bar value and then scaled to fit the image height.

Let's also see the effect of the bins variable. Decreasing the bins will result in grouping intensities together, thus leading to a lower resolution histogram being calculated and visualized. If we run the same code with a bins value of 20, we will get the following histogram:

In case we need a simple graph instead of a bar chart view, we can use the following code in the drawing loop at the end of the previous code:

```
Point p1(0,0), p2(0,0);
for(int i=0; i<bins; i++)
{
    float value = histogram.at<float>(i,0);
    value = maxVal - value; // invert
    value = value / maxVal * outputImage.rows; // scale
    line(outputImage,
        p1,
        Point(p1.x,value),
        Scalar(0,0,0));
    p1.y = p2.y = value;
    p2.x = float(i+1) * float(outputImage.cols) / float(bins);
    line(outputImage,
        p1, p2,
        Scalar(0,0,0));
    p1.x = p2.x;
}
```

It would lead to the following output if again a `bins` value of `256` is used:

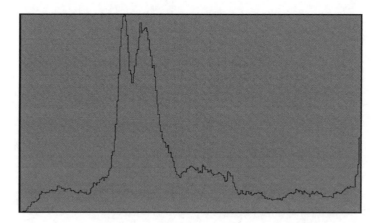

Similarly, we can calculate and visualize the histogram for a color (RGB) image. We simply need to adapt the same code for three individual channels. To be able to do this, first we need to split the input image to its underlying channels and then calculate the histogram for each one as if it was a single-channel image. Here is how you can split an image to get three `Mat` classes each representing a single channel:

```
vector<Mat> planes;
split(inputImage, planes);
```

Now you can use `planes[i]` or something similar in a loop and treat each channel as an image, then calculate and visualize its histograms using the previous code examples. If we visualize each histogram using its own color, we would get something like this as a result (the image resulting in this histogram is the colored image of our previous example that we have used throughout the book):

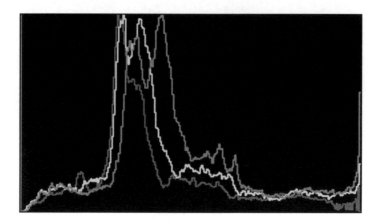

Again, the contents of the result can be interpreted in almost the same way as before. The preceding histogram image is a display of how colors are distributed in different channels of an RGB image. But how can we really use a histogram, other than just to get information about the distribution of pixel values? The next section is going to present the way a histogram can be used to modify an image.

# Understanding back-projection images

Apart from the visual information in a histogram, there is a much more important use for it. This is called back-projection of a histogram, which can be used to modify an image using its histogram, or as we'll see later on in this chapter, to locate objects of interest inside an image. Let's break it down further. As we learned in the previous section, a histogram is the distribution of pixel data over the image, so if we somehow modify the resulting histogram and then re-apply it to the source image (as if it was a lookup table for pixel values), the resulting image would be considered the back-projection image. It is important to note that a back-projection image is always a single-channel image in which the value of each pixel is fetched from its corresponding bin in the histogram.

Let's see this as another example. First of all, here is how a back-projection is calculated in OpenCV:

```
calcBackProject(&image,
    1,
    channels,
    histogram,
    backprojection,
    ranges);
```

The `calcBackProject` function is used in quite a similar way to the `calcHist` function. You only need to make sure you pass an additional `Mat` class instance to get the back-projection of the image. Since in a back-projection image the pixel values are taken from the histogram, they can easily overflow the standard grayscale range, which is between 0 and 255 (inclusive). That is why we need to normalize the result of the histogram accordingly before calculating the back-projection. Here is how:

```
normalize(histogram,
    histogram,
    0,
    255,
    NORM_MINMAX);
```

The `normalize` function will scale all the values in the histogram to fit the provided minimum and maximum values, which are 0 and 255 respectively. Just to repeat once more, this function must be called before `calcBackProject`, otherwise, you'll end up with overflowed data in your back-projection image, which will most likely contain all white pixels if you try to view it using the `imshow` function.

If we view the back-projection image without performing any modifications on the histogram that produced it, then in our example case we'll have the following output image:

The intensity of each pixel in the preceding image is relevant to the number of pixels in the image that contain that specific value. For example, notice the top-right darkest part of the back-projection image. This area contains pixels with values that are not found a lot in comparison to the brighter areas. Or to put it another way, the areas that are bright contain pixel values that exist much more in the image and across various regions of it. So again, how can we use this when processing images and video frames?

In essence, back-projection images can be used to get useful mask images for computer vision operations. Up until now, we didn't really use mask parameters in OpenCV functions (and they exist in most of them). Let's start with an example using the preceding back-projection image. We can modify the histogram with a simple threshold to get a mask for filtering out parts of the image that we do not need. Let's say we want a mask that can be used for getting the pixels that contain the darkest values (from 0 to 39 pixel value for instance). To be able to do this, first we can modify the histogram by setting the first 40 elements (just a threshold for darkest values, it can be set to any other value or range) to the maximum possible value in the grayscale range (255) and the rest to the minimum possible value (zero) and calculate the back-projection image. Here's an example:

```
calcHist(&grayImg,
    1, // number of images
    channels,
    Mat(), // no masks, an empty Mat
    histogram,
    1, // dimensionality
    histSize,
    ranges);

for(int i=0; i<histogram.rows; i++)
{
    if(i < 40) // threshold
        histogram.at<float>(i,0) = 255;
    else
        histogram.at<float>(i,0) = 0;
}

Mat backprojection;
calcBackProject(&grayImg,
    1,
    channels,
    histogram,
    backprojection,
    ranges);
```

By running the preceding example code, we'll get the following output image inside the `backprojection` variable. This is, in fact, a thresholding technique to get a suitable mask for isolating the darkest areas in an image for any computer vision process using OpenCV. The mask that we obtained using this example code can be passed into any OpenCV function that accepts masks for performing operations on pixels that correspond to white locations in the mask, and ignoring the ones that correspond to black locations:

Another technique similar to the thresholding method we just learned can be used for masking out areas in images that contain a specific color, which consequently can be used for processing (for instance modifying the color of) only some parts of an image or even tracking an object that has a specific color, as we'll learn later on in this chapter. But before that, let's first learn about histograms for HSV color spaces (using the hue channel) and how to isolate part of an image that has a specific color. Let's also go through this with an example. Imagine you need to find parts of an image that contain a specific color, for instance the red rose in the following picture:

You can't simply filter out the red channel (in the RGB image) based on a threshold, since it might be simply too bright or too dark, but it can still be a different shade of the red color. Also, you might want to consider colors that are too similar to red to make sure you get the rose as precisely as possible. This, and similar cases where you need to deal with the colors are best handled using the **hue**, **saturation**, **value** (**HSV**) color space, where colors are preserved in a single channel (hue or h channel). This can be demonstrated with an example experiment using OpenCV. Simply try running the following code snippet in a new application. It can be a console application or widgets, it doesn't matter:

```
Mat image(25, 180, CV_8UC3);
for(int i=0; i<image.rows; i++)
{
  for(int j=0; j<image.cols; j++)
  {
    image.at<Vec3b>(i,j)[0] = j;
    image.at<Vec3b>(i,j)[1] = 255;
    image.at<Vec3b>(i,j)[2] = 255;
  }
}
cvtColor(image,image,CV_HSV2BGR);
imshow("Hue", image);
```

Note that we are only changing the first channel in our three-channel image, and the value changes from 0 to 179. This will result in the following output:

The reason for this, as mentioned before, is the fact that hue, single handedly, is responsible for the color of each pixel. The saturation and value channels, on the other hand, can be used to get brighter (using the saturation channel) and darker (using the value channel) variations of the same colors. Note that in HSV color space, unlike RGB, hue is a value between 0 and 360. This is because hue is modeled as a circle, so, whenever its value overflows, the color goes back to the start. This is obvious if you look at the start and end of the previous image, both of which are red, so a hue value around 0 or 360 must be a reddish color.

In OpenCV however, hue is normally divided by two to fit eight bits (unless we use 16 or more bits for pixel data), so the value of hue can vary between 0 and 180. If you go back to the previous code sample, you can notice that the hue value is set from 0 to 180 over the columns of our `Mat` class, which leads to our color spectrum output image.

Now let's create a color histogram using what we just learned, and use it to get a back-projection image to isolate our red rose. To give this a purpose, we can even make it a blue rose using a simple piece of code, but as we'll learn later on in this chapter, this same method is used in conjunction with the MeanShift and CamShift algorithms to track objects that have a specific color. Our histogram will be based on the color distribution or the hue channel in the HSV version of our image. So, we need to first convert it to HSV color space using the following code:

```
Mat hsvImg;
cvtColor(inputImage, hsvImg, CV_BGR2HSV);
```

And then calculate the histogram using the exact same method we used in the preceding example. The main difference (in visualization) this time, is the fact that the histogram needs to also display the colors for each of the bins since it's a color distribution, otherwise, the output would be hard to interpret. To make a proper output, this time we'll use HSV to BGR conversion to create a buffer that contains the color value of all the bins, and then fill each of the bars in the output bar chart accordingly. Here's the source code for correctly visualizing a hue channel histogram (or in other words, color distribution graph), after it is calculated:

```
Mat colors(1, bins, CV_8UC3);
for(int i=0; i<bins; i++)
{
  colors.at<Vec3b>(i) =
  Vec3b(saturate_cast<uchar>(
    (i+1)*180.0/bins), 255, 255);
}
cvtColor(colors, colors, COLOR_HSV2BGR);

Point p1(0,0), p2(0,outputImage.rows-1);
```

```
for(int i=0; i<ui->binsSpin->value(); i++)
{
  float value = histogram.at<float>(i,0);
  value = maxVal - value; // invert
  value = value / maxVal * outputImage.rows; // scale
  p1.y = value;
  p2.x = float(i+1) * float(outputImage.cols) / float(bins);
  rectangle(outputImage,
   p1,
   p2,
   Scalar(colors.at<Vec3b>(i)),
   CV_FILLED);
  p1.x = p2.x;
}
```

As we saw in the previous code examples, maxVal is calculated using the minMaxLoc function from the histogram data. bins are simply the number of bins (or histogram size), which cannot be higher than 180 in this case; as we know, hue can vary only between 0 and 179. The rest is pretty much identical, except setting the fill color value of each bar in the graph. If we execute the preceding code using the maximum bin size (which is 180) in our example rose image, we'll get the following output:

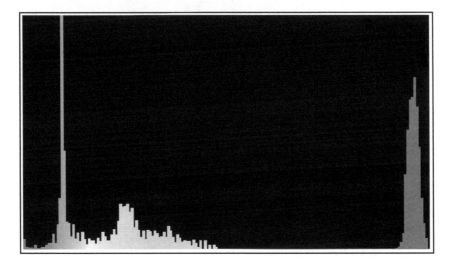

In this histogram, basically all possible colors with our hue precision (eight bits) are considered in the histogram, but we can simplify this even more by reducing the bin size. A bin size of 24 is low enough to simplify and group similar colors together, and at the same time provide enough precision. If we change the bin size to 24, we would get the following output:

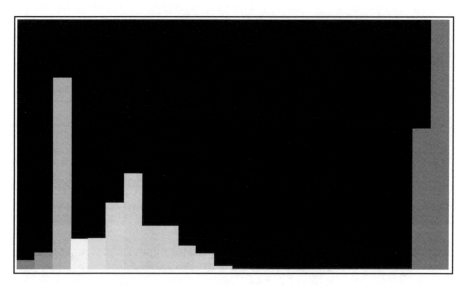

By taking a look at the histogram, it seems obvious that the first (from the left) and last two bars from the 24 bars in the histogram are the most reddish colors. Just like before, we'll simply threshold everything else, except those. Here's how:

```
for(int i=0; i<histogram.rows; i++)
{
   if((i==0) || (i==22) || (i==23)) // filter
     histogram.at<float>(i,0) = 255;
   else
     histogram.at<float>(i,0) = 0;
}
```

A good practice case for this is to make a user interface that allows selecting bins in a histogram and filtering them out. You can do this yourself based on what you have learned so far, by using a QGraphicsScene and QGraphicsRectItem to draw the bar charts and the histogram. You can then enable item selection and make sure when the **Delete** button is pressed, bars are removed and consequently filtered out.

After the simple threshold, we can calculate the back-projection using the following code. Note that since our histogram is a single-dimensional histogram, we can reapply it using the back-project only if the input image is also single-channel. That is why first we need to extract the hue channel from the image. The mixChannels function can be used to copy a channel from one Mat class to another. So, we can use this same function to copy the hue channel from our HSV image into a single-channel Mat class. The mixChannels function simply needs to be provided with the source and destination Mat classes (of the same depth only, not channels necessarily), the number of source and destination images, and a pair of integers (fromto array in the following code) for deciding the source channel index and destination channel index:

```
Mat hue;
int fromto[] = {0, 0};
hue.create(hsvImg.size(), hsvImg.depth());
mixChannels(&hsvImg, 1, &hue, 1, fromto, 1);
Mat backprojection;
calcBackProject(&hue,
    1,
    channels,
    histogram,
    backprojection,
    ranges);
```

Display the back-projection image in an output using imshow as it is, or a Qt Widget, after converting it to RGB color space, and you'll see our perfect mask for the reddish colors in the example rose image:

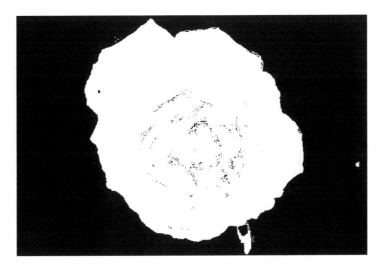

Now if we shift the value in the hue channel by the correct amount, we can get a blue rose out of our red rose; not just the same static blue color, but with the correct shade and brightness values in all corresponding pixels. If you go back to the color spectrum image output that we created earlier on in this chapter, you'll notice that red, green, blue, and red again exactly coincide with the hue values 0, 120, 240, and 360. Of course, again, if we consider the division by two (because 360 can't fit into a byte, but 180 can), they are actually 0, 60, 120, and 180. This means if we want to shift the red color in a hue channel to get the blue color, we must shift it by 120, and similarly for shifting to get other colors. So, we can use something like this to correctly shift the colors, and only in the pixels that are highlighted by our preceding back-projection image. Note that we also need to take care of overflows, since the highest possible hue value should be 179 and not more:

```
for(int i=0; i<hsvImg.rows; i++)
{
  for(int j=0; j<hsvImg.cols; j++)
  {
    if(backprojection.at<uchar>(i, j))
    {
        if(hsvImg.at<Vec3b>(i,j)[0] < 60)
            hsvImg.at<Vec3b>(i,j)[0] += 120;
        else if(hsvImg.at<Vec3b>(i,j)[0] > 120)
            hsvImg.at<Vec3b>(i,j)[0] -= 60;
    }
  }
}

Mat imgHueShift;
cvtColor(hsvImg, imgHueShift, CV_HSV2BGR);
```

By executing the preceding code, we'll get the following result image, which is simply the RGB image that is converted back from an image that has its reddish pixels turned into blue:

Try the same thing with different bin sizes for histograms. Also as an exercise you can try to build a proper GUI for color shifting. You can even try writing a program that can change objects with a specific color (color histogram to be precise) in the image to some other color. A quite similar technique is widely used in movie and photo editing programs to shift the color (hue) of specific regions in an image or continuous video frames.

# Histogram comparison

Two histograms calculated by using the `calcHist` function, or loaded from disk and filled into a `Mat` class, or literally created with any method, can be compared with each other to find the distance or difference (or divergence) between them, by using the `compareHist` method. Note that this is true as long as the `Mat` structure of the histograms is consistent with what we saw before, meaning the number of columns, depth, and channels.

The `compareHist` function takes two histograms stored in `Mat` classes and a `comparison` method, which can be one of the following constants:

- `HISTCMP_CORREL`
- `HISTCMP_CHISQR`
- `HISTCMP_INTERSECT`
- `HISTCMP_BHATTACHARYYA`
- `HISTCMP_HELLINGER`
- `HISTCMP_CHISQR_ALT`
- `HISTCMP_KL_DIV`

Note that the return value of the `compareHist` function and how it should be interpreted is completely dependent on the `comparison` method, and they vary quite a lot, so make sure to check out the OpenCV documentation pages for a detailed list of the underlying comparison equations used in each method. Here is an example code that can be used to calculate the difference between two images (or two video frames) using all of the existing methods:

```
Mat img1 = imread("d:/dev/Packt/testbw1.jpg", IMREAD_GRAYSCALE);
Mat img2 = imread("d:/dev/Packt/testbw2.jpg", IMREAD_GRAYSCALE);

float range[] = {0, 255};
const float* ranges[] = {range};
int bins[] = {100};

Mat hist1, hist2;
```

```
calcHist(&img1, 1, 0, Mat(), hist1, 1, bins, ranges);
calcHist(&img2, 1, 0, Mat(), hist2, 1, bins, ranges);

qDebug() << compareHist(hist1, hist2, HISTCMP_CORREL);

qDebug() << compareHist(hist1, hist2, HISTCMP_CHISQR);

qDebug() << compareHist(hist1, hist2, HISTCMP_INTERSECT);

// Same as HISTCMP_HELLINGER
qDebug() << compareHist(hist1, hist2, HISTCMP_BHATTACHARYYA);

qDebug() << compareHist(hist1, hist2, HISTCMP_CHISQR_ALT);

qDebug() << compareHist(hist1, hist2, HISTCMP_KL_DIV);
```

We can try the preceding code on the following two images:

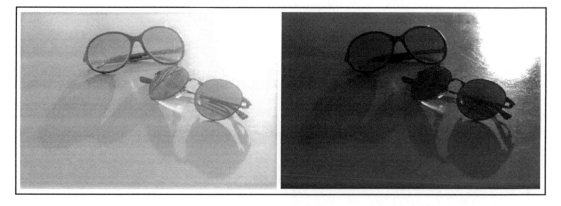

The result of comparisons can be viewed in the Qt Creator output, as seen here:

```
-0.296291
1.07533e+08
19811
0.846377
878302
834340
```

It is a common practice to use the histogram difference to compare images in general. It is also possible to use a similar technique in video frames to detect divergence from a scene or an object existing in the scene. For this reason, a previously prepared histogram should be present that is then compared with the histogram of each incoming video frame.

# Histogram equalization

The histogram of an image can be used to adjust the brightness and contrast of an image. OpenCV offers a function called `equalizeHist` that internally calculates the histogram of a given image, normalizes the histogram, calculates the integral of the histogram (sum of all bins), and then uses the updated histogram as a lookup table to update the input image's pixels, which leads to a normalized brightness and contrast in the input image. Here's how this function is used:

```
equalizeHist(image, equalizedImg);
```

If you try this function on images that have an out-of-place brightness level, or contract, then they will be automatically adjusted to a visually better level in terms of brightness and contrast. This process is called **histogram equalization**. The following example displays two images that have a too low or too high brightness level, along with their histograms, which display the corresponding pixel value distribution. The image on the left is produced by using the `equalizeHist` function, which for both of the images on the left side it looks more or less the same. Notice the change in the histogram of the output image, which in turn leads to a more visually appealing image:

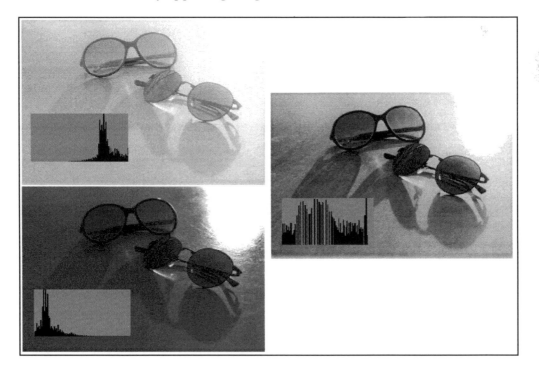

A similar technique is used in most digital cameras to adjust the darkness and brightness of pixels according to the amount of their distribution across the whole image. You can try this with any common smartphone too. Just point your camera towards a bright area and the software on your smartphone will start lowering the brightness level, and vice versa.

# MeanShift and CamShift

What we learned until now in this chapter, apart from the use cases that we already saw, was meant to prepare us for correctly using the MeanShift and CamShift algorithms, since they extensively benefit from histograms and back-projection images. But what are the MeanShift and CAMShift algorithms?

Let's start with the MeanShift and then move on to CamShift, which is basically the enhanced version of the same algorithm. So, a very practical definition for MeanShift (as it is stated in the current OpenCV documentation) is the following:

*Finds an object on a back projection image*

That's quite a simple yet practical definition of the MeanShift algorithm, and we are going to stick to that more or less when we work with it. However, it's worth noting the underlying algorithm, since it helps with using it easily and much more efficiently. To start describing how MeanShift works, first, we need to think about the white pixels in a back-projection image (or binary images in general) as scattered points across a 2D plane. That should be quite easy. With this as a pretext, we can say that MeanShift is, in fact, an iterative method that is used to find the densest location of points on a plane where they are distributed. This algorithm is provided with an initial window (a rectangle that specifies part of the whole image), which is used to search for the mass center, and then shifts the window center to the newly found mass center. This process of finding the mass center and shifting the window center is repeated until either the shift necessary is smaller than a provided threshold (epsilon) or the maximum number of iterations is reached. The following image represents the way the window is shifted after each iteration in the MeanShift algorithm until it reaches the densest location (or even before, if the iteration count is reached):

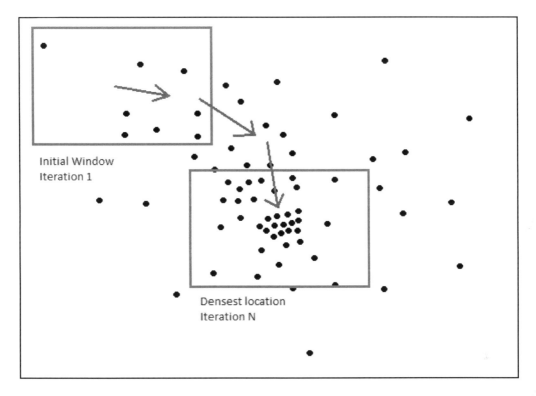

Based on this, the MeanShift algorithm can be used to track an object in a video, by making sure the object is distinguished in the back-projection of each frame. Of course, for this we need to use a similar threshold method as we used before. The most common way to do this is by applying an already prepared histogram and calculating a back-projection using it (in our preceding examples we simply modified the input histogram). Let's go through this step by step with an example. We are going to create a `QThread` subclass for this reason, which can be created from within any standalone Qt application, or used inside a DLL or from a plugin, as we'll use for the `computer_vision` project. No matter what, this thread will stay exactly the same for all project types.

As discussed in Chapter 8, *Multithreading,* processing a video should be done in a separate thread (if we are not looking for any ugly workarounds) so that it does not block the GUI thread and leaves it free to respond to user actions. Note that this same thread can also be used as a template for creating any other (similar) video processing threads. So, let's start:

1. We are going to create a Qt widgets application that can track an object (with any color, but not completely white or black in this case) that will be initially selected using the mouse, on a live feed from the camera, and using the MeanShift algorithm. We will be able to change to another object in the scene, again on the live feed from the camera, anytime after the initial selection. The first time an object is selected, and each time the selection is changed after that, the hue channel of the video frame will be extracted and, using the histogram and back-projection images, calculated and provided to the MeanShift algorithm, and the object will be tracked. So, we need to first create a Qt Widgets application and give it a name such as MeanShiftTracker, then continue with the actual tracker implementation.

2. Create a QThread subclass, as we learned in Chapter 8, *Multithreading.* Name it QCvMeanShiftThread and make sure you include the following in the private and public member areas accordingly. We are going to use the setTrackRect function to set the initial MeanShift track window using this function, but also using this function we'll provide the means to change the tracking to another object. newFrame is quite obvious and it will be emitted after each frame is processed so that the GUI can display it. The members in the private area and the GUI will be described in later steps when they are used, but they pack some of the most important topics we have learned about until now:

```
public slots:
  void setTrackRect(QRect rect);

signals:
  void newFrame(QPixmap pix);

private:
  void run() override;
  cv::Rect trackRect;
  QMutex rectMutex;
  bool updateHistogram;
```

3. The `setTrackRect` function is simply the `setter` function used to update the rectangle (initial window) that we want the MeanShift algorithm to track. Here is how it should be implemented:

```
void QCvMeanShiftThread::setTrackRect(QRect rect)
{
    QMutexLocker locker(&rectMutex);
    if((rect.width()>2) && (rect.height()>2))
    {
        trackRect.x = rect.left();
        trackRect.y = rect.top();
        trackRect.width = rect.width();
        trackRect.height = rect.height();
        updateHistogram = true;
    }
}
```

The `QMutexLocker` in conjunction with `rectMutex` is used for providing access serialization to our `trackRect`. Since we are going to also implement the tracking method in a way that it works in real-time, we need to make sure `trackRect` is not updated while it is being processed. We also make sure it has a reasonable amount of size, otherwise, it is simply ignored.

4. As for the `run` function of our tracker thread, we need to use a `VideoCapture` to open the default camera on the computer and deliver us the frames. Notice that the loop will exit if a frame is empty (broken), the camera is closed, or thread interruption is requested from outside of the thread:

```
VideoCapture video;
video.open(0);
while(video.isOpened() && !this->isInterruptionRequested())
{
    Mat frame;
    video >> frame;
    if(frame.empty())
    break;
    // rest of the process ...
    ....
}
```

Inside the loop, where it's marked as `rest of the process ...`, first we'll use the area function of the `cv::Rect` class to see if a `trackRect` is already set or not. If it is, then we'll lock the access and continue with the tracking operation:

```
if(trackRect.size().area() > 0)
{
   QMutexLocker locker(&rectMutex);
   // tracking code
}
```

As for the MeanShift algorithm and the real tracking, we can use the following source code:

```
Mat hsv, hue, hist;
cvtColor(frame, hsv, CV_BGR2HSV);
hue.create(hsv.size(), hsv.depth());
float hrange[] = {0, 179};
const float* ranges[] = {hrange};
int bins[] = {24};
int fromto[] = {0, 0};
mixChannels(&hsv, 1, &hue, 1, fromto, 1);

if(updateHistogram)
{
   Mat roi(hue, trackRect);
   calcHist(&roi, 1, 0, Mat(), hist, 1, bins, ranges);

   normalize(hist,
       hist,
       0,
       255,
       NORM_MINMAX);

   updateHistogram = false;
}

Mat backProj;
calcBackProject(&hue,
   1,
   0,
   hist,
   backProj,
   ranges);

TermCriteria criteria;
criteria.maxCount = 5;
criteria.epsilon = 3;
```

```
criteria.type = TermCriteria::EPS;
meanShift(backProj, trackRect, criteria);

rectangle(frame, trackRect, Scalar(0,0,255), 2);
```

The preceding code does the following, and exactly in this order:

- Converts the input frame from BGR to HSV color space, using the cvtColor function.
- Extracts the hue channel only, using the mixChannels function.
- If needed, calculates and normalizes the histogram, using the calcHist and normalize functions.
- Calculates the back-projection image, using the calcBackproject function.
- Runs the MeanShift algorithm on the back-projection image, by providing the criteria for iteration. This is done using the TermCriteria class and the meanShift function. meanShift will simply update the provided rectangle (trackRect with a new one at each frame).
- Draws the retrieved rectangle on the original image.

There is nothing new in any of the code you just saw, except the TermCriteria class and the meanShift function itself. As mentioned earlier on, the MeanShift algorithm is an iterative method that needs some stop criteria, based on the amount of shift (epsilon) and the number of iteration. To put it simply, increasing the number of iterations can slow down the algorithm but also make it more accurate. On the other hand, providing a smaller epsilon value would mean a much more sensitive behavior.

After each frame is processed, the thread still needs to send it over to another class using the dedicated signal. Here is how:

```
emit newFrame(
    QPixmap::fromImage(
        QImage(
            frame.data,
            frame.cols,
            frame.rows,
            frame.step,
            QImage::Format_RGB888)
            .rgbSwapped()));
```

Note that apart from sending a QPixmap or QImage and so on, we can also send classes that are not QObject subclasses. To be able to send a non-Qt class over a Qt signal, it must have a public default constructor, a public copy constructor, and a public destructor. It also needs to be registered first. For instance, the Mat class contains the required methods but is not a registered type, so you can register it as seen here: qRegisterMetaType<Mat>("Mat");. After this, you can use the Mat class in Qt signals and slots.

5. We still can't see any results unless we complete the user interface needed for this thread. Let's do it with a QGraphicsView. Just drag and drop one on your mainwindow.ui using the designer, and then add the following to mainwindow.h. We are going to use the rubber band capability of the QGraphicsView class to easily implement object selection:

```
private:
  QCvMeanShiftThread *meanshift;
  QGraphicsPixmapItem pixmap;

private slots:
  void onRubberBandChanged(QRect rect,
  QPointF frScn, QPointF toScn);
  void onNewFrame(QPixmap newFrm);
```

6. In the mainwindow.cpp file and in the constructor of the MainWindow class, make sure to add the following:

```
ui->graphicsView->setScene(new QGraphicsScene(this));
ui->graphicsView->setDragMode(QGraphicsView::RubberBandDrag);
connect(ui->graphicsView,
SIGNAL(rubberBandChanged(QRect,QPointF,QPointF)),
this,
SLOT(onRubberBandChanged(QRect,QPointF,QPointF)));

meanshift = new QCvMeanShiftThread();
connect(meanshift,
  SIGNAL(newFrame(QPixmap)),
  this,
  SLOT(onNewFrame(QPixmap)));
  meanshift->start();

ui->graphicsView->scene()->addItem(&pixmap);
```

How to use the Qt Graphics View Framework was discussed in detail in Chapter 5, *The Graphics View Framework.*

7. Also make sure to take care of the thread when the application is closed, as seen here:

```
meanshift->requestInterruption();
meanshift->wait();
delete meanshift;
```

8. The only thing left is to set the incoming QPixmap on the GUI itself, and also pass the rectangle needed for updating the object that is being tracked:

```
void MainWindow::onRubberBandChanged(QRect rect,
  QPointF frScn,
  QPointF toScn)
  {
    meanshift->setTrackRect(rect);
  }

void MainWindow::onNewFrame(QPixmap newFrm)
{
  pixmap.setPixmap(newFrm);
}
```

Try running the application and choosing an object visible on the camera. The rectangle you draw on the graphics view using your mouse will follow the object you have selected wherever it goes on the screen. Here are a few screenshots of the Qt logo being tracked after it is selected from the view:

It's also a good idea to visualize the back-projection image and see the magic that is going on behind the scenes. Remember, as mentioned before, the MeanShift algorithm is searching for the mass center, which is quite easy to perceive when observed in the back-projection image. Just replace the last few lines we used for visualizing the image inside the thread, with the following code:

```
cvtColor(backProj, backProj, CV_GRAY2BGR);
frame = backProj;
rectangle(frame, trackRect, Scalar(0,0,255), 2);
```

Now try again. You should have the back-projection image in your graphics view:

As can be seen from the results, the MeanShift algorithm, or the `meanShift` function to be precise, is extremely easy to use as long as you provide a grayscale image to it, which isolates the object of interest using any threshold method. And yes, back-projection is also similar to thresholding where you let some pixels pass or some other pixels not pass based on a color, intensity, or other criterion. Now, if we go back to the initial description of the MeanShift algorithm, it will totally make sense to say that it can find and track an object based on the back-projection image.

As easy as the `meanShift` function is to use, it still lacks a couple of very important capabilities. Those are tolerance to scale and orientation changes in the object that is being tracked. No matter what the size of the object or its orientation is, the `camShift` function will provide a window of the exact same size and rotation that just tries to center on the object of interest. These issues are solved in the enhanced version of the MeanShift algorithm, which is called the **Continuously Adaptive MeanShift** algorithm, or CamShift for short.

The `CamShift` function, which is the implementation of the CamShift algorithm in OpenCV, shares a lot with the MeanShift algorithm, and for this same reason, it is used in an almost identical way. To prove this, simply replace the call to the `meanShift` algorithm in the preceding codes with `CamShift`, as seen here:

```
CamShift(backProj, trackRect, criteria);
```

If you run the program again you'll notice that nothing has really changed. But this function also provides a return value of type `RotatedRect`, which is basically a rectangle but with center, size, and angle properties. You can save the returned `RotatedRect` and draw it on the original image, as seen here:

```
RotatedRect rotRec = CamShift(backProj, trackRect, criteria);
rectangle(frame, trackRect, Scalar(0,0,255), 2);
ellipse(frame, rotRec, Scalar(0,255,0), 2);
```

Note that we actually draw an ellipse that fits our `RotatedRect` class properties in this piece of code. We also draw the previously existing rectangle for comparison with the rotated one. Here is the result if you try running the program again:

Notice the rotation of the green ellipse in contrast to the red rectangle, which is the result of the `CamShift` function. Try moving the colored object that is being tracked away from or near to the camera and see how `CamShift` tries to adapt to the changes. Also, try a non-square object to observe the rotation invariant tracking provided by `CamShift`.

The `CamShift` function can also be used to detect an object based on its color; of course, if it is distinguishable from its surrounding environment. For this reason, you need to set a previously prepared histogram instead of setting it on runtime like in our example. You also need to set the initial window size to quite a big one, such as the size of the whole image, or the biggest area in the image where the object is expected to appear. By running the same code, you'll notice that after each frame the window becomes smaller and smaller until it only covers the object of interest to which we provided the histogram for.

# Background/foreground detection

Background/foreground detection, or segmentation, which is often also referred to as background subtraction for quite good reasons, is the method of differentiating between the moving or changing regions in an image (foreground), as opposed to the regions that are more or less constant or static (background). This method is also very effective in detecting motions in an image. OpenCV includes a number of different methods for background subtraction, with two of them being available in the current OpenCV installation by default, namely `BackgroundSubtractorKNN` and `BackgroundSubtractorMOG2`. Similar to the feature detector classes we learned about in Chapter 7, *Features and Descriptors*, these classes also originate from the `cv::Algorithm` class, and they are both used quite easily and similarly since they differ not in the usage or the result, but in the implementation of the classes.

`BackgroundSubtractorMOG2` can be used to detect the background/foreground by using the Gaussian mixture model. `BackgroundSubtractorKNN`, on the other hand, can also be used to achieve the same goal, by using the **kNN** or **k-nearest neighbors** method.

If you are interested in the internal details of these algorithms, or how they are implemented, you can refer to the following papers for more information:

- *Zoran Zivkovic and Ferdinand van der Heijden. Efficient adaptive density estimation per image pixel for the task of background subtraction. Pattern recognition letters, 27(7):773-780, 2006.*
- *Zoran Zivkovic. Improved adaptive gaussian mixture model for background subtraction. In Pattern Recognition, 2004. ICPR 2004. Proceedings of the 17th International Conference on, volume 2, pages 28-31. IEEE, 2004.*

Let's first see how they are both used and then go through some of their important functions. Similar to the QCvMeanShiftThread class that we created in the previous section, we can create a new thread by subclassing QThread. Let's do it and name it QCvBackSubThread, or any name you see fit. The only part with a difference will be the overridden run function, and it will look like the following:

```
void QCvBackgroundDetect::run()
{
    using namespace cv;

    Mat foreground;
    VideoCapture video;
    video.open(0);

    Ptr<BackgroundSubtractorMOG2> subtractor =
        createBackgroundSubtractorMOG2();

    while(video.isOpened() && !this->isInterruptionRequested())
    {
        Mat frame;
        video >> frame;
        if(frame.empty())
            break; // or continue if this should be tolerated

        subtractor->apply(frame, foreground);

        Mat foregroundBgr;
        cvtColor(foreground, foregroundBgr, CV_GRAY2BGR);

        emit newFrame(
            QPixmap::fromImage(
                QImage(
                    foregroundBgr.data,
                    foregroundBgr.cols,
                    foregroundBgr.rows,
                    foregroundBgr.step,
                    QImage::Format_RGB888)
                .rgbSwapped())));

    }
}
```

Notice that the only calls needed for background subtraction are the construction of the `BackgroundSubtractorMOG2` class and calling the `apply` function. There is nothing more in terms of using them, which makes them pretty straightforward and easy to use. At each frame, the foreground, which is a `Mat` class, is updated according to the history of changes in all areas of the image. Since we simply used the default parameters by calling the `createBackgroundSubtractorMOG2` function, we didn't change any of the parameters and continued with the defaults, but in case we want to change the behavior of the algorithm, we need to provide the following parameters to it:

- `history`, which is set to 500 by default, is the number of last frames that affect the background subtraction algorithm. In our example, we also used the default value which is roughly about 15 seconds on a 30 FPS camera or video. This means that if an area is completely unchanged for the past 15 seconds, it will be completely black.
- `varThreshold`, which is set to 16 by default, is the variance threshold of the algorithm.
- `detectShadows`, which is set to true by default, can be used to ignore or count detecting shadow changes.

Try running the preceding example program that uses the default parameters and observes the results. You should see a completely black screen if nothing is moving in front of the camera, but even the slightest movements can be viewed as white areas on the output. You should see something like this:

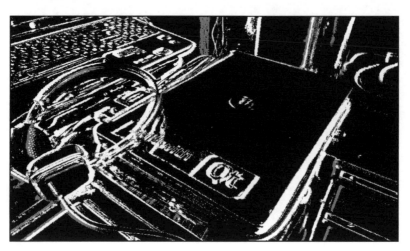

It's quite easy to switch to the `BackgroundSubtractorKNN` class, you simply need to replace the construction line with the following:

```
Ptr<BackgroundSubtractorKNN> subtractor =
    createBackgroundSubtractorKNN();
```

Nothing else needs to change. However, to modify the behavior of this algorithm, you can use the following parameters, some of which are also shared with the `BackgroundSubtractorMOG2` class:

- `history`, is exactly the same as the previous algorithm.
- `detectShadows`, is also the same as the previous algorithm.
- `dist2Threshold`, is set to `400.0` by default and is the threshold value for the squared distance between the pixel and the sample. To better understand this, it is better to take a look at the k-nearest neighbor's algorithm online. You can of course simply go with the default values and use the algorithm without providing any parameters at all.

Nothing can help you become more efficient in using these algorithms than trying out various parameters and observing the results. For example, you can notice that increasing the history value will help with detecting even smaller movements. Try changing the rest of the parameters to observe and compare the results by yourself.

In the previous example, we tried outputting the foreground mask image extracted by using the background subtraction classes. You can also use the same foreground mask in a `copyTo` function to output the actual pixels of the foreground. Here's how:

```
frame.copyTo(outputImage, foreground);
```

Where `frame` is the input frame from the camera, and `foreground` is obtained from the background subtraction algorithm, the same as the previous example. If you try to display the output images, you'll have something similar to this:

Note that the output seen here is a result of moving the camera, which is basically the same as moving the objects in the video. However, if you try the same example with a video in which any other colored object is being moved around on a static background, you can use the CamShift algorithm to get a bounding box around the moving object for extracting it, or further processing it for any reason.

The opportunities for writing applications using the existing video analysis classes in OpenCV are immense, and it only depends on how familiar you are with using them. For instance, by using background subtraction algorithms you can try writing an application that runs an alarm, or executes another process in case of movement detection. Something like this can be easily done by measuring the sum or average of pixels in the extracted foreground image that we saw in the previous examples, and then detecting sudden increases above certain thresholds. We cannot even begin to name all the possibilities, but one thing is for sure, which is you are the master of mixing these algorithms to solve a specific task and any guide, including this book, is merely a collection of signposts to how you can use the existing algorithms.

# Summary

Writing computer vision applications that perform real-time image processing is one of the hot topics of today, and OpenCV contains many classes and functions to help with simplifying the development of such applications. In this chapter, we tried to cover some of the most important classes and functions provided by OpenCV for real-time processing of videos and images. We learned about the MeanShift, CamShift, and background subtraction algorithms in OpenCV, which are packed into fast and efficient classes which are, at the same time, very easy to use, provided that you are familiar with the basic concepts used in most of them, such as histograms and back-projection images. That is why we started by learning all about histograms, how they are calculated, visualized, and compared with each other. We also learned how back-projection images are calculated and used as a lookup table to update images. We used the same also in the MeanShift/CamShift algorithms to track objects of specific colors. By now, we should be efficient in writing applications that process videos and images based on the movement of parts and pieces within them.

This chapter was the last chapter in which we will cover details of both OpenCV and the Qt framework. A book, or even a pack of books, can never be enough for covering all the existing materials within OpenCV and the Qt Framework, but we tried to present an overview of the whole picture in a way that you can follow up with the rest of the existing classes and functions on your own and develop interesting computer vision applications. Make sure to keep yourself up to date with the new developments of OpenCV and the Qt Framework, as they are living and breathing projects with an ongoing progress that doesn't look like it's going to stop anytime soon.

The next chapter of the book will be dedicated to how Qt and OpenCV applications are debugged, tested, and deployed to the users. We will first learn about the debugging capabilities of Qt Creator, then we'll continue with the Qt Test Namespace and its underlying functions that can be used for easy unit testing of Qt applications. In the next chapter, we'll also be introduced to the Qt Installer Framework, and we'll even create a simple installer for our applications.

# 10
# Debugging and Testing

We have come a long way since the start of our computer vision journey with OpenCV 3 and Qt5 Frameworks. We can now very easily install these powerful frameworks and configure a computer running a Windows, macOS, or Linux operating system so that we can design and build computer vision applications. Over the course of the previous chapters, we learned how to use the Qt plugin system to build modular and plugin-based applications. We learned how to style our apps using Qt Style Sheets and also make them support multiple languages by using the internationalization technologies in Qt. We built powerful graphics viewer applications using the Qt Graphics View Framework. The classes in this framework helped us deal with displaying graphical items much more efficiently and with much more flexibility. We were able to build graphics viewers that could zoom in and out of images without having to deal with the source image itself (thanks to the Scene-View-Item Architecture). Later on, we started to dig deeper into the OpenCV Framework, and we learned about many of its classes and functions that allow us to transform images in many ways and process them to achieve a specific computer vision goal. We learned about feature detection and descriptor extraction, which we used for detecting objects in a scene. We browsed through many of the existing algorithms in OpenCV meant for dealing with image content in a much smarter way instead of just their raw pixel values. In more recent chapters, we learned about multithreading and thread synchronization tools provided by Qt. We learned about both the low-level (`QThread`) and the high-level (`QtConcurrent`) technologies provided by Qt Framework for dealing with multithreading in applications, independent of the platform. Finally, in the last chapter, we learned about the real-time image processing of videos and OpenCV algorithms that can track objects with a specific color. By now, we should be familiar with many aspects of both the Qt and OpenCV Frameworks in such a way that we follow up with more advanced topics by ourselves and simply depend on the documentation.

Apart from all that was mentioned, and the long list of our achievements through the previous chapters, we still haven't talked about a very important aspect of software development and how it is handled when working with Qt and OpenCV, that is, the testing process. A computer program, whether it is a simple and small binary file, a huge computer vision application, or any application in general, must be tested before it is deployed to the users of that application. Testing is a never-ending phase of the development process, and it is performed right after an application is developed and, every now and then, when a problem is fixed or a new feature is added. In this chapter, we will learn about the existing technologies to test the applications we built using Qt and OpenCV. We'll learn about development time testing and debugging. We'll also learn how to use the Qt Test Framework for unit testing our applications. This is the most important process prior to shipping applications to the end users.

The topics that we will cover in this chapter are as follows:

- Debugging features of Qt Creator
- How to use Qt Test Namespace for unit testing
- Data-driven testing
- GUI Testing and Replaying GUI Events
- Creating testcase projects

# Debugging with Qt Creator

A debugger is a program that can be used to test and debug other programs, in case of a sudden crash during the program execution or an unexpected behavior in the logic of the program. Most of the time (if not always), debuggers are used in the development environment and in conjunction with an IDE. In our case, we will learn how to use a debugger with Qt Creator. It is important to note that debuggers are not part of the Qt Framework, and, just like compilers, they are usually provided by the operating system SDK. Qt Creator automatically detects and uses debuggers if they are present on a system. This can be checked by navigating into the Qt Creator Options page via the main menu **Tools** and then **Options**. Make sure to select **Build & Run** from the list on the left side and then switch to the **Debuggers** tab from the top. You should be able to see one or more auto-detected debuggers on the list.

**Windows Users**: You should see something similar to the screenshot after this information box. If not, this means you have not installed any debuggers. You can easily download and install it using the instructions provided here:

`https://docs.microsoft.com/en-us/windows-hardware/drivers/debugger/`

Or, you can independently search for the following topic online: Debugging Tools for Windows (WinDbg, KD, CDB, NTSD).

Nevertheless, after the debugger is installed (assumingly, CDB or Microsoft Console Debugger for Microsoft Visual C++ Compilers and GDB for GCC Compilers), you can restart Qt Creator and return to this page. You should be able to have one or more entries similar to the following. Since we have installed a 32-bit version of the Qt and OpenCV Frameworks, choose the entry with x86 in its name to view its path, type, and other properties.

**macOS and Linux Users**:
There shouldn't be any action needed on your part and, depending on the OS, you'll see a GDB, LLDB, or some other debugger in the entries.

Here's the screenshot of the **Build & Run** tab on the **Options** page:

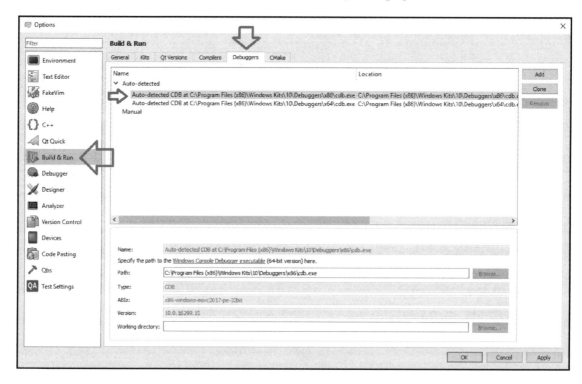

Depending on the operating system and the installed debugger, the preceding screenshot might be slightly different. Nevertheless, you'll have a debugger that you need to make sure is correctly set as the debugger for the Qt Kit you are using. So, make a note of the debugger path and name and switch to the **Kits** tab, and, after selecting the Qt Kit you were using, make sure the debugger for it is correctly set, as you can see in the following screenshot:

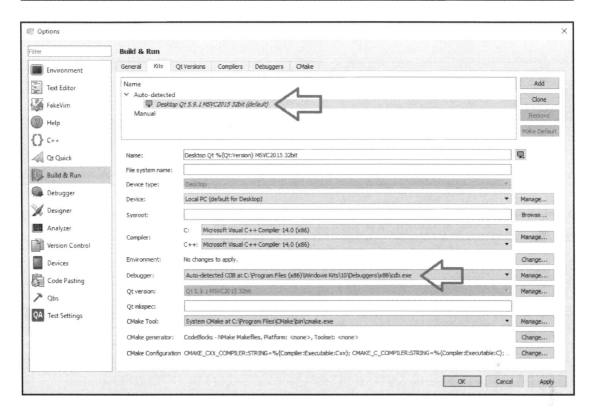

Don't worry about choosing the wrong debugger, or any other options, since you'll be warned with relevant icons beside the Qt Kit icon selected at the top. The icon seen in the following image on the left side is usually displayed when everything is okay with the Kit, the second one from the left is an indication that something is not right, and the one on the right means a critical error. Move your mouse over the icon when it appears to see more information about the required actions needed to fix the issue:

Critical issues with Qt Kits can be caused by many different factors such as a missing compiler which will make the kit completely useless until the issue is resolved. An example of a warning message in a Qt Kit would be a missing debugger, which will not make the kit useless, but you won't be able to use the debugger with it, thus it means less functionality than a completely configured Qt Kit.

After the debugger is correctly set, you can start debugging your applications in one of the following ways, which basically have the same result: ending up in the Debugger view of the Qt Creator:

- Starting an application in Debugging mode
- Attaching to a running application (or process)

Note that a debugging process can be started in many ways, such as remotely, by attaching to a process running on a separate machine and so on. However, the preceding methods will suffice for most cases and especially for the ones relevant to the Qt+OpenCV application development and what we learned throughout this book.

# Getting started with the debugging mode

To start an application in the debugging mode, after opening a Qt project, you can use one of the following methods:

- Pressing the *F5* button
- Using the **Start Debugging** button, right below the usual **Run** button with a similar icon, but with a small bug on it
- Using the main menu entries in the following order: **Debug/Start Debugging/Start Debugging**

To attach the debugger to a running application, you can use the main menu entries in the following order: **Debug/Start Debugging/Attach to Running Application**. This will open up the **List of Processes** window, from which you can choose your application or any other process you want to debug using its process ID or executable name. You can also use the **Filter** field (as seen in the following image) to find your application, since, most probably, the list of processes will be quite a long one. After choosing the correct process, make sure to press the **Attach to Process** button.

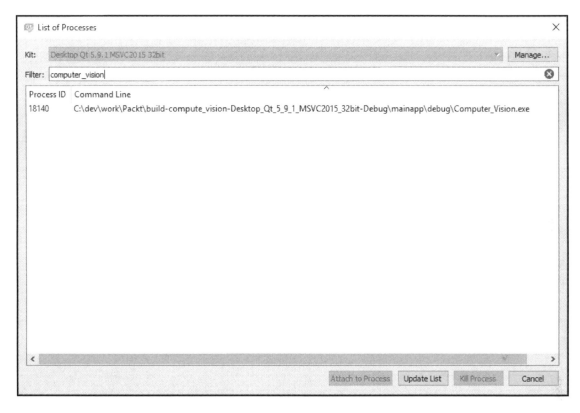

No matter which one of the preceding methods you use, you will end up in the Qt Creator Debug mode, which is quite similar to the Edit mode, but it also allows you to do the following, among many others:

- Add, Enable, Disable, and View Breakpoints in the code (a Breakpoint is simply a point or a line in the code that we want the debugger to pause in the process and allow us to do a more detailed analysis of the status of the program)
- Interrupt running programs and processes to view and examine the code
- View and examine the function call stack (the call stack is a stack containing the hierarchical list of functions that led to a breakpoint or interrupted state)
- View and examine the variables
- Disassemble the source codes (disassembling in this sense means extracting the exact instructions that correspond to the function calls and other C++ codes in our program)

You'll notice a performance drop in the application when it is started in debugging mode, which is obviously because of the fact that codes are being monitored and traced by the debugger. Here's a screenshot of the Qt Creator Debug mode, in which all of the capabilities mentioned earlier are visible in a single window and in the Debug mode of the Qt Creator:

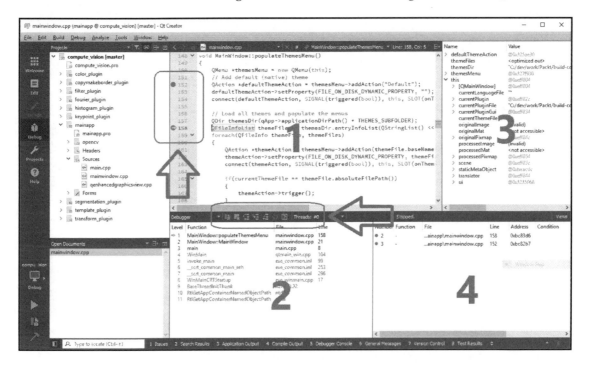

The area specified with the number **1** in the preceding screenshot in the code editor that you have already used through the book and are quite familiar with. Each line of code has a line number; you can click on their left side to toggle a breakpoint anywhere you want in the code. You can also right-click on the line numbers to set, remove, disable, or enable a breakpoint by selecting **Set Breakpoint at Line X**, **Remove Breakpoint X**, **Disable Breakpoint X**, or **Enable Breakpoint X**, where X in all of the commands mentioned here needs to be replaced by the line number. Apart from the code editor, you can also use the area mentioned with number **4** in the preceding screenshot to add, delete, edit, and further modify breakpoints in the code.

After a Breakpoint is set in the code, whenever the program reaches that line in the code, it will be interrupted, and you will be allowed to use the controls right below the code editor to perform the following tasks:

- **Continue**: This means continuing with the remaining flow of the program (or by pressing *F5* again).
- **Step Over**: This is used to execute the next step (line of code) without entering into function calls or similar codes that may change the current position of the debugging cursor. Note that the debugging cursor is simply an indicator of the current line of code being executed. (This can also be done by pressing *F10*.)
- **Step Into**: This, as opposed to Step Over, can be used to go further down into the function calls for a more detailed analysis of the code and debugging. (It is the same as pressing *F11*.)
- **Step Out**: This can be used to step out of the function calls and return to the calling point while debugging. (It is the same as pressing *Shift + F11*.)

You can also right-click on the same toolbar below the code editor that contains the debugger controls to open up the following menu and add or remove more panes to display additional debug and analysis information. We will cover the default debugger view, but make sure to check out each one of the following options on your own to familiarize yourself with the debugger even more:

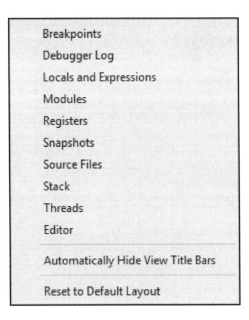

Breakpoints

Debugger Log

Locals and Expressions

Modules

Registers

Snapshots

Source Files

Stack

Threads

Editor

Automatically Hide View Title Bars

Reset to Default Layout

The area specified with number **2** in the preceding code can be used to view the call stack. Whether you interrupt the program by pressing the Interrupt button or choosing Debug/Interrupt from the menu while the it is running, set a breakpoint and stop the program in a specific line of code, or a malfunctioning code causes the program to fall into a trap and pause the process (since a crash and exception will be caught by the debugger), you can always view the hierarchy of function calls that led to the interrupted state, or further analyze them by checking the area 2 in the preceding Qt Creator screenshot.

Finally, you can use the third area in the previous screenshot to view the local and global variables of the program in the interrupted location in the code. You can see the contents of the variables, whether they are standard data types, such as integers and floats or structures and classes, and also you can further expand and analyze their content to test and analyze any possible issues in your code.

Using a debugger efficiently can mean hours of difference in testing and solving the issues in your code. In terms of practical usage of the debuggers, there is really no other way but to use it as much as you can and develop habits of your own to use the debugger, but also make note of good practices and tricks you found along the way and the ones we just went through. If you are interested, you can also read online about other possible methods of debugging, such as remote debugging, debugging using crash dump files (on Windows), and more.

# Qt Test Framework

Debugging and testing while developing your applications is completely unavoidable, but the one thing that many developers tend to miss is to take care of unit testing, which is even more important, especially in big projects and applications that are hard to fully test manually, every time they are built or a bug is fixed somewhere in their code. Unit testing refers to a method of testing parts and pieces (units) in an application to make sure they are working as intended. It's also worth noting that Test Automation, which is one of the hot topics of software development nowadays, is the process of automating unit tests using third-party software or programming.

In this section, we will learn about using the Qt Test Framework, or Qt Test Namespace, to be precise (along with a few additional test-related classes), that can be used to develop unit tests for applications built with Qt. As opposed to third-party testing frameworks, the Qt Test Framework is an in-house (based on Qt Framework itself) and lightweight test framework, and, among the many capabilities it has, it offers benchmarking, data-driven testing, and GUI testing: Benchmarking can be used to measure the performance of a function or a specific piece of code and a data-driven test can help with running unit tests using different datasets as input. On the other hand, GUI testing is made possible by simulating mouse and keyboard interactions, which, again, is another aspect covered by the Qt Test Framework.

# Creating a Unit Test

A unit test can be created by subclassing the QObject class and adding the slots required by the Qt Test Framework into it, along with one or more slots (test functions) for performing various tests. The following slots (private slots) can exist in each test class and are called by Qt Test, in addition to test functions:

- initTestCase: This is called before the first test function is called. If this function fails, the entire test will fail and no test function will be called.
- cleanupTestCase: This is called after the last test function is called.
- init: This is called before each test function is called. If this function fails, the preceding test function will not be executed.
- cleanup: This is called after each test function is called.

Let's create our first unit test with a real example to see how the functions we just mentioned are added to a test class and how test functions are written. To make sure our example is realistic and easy to follow at the same time, we will avoid bothering too much with the implementation details of the classes we want to test and mostly focus on how they are tested. Basically, the same approach can be used to test literally any class with any level of complexity.

So, as our first example, we'll assume that we have a class that returns the number of pixels in an image (the width multiplied by the height of an image), and we want to test it using a Unit Test:

1. A unit test can be created using Qt Creator, similar to creating Qt Applications or Libraries, using the **New Project** button in Welcome mode or by selecting **New File or Project** from the **File** menu. Make sure to choose the following as the project template:

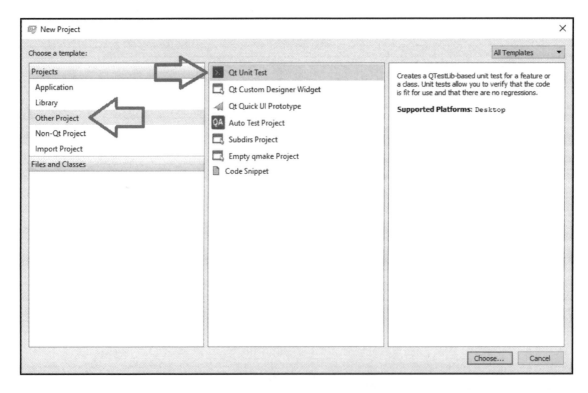

2. Click on **Choose** and enter HelloTest as the name of the Unit Test project, then click on **Next**.
3. Choose the Kit exactly as you would for your Qt Project, then click on **Next** again.

4. In the **Modules** page, which is seen in the next screenshot, you'll notice that the **QtCore** and **QtTest** modules are selected by default and they cannot be deselected. This page is simply a helper, or a so-called wizard that helps you choose the required modules interactively. You can also add or remove modules later on using the project ∗.pro file if you forget adding a module that your classes need in order to work correctly. This makes it necessary to repeat an important point once again. A Unit Test is just like an application that uses your classes and functions. The only difference is that you just use it for testing purposes and it is only meant for making sure things work as they are supposed to, and that there are no Regressions:

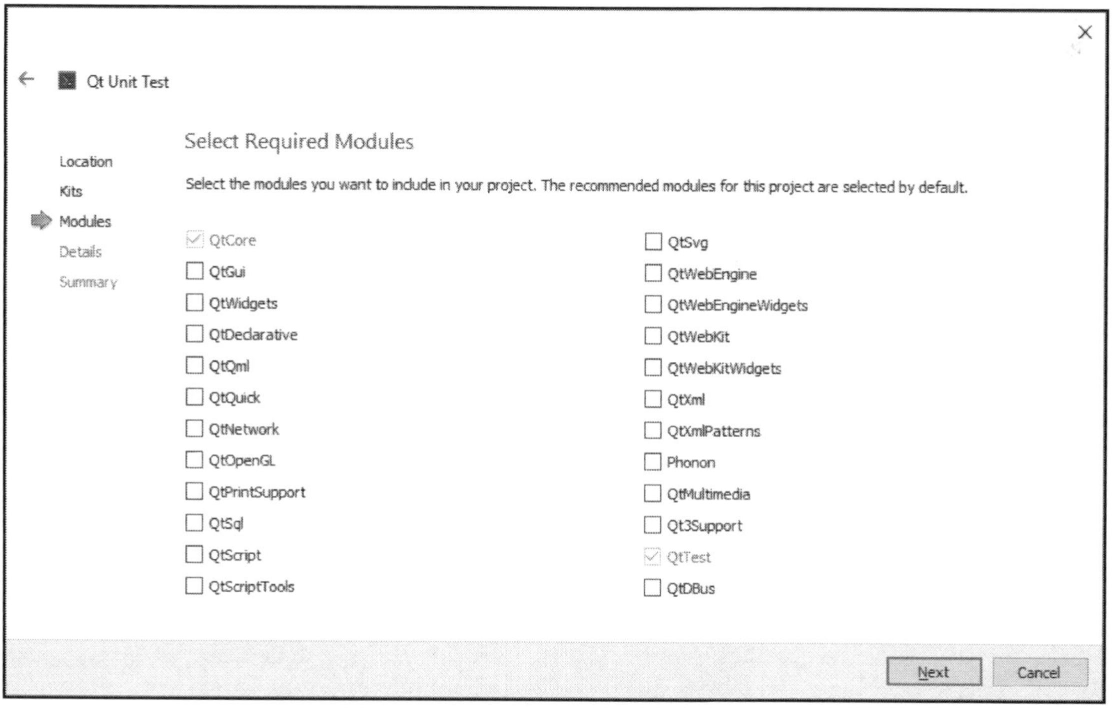

5. After choosing the modules and clicking on **Next**, the **Details** page, or the **Test Class Information** page, appears. Enter `testPixelCount` at the **Test Slot** field seen in the following screenshot and click on **Next**. The rest of the options, like the previous window, are simply helpers to easily and interactively add the required functions and include directives to the Test Unit, which can be also added later on in the source files if anything is missing. Nevertheless, we'll learn about what they mean and how they are used in detail later on in this chapter.

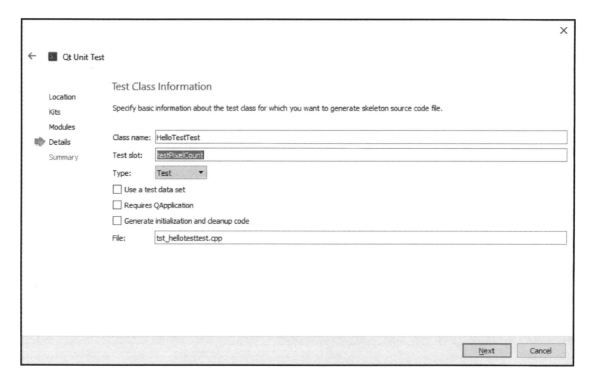

6. After confirming all of the dialog boxes, we'll end up in the code editor in the Qt Creator Edit mode. Check the `HelloTest.pro` file and you'll notice it's quite similar to a `*.pro` file for a standard Qt Project (Widgets or Console app), with the following module definition that imports the Qt Test module into the project. This is how you can use Qt Test in any Unit Test project; if you do not use the **New File or Project** wizard, however, with the wizard, this gets added automatically:

```
QT += testlib
```

Before moving on to the next step, make sure to add OpenCV libraries to the pro file like you would do in a Qt Widgets application. (Refer to the initial chapters of the book for more on this.)

7. Now, add the class you have created in order to count the pixels of an image into this project. Note that adding and copying is not the same thing in this context. You can add a class header and source file that belongs to another project in a separate folder, into your project without copying it into your project folder. You just need to make sure they are included in your HEADERS and SOURCES list in the *.pro file, and, optionally, also add the folder where the class is located to the INCLUDEPATH variable.

In practice, you should never copy the source files of the classes you are testing into the test project, and as we'll discuss further in this section, you should always make a project using the subdirs template, even if it contains a single project, in order to at least add one Unit Test into the project and also execute the tests automatically every time your main project is built. However, strictly speaking, your Unit Test will work the same way, whether you copy the class files into it or simply add them where they are located.

8. It is time to write our test class, so open tst_hellotesttest.cpp in the Qt Creator code editor. Apart from the obvious #include directives, there are a few things to note here: one is HelloTestTest class, which is the class name provided during the **New File or Project** wizard. It is nothing more than a QObject subclass, so don't look for anything hidden here. It has a single private slot called testPixelCount, which, again, was set during the wizard. Its implementation includes a single line with a QVERIFY2 macro, which we'll get to in the later steps. However, the last couple of lines, as shown here, are new:

```
QTEST_APPLESS_MAIN(HelloTestTest)
#include "tst_hellotesttest.moc"
```

QTEST_APPLESS_MAIN is a macro that is expanded by the C++ compiler and moc (refer to Chapter 3, *Creating a Comprehensive Qt+OpenCV Project*, for more information about moc) to create a proper C++ main function for executing the test functions we have written in the HelloTestTest class. It merely creates an instance of our test class and calls the QTest::qExec function in order to start the testing process. The test process automatically calls all of the private slots in the test classes and outputs the test results. Finally, the last line is required by the Qt framework in case we create our test class in a single cpp source file, instead of a separate header and a source. Make sure to add the class that will be tested, into the tst_hellotesttest.cpp file using an include directive. (For an easier referral to it, we'll assume that it's called PixelCounter.)

9. Now, you can use one of the suitable test macros to test the function in this class that is responsible for counting the pixels of an image. Assumingly, it's a function that takes a file name and path (QString type) and returns an integer number. Let's use the already existing VERIFY2 macro within the testPixelCount slot, as seen here:

```
void HelloTestTest::testPixelCount()
{
    int width = 640, height = 427;
    QString fname = "c:/dev/test.jpg";
    PixelCounter c;
    QVERIFY2(c.countPixels(fname) == width*height, "Failure");
}
```

In this test, we simply provided an image file with a known pixel count (width multiplied by height) to test if our function works correctly or not. Then, we will create an instance of the PixelCounter class, and finally execute the QVERIFY2 macro, which will execute the countPixels function (assuming that's the name of its public function we want to test), and cause the test to fail or pass based on the comparison. In case of test failure, it also outputs the Failure string.

We just built our first Unit Test project. Click on the **Run** button to run this test and view the results in the Qt Creator output pane. If the test passes, then you'll see something similar to this:

```
********* Start testing of HelloTestTest *********
Config: Using QtTest library 5.9.1, Qt 5.9.1 (i386-
little_endian-ilp32 shared (dynamic) debug build; by MSVC 2015)
PASS    : HelloTestTest::initTestCase()
PASS    : HelloTestTest::testPixelCount()
PASS    : HelloTestTest::cleanupTestCase()
Totals: 3 passed, 0 failed, 0 skipped, 0 blacklisted, 26ms
********* Finished testing of HelloTestTest *********
```

In case of failure, you'll see the following in the output:

```
********* Start testing of HelloTestTest *********
Config: Using QtTest library 5.9.1, Qt 5.9.1 (i386-little_endian-
ilp32 shared (dynamic) debug build; by MSVC 2015)
PASS    : HelloTestTest::initTestCase()
FAIL!   : HelloTestTest::testPixelCount() 'c.countPixels(fname) ==
width*height' returned FALSE. (Failure)
..HelloTesttst_hellotesttest.cpp(26) : failure location
PASS    : HelloTestTest::cleanupTestCase()
Totals: 2 passed, 1 failed, 0 skipped, 0 blacklisted, 26ms
********* Finished testing of HelloTestTest *********
```

The results are pretty much self-explanatory, but there is one thing we may need to take note of here, and that is the fact that `initTestCase` was called before all test functions, and `cleanupTestCase` was called after all test functions, as we mentioned earlier. However, since those functions weren't really existent, they were just marked as PASS. This can change if you implement those functions and do real initialization and finalization tasks.

In the preceding example, we saw the simplest form of a Unit Test, but the reality is that writing an efficient and reliable Unit Test, which takes care of all possible issues, is quite a hard task and much more complex in comparison to what we faced. To be able to write a proper Unit Test, you can use the following macros inside each one of the test functions. These macros are defined in the `QTest` as follows:

- `QVERIFY`: This can be used to check if a condition is met or not. The condition is simply a Boolean value or any expression that evaluates to a Boolean value. If the condition is not met, the test stops, fails, and gets logged in the output; otherwise, it continues.

- QTRY_VERIFY_WITH_TIMEOUT: This is similar to QVERIFY, but this function tries checking for the provided condition, either until the given timeout (in milliseconds) is reached or the condition is met.
- QTRY_VERIFY: This is similar to QTRY_VERIFY_WITH_TIMEOUT, but the timeout is set to a default of five seconds.
- QVERIFY2, QTRY_VERIFY2_WITH_TIMEOUT, and QTRY_VERIFY2: These macros are quite similar to the previous macros with strikingly similar names, except that functions also output a given message in case of a test failure.
- QCOMPARE: This can be used to compare an *actual* value with an *expected* one. It is quite similar to QVERIFY, except that this macro also outputs the actual and expected values for later reference purposes.
- QTRY_COMPARE_WITH_TIMEOUT: This is similar to QCOMPARE, but this function tries comparing the actual and expected values, either until the given timeout (in milliseconds) is reached or they are equal.
- QTRY_COMPARE: This is similar to QTRY_COMPARE_WITH_TIMEOUT, but the timeout is set to a default of 5 seconds.

# Data-driven testing

Apart from simple comparisons with input data provided inside each test function, QTest also provides the means to perform unit tests with a more organized and structured set of input data to perform data-driven testing, or, in other words, testing functionalities with different sets of input data. This is done using the QFETCH macro along with the QTest::addColumn and QTest::newRow functions. The QFETCH function can be used inside a test function to fetch the required test data. This needs a data function to be created for our test function. A data function is again another private slot with the exact same name as the test function, but with _data appended to its name. So, if we go back to our previous example, to have a data-driven test, we would need to add a new private slot to our test class, something similar to this:

```cpp
void HelloTestTest::testPixelCount_data()
{
    QTest::addColumn<QString>("filename");
    QTest::addColumn<int>("pixelcount");

    QTest::newRow("huge image") <<
        "c:/dev/imagehd.jpg" << 2280000;
    QTest::newRow("small image") <<
        "c:/dev/tiny.jpg" << 51200;
}
```

Notice that the data function name has an appended _data at the end of its name. Test data in QTest is treated like a table; that is why, inside the data function, the addColumn function is used to create new columns (or fields) and addRow is used to add new rows (or records) to it. The preceding code will result in a test data table similar to the following:

| Index | Name (or label) | filename | pixelcount |
|-------|-----------------|-----------------------|------------|
| 0 | huge image | c:/dev/imagehd.jpg | 2280000 |
| 1 | small image | c:/dev/tiny.jpg | 51200 |

We can now modify our test function, testPixelCount, to use this test data instead of the provided single filename inside the same function. Our new testPixelCount will look similar to this (in the meantime, let's also replace QVERIFY with QCOMPARE for a better test log output):

```
void HelloTestTest::testPixelCount()
{
    PixelCounter c;
    QFETCH(QString, filename);
    QFETCH(int, pixelcount);
    QCOMPARE(c.countPixels(filename), pixelcount);
}
```

It is important to note that QFETCH must be provided with the exact data type and element name for each column in the test data that was created inside the data function. If we execute the test again, testPixelCount will be called by the test framework as much as there are rows in the test data, each time it will run the test function by fetching and using a new row and logging the outputs. Using data-driven testing capabilities helps with keeping the actual test function intact, and instead of creating test data inside the test function, they are fetched from a simple and structured data function. Needless to say, you can extend this to get the test data from a file on disk or other input methods, such as a network location. No matter where the data is gotten from, it should be completely present and correctly structured when the data function exists.

# Benchmarking

QTest offers the QBENCHMARK and QBENCHMARK_ONCE macros to measure the performance (benchmark) of function calls or any other piece of code. These two macros differ only in the number of times they repeat a piece of code to measure its performance, with the latter, obviously, running the code only once. You can use these macros in the following way:

```
QBENCHMARK
{
    // Piece of code to be benchmarked
}
```

Again, we can use this in our previous example to measure the performance of the PixelCounter class. You can simply add the following line to the end of the testPixelCount function:

```
QBENCHMARK
{
    c.countPixels(filename);
}
```

If you run the test again, you'll see outputs similar to the following in the test log output. Note that the numbers are just examples running on a random test PC and they can be significantly different on various systems:

```
23 msecs per iteration (total: 95, iterations: 4)
```

The preceding test output means that it took 23 milliseconds each time the function was tested with a particular test image. The numbers of iteration, on the other hand, was 4 and the total time it took for the benchmarking was about 95 milliseconds.

# GUI testing

Similar to testing classes that perform a specific task, it is also possible to create Unit Tests that are meant for testing GUI functionality or a widget's behavior. The only difference in this case is that GUIs need to be provided with mouse clicks, key presses, and similar user interactions. QTest supports testing GUIs created with Qt by simulating mouse clicks and other user interactions. The following functions are available in the QTest namespace to write Unit Tests capable of performing GUI tests. Note that almost all of them rely on the fact that all widgets and GUI components in Qt are subclasses of QWidget:

- keyClick: This can be used to simulate clicking a key on the keyboard. This function has many overloaded versions for convenience. You can optionally provide a modifier key (ALT, CTRL, and so on) and/or a delay time before the key is clicked on. A keyClick should not be confused with mouseClick, which we'll get to a bit later, and it refers to a single keypress and release, thus leading to a click.

- keyClicks: This is quite similar to keyClick, but it can be used to simulate clicking on the keys in a sequence, again with optional modifier or delays in between.

- keyPress: This again is quite similar to keyClick, but it only simulates the pressing of keys, not releasing them. This is very useful if we need to simulate holding down a key.

- keyRelease: This is the opposite of keyPress, which means it only simulates the releasing of the key and not pressing them. This can be useful if we want to simulate releasing a key that was held down previously, by using keyPress.

- keyEvent: This is the more advanced version of the keyboard simulating functions, with an additional action parameter that defines if the key is pressed, released, clicked (press and release), or if it is a shortcut.

- mouseClick: This is similar to keyClick, but it works with mouse clicks. That's why the key provided to this function is a mouse button such as left, right, middle, and so on. The value for the key should be an entry from the Qt::MouseButton enum. It also supports a keyboard modifier and a delay time before the click is simulated. In addition, this function and all other mouse simulation functions, also take an optional point (QPoint) which contains the position inside the widget (or window) that will be clicked. If an empty point is provided, or if this parameter is omitted, the simulated click will happen in the middle of the widget.

- `mouseDClick`: This is the double-click version of the `mouseClick` function.
- `mousePress`: This is quite similar to `mouseClick`, but only the pressing of the mouse button is simulated and not releasing it. This can be useful if you want to simulate holding down a mouse button.
- `mouseRelease`: This is the opposite of `mousePress`, which means it only simulates the releasing of the mouse button and not pressing it. This can be used to simulate releasing a mouse button after a period of time.
- `mouseMove`: This can be used to simulate moving the mouse cursor over a widget. This function must be provided with a point and delay. Similar to other mouse interaction functions, if no point is set, then the mouse is moved to the middle point of the widget. This function can be used to simulate and test drag and drop when used in conjunction with `mousePress` and `mouseRelease`.

Let's create a simple GUI test to familiarize ourselves with how the preceding functions are used in practice. Assuming that you want to test an already created window or widget, you have to first include it in a Qt Unit Test Project. So, start by creating the Unit Test project similar to the way we did in the previous example and also in our first test project. During the project creation, make sure you also choose `QtWidgets` as one of the required modules. Then, add the widget class files (probably a header, source, and a UI file) to the test project. In our example, we assume that we have a simple GUI with a button and label on it. Each time the button is pressed, the number on the label is multiplied by two. To be able to test this functionality, or any other GUI functionality, we must first make sure that the widgets on the form, container widget, or the window are exposed to the test class by making them public. Among the many methods to achieve this, the quickest and most simple one is to define the same widgets also in the class declaration and as public members. Then, simply assign the classes in the `ui` variable (found in all Qt Widgets created using the **New File or Project** wizard) to the class-wide members. Let's say the button and label on our window are named `nextBtn` and `infoLabel` respectively (when they were designed using the designer), then we have to define the following in the class declaration public members:

```
QPushButton *nextBtn;
QLabel *infoLabel;
```

And, we have to assign them in the constructor, as shown here:

```
ui->setupUi(this);
this->nextBtn = ui->nextBtn;
this->infoLabel = ui->infoLabel;
```

Make sure to always assign the widgets created using the Designer and UI files after the setupUi call; otherwise, your application will definitely crash since no widget is really created until setupUi is called. Now, assuming our widget class is called TestableForm, we can have a private testGui slot in our test class. Remember, each time the nextBtn is pressed, the number on the infoLabel is multiplied by 2, so we can have something like the following in the testGui function:

```
void GuiTestTest::testGui()
{
    TestableForm t;

    QTest::mouseClick(t.nextBtn, Qt::LeftButton);
    QCOMPARE(t.infoLabel->text(), QString::number(1));

    QTest::mouseClick(t.nextBtn, Qt::LeftButton);
    QCOMPARE(t.infoLabel->text(), QString::number(2));

    QTest::mouseClick(t.nextBtn, Qt::LeftButton);
    QCOMPARE(t.infoLabel->text(), QString::number(4));

    // repeated until necessary
}
```

It is extremely important to also replace the following line:

```
QTEST_APPLESS_MAIN(GuiTestTest)
```

The following line is added:

```
QTEST_MAIN(GuiTestTest)
```

Otherwise, no `QApplication` is created behind the scenes and the test will simply fail. This is important to remember when testing GUIs with the Qt Test Framework. Now, if you try and run the Unit Test, the `nextBtn` widget will be clicked three times and, after each time, the value displayed by the `infoLabel` is checked to see if it is correct or not. In case of a failure, it will be logged in the output. This is quite easy, but the problem is, what if the number of required interactions increases? What if you have to perform a long set of GUI interactions? To overcome this, you can use data-driven testing along with GUI testing to easily replay GUI interactions (or events, as it is called in the Qt Framework). Remember, to have a data function for a test function in a test class, you must create a new function with exactly the same name that has `_data` appended to it. So, we can create a new function called `testGui_data`, which prepares the set of interactions and the results and passes it to test function using `QFETCH`, as we used in the previous example:

```cpp
void GuiTestTest::testGui_data()
{
    QTest::addColumn<QTestEventList>("events");
    QTest::addColumn<QString>("result");

    QTestEventList mouseEvents; // three times
    mouseEvents.addMouseClick(Qt::LeftButton);
    mouseEvents.addMouseClick(Qt::LeftButton);
    mouseEvents.addMouseClick(Qt::LeftButton);
    QTest::newRow("mouse") << mouseEvents << "4";

    QTestEventList keybEvents; // four times
    keybEvents.addKeyClick(Qt::Key_Space);
    keybEvents.addDelay(250);
    keybEvents.addKeyClick(Qt::Key_Space);
    keybEvents.addDelay(250);
    keybEvents.addKeyClick(Qt::Key_Space);
    keybEvents.addDelay(250);
    keybEvents.addKeyClick(Qt::Key_Space);
    QTest::newRow("keyboard") << keybEvents << "8";
}
```

The `QTestEventList` class is a convenience class in the Qt Test Framework that can be used to easily create lists of GUI interactions and simulate them. It contains functions to add all of the possible interactions we previously mentioned as part of possible events that can be performed using Qt Test.

To use this data function, we need to rewrite our `testGui` function, as seen here:

```
void GuiTestTest::testGui()
{
    TestableForm t;
    QFETCH(QTestEventList, events);
    QFETCH(QString, result);
    events.simulate(t.nextBtn);
    QCOMPARE(t.infoLabel->text(), result);
}
```

Similar to any data-driven test, `QFETCH` gets the data provided by the data function. In this case, however, the data stored is a `QEventList` and it is populated with the series of required interactions. This testing method is highly effective in replaying a series of events from an error report to reproduce, fix, and further, test a specific issue.

# testcase projects

In the previous sections and their corresponding examples, we saw some simple testing cases and solved them using the Qt Test functions. We learned about data-driven and GUI testing, and how to combine both to replay GUI events and perform more complicated GUI tests. The same approaches that we learned in each case, can be further extended to apply to much more complex test cases. What we'll learn in this section is making sure tests are performed automatically when we build a project. Of course, depending on the time it takes for the test and our preferences, we may want to easily skip automatic testing temporarily, but, ultimately, we will need our tests to be easily performed when we build our projects. To be able to automate running test units of your Qt project (let's call this our main project), first, we need to make sure they are always created using a subdirs template, and then configure unit test projects as testcase projects. This can also be done with the projects that already exist and are not inside a subdirs template. Just follow the steps provided in this section to add an existing project to a subdirs template and create a unit test (configured as a testcase) for it that runs automatically whenever you build your main project:

1. Start by creating a new project using the **New Project** button from the **Welcome** mode in Qt Creator, or choose the **New File or Project** item from the **File** menu.

2. Make sure you select **Subdirs Project**, as seen in the following screenshot, and click on **Choose**:

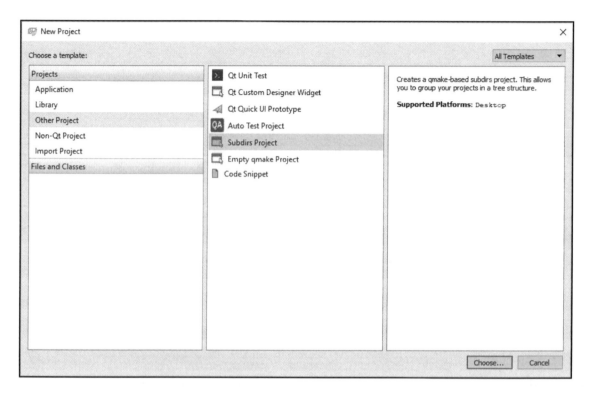

3. Choose a name for your project. This can be the same as your main project name. Let's assume it's called `computer_vision`. Continue forward, and in the final dialog, click on the **Finish & Add Subproject** button. If you are creating a project from scratch, then you can simply create your project the same way you did throughout the book. Otherwise, meaning if you want to add an existing project (inside a folder that is called `src`, assumingly), just click on **Cancel** and copy your existing project that you want to build a test for, into this newly created `subdirs` project folder. Then, open the `computer_vision.pro` file, and modify it to look like the following lines of code:

```
TEMPLATE = subdirs
SUBDIRS += src
```

4. Now, you can create a Unit Test project that is also a sub-project of the `computer_vision` subdirs project, and program it to test the classes that exist inside the `src` folder (your main project, which is the actual application itself). So, right-click on `computer_vision` from the projects pane once again, and by choosing **New Subproject**, start creating a Unit Test using everything you learned in the previous sections.

5. After you have created your test, you should be able to run it individually, regardless of the main project to see the test results. However, to make sure it's marked as a testcase project, you need to add the following line of code to the `*.pro` file of your Unit Test project:

```
CONFIG += testcase
```

6. Finally, you need to switch to Projects mode in Qt Creator and add check to the **Make arguments** field, as seen in the following screenshot. Make sure to first expand the Make section using the **Details** expander button; otherwise, it won't be visible:

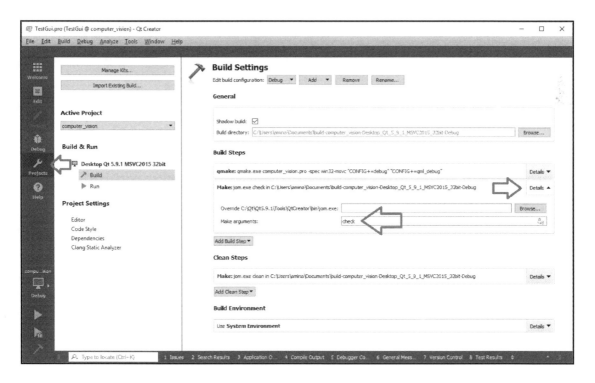

It doesn't matter now if you specifically run the Unit Test project or not, and every time you run your main project or try to build it, the test will be executed automatically. This is a very useful technique to make sure changes from one library don't have a negative effect on another library. The important thing to note about this technique is that the test results will, in fact, affect the build results. Meaning, you'll notice if there was a failure in the tests automatically when you build them, and the test results will be visible in the compiler output pane in Qt Creator that can be activated using the bottom bar or pressing *ALT + 4* keys.

# Summary

In this chapter, you learned about debugging using Qt Creator and the capabilities it offers in order to further analyze the codes, find issues, and try to fix them using breakpoints, call stack viewer, and so on. This was but a small taste of what can be done using a debugger, and it was meant to prepare you to take on using the debugger on your own and develop coding and debugging habits of your own that can help you overcome programming issues with much more ease. Apart from debugging and developer-level tests, we also learned about Unit Testing in Qt, which is especially important with the ever-growing number of applications and projects written using the Qt Framework. Test Automation is one of the hot topics in the application development industry nowadays, and having a clear idea about the Qt Test Framework will help you develop better and reliable tests. It is important to get used to writing Unit Tests for your projects, and yes, even for the very small ones. The cost of testing an application and avoiding regressions is not easily visible for beginners or hobbyists, so it is a good idea to be prepared for what you will definitely face in the later stages of your development career.

As we're nearing the final chapters of the book, we are also focusing more and more on the final stages of the application development using Qt and OpenCV. So, in the next chapter, you'll learn about deploying applications to the end users. You'll also learn about dynamic and static linking of applications, and creating application packages that can be easily installed on computers with different operating systems. The next chapter will be the final chapter we'll go through in our computer vision journey with OpenCV and Qt on desktop platforms.

# 11
# Linking and Deployment

After learning about debugging and testing applications using Qt Creator and the Qt Test framework in the previous chapters, we are down to one of the last phases in application development, which is the deployment of applications to the end users. This process itself has many variations and can take quite a lot of different forms depending on the target platform, but one thing they all have in common is the packaging of an application in a way that it can be simply executed in the target platform and without bothering with the dependencies of the application. Remember, not all target platforms (whether it is Windows, macOS, or Linux) have Qt and OpenCV libraries on them. So, if you go on and just provide the users of your application with only the executable of your application, it will most probably not even start executing, much less working correctly.

In this chapter, we are going to tackle exactly that, by learning about the correct way of creating an application package (usually a folder with all the required files) that can be simply executed on computers other than our own, and other than the development environment, and without the need for a user taking care of any required libraries. To be able to understand some of the concepts described in this chapter, we need to first go through some of the basics of what happens behind the scenes when an application executable is created. We will talk about the three major phases of the build process, which are preprocessing, compiling, and linking of an application executable (or library). Then, we will learn that linking can be done in two different ways, namely dynamic and static linking. We will talk about their differences and how they affect the deployment, and how to build both Qt and OpenCV libraries dynamically or statically on Windows, macOS, and Linux operating systems. After that, we'll create and deploy a simple application for all of the mentioned platforms. We'll take this chance to also learn about Qt Installer Framework and how to create installers that are shipped to the end users from a website download link, on a flash drive, or literally any other media. By the end of this chapter, we will be able to provide our end users with only what they need to execute our application, nothing more and nothing less.

Topics that will be covered in this chapter include:

- Dynamic and static linking of Qt and OpenCV frameworks
- Configuring Qt projects to use static libraries
- Deploying applications written using Qt and OpenCV
- Creating cross-platform installers using Qt Installer Framework

# The build process, behind the scenes

It all seems quite natural when we write an application by editing some C++ header or source files, adding some modules in the project file, and finally pressing the run button. However, there are a few processes going on behind the scenes which, by working in the correct order, executed by the IDE (in our case Qt Creator), allow this smooth and natural sense of development. In general, there are three major processes that lead to the creation of an executable (such as *.exe) when we press the run or **Build** button in Qt Creator, or any other IDE for that matter. Here are those three processes:

- Preprocessing
- Compiling
- Linking

This is a very high-level categorization of the processes and phases going when an application is created from the source files. This categorization allows a much simpler overview of the processes and an easier way to understand their purpose in general. However, these processes include many subprocesses and phases that are out of the scope of this book, since we are mostly interested in the processes that affect the deployment process one way or another. However, you can read about them online or by grabbing any book about compilers and linkers.

# Preprocessing

This phase is the process of transforming source codes into their final states before being passed onto the actual compiler. To further explain this, think about all of the included files, various compiler directives, or more importantly in the case of Qt Framework, think about the Qt-specific macros and codes that are not part of the standard C++ language. In Chapter 3, *Creating a Comprehensive Qt+OpenCV Project*, we learned about uic and moc, which transform UI files and C++ codes written using Qt-specific macros and guidelines into standard C++ codes (in recent versions of Qt, into C++11 or later, to be precise). Even though these are not part of the standard preprocessing performed on C++ source codes, they are still pretty much in the same phase when we work with Qt Framework or frameworks that generate code based on their own set of rules.

The following image is a description of the preprocessing phase when it's combined with Qt-specific code generation using uic, moc, and so on:

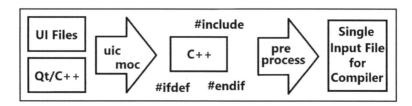

The output of this process, which is marked as the **Single Input File for Compiler** in the preceding image, is rather obviously a single file that contains all the required tokens and information for compiling source codes. This file is then passed to the compiler and the compilation phase beings.

# Compiling

At the second major phase of the build process, the compiler takes the output of the preprocessor, or in our case, the preprocess phase, which also includes the codes generated by uic and moc, and compiles it into the machine code. This machine code can be saved and reused during the build process, since as long as source files are not changed, then the produced machine code also stays the same. This process helps save a lot of time when building applications, by making sure that individual and separately compiled objects (such as *.obj or *.lib files) are reused instead of being produced each and every time the project is built. The good thing about all this is that it is taken care of by the IDEs and we usually don't need to bother with it. The output files produced by the compiler are then passed into the linker, and we enter the linking phase.

# Linking

The linker is the last program that is called in the chain of build processes, and its goal is to link the objects produced by the compiler to produce executables or libraries. This process is of the utmost importance for us because it can have tremendous effects on the way you deploy your application, its executable size, and so on. To better understand this, first we need to talk about the difference between the two possible linking types:

- Dynamic linking
- Static linking

Dynamic linking is the process of linking the objects produced by the compiler, by putting the names of the functions inside the produced executable or library, so that the actual codes of that specific function reside inside a shared library (such as a *.dll file) and the actual linking and loading of the library is done at runtime. The most obvious advantages and disadvantages of dynamic linking are:

- Your application will need the shared libraries at runtime, so you must deploy them along with your application's executable and make sure that it can reach them. For instance, on Windows, this can be done by copying it to the same folder as the application executable, or on Linux by putting them inside default library paths such as /lib/.
- Dynamic linking allows a high amount of flexibility by keeping separate parts of an application in separate shared library files. This way, a shared library can be updated individually without the need to recompile each and every part of an application.

As opposed to dynamic linking, static linking can be used to link all of the required codes into the produced executable, thus creating a static library or executable. You can guess that using static libraries has the complete opposite advantages and disadvantages to using shared libraries, which are:

- You don't need to deploy the static libraries you have used to build your application since all of their codes are actually copied into the produced executable
- Your application executable size will get bigger, which can mean longer initial load times and bigger files to deploy
- Any change to a library or any part of the application needs a complete rebuild process for all of its consisting parts

Throughout the whole book, especially when developing plugins for our comprehensive computer vision application, we used shared libraries and dynamic linking. This is because when we built OpenCV by using all of the default CMake settings, and installed Qt Framework by using the official installers in Chapter 1, *Introduction to OpenCV and Qt*, they were both dynamically linked and shared libraries (*.dll on Windows, *.dylib on macOS, and so on). In the next sections, though, we are going to learn how to build both Qt and OpenCV libraries statically, using their source codes. By using statically linked libraries, we can create applications that do not require any shared libraries to be present on the target system. This can help extremely reduce the effort needed to deploy your applications. It is especially felt with OpenCV in macOS and Linux operating systems, where your users need to do absolutely nothing except copying and running your applications, whereas they would be required to take some actions or you would have to do some scripting in order to make sure all of the required dependencies are in place when your application is executed.

# Building OpenCV static libraries

Let's start with OpenCV, which follows almost the same set of instructions for building static libraries as we did for dynamic libraries. You can refer to Chapter 1, *Introduction to OpenCV and Qt*, for more information about this. Simply download the source codes, extract, and use CMake to configure your build, as it is mentioned in that chapter. This time though, in addition to checking the checkbox next to the BUILD_opencv_world option, also make sure that all of the following options are turned off by unchecking the checkbox next to each one of them:

- BUILD_DOCS
- BUILD_EXAMPLES
- BUILD_PERF_TESTS
- BUILD_TESTS
- BUILD_SHARED_LIBS
- BUILD_WITH_STATIC_CRT (only available on Windows)

Turning off the first four parameters is merely for speeding up the build process and is completely optional. Disabling `BUILD_SHARED_LIBS` simply enables the static (non-shared) build mode of OpenCV libraries, and the last parameter (on Windows) helps with avoiding incompatible library files. Now, if you start the build process by using the same instructions provided in Chapter 1, *Introduction to OpenCV and Qt*, this time, instead of shared libraries (for instance, on Windows, `*.lib` and `*.dll` files), you will end up with the statically linked OpenCV libraries (again, on Windows, only `*.lib` files, without any `*.dll` files) in the install folder. What you need to do next is configure your project to use the OpenCV static libraries. Either by using a `*.pri` file, or directly adding them to your Qt project `*.pro` file, you need the following lines so that your project can use the OpenCV static libraries:

```
win32: {
  INCLUDEPATH += "C:/path_to_opencv_install/include"
  Debug: {
    LIBS += -L"C:/path_to_opencv_install/x86/vc14/staticlib"
        -lopencv_world330d
        -llibjpegd
        -llibjasperd
        -littnotifyd
        -lIlmImfd
        -llibwebpd
        -llibtiffd
        -llibprotobufd
        -llibpngd
        -lzlibd
        -lipp_iw
        -lippicvmt
  }
  Release: {
    LIBS += -L"C:/path_to_opencv_install/x86/vc14/staticlib"
        -lopencv_world330
        -llibjpeg
        -llibjasper
        -littnotify
        -lIlmImf
        -llibwebp
        -llibtiff
        -llibprotobuf
        -llibpng
        -lzlib
        -lipp_iw
        -lippicvmt
  }
}
```

The order of the libraries in the preceding code is not random. These libraries need to be included in the correct order of their dependencies. You can check this out for yourself in Visual Studio 2015, by selecting **Project** and then **Project Build Order...** from the main menu. For macOS users, `win32` must be replaced with `unix: macx` in the preceding code, and also the path to the libraries must match the ones in your build folder. As for Linux, you can use the same `pkgconfig` lines that we were using for dynamic libraries, as seen here:

```
unix: !macx{
  CONFIG += link_pkgconfig
  PKGCONFIG += opencv
}
```

Note that even when you build OpenCV statically, on Windows OS, there is still one library that will be in the output folder as a dynamic one, and that is `opencv_ffmpeg330.dll`. You won't need to include it in your `*.pro` file; however, you still need to deploy it along with your application executable since OpenCV itself depends on it to be able to support some of the well-known video formats and encodings.

# Building Qt static libraries

By default, only dynamic Qt libraries are provided with the official Qt installers. This was also the case in `Chapter 1`, *Introduction to OpenCV and Qt*, when we installed Qt in our development environment by using the installers provided by the following link:

`https://download.qt.io/official_releases/qt/5.9/5.9.1/`

So, to put it simply, if you want to use the static Qt libraries, you must build them on your own using their source codes. You can follow the steps provided here in order to configure, build, and use static Qt libraries:

1. To be able to build a set of static Qt libraries, you need to start by downloading the source codes from the Qt downloads website. They are usually provided as a single compressed file (`*.zip`, `*.tar.xz`, and so on) that contains all of the required source codes. In our case (Qt version 5.9.1), you can use the following link to download the Qt source codes:

   `https://download.qt.io/official_releases/qt/5.9/5.9.1/single/`

Download `qt-everywhere-opensource-src-5.9.1.zip` (or `*.tar.xz`) and proceed to the next step.

2. Extract the source codes to a folder of your choice. We'll assume the extracted folder is called `Qt_Src` and it is located in the `c:/dev` folder (on the Windows operating system). So, the complete path to our extracted Qt source codes is assumingly `c:/dev/Qt_Src`.

For macOS and Linux users, the path might be something like `Users/amin/dev/Qt_Src`, so in case you are using one of the mentioned operating systems instead of Windows, you will need to replace it in all of the provided instructions that refer to it, which should be quite obvious by now.

3. Now, you need to take care of some dependencies before proceeding further with the next steps; macOS and Linux users usually do not need to do anything at this step since all of the required dependencies exist by default on those operating systems. However, the same doesn't apply to Windows users. In general, the following dependencies must exist on your computer before you can build Qt from source codes:

   - ActivePerl (`https://www.activestate.com/activeperl/downloads`).
   - Python (`https://www.python.org`), you need version 2.7.X, whereas X is replaced by the latest existing version, which is 14 at the time of writing this book.
   - Bison is provided inside the `gnuwin32` subfolder in the Qt source codes ZIP file for convenience of Windows users. Just make sure to add `c:/dev/Qt_Src/gnuwin32/bin` to the `PATH` environment variable.
   - Flex, the same as Bison, is provided inside the `gnuwin32` subfolder, which needs to be added to the `PATH`.
   - GNU `gperf`, the same as Bison and Flex, is provided inside the `gnuwin32` subfolder, which needs to be added to the `PATH`.

To make sure everything is in order, try to run the relevant commands that execute each one of the dependencies we just mentioned. It might be the case that you have forgotten to add one of the dependencies to the PATH, or in the case of macOS and Linux users, they are removed and don't exist for any possible reason. It should be enough to just execute each one of the following commands in a Command Prompt (or Terminal) and make sure you don't face a **not recognized** or **not found** type of error:

```
perl
python
bison
flex
gperf
```

4. Now, run **Developer Command Prompt for VS2015** on Windows. On macOS or Linux, run the Terminal. You'll need to run a set of consecutive commands to configure and build Qt from source codes. The configuration, which is the most crucial part of this step, is done by using the `configure` command. The `configure` command, which resides in the root of the Qt source folders, accepts the following parameters (note that the actual set of parameters is a very long list, so we will suffice with the ones that are most widely used):

   - `-help` or `-h`: This can be used to display the help contents for the `configure` command.
   - `-verbose` or `-v`: This can be used to display more detailed messages while building.
   - `-opensource`: This is used to build the open source edition of the Qt Framework.
   - `-commercial`: This is used to build the commercial edition of the Qt Framework.
   - `-confirm-license`: This can be used to automatically confirm (acknowledge) the selected license or the edition of the Qt Framework.
   - `-shared`: This can be used to build Qt dynamically, or in other words, shared Qt libraries.
   - `-static`: This can be used to build Qt statically.

- `-platform`: This is used to set the target platform. This parameter must be followed by a supported platform. By default, Qt supports many platforms, which you can check out by taking a peek inside the `qtbase/mkspecs` folder, which is a subfolder inside the extracted Qt source codes. If you omit this parameter, then the platform will be automatically detected.
- `-prefix`: This followed by a path, can be used to set the installation folder of the built libraries.
- `-skip`: This, followed by a repository name, can be used to skip building a specific Qt module. By default, meaning if we omit this parameter, all repositories inside the Qt sources folder will be built. If you want to skip building a module for any reason, you can simply pass it to the `configure` command using a `-skip` parameter. Just make sure to omit the starting `qt` from the repository name. For instance, if you want to skip building the Qt WebEngine module, which has a folder named `qtwebengine` inside the Qt source codes folder, you need to pass `-skip webengine` to the `configure` command.
- `-make`: This can be used to include a so-called *part* in the Qt build. A *part* can be libs for libraries, tests for tests, examples for examples, and so on.
- `-nomake`: This is the opposite of `-make`, and it can be used to exclude a *part* from the Qt build. This can be useful especially in case we need to speed up the build process since we don't usually need to build the tests or examples.

The list of parameters provided here should be more than enough for building a static version of Qt Framework with more or fewer default settings:

5. It's time to configure our Qt build. First things first, we need to switch to the Qt source codes folder by using the following command:

```
cd c:/dev/Qt_Src"
```

6. And then start the configuration by typing the following command:

```
configure -opensource -confirm-license -static -skip webengine
    -prefix "c:devQtStatic" -platform win32-msvc
```

The reason why we provide -skip webengine is because at the moment (of writing this book), building the Qt WebEngine module statically is not supported. Also note that we provide a -prefix parameter, which is the folder that we want to get our static libraries in. You need to be careful with this parameter since you cannot just copy it around later on and because of your build configuration, the static libraries will only work when they remain in that location on disk. The rest of the parameters we already described in the parameters list.

You can also add the following to the configure command to skip the parts that you probably won't need and speed up the build process, since it will take a long time:

```
-nomake tests -nomake examples
```

On macOS and Linux, you must omit the following part from the configure command. The reason for this is simply the fact that the platform will be automatically detected. This of course is also the case on Windows, but since we want to force a 32-bit build of the Qt libraries (to support a wider range of Windows versions), we'll stick to using this parameter:

```
-platform win32-msvc
```

The configuration process should not take too long, depending on your computer specifications. You should see an output similar to the following after the configuration is completed, otherwise, you need to carefully go through the previous steps again:

```
Qt is now configured for building. Just run 'nmake'.
Once everything is built, you must run 'nmake install'.
Qt will be installed into 'c:devQtStatic'.

Prior to reconfiguration, make sure you remove any leftovers
from
the previous build.
```

Note that on macOS and Linux, nmake will be replaced by make in the preceding output.

7. As it is mentioned in the configuration output, you need to type the build and install commands.

On Windows, use the following commands:

```
nmake
nmake install
```

On macOS and Linux, use the following commands:

```
make
make install
```

Note that the first command usually takes a long time to complete (depending on your computer specs), since Qt Framework contains a lot of modules and libraries that need to be built, so you need to be patient at this step. In any case, it should be built without any issues if you have exactly followed all of the provided steps until now.

It is important to note that if you use an install folder (-prefix parameter) that is in a restricted area on your computer, you must make sure to run the Command Prompt instance using administrator level (if you are using Windows) or execute the build and install commands with a sudo prefix (if you are on macOS or Linux).

8. After running the `install` command, you should get your static Qt libraries inside the folder you provided as the prefix parameter during the configuration, or in other words, the installation folder. So, at this step, you need to add this newly built set of Qt static libraries as a kit in Qt Creator. To do this, open Qt Creator and select **Tools** from the main menu, then select **Options**. From the list on the left side, select **Build & Run**, and then select the **Qt Versions** tab. Now, press the **Add** button and by browsing to the Qt build installation folder, select **qmake.exe**, which should be inside the `C:devQtStaticbin` folder in our case. The following screenshot shows the status in the **Qt Versions** tab after correctly adding the new Qt build:

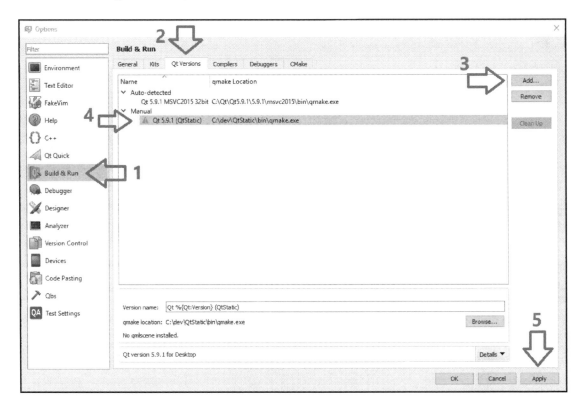

9. Now, switch to the **Kits** tab. You should be able to see the Kit that you have been using throughout the whole book to build Qt applications. For instance, on Windows, it should be **Desktop Qt 5.9.1 MSVC2015 32bit**. Select it and press the **Clone** button, then choose the **Qt Version** that we set in the **Qt Versions** tab in the previous step (if you don't see your build there, you probably need to press the **Apply** button once, and then it'll appear in the combo box). Also, make sure to remove the `Clone of` from its name and instead, append the word `Static` to it so that it is easily distinguished. The following screenshot represents the status of the **Kits** tab and the way it needs to be configured:

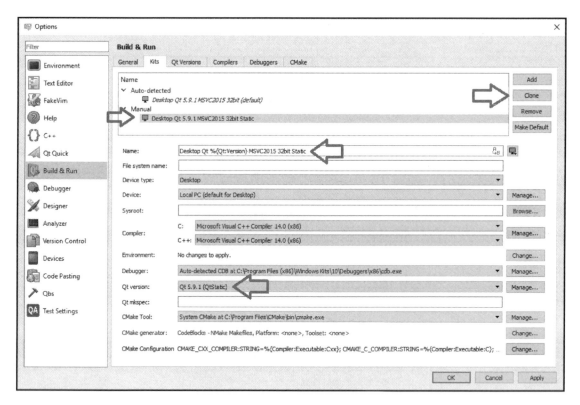

That's about it for building and configuring a static Qt kit. You can now start creating your Qt projects with it exactly the same way as you did with the default Qt kit (which was a dynamic kit). The only thing you need to take care of is to select it as the target kit when you create and configure your Qt project. Let us do this with a simple example. Start by creating a Qt Widgets application, and name it `StaticApp`. At the **Kit Selection** page, make sure you select your newly built static Qt kit and continue pressing **Next** until you are in the Qt code editor. The following screenshot depicts the **Kit Selection** page and how it should look (on a Window OS):

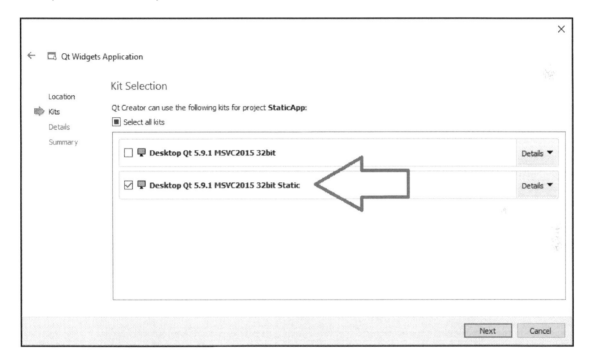

Without making much of a change, or adding any codes, simply press the **Run** button to build and execute this project. Now, if you browse to the build folder of this project, you will notice that the executable size is a lot bigger than it was before when we were building it using the default dynamic kit. To give you a comparison, on Windows OS and debug mode, the dynamically built version should be much smaller than one megabyte, whereas the statically built version is about 30 megabytes, which is much more. The reason for this is, as we mentioned before, all of the required Qt codes are now linked into the executable. Although strictly speaking it is not technically correct, you can think of it as embedding the libraries (*.dll files and so on) inside the executable itself.

Now, let us try to also use static OpenCV libraries in our example project. Just add the required additions to the StaticApp.pro file and additionally try a couple of simple OpenCV functions such as imread, dilate, and imshow to test your set of static OpenCV libraries. If you now check the size of your statically linked executable, you will notice that the file size is even bigger now. The obvious reason for this is that all of the required OpenCV codes are linked into the executable itself.

# Deploying Qt+OpenCV applications

It is extremely important to provide the end users with an application package that contains everything it needs to be able to run on the target platform and demand very little or no effort at all from the users in terms of taking care of the required dependencies. Achieving this kind of *works-out-of-the-box* condition for an application relies mostly on the type of the linking (dynamic or static) that is used to create an application, and also the specifications of the target operating system.

# Deploying using static linking

Deploying an application statically means that your application will run on its own and it eliminates having to take care of almost all of the needed dependencies, since they are already inside the executable itself. It is enough to simply make sure you select the **Release** mode while building your application, as seen in the following screenshot:

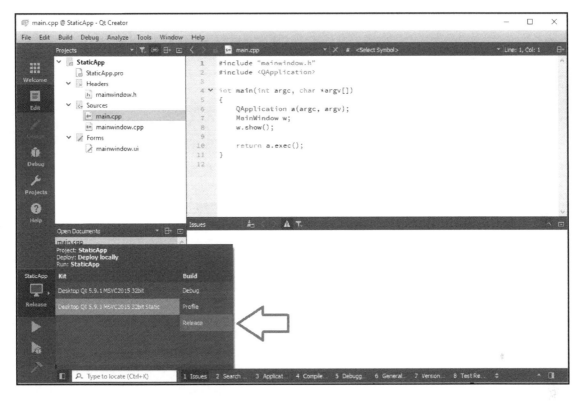

When your application is built in the **Release** mode, you can simply pick up the produced executable file and ship it to your users.

> If you try to deploy your application to Windows users, you might face an error similar to the following when your application is executed:

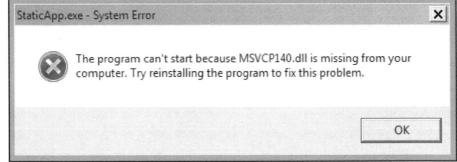

The reason for this error is that on Windows, even when building your Qt application statically, you still need to make sure that Visual C++ Redistributables exist on the target system. This is required for C++ applications that are built by using Microsoft Visual C++, and the version of the required redistributables correspond to the Microsoft Visual Studio installed on your computer. In our case, the official title of the installer for these libraries is Visual C++ Redistributables for Visual Studio 2015, and it can be downloaded from the following link: `https://www.microsoft.com/en-us/download/details.aspx?id=48145`.

It is a common practice to include the redistributables installer inside the installer for our application and perform a silent installation of them if they are not already installed. This process happens with most of the applications you use on your Windows PCs, most of the time, without you even noticing it.

We already quite briefly talked about the advantages (fewer files to deploy) and disadvantages (bigger executable size) of static linking. But when it is meant in the context of deployment, there are some more complexities that need to be considered. So, here is another (more complete) list of disadvantages, when using static linking to deploy your applications:

- The building takes more time and the executable size gets bigger and bigger.
- You can't mix static and shared (dynamic) Qt libraries, which means you can't use the power of plugins and extending your application without building everything from scratch.
- Static linking, in a sense, means hiding the libraries used to build an application. Unfortunately, this option is not offered with all libraries, and failing to comply with it can lead to licensing issues with your application. This complexity arises partly because of the fact that Qt Framework uses some third-party libraries that do not offer the same set of licensing options as Qt itself. Talking about licensing issues is not a discussion suitable for this book, so we'll suffice with mentioning that you *must* be careful when you plan to create commercial applications using static linking of Qt libraries. For a detailed list of licenses used by third-party libraries within Qt, you can always refer to the *Licenses Used in Qt* web page from the following link:

      http://doc.qt.io/qt-5/licenses-used-in-qt.html

For a complete reference of various LGPL licenses and their versions used throughout the Qt modules (and many other open source software that can be found online), you can refer to the following link: https://www.gnu.org/licenses/.

You can also use the following link for a complete discussion about what you need to know before choosing a Qt open source license: https://www.qt.io/qt-licensing-terms/.

Static linking, even with all of its disadvantages that we just mentioned, is still an option, and a good one in some cases, provided that you can comply with the licensing options of the Qt Framework. For instance, in Linux operating systems where creating an installer for our application requires some extra work and care, static linking can help extremely reduce the effort needed to deploy applications (merely a copy and paste). So, the final decision of whether to use static linking or not is mostly on you and how you plan to deploy your application. Making this important decision will be much easier by the end of this chapter, when you have an overview of the possible linking and deployment methods.

# Deploying using dynamic linking

When you deploy an application built with Qt and OpenCV using shared libraries (or dynamic linking), you need to make sure that the executable of your application is able to reach the runtime libraries of Qt and OpenCV, in order to load and use them. This reachability or visibility of runtime libraries can have different meanings depending on the operating system. For instance, on Windows, you need to copy the runtime libraries to the same folder where your application executable resides, or put them in a folder that is appended to the **PATH** environment value.

Qt Framework offers command-line tools to simplify the deployment of Qt applications on Windows and macOS. As mentioned before, the first thing you need to do is to make sure your application is built in the **Release** mode, and not **Debug** mode. Then, if you are on Windows, first copy the executable (let us assume it is called app.exe) from the build folder into a separate folder (which we will refer to as deploy_path) and execute the following commands using a command-line instance:

```
cd deploy_path
QT_PATHbinwindeployqt app.exe
```

The `windeployqt` tool is a deployment helper tool that simplifies the process of copying the required Qt runtime libraries into the same folder as the application executable. It simply takes an executable as a parameter and after determining the modules used to create it, copies all required runtime libraries and any additional required dependencies, such as Qt plugins, translations, and so on. This takes care of all the required Qt runtime libraries, but we still need to take care of OpenCV runtime libraries. If you followed all of the steps in `Chapter 1`, *Introduction to OpenCV and Qt*, for building OpenCV libraries dynamically, then you only need to manually copy the `opencv_world330.dll` and `opencv_ffmpeg330.dll` files from OpenCV installation folder (inside the `x86vc14bin` folder) into the same folder where your application executable resides.

We didn't really go into the benefits of turning on the `BUILD_opencv_world` option when we built OpenCV in the early chapters of the book; however, it should be clear now that this simplifies the deployment and usage of the OpenCV libraries, by requiring only a single entry for LIBS in the `*.pro` file and manually copying only a single file (not counting the `ffmpeg` library) when deploying OpenCV applications. It should be also noted that this method has the disadvantage of copying all OpenCV codes (in a single library) along your application even when you do not need or use all of its modules in a project.

Also note that on Windows, as mentioned in the *Deploying using static linking* section, you still need to similarly provide the end users of your application with Microsoft Visual C++ Redistributables.

On a macOS operating system, it is also possible to easily deploy applications written using Qt Framework. For this reason, you can use the `macdeployqt` command-line tool provided by Qt. Similar to `windeployqt`, which accepts a Windows executable and fills the same folder with the required libraries, `macdeployqt` accepts a macOS application bundle and makes it deployable by copying all of the required Qt runtimes as private frameworks inside the bundle itself. Here is an example:

```
cd deploy_path
QT_PATH/bin/macdeployqt my_app_bundle
```

Optionally, you can also provide an additional –dmg parameter, which leads to the creation of a macOS * . dmg (disk image) file. As for the deployment of OpenCV libraries when dynamic linking is used, you can create an installer using Qt Installer Framework (which we will learn about in the next section), a third-party provider, or a script that makes sure the required runtime libraries are copied to their required folders. This is because of the fact that simply copying your runtime libraries (whether it is OpenCV or anything else) to the same folder as the application executable does not help with making them visible to an application on macOS. The same also applies to the Linux operating system, where unfortunately even a tool for deploying Qt runtime libraries does not exist (at least for the moment), so we also need to take care of Qt libraries in addition to OpenCV libraries, either by using a trusted third-party provider (which you can search for online) or by using the cross-platform installer provided by Qt itself, combined with some scripting to make sure everything is in place when our application is executed.

# Qt Installer Framework

Qt Installer Framework allows you to create cross-platform installers of your Qt applications for Windows, macOS, and Linux operating systems. It allows for creating standard installer wizards where the user is taken through consecutive dialogs that provide all the necessary information, and finally display the progress for when the application is being installed and so on, similar to most of installations you have probably faced, and especially the installation of Qt Framework itself. Qt Installer Framework is based on Qt Framework itself but is provided as a different package and does not require Qt SDK (Qt Framework, Qt Creator, and so on) to be present on a computer. It is also possible to use Qt Installer Framework in order to create installer packages for any application, not just Qt applications.

In this section, we are going to learn how to create a basic installer using Qt Installer Framework, which takes care of installing your application on a target computer and copying all the necessary dependencies. The result will be a single executable installer file that you can put on a web server to be downloaded or provide it in a USB stick or CD, or any other media type. This example project will help you get started with working your way around the many great capabilities of Qt Installer Framework by yourself.

You can use the following link to download and install the Qt Installer Framework. Make sure to simply download the latest version when you use this link, or any other source for downloading it. At the moment, the latest version is 3.0.2:

```
https://download.qt.io/official_releases/qt-installer-framework
```

After you have downloaded and installed Qt Installer Framework, you can start creating the required files that Qt Installer Framework needs in order to create an installer. You can do this by simply browsing to the Qt Installer Framework, and from the `examples` folder copying the `tutorial` folder, which is also a template in case you want to quickly rename and re-edit all of the files and create your installer quickly. We will go the other way and create them manually; first because we want to understand the structure of the required files and folders for the Qt Installer Framework, and second, because it is still quite easy and simple. Here are the required steps for creating an installer:

1. Assuming that you have already finished developing your Qt and OpenCV application, you can start by creating a new folder that will contain the installer files. Let's assume this folder is called `deploy`.
2. Create an XML file inside the `deploy` folder and name it `config.xml`. This XML file must contain the following:

```xml
<?xml version="1.0" encoding="UTF-8"?>
<Installer>
    <Name>Your application</Name>
    <Version>1.0.0</Version>
    <Title>Your application Installer</Title>
    <Publisher>Your vendor</Publisher>
    <StartMenuDir>Super App</StartMenuDir>
    <TargetDir>@HomeDir@/InstallationDirectory</TargetDir>
</Installer>
```

Make sure to replace the required XML fields in the preceding code with information relevant to your application and then save and close this file:

1. Now, create a folder named `packages` inside the `deploy` folder. This folder will contain the individual packages that you want the user to be able to install, or make them mandatory or optional so that the user can review and decide what will be installed.

2. In the case of simpler Windows applications that are written using Qt and OpenCV, usually it is enough to have just a single package that includes the required files to run your application, and even do silent installation of Microsoft Visual C++ Redistributables. But for more complex cases, and especially when you want to have more control over individual installable elements of your application, you can also go for two or more packages, or even sub-packages. This is done by using domain-like folder names for each package. Each package folder can have a name like `com.vendor.product`, where vendor and product are replaced by the developer name or company and the application. A sub-package (or sub-component) of a package can be identified by adding `.subproduct` to the name of the parent package. For instance, you can have the following folders inside the `packages` folder:

```
com.vendor.product
com.vendor.product.subproduct1
com.vendor.product.subproduct2
com.vendor.product.subproduct1.subsubproduct1
. . .
```

This can go on for as many products (packages) and sub-products (sub-packages) as we like. For our example case, let's create a single folder that contains our executable, since it describes it all and you can create additional packages by simply adding them to the `packages` folder. Let's name it something like `com.amin.qtcvapp`. Now, follow these required steps:

1. Now, create two folders inside the new package folder that we created, the `com.amin.qtcvapp` folder. Rename them to `data` and `meta`. These two folders must exist inside all packages.

2. Copy your application files inside the `data` folder. This folder will be extracted into the target folder exactly as it is (we will talk about setting the target folder of a package in the later steps). In case you are planning to create more than one package, then make sure to separate their data correctly and in a way that it makes sense. Of course, you won't be faced with any errors if you fail to do so, but the users of your application will probably be confused, for instance by skipping a package that should be installed at all times and ending up with an installed application that does not work.

3. Now, switch to the `meta` folder and create the following two files inside that folder, and fill them with the codes provided for each one of them.

The `package.xml` file should contain the following. There's no need to mention that you must fill the fields inside the XML with values relevant to your package:

```xml
<?xml version="1.0" encoding="UTF-8"?>
<Package>
    <DisplayName>The component</DisplayName>
    <Description>Install this component.</Description>
    <Version>1.0.0</Version>
    <ReleaseDate>1984-09-16</ReleaseDate>
    <Default>script</Default>
    <Script>installscript.qs</Script>
</Package>
```

The script in the previous XML file, which is probably the most important part of the creation of an installer, refers to a Qt Installer Script (`*.qs` file), which is named `installerscript.qs` and can be used to further customize the package, its target folder, and so on. So, let us create a file with the same name (`installscript.qs`) inside the `meta` folder, and use the following code inside it:

```javascript
function Component()
{
  // initializations go here
}


Component.prototype.isDefault = function()
{
  // select (true) or unselect (false) the component by default
  return true;
}


Component.prototype.createOperations = function()
{
  try {
    // call the base create operations function
    component.createOperations();
  } catch (e) {
    console.log(e);
  }
}
```

This is the most basic component script, which customizes our package (well, it only performs the default actions) and it can optionally be extended to change the target folder, create shortcuts in the Start menu or desktop (on Windows), and so on. It is a good idea to keep an eye on the Qt Installer Framework documentation and learn about its scripting to be able to create more powerful installers that can put all of the required dependencies of your app in place, and automatically. You can also browse through all of the examples inside the `examples` folder of the Qt Installer Framework and learn how to deal with different deployment cases. For instance, you can try to create individual packages for Qt and OpenCV dependencies and allow the users to deselect them, in case they already have the Qt runtime libraries on their computer.

1. The last step is to use the `binarycreator` tool to create our single and stand-alone installer. Simply run the following command by using a Command Prompt (or Terminal) instance:

```
binarycreator -p packages -c config.xml myinstaller
```

The `binarycreator` is located inside the Qt Installer Framework `bin` folder. It requires two parameters that we have already prepared. `-p` must be followed by our `packages` folder and `-c` must be followed by the configuration file (or `config.xml`) file. After executing this command, you will get `myinstaller` (on Windows, you can append `*.exe` to it), which you can execute to install your application. This single file should contain all of the required files needed to run your application, and the rest is taken care of. You only need to provide a download link to this file, or provide it on a CD to your users.

The following are the dialogs you will face in this default and most basic installer, which contains most of the usual dialogs you would expect when installing an application:

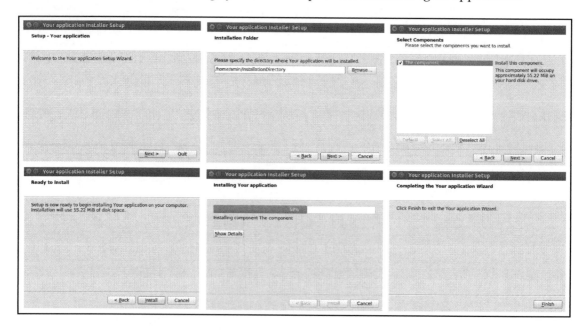

If you go to the installation folder, you will notice that it contains a few more files than you put inside the data folder of your package. Those files are required by the installer to handle modifications and uninstall your application. For instance, the users of your application can easily uninstall your application by executing the maintenancetool executable, which would produce another simple and user-friendly dialog to handle the uninstall process:

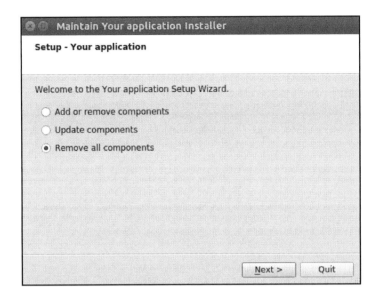

# Summary

Whether your application can be *easily* installed and used on a target computer or not, it can mean winning or losing a significant number of users. Especially with the ones that are not professional users, you must make sure to create and deploy installers that contain all of the required dependencies and work out of the box on the target platform. In this chapter, we talked a fair amount about just that. We learned about the build process and how the linking method that we choose can completely alter the deployment experience. We learned about existing Qt tools to simplify the deployment process on Windows and macOS. Note that these tools contain many more parameters than we saw in this chapter, and they are worth taking a deeper look at by yourself, and trying out various parameters to see their effect for yourself. In the last section of this chapter, we learned about Qt Installer Framework and also created a simple installer by using it. We learned how to create packages that get extracted on a target system using the installer. This same skill can be used to put all of the dependencies in their required folders. For instance, OpenCV libraries can be added in a package and when installed, they are put inside `/usr/lib/` or `/usr/local/lib/` on Linux operating systems, so that your application can access them without any issues. With this last set of skills, we are now familiar with most of the existing phases of the development cycle that a developer (especially a computer vision developer) must be aware of.

In the final chapter of this book, we will be introduced to Qt Quick and QML. We will learn how to create beautiful UIs with the power of Qt and with the simplicity of QML. We will also learn how to combine C++ and QML codes in order to write classes that use a third-party framework such as OpenCV, which are easily usable from within our QML codes. The final chapter of this book is meant to help you get started with developing computer vision applications for mobile (Android and iOS), using OpenCV combined with extremely easy-to-use and beautiful Qt Quick Controls.

# 12
# Qt Quick Applications

Using **Qt Widgets Application** projects allows the creation of flexible and powerful GUIs by using the Qt Creator Design mode, or manually modifying the GUI files (`*.ui`) in a text editor. Up until now and throughout the chapters of this book, we relied on **Qt Widgets applications** as the basis for the GUIs that we created, and as we learned in Chapter 3, *Creating a Comprehensive Qt+OpenCV Project*, we can use style sheets to effectively alter the look and feel of our Qt applications. But apart from Qt Widgets applications and using `QtWidgets` and `QtGui` modules, there is another approach to the creation of GUIs that is offered by the Qt Framework. This approach is based on the `QtQuick` module and the QML language, and it allows the creation of far more flexible (in terms of the look, feel, animations, effects, and so on) GUIs and with much more ease. Applications created by using this approach are referred to as Qt Quick applications. Note that in more recent Qt versions (5.7 and later), you can also create Qt Quick Controls 2 applications, which offers more improved types for the creation of Qt Quick applications, and we'll also mainly focus on that.

The `QtQuick` module, along with `QtQml` module, are the modules that contain all of the required classes in order to use Qt Quick and QML programming within a C++ application. QML itself, on the other hand, is a highly readable declarative language that uses a JSON-like syntax (combined with scripting) to describe user interfaces in terms of various components and the way they interact with each other. In this chapter, we are going to be introduced to the QML language and how it is used to simplify the process of creating GUI applications. We'll learn about its simple and readable syntax and how it is used in practice, by creating an example QML-based GUI application, or to be precise, a **Qt Quick Controls 2 Application**. Even though using the QML language does not necessarily require a deep knowledge of the C++ language, it is still quite useful to understand the structure of a Qt Quick project, so we'll briefly go through the structure of a most basic Qt Quick application. By going through some of the most important QML libraries, we'll learn about the existing visual and non-visual QML types that can be used to create user interfaces, add animations to them, access hardware, and so on. We'll learn how to use the Qt Quick Designer, which is integrated into the Qt Creator, to modify QML files using a graphical designer. Later on, by learning about the integration of C++ and QML, we'll fill the gap between them and learn how to use the OpenCV framework within a **Qt Quick Application**. In this final chapter, we'll also learn about how to use the same desktop projects that use Qt and OpenCV to create mobile computer vision applications and expand our cross-platform reach beyond the desktop platforms and into the mobile world.

The topics covered in this chapter include:

- Introduction to QML
- Structure of a **Qt Quick Application** project
- Creating a **Qt Quick Controls 2 Application**
- Using Qt Quick Designer
- Integrating C++ and QML
- Running Qt and OpenCV applications on Android and iOS

# Introduction to QML

As mentioned in the introduction, QML has a JSON-like structure that can be used to describe the elements on a user interface. A QML code imports one or more libraries and has a root element that contains all of the other visual and non-visual elements. The following is an example of a QML code that results in the creation of an empty window (ApplicationWindow type) with a specified width, height, and title:

```
import QtQuick 2.7
import QtQuick.Controls 2.2

ApplicationWindow
{
  visible: true
  width: 300
  height: 500
  title: "Hello QML"
}
```

Each import statement must be followed with a QML library name and version. In the preceding code, two of the main QML libraries that include most of the default types are imported. For instance, ApplicationWindow is defined inside the QtQuick.Controls 2.2 library. The only source of truth for existing QML libraries and their correct versions is the Qt documentation, so make sure to always refer to it in case you need to use any other classes. If you search for ApplicationWindow using the Qt Creator Help mode, you'll find out that the required import statement is what we just used. Another thing worth mentioning is that ApplicationWindow in the previous code is the single root element, and all additional UI elements must be created inside it. Let's expand our code even further by adding a Label element that displays some text:

```
ApplicationWindow
{
  visible: true
  width: 300
  height: 500
  title: "Hello QML"

  Label
  {
    x: 25
    y: 25
    text: "This is a label<br>that contains<br>multiple lines!"
  }
}
```

We skipped the import statements in the preceding code since they are the same as before. Notice that the newly added `Label` has a `text` property, which is the text shown on the label. `x` and `y` simply refer to the position of the `Label` inside the `ApplicationWindow`. Container items such as group boxes can be added in a quite similar way. Let's add one and see how it's done:

```
ApplicationWindow
{
  visible: true
  width: 300
  height: 500
  title: "Hello QML"
  GroupBox
  {
    x: 50
    y: 50
    width: 150
    height: 150
    Label
    {
      x: 25
      y: 25
      text: "This is a label<br>that contains<br>multiple lines!"
    }
  }
}
```

This QML code will result in a window similar to what is shown here:

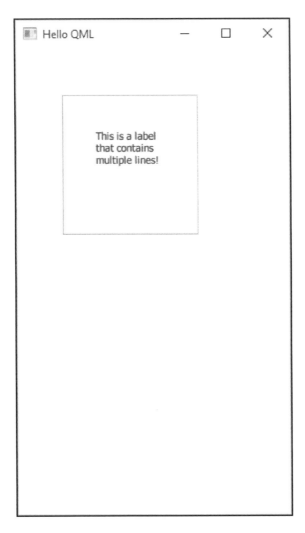

Note that the position of each element is an offset from its parent element. For instance, the x and y values provided to the `Label` inside the `GroupBox` are added to the x and y properties of the `GroupBox` itself, and that is how the final position of a UI element is decided within a root element (in this case, `ApplicationWindow`).

Similar to Qt Widgets, you can also use layouts in QML code to control and organize the UI elements. For this purpose, you can use `GridLayout`, `ColumnLayout`, and `RowLayout` QML types, but first, you need to import them using the following statement:

```
import QtQuick.Layouts 1.3
```

Now, you can add QML user interface elements as child items to a layout and they'll be managed by it automatically. Let's add a few buttons in a `ColumnLayout` and see how this is done:

```
ApplicationWindow
{
  visible: true
  width: 300
  height: 500
  title: "Hello QML"

  ColumnLayout
  {
    anchors.fill: parent
    Button
    {
      text: "First Button"
      Layout.alignment: Qt.AlignHCenter | Qt.AlignVCenter
    }
    Button
    {
      text: "Second Button"
      Layout.alignment: Qt.AlignHCenter | Qt.AlignVCenter
    }
    Button
    {
      text: "Third Button"
      Layout.alignment: Qt.AlignHCenter | Qt.AlignVCenter
    }
  }
}
```

This would result in a window similar to this:

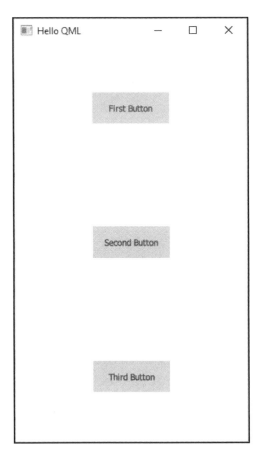

In the preceding code, ColumnLayout acts in a similar way to the vertical layouts that we used in Qt Widgets applications. From top to bottom, each element added as a child into ColumnLayout is displayed after the previous one and no matter the size of the ColumnLayout, the items within it are always resized and relocated to keep the vertical layout view. There are a couple more things to note about the preceding. First, the size of the ColumnLayout itself is set to the parent size by using the following code:

```
anchors.fill: parent
```

anchors is one of the most important properties of QML visual elements, and it takes care of the size and positioning of an element. In this case, and by setting the fill value of anchors to another object (the parent object), we're describing the size and position of our ColumnLayout to be the same as ApplicationWindow. By correctly using the anchors, we can handle the size and position of objects with much more power and flexibility. As another example, replace the anchors.fill line in the code with the following and see what happens:

```
width: 100
height: 100
anchors.centerIn: parent
```

Obviously, our ColumnLayout now has a constant size and it does not change when the ApplicationWindow is resized; however, the layout always keeps to the center of the ApplicationWindow. One last note about the preceding code is the following:

```
Layout.alignment: Qt.AlignHCenter | Qt.AlignVCenter
```

This line inside each item that is added to the ColumnLayout causes that item to position itself at the center of its cell, vertically and horizontally. Notice that a cell in this sense does not contain any visual borders and like the layout itself, cells within a layout are also non-visual ways of organizing the items within them.

The expansion of a QML code follows the same pattern no matter how many items are added or required. However, as the number of UI elements becomes bigger and bigger, it is better to separate the user interface into separate files. QML files that are in the same folder can be used as if they are predefined and important items. Let's say we have a QML file called MyRadios.qml that contains the following code:

```
import QtQuick 2.7
import QtQuick.Controls 2.2
import QtQuick.Layouts 1.3

Item
{
  ColumnLayout
  {
    anchors.centerIn: parent

    RadioButton
    {
        text: "Video"
    }
    RadioButton
    {
```

```
        text: "Image"
    }
  }
}
```

You can use this QML file and its `Item` inside another QML file in the same folder. Let's assume we have a `main.qml` file in the same folder with `MyRadios.qml`. Then, you can use it like this:

```
import QtQuick 2.7
import QtQuick.Controls 2.2
import QtQuick.Layouts 1.3

ApplicationWindow
{
  visible: true
  width: 300
  height: 500
  title: "Hello QML"

  ColumnLayout
  {
    anchors.fill: parent

    MyRadios
    {
        width: 100
        height: 200
    }
  }
}
```

Notice that no import statement is required as long as the QML files are both in the same folder. In case the QML file that you want to use in code is in a separate folder (a sub-folder in the same folder), then you have to import it with a statement, like this:

```
import "other_qml_path"
```

Obviously, in the preceding code, `other_qml_path` is the relative path to our QML file.

# User interaction and scripting in QML

Responding to user actions and events in QML code is done by adding scripts to slots of the items, in quite a similar way to Qt Widgets. The major difference here is that each signal defined internally within a QML type also has a corresponding slot for it which is automatically generated and can be filled with a script to perform an action when the relevant signal is emitted. Well, let's see this with another example. A QML `Button` type has a pressed signal. This automatically means that there is an `onPressed` slot that you can use to code the required action of the specific button. Here's an example code:

```
Button
{
  onPressed:
  {
    // code goes here
  }
}
```

For a list of available slots in QML types, you can refer to the Qt documentation. As mentioned before, you can easily guess the slot name of each signal by capitalizing the first letter of the signal name and prepending `on` to it. Thus, for the `pressed` signal you'll have an `onPressed` slot, for the `released` signal you'll have an `onReleased` slot, and so on.

To be able to access other QML items from within a script or a slot, first, you must assign a unique identifier to them. Note that this is only required for the items that you want to access and modify, or interact with. In all of the previous examples of this chapter we simply created items without assigning any identifiers to them. This can be easily done by assigning the unique identifier to the `id` property of an item. The value of the `id` property follows the variable naming conventions, meaning that it is case sensitive, cannot start with numbers, and so on. Here's an example code that demonstrates how `id` is assigned and used in a QML code:

```
ApplicationWindow
{
  id: mainWindow
  visible: true
  width: 300
  height: 500
  title: "Hello QML"

  ColumnLayout
  {
    anchors.fill: parent
    Button
```

```
    {
      text: "Close"
      Layout.alignment: Qt.AlignVCenter | Qt.AlignHCenter

      onPressed:
      {
        mainWindow.close()
      }
    }
  }
}
```

In the preceding code, the ApplicationWindow has an ID assigned to it; that is, mainWindow, which is used inside the onPressed slot of the Button to access it. You can guess that pressing the **Close** button in the preceding code will result in mainWindow being closed. Regardless of where an ID is defined in a QML file, it can be accessed everywhere within that specific QML file. This means the scope of an ID is not limited to a same group of items, or children of an item, and so on. Simply put, any ID is visible to all items in a QML file. But what about the id of an item in a separate QML file? To be able to access an item in a separate QML file, we need to export it by assigning it to a property alias, as seen in the following example:

```
Item
{
  property alias videoRadio: videoRadio
  property alias imageRadio: imageRadio
  ColumnLayout
  {
    anchors.centerIn: parent
    RadioButton
    {
      id: videoRadio
      text: "Video"
    }
    RadioButton
    {
      id: imageRadio
      text: "Image"
    }
  }
}
```

The preceding code is the same `MyRadios.qml` file, but this time, we have exported the two `RadioButton` items inside it by using alias properties of the root item. This way, we can access these items in a separate QML file where we use `MyRadios`. In addition to exporting items within an item, a property can be used to contain any other value that is required for a specific item. So, here is the general syntax for defining an additional property within a QML item:

```
property TYPE NAME: VALUE
```

Where `TYPE` can contain any QML type, `NAME` is a given name to the property and `VALUE` is the value of the property, which must be compatible with the provided type.

# Using Qt Quick Designer

QML files, because of their simple and readable syntax, are quite easy to modify and extend using any code editor; however, you can also use the integrated Quick Designer in Qt Creator for easier design and modification of a QML file. If you try to open a QML file in Qt Creator and switch to Design mode, then you'll be presented with the following Design mode, which is quite different from the standard Qt Widgets designer (used with `*.ui` files), and it contains most of what you need for quickly designing your user interfaces using a QML file:

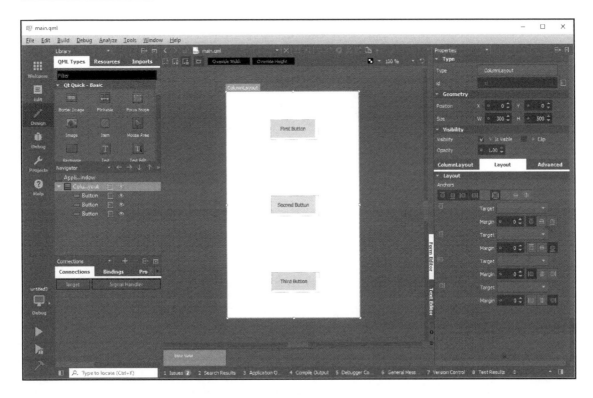

On the left side of the Qt Quick Designer screen, you can see the library of QML types that can be added to the user interface in the **Library** pane. It's similar to the Qt Widgets toolbox, but definitely with more components that you can use to design the user interface of your applications. You can simply drag and drop each one of them on the user interface and they'll be automatically added to your QML file:

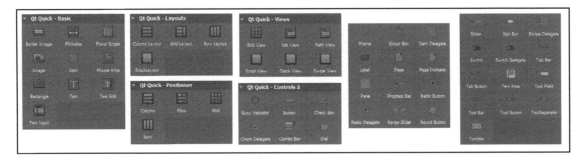

Right below the **Library** pane is the **Navigator** pane, which displays a hierarchical view of the components on the user interface. You can use the Navigator pane to quickly set the ID of the items on your QML file, by simply double-clicking on them. Additionally, you can export an item as an alias so that it can be used in other QML files or hide it during the design time (to be able to view the overlapping QML items). In the following screenshot on the **Navigator** pane, notice how the small icons beside the components have changed after **button2** is exported as an alias and **button3** is made hidden during design time:

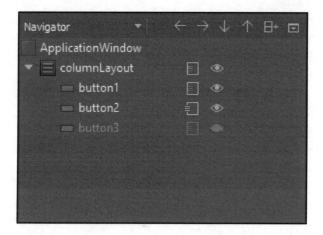

At the right side of the Qt Quick Designer, you can find the **Properties** pane. Similar to the **Properties** pane in the standard Qt Design mode, this pane can be used to manipulate and modify the properties of a QML item in detail. The content of this pane changes depending on the selected item on the user interface. In addition to the standard properties of a QML item, this pane also allows modifying the properties related to the layout of an individual item. The following screenshot depicts the different views of the **Properties** pane when a Button item is selected on the user interface:

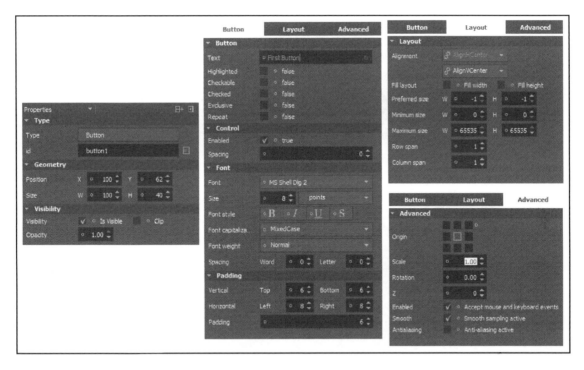

Apart from a helper tool for designing QML user interfaces, Qt Quick Designer can help you learn about the QML language itself, since all of the modifications done in the designer are converted to QML codes and stored in the same QML file. Make sure to familiarize yourself with how it's used by designing your user interfaces with it. For example, you can try to design some of the same user interfaces you have designed when you created Qt Widgets applications, but this time using the Qt Quick Designer and in QML files.

# Structure of a Qt Quick Application

In this section, we are going to learn about the structure of a **Qt Quick Application** project. Similar to **Qt Widgets Application** projects, most of the files required for a **Qt Quick Application** project are created automatically when you create a new project using Qt Creator, so you don't really need to memorize all of what is needed as a minimum, but still it is important to understand some of the basic concepts of how a **Qt Quick Application** is handled in order to be able to further extend it, or, as we'll learn in a later section of this chapter, to integrate and use C++ codes inside a QML file.

Let's go through this by creating an example application. Start by opening Qt Creator and pressing the **New Project** button from the welcome screen, or by choosing **New File or Project** from the **File** menu. Choose **Qt Quick Controls 2 Application** as the template type and press **Choose**, as seen in the following screenshot:

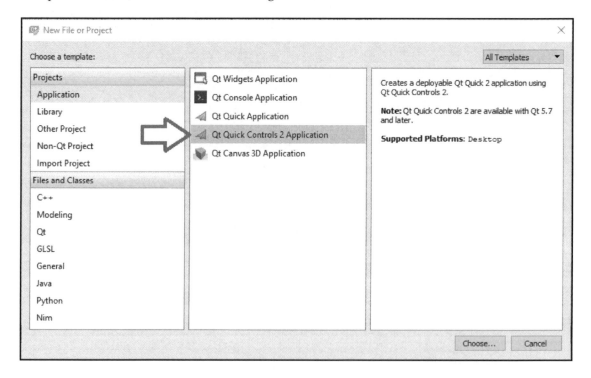

Set the name of the project as CvQml and press **Next**. In the **Define Build System** page, leave the **Build system** as **qmake**, which should be selected by default. In the **Define Project Details** page, you can choose one of the following for the Qt Quick Controls 2 style:

- **Default**
- **Material**
- **Universal**

The option you choose in this screen affects the overall style of your application.
The **Default** option leads to the default style, which allows the highest performance for Qt
Quick Controls 2 and consequently to our **Qt Quick Application**. The **Material** style can be
used to create applications based on the Google Material Design guidelines. It offers much
more appealing components but also requires more resources. Finally, **Universal** style can
be used to create applications based on the Microsoft Universal Design guidelines. Similar
to **Material** style, this also requires more resources but offers another appealing set of user
interface components.

 You can refer to the following links for more information about the
guidelines used to create the **Material** and **Universal** styles:

```
https://goo.gl/TiQEYB
```

```
https://dev.windows.com/design
```

The following screenshot depicts the differences between some of the common components,
and how your application will look when each one of the three possible style options is
selected:

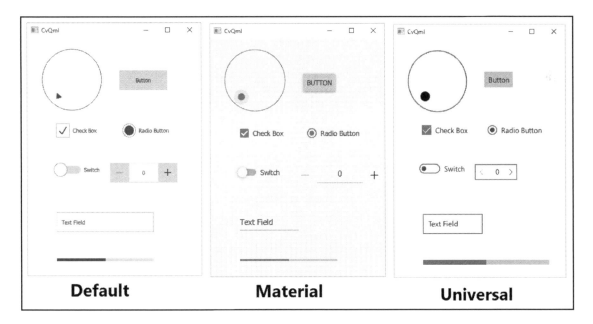

No matter what you choose, you can easily change this later on in a dedicated settings file called `qtquickcontrols2.conf` that is automatically included in your new project. Even the colors can be altered later on to match a dark or light theme, or any other set of colors. In any case, choose the one you like (or leave it as **Default**) and continue pressing **Next** until you end up in the Qt Code Editor. Your project now contains almost the minimum required files for a **Qt Quick Application**.

 Note that whenever we mention **Qt Quick Application** in this chapter, we actually mean **Qt Quick Controls 2 Application**, which is the new and enhanced type of **Qt Quick Application** (available in Qt 5.7 and later) that we just created and are going to extend to a complete and beautiful cross-platform computer vision application.

First things first, let's see the difference in the project (`*.pro`) file. In a **Qt Quick Application** as opposed to a **Qt Widgets Application**, instead of the `QtCore`, `QtGui` and `QtWidgets` modules, the `QtQml` and `QtQuick` modules are used by default. You can check this out by opening the `CvQml.pro` file, which has the following line at the top:

```
QT += qml quick
```

The two files that you can expect in a Qt project, whether it is a **Qt Widgets Application** or a **Qt Quick Application**, are a project and a C++ source file that contains the main function. So, apart from the `CvQml.pro` file, there is a single `main.cpp` file that contains the following:

```cpp
#include <QGuiApplication>
#include <QQmlApplicationEngine>

int main(int argc, char *argv[])
{
  QCoreApplication::setAttribute(Qt::AA_EnableHighDpiScaling);
  QGuiApplication app(argc, argv);

  QQmlApplicationEngine engine;
  engine.load(QUrl(QLatin1String("qrc:/main.qml")));
  if (engine.rootObjects().isEmpty())
    return -1;

  return app.exec();
}
```

This `main.cpp` is quite different from what we saw when creating Qt Widgets applications. Remember, in a **Qt Widgets Application**, inside the `main.cpp` and in the main function, a `QApplication` was created, then the main window was displayed and the program entered the event loop so that the window stays alive and all the events are processed, as seen here:

```
#include "mainwindow.h"
#include <QApplication>

int main(int argc, char *argv[])
{
  QApplication a(argc, argv);
  MainWindow w;
  w.show();

  return a.exec();
}
```

Similarly, in a **Qt Quick Application**, a `QGuiApplication` is created but this time instead of loading any windows, the QML file is loaded by using a `QQmlApplicationEngine`, as seen here:

```
QQmlApplicationEngine engine;
engine.load(QUrl(QLatin1String("qrc:/main.qml")));
if (engine.rootObjects().isEmpty())
  return -1;
```

This makes it clear that QML files are in fact loaded at runtime, so you can load them from disk, or in our example case from the `main.qml` file stored as a resource inside the `qml.qrc` file and embedded into the executable. This is, in fact, the common method of developing Qt Quick applications, and if you check the newly created `CvQml` project, you'll notice that it contains a Qt Resource file called `qml.qrc` that contains all of the project's QML files. Included in the `qml.qrc` file are the following files:

- `main.qml`, which is the QML file that is loaded in the `main.cpp` file and it is the entry point of our QML codes.
- `Page1.qml` contains the interactions and scripts for the `Page1Form` QML type.
- `Page1Form.ui.qml` contains the user interface and QML items within the `Page1Form` type. Note that the pair of `Page1.qml` and `Page1Form.ui.qml` is a common way of separating the user interface and its underlying codes, similar to that of using the `mainwindow.ui`, `mainwindow.h`, and `mainwindow.cpp` files when developing Qt Widgets applications.

- The `qtquickcontrols2.conf` file is the configuration file that can be used to change the style of our **Qt Quick Application**. It contains the following:

```
; This file can be edited to change the style of the application
; See Styling Qt Quick Controls 2 in the documentation ...
; http://doc.qt.io/qt-5/qtquickcontrols2-styles.html

[Controls]
Style=Default

[Universal]
Theme=Light
;Accent=Steel

[Material]
Theme=Light
;Accent=BlueGrey
;Primary=BlueGray
```

A semicolon `;` at the beginning of a line means it's just a comment. You can change the value of the `Style` variable in the preceding code to `Material` and `Universal` to change the overall style of your application. Depending on the style that is set, you can use `Theme`, `Accent`, or `Primary` values in the preceding code to alter the theme used in your application.

For a complete list of themes and colors and additional information on how you can use the wide range of available customizations in each theme, you can refer to the following links:

`https://goo.gl/jDZGPm` (For Default style)

`https://goo.gl/Um9qJ4` (For Material style)

`https://goo.gl/U6uxrh` (For Universal Style)

That's about it for the general structure of Qt Quick applications. This structure can be used to develop any kind of application for any platform in no time. Note that you are not obliged to use the automatically created files and you can simply start with an empty project or remove the unnecessary default files and start from scratch. For instance, in our example **Qt Quick Application** (titled CvQml), we won't be needing the Page1.qml and Page1Form.ui.qml files, so simply select them from inside the qml.qrc file and remove them by right-clicking and choosing **Remove File**. Of course, this will result in missing codes in your main.qml file. So, make sure you update it to the following, before proceeding to the next section:

```
import QtQuick 2.7
import QtQuick.Controls 2.0
import QtQuick.Layouts 1.3

ApplicationWindow
{
  visible: true
  width: 300
  height: 500
  title: qsTr("CvQml")
}
```

# Integrating C++ and QML codes

Even though the QML libraries have grown into a fully-fledged collection of types that can handle visuals, networking, cameras, and so on, it's still important to be able to extend them by using the power of C++ classes. Fortunately, QML and the Qt Framework provides enough provisions to be able to easily handle this. In this section, we are going to learn how to create a non-visual C++ class that can be used within QML codes to process images using OpenCV. Then, we'll create a C++ class that can be used as a visual item within QML codes to display images.

Note that there is an Image type by default in QML that can be used to display images saved on disk by providing their URL to the Image item. However, we'll be creating an image viewer QML type that can be used to display QImage objects, and use this opportunity to learn about the integration of C++ classes (visual) in QML codes.

Start by adding the OpenCV framework to our project that we created in the previous section. This is done exactly the same way as we did when creating Qt Widgets applications, and by including the required lines in the `*.pro` file. Then, add a new C++ class to the project by right-clicking on it from the projects pane and choosing **Add New**. Make sure the class name is `QImageProcessor` and its base class is `QObject`, as seen in the following screenshot:

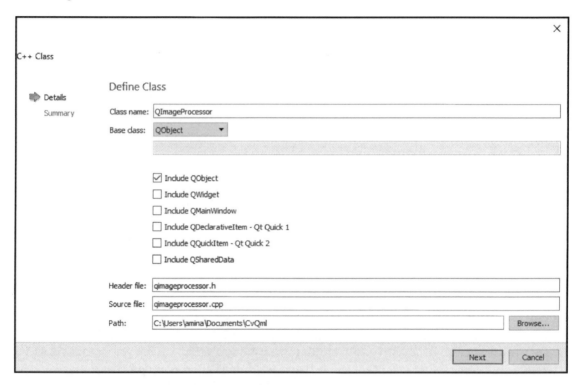

Add the following `#include` directives to `qimageprocessor.h` file:

```
#include <QImage>
#include "opencv2/opencv.hpp"
```

And then add the following function to the public members area of the `QImageProcessor` class:

```
Q_INVOKABLE void processImage(const QString &path);
```

Q_INVOKABLE is a Qt macro that allows a function to be called (invoked) by using the Qt Meta Object system. As QML uses the same Qt Meta Object for its underlying communication mechanism between objects, it is enough to mark a function with the Q_INVOKABLE macro so that it can be called from QML codes. Also, add the following signal to the QImageProcessor class:

```
signals:
    void imageProcessed(const QImage &image);
```

We'll use this signal to pass on a processed image to an image viewer class that we'll create later on. Finally, for the implementation of the processImage function, add the following to the qimageprocessor.cpp file:

```
void QImageProcessor::processImage(const QString &path)
{
    using namespace cv;
    Mat imageM = imread(path.toStdString());
    if(!imageM.empty())
    {
        bitwise_not(imageM, imageM); // or any OpenCV code
        QImage imageQ(imageM.data,
                      imageM.cols,
                      imageM.rows,
                      imageM.step,
                      QImage::Format_RGB888);
        emit imageProcessed(imageQ.rgbSwapped());
    }
    else
    {
        qDebug() << path << "does not exist!";
    }
}
```

There is nothing new here that we haven't seen or used. This function simply takes the path to an image, reads it from disk, performs an image processing, which can be anything but for simplicity's sake we used the bitwise_not function to invert the value of pixels in all channels, and finally emit the result image using the signal we defined.

Our image processor is complete now. Now, we need to create a Visual C++ type that can be used in QML to display QImage objects. So, create another class and name it QImageViewer, but this time make sure it is a QQuickItem sub-class, as seen in the following new class wizard screenshot:

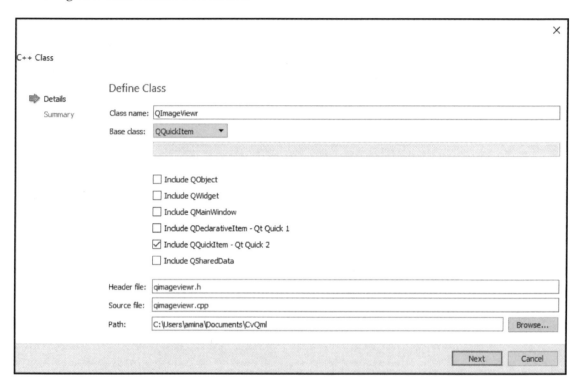

Modify the qimageviewer.h file, as seen here:

```cpp
#include <QQuickItem>
#include <QQuickPaintedItem>
#include <QImage>
#include <QPainter>

class QImageViewer : public QQuickPaintedItem
{
  Q_OBJECT
  public:
    QImageViewer(QQuickItem *parent = Q_NULLPTR);
    Q_INVOKABLE void setImage(const QImage &img);

  private:
```

```
QImage currentImage;
void paint(QPainter *painter);

};
```

We have made our `QImageViewer` class a sub-class of `QQuickPaintedItem`. Also, the constructor is updated to match this modification. We have defined another function using the `Q_INVOKABLE` macro in this class, which will be used to set the QImage we want to display on instances of this class, or to be precise, QML items that will be created using this type. `QQuickPaintedItem` offers a simple method of creating new visual QML types; that is, by subclassing it and reimplementing the paint function, as seen in the preceding code. The painter pointer passed to the paint function in this class can be used to draw anything we require. In this case, we simply want to draw an image on it; that is, we have defined `currentImage` which is a `QImage` that will hold the image we want to draw on the `QImageViewer` class.

Now, we need to add the implementation of the `setImage` and paint functions and update the constructor according to what we changed in the header file. So, make sure the `qimageviewer.cpp` file looks like this:

```
#include "qimageviewer.h"

QImageViewer::QImageViewer(QQuickItem *parent)
  : QQuickPaintedItem(parent)
{
}

void QImageViewer::setImage(const QImage &img)
{
  currentImage = img.copy(); // perform a copy
  update();
}

void QImageViewer::paint(QPainter *painter)
{
  QSizeF scaled = QSizeF(currentImage.width(),
                    currentImage.height())
        .scaled(boundingRect().size(), Qt::KeepAspectRatio);
  QRect centerRect(qAbs(scaled.width() - width()) / 2.0f,
                   qAbs(scaled.height() - height()) / 2.0f,
                   scaled.width(),
                   scaled.height());
  painter->drawImage(centerRect, currentImage);
}
```

In the preceding code, the `setImage` function is quite simple; it makes a copy of the image and holds it, then calls the update function of the `QImageViwer` class. `update` will result in a repaint when it is called inside a `QQuickPaintedItem` (similar to `QWidget`), thus our paint function will be called. In case we want to stretch the image over the whole displayable area of the `QImageViewer`, then this function only needs the last line (`centerRect` replaced by `boundingRect`); however, we'd like our result image to fit the screen and also preserve the aspect ratio. So, we do a scale conversion and then make sure the image is always at the center of the displayable area.

We are almost there, and both our new C++ classes (`QImageProcessor` and `QImageViewer`) are ready to be used in QML codes. The only thing left to do is to make sure they are visible to our QML codes. For this reason, we need to make sure they are registered by using the `qmlRegisterType` function. This function must be called in our `main.cpp` file, as seen here:

```
qmlRegisterType<QImageProcessor>("com.amin.classes",
    1, 0, "ImageProcessor");
qmlRegisterType<QImageViewer>("com.amin.classes",
    1, 0, "ImageViewer");
```

Place then right before where the `QQmlApplicationEngine` is defined in the `main.cpp` file. Needless to say, you have to include both our new classes in the `main.cpp` file by using the following `#include` directives:

```
#include "qimageprocessor.h"
#include "qimageviewer.h"
```

Note that `com.amin.classes` in the `qmlRegisterType` function call can be replaced with a domain-like identifier of your own, and it is the name we have given to the library that includes the `QImageProcessor` and `QImageViewer` classes. The following 1 and 0 refer to the version 1.0 of the library, and the last literal string is the type identifier that can be used inside our QML type to access and use these new classes.

Finally, we can start using our C++ classes in the `main.qml` file. First of all, make sure your `import` statements match the following:

```
import QtQuick 2.7
import QtQuick.Controls 2.0
import QtQuick.Layouts 1.3
import QtMultimedia 5.8
import com.amin.classes 1.0
```

The last line includes the `ImageProcessor` and `ImageViewer` QML types that we just created. We are going to use the QML Camera type to access the camera and capture images using it. So, add the following as a direct child of the `ApplicationWindow` item in the `main.qml` file:

```
Camera
{
  id: camera
  imageCapture
  {
    onImageSaved:
    {
      imgProcessor.processImage(path)
    }
  }
}
```

In the preceding code, `imgProcessor` is the `id` of our `ImageProcessor` type, which also needs to be defined as a child item of the `ApplicationWindow`, as seen here:

```
ImageProcessor
{
  id: imgProcessor
  onImageProcessed:
  {
    imgViewer.setImage(image);
    imageDrawer.open()
  }
}
```

Note that the `onImageProcessed` slot in the preceding code is automatically generated because of the `imageProcessed` signal that we created inside the `QImageProcessor` class. You can guess that `imgViewer` is the `QImageViewer` class that we had created earlier, and we set its image inside the `onImageProcessed` slot. In this example, we are also using a QML `Drawer` that slides over another window when its open function is called, and we have embedded `imgViewer` as a child item of this `Drawer`. Here is how the `Drawer` and `ImageViewer` are defined:

```
Drawer
{
  id: imageDrawer
  width: parent.width
  height: parent.height
  ImageViewer
  {
```

```
            id: imgViewer
            anchors.fill: parent
            Label
            {
               text: "Swipe from right to left<br>to return to capture mode!"
               color: "red"
            }
          }
       }
     }
```

That's about it. The only thing left to do is to add a QML `VideoOutput` that allows a preview of the camera. We'll use this `VideoOutput` to capture images, which consequently invokes the `imageCapture.onImageSaved` slot of the QML `Camera` type, as seen here:

```
        VideoOutput
        {
          source: camera
          anchors.fill: parent
          MouseArea
          {
            anchors.fill: parent
            onClicked:
            {
              camera.imageCapture.capture()
            }
          }
          Label
          {
              text: "Touch the screen to take a photo<br>and process it using
    OpenCV!"
              color: "red"
          }
        }
```

If you start the application now, you'll be faced immediately with the output from the default camera on the computer. If you click inside the video output, an image will be captured and processed and then displayed on a `Drawer` that slides over the current page from left to right. The following are a couple of screenshots of how this application looks when it is executed:

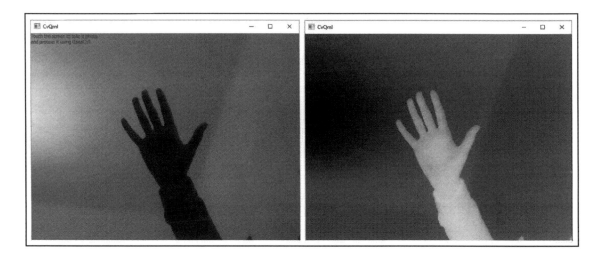

# Qt and OpenCV apps on Android and iOS

Ideally, you can build and run the applications created by using Qt and OpenCV frameworks on desktop and mobile platforms alike, without having the need to write any platform-specific codes. However, in practice, this is not as easy as it seems, since frameworks like Qt and OpenCV act as wrappers over the capabilities of the operating system itself (in some cases), and since they are still undergoing extensive development, there might be some cases that are not yet fully implemented in a particular operating system, such as Android or iOS. The good news is that those cases are getting rarer as new versions of the Qt and OpenCV frameworks are released, and even now (Qt 5.9 and OpenCV 3.3), most of the classes and functions in both of these frameworks can be easily used in Windows, Linux, macOS, Android, and iOS operating systems.

So, first of all by keeping what we just mentioned in mind, we can say that practically (as opposed to ideally), to be able to build and run applications written using Qt and OpenCV on Android and iOS, we need to make sure of the following:

- Corresponding Qt kits for Android and iOS must be installed. This can be done during the initial installation of the Qt Framework (refer to `Chapter 1`, *Introduction to OpenCV and Qt*, for more information about this).

 Note that Android kits are available on Windows, Linux, and macOS, whereas iOS kits only exist for macOS, since the development of iOS applications using Qt is limited to macOS only (at the moment).

- Pre-built OpenCV libraries for Android and iOS must be downloaded from the OpenCV website (at the moment, they are provided from `opencv.org`) and extracted in your computer. They must be added to the Qt project files the way they are added in Windows or any other desktop platforms.
- For iOS, it is enough to have the latest version of Xcode on your macOS operating system.
- For Android, you must make sure to install JDK, Android SDK, Android NDK, and Apache Ant on your computer. Qt Creator simplifies the configuration of the Android development environment, provided that the required programs are downloaded and installed on your computer, using the **Android** tab in the **Devices** page inside the Qt Creator **Options** (see the following screenshot):

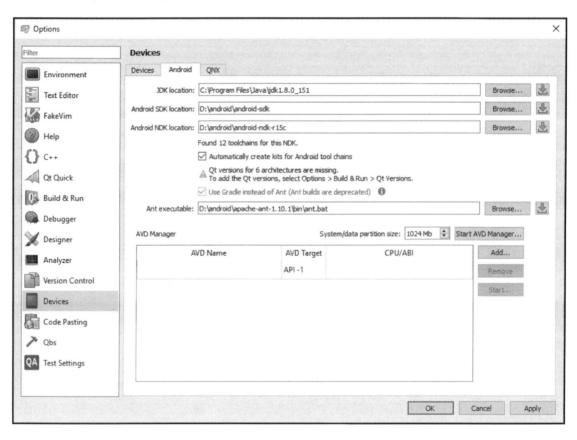

Note the buttons beside the **Browse** buttons in the preceding image. They provide the link to the download page and the online link from which you can get a copy of all the required dependencies.

That is all you need to take care of if you want to build your applications for Android and iOS operating systems. Applications built by using Qt and OpenCV can also be published in application stores for Windows, macOS, Android, and iOS. This process usually involves being signed up as a developer with the providers of these operating systems. You can find the guidelines and requirements for publishing your apps online and globally in the mentioned application stores.

# Summary

In this chapter, we learned about the **Qt Quick Application** development and the QML language. We started with the bare syntax of this highly readable and easy-to-use language, and then moved our way to developing applications that contain components that can interact with each other in order to achieve a common goal. We learned how to fill the gap between the QML and C++ codes and then built a visual and a non-visual class to process and display images processed using OpenCV. We also went through a brief introduction of the tools required in order to build and run the same applications on Android and iOS platforms. The final chapter of this book was meant to help you get up on your feet by starting to develop quick and beautiful applications using the new Qt Quick Controls 2 module, and also combining the power of C++ codes and third-party frameworks such as OpenCV to achieve the maximum power and flexibility in developing mobile and desktop applications.

Building cross-platform and visually appealing applications has never been so easy. By using the Qt and OpenCV frameworks, and especially the power of QML for building applications quickly and easily, you can start realizing all of your computer vision ideas right now. What we learned in this chapter was just an introduction to all of the possibilities that Qt Quick and the QML language have to offer; however, you are the one who needs to put these pieces together in order to build applications that solve the existing problems in the field.

# Other Books You May Enjoy

If you enjoyed this book, you may be interested in these other books by Packt:

**Mastering OpenCV 3**

Daniel Lelis Baggio, Shervin Emami, David Millán Escrivá, Khvedchenia
Ievgen, Jason Saragih, Roy Shilkrot

ISBN: 978-1-78646-717-1

- Execute basic image processing operations and cartoonify an image
- Build an OpenCV project natively with Raspberry Pi and cross-compile it for
  Raspberry Pi.text
- Extend the natural feature tracking algorithm to support the tracking of multiple
  image targets on a video
- Use OpenCV 3's new 3D visualization framework to illustrate the 3D scene
  geometry
- Create an application for Automatic Number Plate Recognition (ANPR) using a
  support vector machine and Artificial Neural Networks
- Train and predict pattern-recognition algorithms to decide whether an image is a
  number plate
- Use POSIT for the six degrees of freedom head pose
- Train a face recognition database using deep learning and recognize faces from
  that database

## Machine Learning for OpenCV
Michael Beyeler

ISBN: 978-1-78398-028-4

- Explore and make effective use of OpenCV's Machine Learning module
- Learn deep learning for computer vision with Python
- Master linear regression and regularization techniques
- Classify objects such as flower species, handwritten digits, and pedestrians
- Explore the effective use of support vector machines, boosted decision trees, and random forests
- Get acquainted with neural networks and Deep Learning to address real-world problems
- Discover hidden structures in your data using k-means clustering
- Get to grips with data pre-processing and feature engineering

# Leave a review - let other readers know what you think

Please share your thoughts on this book with others by leaving a review on the site that you bought it from. If you purchased the book from Amazon, please leave us an honest review on this book's Amazon page. This is vital so that other potential readers can see and use your unbiased opinion to make purchasing decisions, we can understand what our customers think about our products, and our authors can see your feedback on the title that they have worked with Packt to create. It will only take a few minutes of your time, but is valuable to other potential customers, our authors, and Packt. Thank you!

# Index

64808448R00269

Made in the USA
Middletown, DE
18 February 2018